ADMINISTERING SMS

Administering SMS

Mark Wilkins

McGraw-Hill

New York San Francisco Washington, D.C.
Auckland Bogotá Caracas Lisbon London
Madrid Mexico City Milan Montreal New Delhi
San Juan Singapore Sydney Tokyo Toronto

McGraw-Hill

A Division of The ***McGraw-Hill*** *Companies*

1 2 3 4 5 6 7 8 9 0 AGM/AGM 0 5 4 3 2 1 0

ISBN 0-07-212421-0

The sponsoring editor for this book was Michael Sprague, the editing supervisor was Penny Linskey, and the production supervisor was Clare Stanley. It was set in Century Schoolbook by Don Feldman of McGraw-Hill's Professional Book Group composition unit in cooperation with Spring Point Publishing Services.

Printed and bound by Quebecor/Martinsburg.

This book is printed on recycled, acid-free paper containing a minimum of 50% recycled de-inked fiber.

CONTENTS

PREFACE

Systems Management Server 2.0 (SMS) is a Microsoft product originally developed for the Microsoft BackOffice family of products. You may not have any experience with the BackOffice platform, but it's been around for a few years, gathering steam and popularity as a backroom service platform running on the NT operating system linked primarily with Exchange Server and SQL Server.

The initial release of SMS version 1.0 was focused completely on remote desktop management. It resembled some of the other desktop management products that were out in the computer field at the time—for example, Symantec's Norton Administrator, Intel LANDesk, and others.

The next release was SMS version 1.2. In this version, more network management with SNMP features was introduced to allow increased fault management from remote locations. NT Remote Control was also introduced, which allowed the remote control of servers, as well as the unattended administration of NT workstations.

In 1999 the beta versions of SMS version 2.0 started appearing to beta testers and Microsoft developers. This current release really has to be viewed as a completely new product because of the vast amount of features included. Understand, however, that SMS 2.0 is primarily an NT product for the NT platform on dedicated NT servers. There is support for the bindery and NDS NetWare environments, but the major support will be for the Microsoft product line.

At this writing, NetWare version 5.0 is slowly being implemented in NetWare shops that still exist. NetWare version 5 supports native IP. This is an important change for NetWare. For years, their IPX protocol had been the standard in the computer industry. Now, as we all know, Microsoft has taken away a large portion of their market due to their timely and, as some might say, lucky adoption of TCP/IP. Since NetWare now supports the same basic protocol, we have NT Server 4.0, Windows 2000 (the new version of NT), and UNIX now fighting it out for the huge enterprise network world.

As our networks get larger, one of the major needs for the enterprise network administrator is the ability for desktop management and remote control. Microsoft is intending SMS version 2 to provide that capability as Windows 2000 assumes a bigger role on larger networks in major corporations in the coming years.

SMS 2.0 is Microsoft's foray into network management. Their Windows-based client operating systems released over the last few years have also included the ability for remote management and control from remote locations. These include Windows 95, Windows 98, and Windows NT Workstation 4.0—in short, all currently available Windows 32-bit platforms support the principle of remote access and control. The structure/feature that makes Systems Management Server even possible is the Windows Registry, which is the central database in all Windows-based PCs.

The features that SMS offers are by themselves nothing new, as there are lots of third-party vendors that are competing with SMS. However, the advantage that Microsoft has is that SMS was designed for running on NT 4.0, and since they wrote the NT platform, they hold all the answers to its internals and to its architecture.

In my travels as a consultant and speaker, the one common theme I hear is that "we are throwing NetWare away and replacing it with NT." When I ask why, the answer is usually "I don't know; it wasn't my decision, but that's what we're doing."

Talk about a ready-made market. Upper corporate management has bought into the elusive promise of Microsoft programs and products solving all their problems.

Many times the background work and testing is never performed. The reality in the computer field is that the product that we standardize on is usually not the best—just the most popular. That said, you probably think I'm starting to slight Microsoft already, but in fact, I like Microsoft products. I just wish that sometimes they initially worked a little better.

So on to SMS and what it can do for us. Let's take a look at the features that make version 2.0 so powerful.

MARK WILKINS

CHAPTER 1

Introduction to Systems Management Server 2.0

In this chapter you will be introduced to the features of SMS 2.0. You will learn about:

- Network management and SMS
- SMS Administrator console and Microsoft Management Console (MMC)
- What type of clients and servers best take advantage of SMS 2.0
- How SMS discovers network resources
- Where Windows 2000 fits with SMS

What Is Systems Management Server 2.0?

The key to SMS is contained in the name of the product itself: *management*, the management of workstations, servers, software and hardware, and many other management tasks performed through the network infrastructure. Another way to describe this software offering is as a system management tool that centralizes the control of all your network resources. SMS is also designed to be part of the Microsoft BackOffice family of products—Exchange Server, IIS, and SQL Server, to name a few.

The current network structure for NT Server 4.0 is made up of primary and backup domain controllers, and multiple master domains linked together with trusts across wide area networks (WANs), that ultimately link companies like yours across the globe. The network user of today is on the move, around the local network and around the world.

Hiring IP professionals and the needed support staff is a huge task for the network administrator, especially in these times of restraint. Upper management's illusion that the installation of Microsoft networking products requires less network support is just that, an illusion. As IT and support staff is being downsized, in fact, support should be upsized.

You and I both know that won't happen anytime soon. Therefore, Systems Management Server may be the answer for networks that are running 24 hours a day, 7 days a week. Working and executing as a collection of network services, SMS works tirelessly in the background, providing administrative support, and to the best of my knowledge, it will not ask for a raise or quit on you suddenly.

How Can SMS Help?

Let's look at what SMS will do for us from both the user's and administrator's point of view. When network users have a problem on their PC and get stuck, they usually (hopefully) call the help desk or some support personnel for some assistance. As we all know, help desk personnel are overworked, and if you don't even have a help desk, you or your support staff will take the call. Without SMS installed, some nagging user problems require that you actually go to the user's PC to look at the real problem (if indeed a problem exists) and talk the user through it or assist in fixing the problem quickly.

If SMS 2.0 is installed, when users call you or the help desk for support, you, or other support staff, can use SMS 2.0 to diagnose and possibly solve the problem across the network without taking the journey to the user's local PC. This makes at least one person happy: the support person, and since the problem is solved, the user is happy as well.

In a nutshell, what I've just described is an SMS feature called Remote Control. The remote control features of SMS allow user support across the network without support personnel having to leave their desks. This feature can be also summarized as advanced network management with remote control. In addition, if the user needs a new file or a new version of software to be installed, through Remote Control, files can be transferred to the user's PC. SMS can also be tailored to provide custom packages for the installation of applications, operating system, and virus updates; the bottom line is this: If you can package it, SMS can install it for you.

Does Network Size Matter?

At this point, you might be thinking "I've got 60 users max and two servers; how can SMS help me?" True, SMS is primarily designed for much larger networks than 60 workstations. However, it really depends on the tasks being performed by the users. If software updates and virus updates are weekly, and you are wearing many hats as the network administrator and Mr. or Ms. Fix-It, plus the chief bottle washer, SMS can help you stay organized as your network grows.

Installing SMS on a smaller network that will be getting larger with more and more users *is* the best time. SMS allows us to be proactive and not reactive.

Plan to Be Proactive

Deploying SMS and network management before there's a problem allows you to plan and set your network infrastructure up properly. This allows you to complement the SMS features that will work best on your network, and as I've just said, the key to long-term success is to be proactive, fixing potential problems before they become problems. Being proactive rather than reactive must be our long-term goal.

Let's walk through the features of SMS 2.0 so you can see how this software can possibly help you as a network administrator. But before we do, keep in mind whom SMS has been really designed for. No surprises here, if you wish to deploy every feature of SMS, then this is a software solution for Microsoft Windows NT network shops. You'll find details in this book on how to integrate SMS with NetWare through bindery and NDS (NetWare Directory Services).

However, in order to use SMS fully, we are talking NT servers and Windows-based clients. The full version of SMS 2.0 is designed for the NT 4.0 platform. By the time you read this book, Windows 2000 will have been released; however, this book is still quite valid, since SMS is a standalone product. Some SMS features have been integrated into Windows 2000, but how many of your network clients will be Windows 2000 Professional by the end of 2000? Quite possibly, some will have been upgraded, but definitely not all.

SMS Administrator Console

Command Central for running SMS is in the SMS Administrator console. This utility is viewed and used through a new graphical "front end" called the Microsoft Management Console (MMC).

The MMC is by itself just an empty shell. Through the MMC, you will set up and use the SMS Administrator console, shown in Figure 1-1, as a utility that you "snap in" to the MMC. The way you snap in the SMS Administrator console, or any other MMC-supported utility, is by selecting the available utilities that are installed on your PC, and selecting and adding and saving the desired utilities so that they show up the next time you execute the MMC.

This interface is the standard interface for all administrator functions for a Windows 2000 server and most new NT 4.0 companion products,

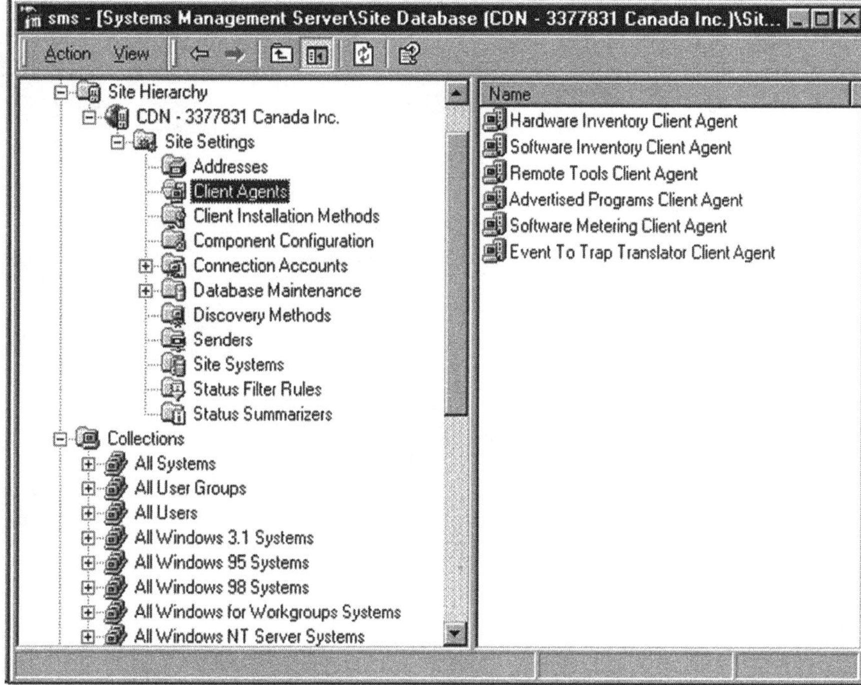

Figure 1-1 Viewing the SMS Administrative console.

such as Internet Information Server 4. Microsoft is trying to standardize how all 32-bit software tools and utilities look and feel through Windows 2000 with the MMC interface.

Remember, the MMC is nothing more than a set of available 32-bit application programming interfaces (APIs) and an empty graphic shell that you use as your framework.

You can customize, mix, and match the different tools inside an MMC for your administrators, providing them the software tools and the associated permissions to the utilities that they need. The custom MMC can be saved as an MSC file and delivered to the person responsible for performing these administrative tasks. Special toolsets can be then created for end users, power users, and administrators.

Any third-party software developer must soon support the MMC interface. Microsoft has announced that in order for developers of server applications to be BackOffice-compliant, the use of MMC snap-ins for their third-party software applications and utilities is required.

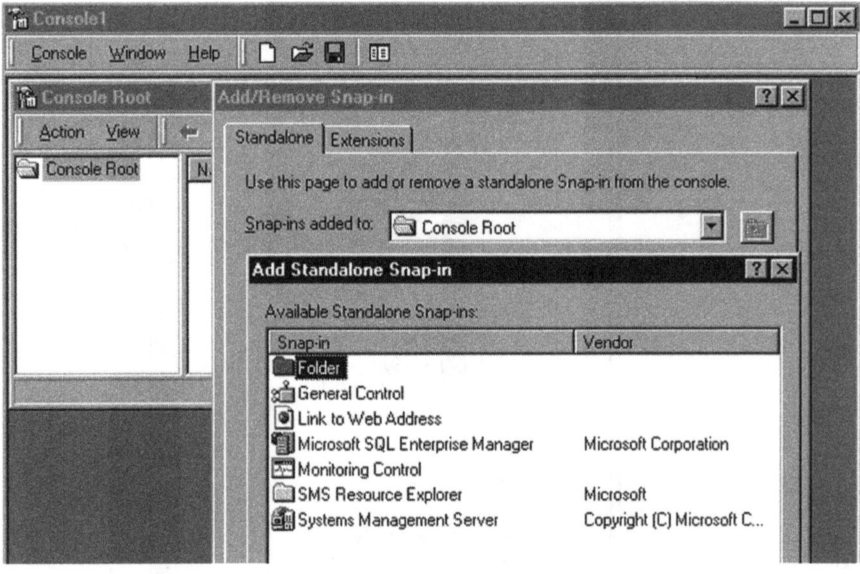

Figure 1-2
Start the MMC by entering "MMC" at the Run box.

Figure 1-3 shows another view of the MMC with the SMS Administrator console running.

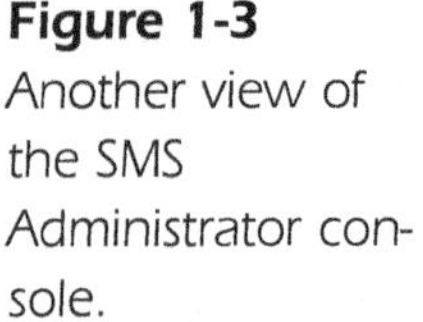

Figure 1-3
Another view of the SMS Administrator console.

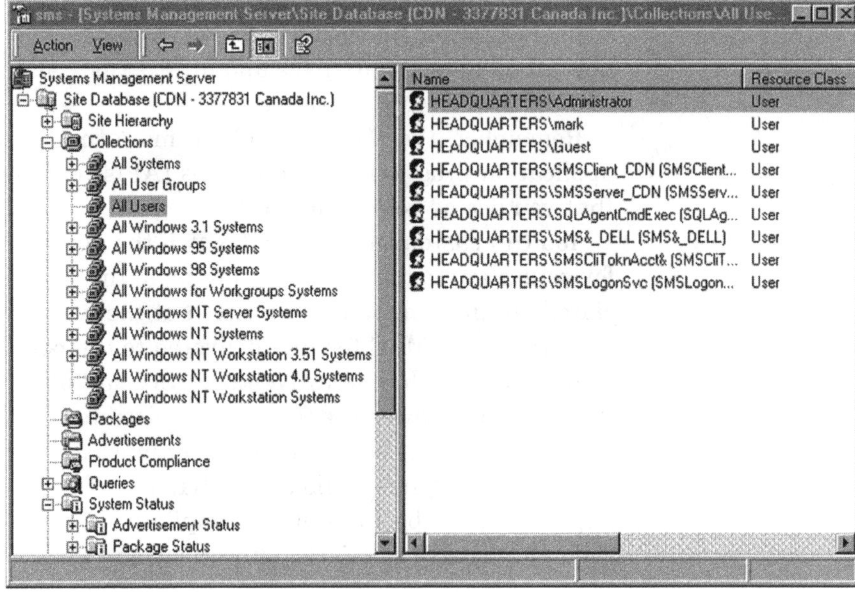

Overview: Features of SMS 2.0

This overview section has been written as a starting point so that you can quickly read through this chapter and have a summary of SMS 2.0 and its features. You'll then know where to go in the book for the details on the features that you are most interested in.

Resource Discovery

A process called *resource discovery* is the fundamental backbone of how SMS communicates. Complete network management of your network cannot be accomplished until SMS figures out the clients attached to your network—the network devices such as hubs, routers, bridges, network printers, and any other device that can communicate using one of the two network protocols supported by SMS. SMS 2.0 supports the following Microsoft operating systems:

- Windows NT 4.0 Server, Server Enterprise Edition, and Workstation
- Windows NT 3.51, both Workstation and Server
- Windows 98, Windows 98 2nd Edition, and Windows 95
- Windows for Workgroups 3.11 using the Windows Network Client for MS-DOS
- Windows 3.1/3.11 using the Windows Network Client for MS-DOS

If you're supporting Windows NT 4.0 Terminal Server, only the following client-based functions are supported:

- Remote Windows NT client installation
- Hardware inventory
- Software inventory

Protocols supported by SMS 2.0 are TCP/IP (the IP portion of the protocol is used to identify the devices across your network) and IPX/SPX. Resource discovery can be further categorized into four main methods: Windows Networking Logon Discovery, Heartbeat Discovery, Windows NT User Account and Group Discovery, and SMS Server Discovery.

Windows Networking Logon Discovery

Windows Networking Logon Discovery uses the simple network Management Protocol (SNMP) combined with information provided from

Dynamic Host Configuration Protocol (DHCP) servers, domain controllers, and network addresses, along with LAN manager system calls, to sniff out the existing devices across your network. Windows Networking Logon Discovery is the most basic SMS procedure for gathering the facts and data about all of the installed devices on your network.

During the process of Logon Discovery, when computers are found, SMS also can install SMS client discovery software onto the client's computer. You can also choose to install the client agent on your user's PC before the discovery process begins.

So we have two methods for the client agents to be installed, either through Logon Discovery or through manual installation at the client PC. There are several additional types of discovery methods that we will look at in detail in Chapter 7 "Resource Discovery and Client Installation."

Heartbeat Discovery

The rediscovery of computer resources that were discovered previously through a network logon is called *Heartbeat Discovery*. The purpose of this discovery method is to keep the discovery database up-to-date. This can be helpful for dedicated servers that rarely are turned off or on, such as Internet servers, the mail servers, or database servers.

Windows NT User Account and Group Discovery

The third option for the discovery of resources is called *User Account and User Group Discovery*. This method allows you to distribute software to domain users and groups. You can also specifically target software installations and upgrades to specific users or groups.

SMS Server Discovery

SMS Server Discovery finds the computers on your network that have been installed as an SMS primary or secondary site system. You cannot disable this discovery method, since recognizing existing site systems is essential for SMS to operate properly.

All of these discovery methods can be configured through the SMS Administrator console. Some SMS management tasks such as software metering, software distribution, and hardware and software inventory cannot be started until after the SMS client has been discovered and client agent software installed.

SQL and Its Role in SMS

SMS works hand in hand with a mandatory installed SQL Server database. All of the above discovery methods create a *discovery data record* (DDR) that contains several fields of data about the discovered resources. The DDRs are then sent to the primary site server where they are processed and then stored in the SQL Server database.

NOTE *Any device with a valid IP (Internet Protocol) address will be discovered through the resource discovery process.*

Hardware Inventory

By default, hardware inventory is enabled for all clients across the entire SMS site. After a computer resource has been discovered, at the client location, the Hardware Inventory Client Agent collects the hardware data stored on the client and the site server.

During the very next inventory cycle, the agent collects any new hardware data and updates the new inventory data to the existing site server, where it will be processed and stored in the SQL database. The Hardware Inventory Agent will inventory 16-bit and 32-bit hardware data. The collection is performed based on a defined template that can be modified to collect more or less inventory data.

For 32-bit Windows clients, the hardware inventory is stored on the client's PC. The initial inventory capture is sent to the site server, but from that point on, only the changes to the client's inventory are sent across the network. You can choose to synchronize the entire client inventory for complete update.

A 16-bit Windows client always sends the complete inventory to the site server. The site server does the work, pinpointing any changes to the client inventory and then storing only the change information in the site database. Figure 1-4 shows the hardware inventory detail for a site server on NT 4.0.

Software Inventory

Software inventory is also enabled by default for all clients across the entire SMS site. The software inventory is collected using the headers of

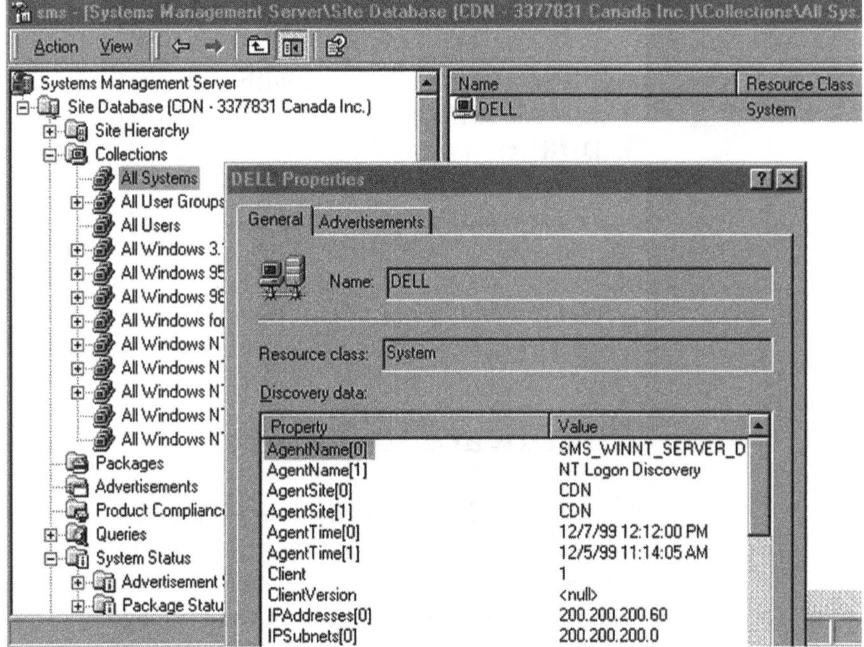

Figure 1-4
Hardware inventory as viewed through the SMS Administrator console.

the program files installed on the local computer. An attempt is made to categorize them by manufacturer type and version number. The internal Windows Registry holds most of this information for registered file types, making the search on a 32-bit system much easier.

Users who decide to hide software by renaming the EXE file will have no luck in their attempt to avoid detection, as the file header won't lie. Files can also be collected and then stored on the site server. (Ouch! I guess noontime game playing is out.)

The Software Inventory Client Agent searches for EXE files by default, but it can be configured to inventory additional file extensions, for example, DLL, REG, and so on. Wildcard characters are also supported. The software agent collects the software inventory data found at each client storing the inventory data in a software inventory complete file. This data file is passed to the client access point (CAP) and then forwarded to the site server, where it is stored in the SMS site database.

The next time software inventory is performed, an incremental update file containing just the changes or updates will be uploaded to the SMS site server for processing.

Using the SMS Resource Explorer, you can access hardware and software inventory for a specific client computer. You can also draw on reports of existing inventory data that can be displayed and customized used Crystal Reports and Crystal Info.

Software Distribution

Probably one of the best features of SMS is the ability to distribute software packages automating software distribution and installation at all clients' computers. The SMS components supporting software distribution are Collections, Advertisements, Packages, Programs, the SMS Installer, and the Software Distribution Agent. Details on these components are found in Table 1-1.

The installation can also be based on the collected discovery and inventory data on a specific client or a group of clients. Software can then be targeted to specific computers, users, and user groups. This feature could be used in many day-to-day operations, for example:

- Installing service packs
- Installing software updates

TABLE 1-1

Software components for SMS 2.0.

SMS Software Components	Description
Collections	Used for software installations, software updates, and reconfigurations.
Advertisements	Combines a collection, package, and software program, and uses the Software Distribution Client Agent to distribute software to the client computers.
Packages	Contains files to be distributed.
Programs	Contained in a package; contains command lines that will execute a package installation.
SMS Installer	Used to create custom installation routines for software to be distributed. This offer tool allows you to automate installation of any software application that can run on a client PC.
Software Distribution Agent	Contains the Advertised Programs Monitor plus the Advertised Programs Wizard. These two software applets run on the client's computer, allowing advertised programs to be installed. The monitor keeps track of any software ready for installation, and the wizard provides the end user with a step-by-step installation interface for installing an application.

- Installing complete operating systems
- Installing virus signature updates

You could even set up software distribution for new users not yet working at your company or new computer systems that have not yet arrived. During the first day on the job the first logon by the new user would prompt the installation of a mix of software automatically to the new client's PC.

SMS Installer

Another feature of software distribution is called the *SMS Installer*. Using this new feature, you can silently install software in the background without the user being aware that it is happening.

Before an actual real-time installation, the SMS Installer first monitors a PC called a *reference computer* before any software is actually installed. Sitting in the background as the softer installation runs, the SMS Installer records all changes to the reference computer made by the software installation. This covers folder or directory creation, file activity, and Registry modifications.

Once the software installation is complete, the installer creates an automated installation script that you can customize further using scripting language. The script is compiled into an executable installation routine that can be used with bundled package instructions to install software to client computers using SMS advertisements and collections.

Software Metering

You may not be aware that your proverbial neck is on the line with regard to the licensing and legality of software run by your company and its employees. Be aware that if you are ever faced with a visit by the software police, they are much more savvy than they used to be; they are usually representatives of Dun & Bradstreet or some large consulting firm. Showing them a bunch of floppies or CD-ROMs won't do the trick; they will want to see licensing information. With software metering you can set the license rules for your organization. Careful attention to this SMS feature means that you can prove that you are doing your job legally and can pin the blame on the specific user who brings in an unlicensed software application and installs it on his or her PC. See Figure 1-5.

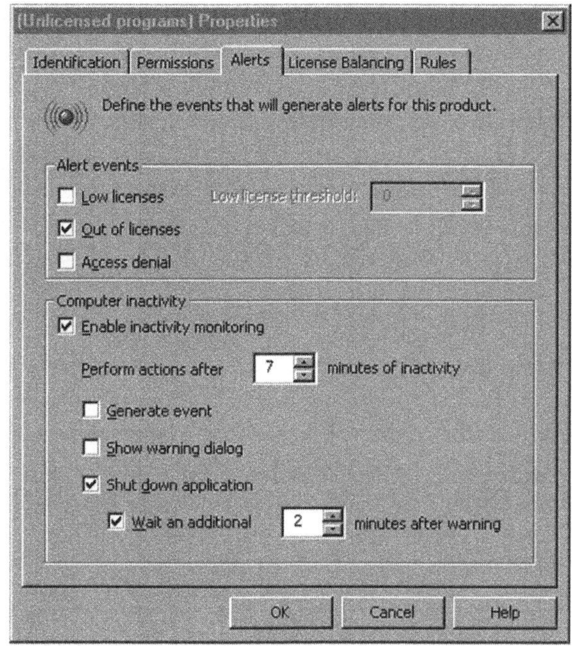

Figure 1-5 Setting the rules for unlicensed software applications.

If you haven't had a visit from the software police, rest assured the visit is usually sparked from disgruntled employees who decide to take it out on their former company. SMS can help you with this huge task of keeping software legal.

In a large company with many computers and many more arriving every month, it is not uncommon to have no real idea at any given point in the day, month, or week what software is perfectly legal and what software isn't. SMS allows you to monitor in the background the copies in use of any particular software application.

In addition, even if you have a site license for a particular software suite, there will still be a legal limit on the number of people that can be running the software at any given time. Software metering can enforce the legal licensing restrictions by requiring the client to request a valid license before running an application.

No doubt you can now see how software metering can help you control your software licensing.

I'm a firm believer (in my legal mind, anyway) that the licensing rules prescribed by Microsoft and other major software companies would not hold up in a court of law. For example, Office 97 allowed you to install the software suite at work and at home. Office 2000 has changed the licensing rules.

Suppose that your company is going to upgrade to Office 2000. It will need upgrades for the existing computers running Office 97 and full packages of Office 2000 for all new computers. SMS can provide quickly a report of how many computers are running any version of Office 97 and what computers are not running it. As Figure 1-6 shows, software metering stores the legal details of a software application, in this case, Office 97. The properties of an existing application can also be easily modified to match the current reality of how many copies your company owns and has installed.

The Software Metering Client Agent and the network servers that function as metering servers on your network are configured through the SMS Administrator console. The License Manager is used to configure the software for metering and reporting, and also to carry out real-time monitoring of the registered application usage. If you have older clients, it's time to upgrade them, since software metering is a 32-bit tool that only executes on Windows 95/98, Windows NT 3.51 to 4.0, and Windows

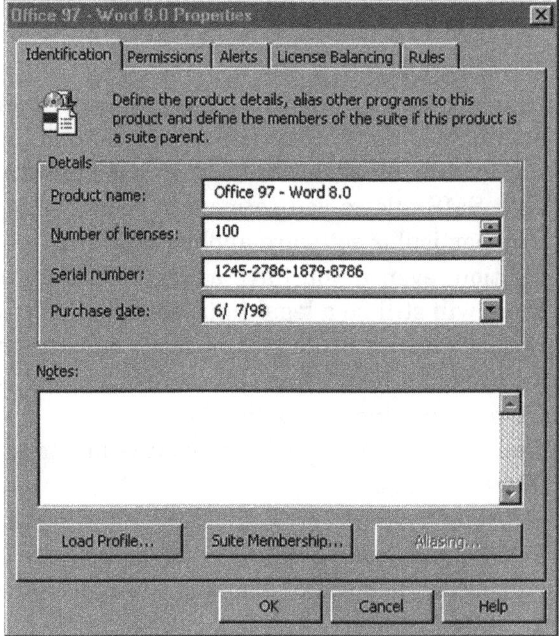

Figure 1-6 Office 97 license properties for software metering.

2000. 16-bit client operating systems such as Windows 3.1 and Windows for Workgroups are not supported.

Software-metering features supported for 32-bit Windows clients include:

- *Concurrent Usage* Records the simultaneous usage of applications across the network.
- *Application Monitoring* Tracks what programs (registered and unregistered software applications) are running on all 32 computers and servers across the wide area network.
- *Allocation Control* Restricts applications to the users and groups of users based on preset policies. Restrictions can be based on the number of current licenses, user accounts, group accounts, the number of computers, time zones, or any other preset quota levels.
- *Record Keeping* Can log, on a real-time basis, the successful and not so successful attempt to use applications.
- *Check-In and Checkout* Allows users to check out a software license and check it back in when they're finished with the licensed program. (I can see very soon in the future when the normal method of software distribution will be performed through renting software applications across the Internet. We won't actually own the software anymore; we'll just rent it for a period of time. In fact, it's actually available right now, but, as always, bandwidth is a problem.)

TCO—Total Cost of Ownership

The buzzword today is TCO, or your total cost of ownership. TCO is bandied about as the total cost of having the pleasure of a network at your company. This includes hardware/software installation, training, maintenance, upgrades, and on and on. Although SMS promises to, and in fact could, reduce your TCO, in my humble opinion, you have to be incredibly organized to reduce your total cost of ownership.

My favorite (and true) TCO example is of a statistical group that analyzed the cost of having a coffeepot in the workplace. It was found that having a coffeepot in a medium-sized department could actually cost your company about $45,000 a year when you factored in the wasted time of employees getting a cup of coffee and standing around the coffeepot shooting the breeze. (Hmmm...Starbucks doesn't seem so expensive now, does it?)

Help Desk Troubleshooting through the Network

At some point during the day a user on your network will need help. Using the SMS Remote Control feature allows you to provide remote support when and where it is needed. As mentioned, this tool allows you to control and troubleshoot a network client without having to go to the actual computer system yourself. Figure 1-7 details the default settings used for a Remote Control session.

Remote Control also allows you to view the remote client video output and even take control of the user's mouse and keyboard. You can also execute programs or batch files and even run commands on the remote client using Remote Execute.

Using the Remote Reboot feature, you can also restart the client's PC. In addition, with File Transfer, you have the ability to transfer files to and from the remote location, allowing you to troubleshoot problems effectively and swiftly. And if all else fails, you can chat with the user using Remote Chat.

SMS Tools for Network Administration

There are also times when you want to diagnose the network itself—that is, the current network activity and any real-time bandwidth problems.

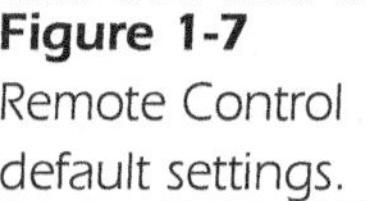

Figure 1-7
Remote Control default settings.

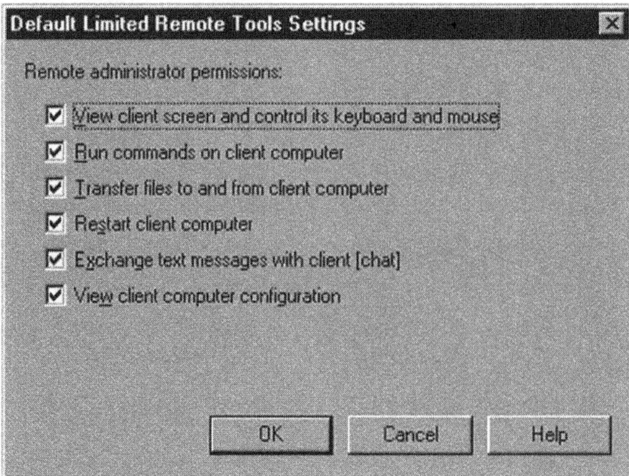

SMS version 2.0 includes a new set of maintenance tools that will help you to monitor, capture, and analyze current network data. The new network tools are Network Monitor 2.0, the Network Monitor Control tool, Network Trace, and Health Monitor.

Network Monitor

If you're a savvy NT administrator with lots of network experience, Network Monitor may not be a new feature. Network Monitor first appeared in Microsoft BackOffice and next appeared in a slightly disabled version with NT 4.0 Server.

This new version allows you to capture frames directly from the current network traffic, open them up, and examine them. The information contained inside the packet can tell you many things about your network, such as the protocols being used, where the packet came from, and the packet's destination.

Using Network Monitor toggles the network interface card on the computer you are using into "promiscuous mode." In this mode of operation, also called p-mode, the network interface card transfers all the packets that flow by its port into a temporary capture file regardless of the destination address of each packet.

All packets will contain control information, source and destination addresses, protocol information, air checking, and, of course, data. Figure 1-8 show what's inside a packet by using Network Monitor and drilling down into the fields of the captured data gram exposing the source and destination address, and the Media Access Control (MAC) address. In fact, you can search for names that are found in the total packet capture.

You can also design a filter to capture specific frames from specific sites or sources using a particular protocol. Network Monitor will frame the data in layers for useful analysis. Network analysis can be helpful when benchmarking your network structure to see how much of a load SMS will place or is placing on your network during day-to-day operations. You may find that your existing network is not up to the task of performing all of the SMS features you expect to carry out.

You may also use the Network Monitor Agent on remote Windows NT computer systems in order to capture network traffic that is flowing by the client's network interface card. The network interface card installed in the remote PC must also support promiscuous mode. (Think of promiscuous mode as electronic gossiping according to George Orwell.)

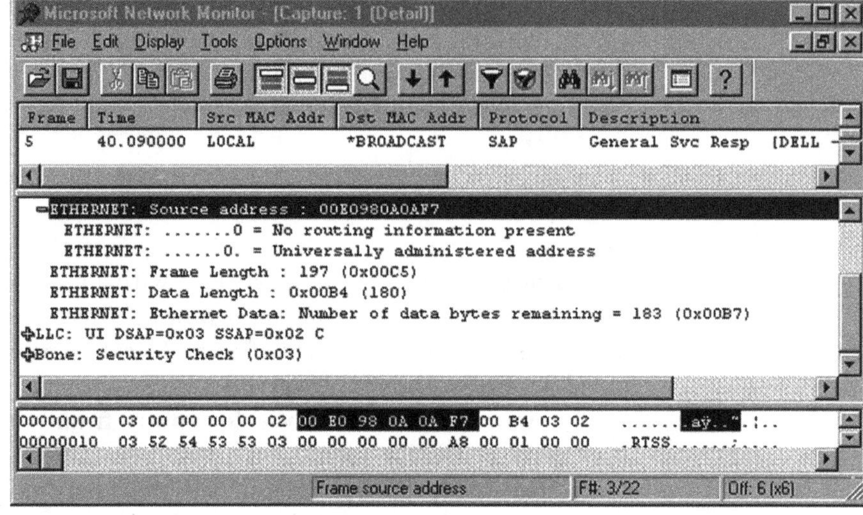

Figure 1-8 Snooping on the contents of a packet with Network Monitor.

The Network Monitor Control Tool

This new utility allows you to be proactive with your network analysis. The Network Monitor Control tool permits you to monitor your live network constantly for any network event, catastrophic or otherwise, that occurs. Running in the background, the monitor can alert you when it discovers hardware failure, such as router or hub failure. Keep in mind, however, that this feature can be very bandwidth-intensive if it is always running in the background.

Network Trace

Another new feature of SMS 2.0 is a diagnostic tool called Network Trace. This utility can trace the routes between the SMS site server you are running Network Trace from and a selective SMS site system. It can be used to confirm communication between the site systems and also to display a graphical view of the site system and component information. Network Trace diagrams will display the following objects:

- Servers found along each route
- The SMS role each server provides
- Active network devices such as routers and hubs

- Subnets
- IP addresses

Figure 1-9 shows the result of a network trace across a complete SMS site. Network Discovery can also be used to trace site devices outside your local subnets. Some of the other features of Network Trace include ping polling and SMS component polling.

Health Monitor

Health Monitor is also a new tool to SMS 2.0 that you can choose to install, since it is not installed by default. Health Monitor usage only applies to NT systems, specifically, NT workstations and NT servers, and not to Windows 95/98 systems. You may have used Performance Monitor before on NT servers. The SMS Health Monitor deals with a subset of new SMS counters that you view through the Health Monitor, giving you a real-time view of the overall health of your NT/2000 workstations and servers. The Health Monitor console communicates with the Health Monitor Client Agent.

In addition, Health Monitor handles monitoring of other Back Office software components: SQL Server, Exchange Server, and Internet Information Server. When system events occur that match a predefined policy trigger, an event is written to the Windows NT Event Log. Some of the counters that can be used are paging file, physical desk, network

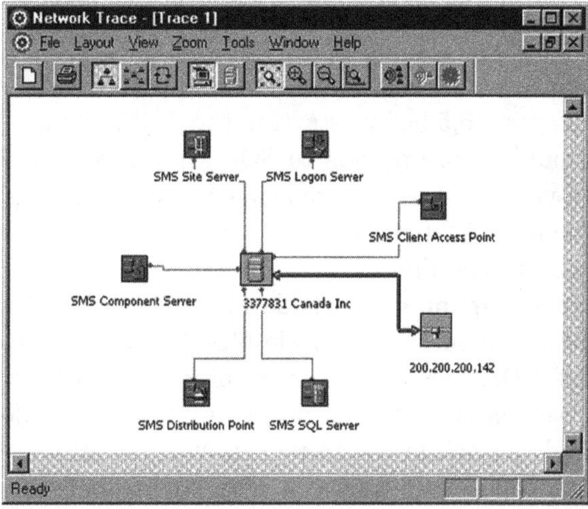

Figure 1-9 Output from Network Trace.

interface, server work queues, logical desk, and memory, to name but a few. You can then drill down into single parts of your system and obtain even more detail.

SMS Versions

Realistically, the first version you may come across is SMS version 1.2. This version had some market penetration, and it can be upgraded to version 2.0. In fact, you may find that they you may be managing an SMS version 1.2 and version 2.0 mixed environment. It almost goes without saying that a mixed SMS environment will experience problems with database storage and the synchronization of mixed SMS sites.

Version 2.0 of SMS has changed much of the terminology used in version 1.2. Table 1-2 will help you understand SMS 2.0 technology if you're upgrading, or still using SMS 1.2. For more details and explanation, see the complete glossary at the back of the book.

Upgrading SMS

SMS 1.2 can be upgraded to SMS 2.0, or it can interoperate with SMS 2.0. However, SMS 1.2 is primarily designed for Windows NT Server 3.51 running Service Pack 4 and operating as a domain controller. SMS 2.0 Site Server can only be installed on Windows NT Server 4.0 with Service Pack 4 installed. A site server does not have to be a domain controller, but it must be a member server in a domain.

SMS 1.2 was also designed for SQL Server version 6.0, whereas SMS 2.0 requires SQL Server version 6.5. SQL Server must be upgraded to either version 6.5 before starting the SMS 2.0 upgrade process. The best path would be to upgrade to SQL Server version 7.0 and Windows NT Server version 4.0 with Service Pack 4 before performing any SMS upgrade from 1.2 to 2.0.

If you are running SMS 1.0 or 1.1, you must upgrade to SMS version 1.2 before starting an upgrade to SMS 2.0. Taking a look at the client side, SMS 2.0 does not include MS-DOS 5.0 or later, Macintosh System 7, or IBM OS/2 client agents, whereas SMS 1.0 does. Therefore, if your client base is older and is not about to be upgraded anytime soon, you may find yourself forced to coexist with two different versions of SMS.

If at all possible, upgrade your client operating systems to support SMS 2.0 client agents. Steps will be provided in Chapter 4 on how to

TABLE 1-2

SMS terminology.

SMS 1.0 Terminology	SMS 2.0 Terminology
Distribution server	Distribution point
Helper server	Component server
Logon server	Logon point
Machine group	Static collection
Named queries	Dynamic collection
Package command	Packages node
Manager	Not available
Not available	Resource discovery
Software auditing	Software inventory
Jobs	Advertisements
Help desk utilities	Remote tools
LAN sender	Standard Sender
SNA sender	SNA RAS Sender
Database Manager	Database Maintenance Node
SMS Security Manager	WBEM namespace/SMS Provider
SMS Sender Manager	Not available
SMS Service Manager	SMS Service Manager
SMS Event Viewer	SMS Status Node
SMS Administrator	SMS Administrator console

install both primary and secondary site servers, along with tips on successful upgrades for SMS and SQL Server.

Where Windows 2000 and SMS Fit Together

As you may have guessed by now, SMS and the features of version 2.0 are not all entirely new. Whenever Microsoft announces a grand scheme, I usually think, “Gee, I wonder what they’ve renamed this time?” SMS 2.0 certainly has some new features but there are some old tried-and-true pieces as well, such as the Performance Monitor, which holds the data used by the Health Monitor. Moreover, if you have carried out any NT network support over the last couple of years, you probably have heard of another Microsoft initiative called *Zero Administration for Windows* (ZAW). Zero administration of the desktop is really what SMS is doing for us through hardware and software inventory, software installation, and remote desktop management.

The code name for the next release of SMS 2.X at this point is "Emerald." It will ship after Windows 2000 has been released and will include support for the Active Directory (AD). At some point in the future, it is conceivable that Windows 2000 will swallow up SMS as standalone product, becoming an in-house management and network service. I say *conceivable* because Windows 2000 contains all of the building blocks of SMS 2.0. Since designing and implementing a medium-to-large Windows 2000 network will take months if not several years, SMS still has a few good years left.

The next few pages are a primer and discussion of Windows 2000 concepts and features that impact or change the current SMS world.

IntelliMirror

The feature set of Windows 2000 that relates to the SMS initiative is grouped under the buzzword "IntelliMirror." The promise of IntelliMirror is grouped under these stated goals:

1. Reduced total cost of ownership by supporting the centralized administration of your network through Active Directory and Group Policy templates.
2. Software management control through each step of the application software cycle, from the initial installation through upgrades and removal.
3. Support for the mobile user: Roaming users can now have their documents, user settings, and applications follow them across the network.

IntelliMirror is not an entirely new technology but a collection of former Microsoft experiments. Because IntelliMirror depends on both the dedicated server and the client, it will only work completely with the combination of Windows 2000 servers, Windows 2000 Professional workstations, and software applications, such as Office 2000, that can take advantage of IntelliMirror features. The supporting players that make IntelliMirror function are as follows:

- Active Directory
- Group Policy
- Windows Installer Service
- Remote OS Installation Service

Active Directory

Active Directory is the big change for Windows 2000. Plan on spending months to implement AD properly, and keep in mind that all of your NT 4.0 knowledge is not required for Active Directory implementation. Active Directory is similar in nature to NetWare's NDS and Banyan VINES StreetTalk directory services offerings. However, the huge advantage that Microsoft has on their side is their relationship with many hardware vendors and software developers that have bought into the Active Directory concept. This level of support is something that NetWare and Banyan never managed to achieve.

Although the base design of Active Directory is the X.500 schema using defined objects, object classes, and attributes, Microsoft uses some additional twists for its owner implementation of Active Directory. Active Directory uses the dynamic DNS protocol to communicate with linked copies of the directory schema using the Lightweight Directory Access Protocol (LDAP) for querying the Active Directory objects. TCP/IP must be deployed as the standard protocol for Windows 2000. Older protocols like NetBEUI and WINS are available for older legacy solutions and for backward-compatibility with NT 4.0.

In order to ensure that the current Active Directory is always available to all servers linked together with Active Directory, Windows 2000 is designed and based on *multimaster replication*. This means each domain controller will contain a master replica of the directory and every change is automatically replicated to all domain controller servers.

There are no primary and backup domain controllers found in the Active Directory environment and Windows 2000. However, a Windows 2000 server can still act as a primary domain controller (PDC) for older NT 4.0 environments. SMS 2.0 does not fully support Active Directory, and so it is primarily a tool for the existing NT 4.0 environment. I realize that Microsoft is pushing SMS 2.0 to complement Active Directory, but at this writing SMS, 2.0 does not fully support AD. This will change over the next few years, however.

Windows 2000 Server Replication

Each server within a domain running Active Directory will store and maintain a complete copy of the domain directory. Anytime information is changed at one of the servers running Active Directory, it is replicated to the other servers through a process called multimaster replication, mentioned in the previous section.

The directory of each domain stores information only about the objects located in its domain. Active Directory is completely extensible, which means that you can add new attributes to existing objects by custom programming or by using the Active Directory Schema Manager utility. Active Directory also uses the Domain Naming System (DNS) for name resolution and name-to-address resolution. An Active Directory server will have a name in DNS format such as Mainoffice.companyname.com, as domain names are stored and referred to in DNS format. Active Directory fully supports versions 2 and 3 of the LDAP. As Figure 1-10 shows, the Windows 2000 server has a DNS name.

Active Directory and Domains

Domains within Active Directory use a new domain model; the MultiMaster Peer Control Model. This means that all domain controllers (DCs) within a domain can receive changes and replicate those changes; there are no primary or backup domain controllers within Active Directory. Each domain has its own security boundary, so security policies and settings will not cross from one domain into another. The admin-

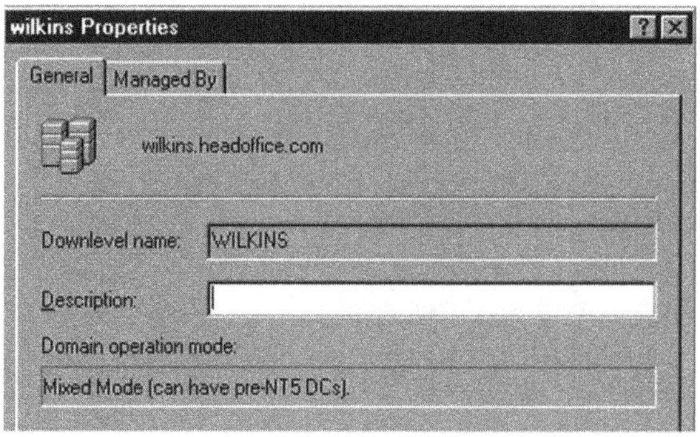

Figure 1-10 DNS names are used for defining Active Directory servers.

istrator of a domain has the absolute right to set group policy within that domain only.

Domain Trees

A *domain tree* is constructed by several domains that share a common schema, forming a seamless namespace. The first domain in a tree is called the *root* of the tree; the additional domains in the same tree are called *child* domains. The domain immediately above a domain in the same tree is called the *parent* of the child domain.

All domains that are in trees are associated with each other by two-way transitive trust relationships. Trust relationships in Active Directory and Windows 2000 are based on the Kerberos security protocol. A trust relationship is now "transitive and hierarchical," which means if Domain A trusts B and Domain B trusts C, Domain A will also trust C. Trusts can also be viewed through the namespace of the domain tree.

Windows 2000: Forests and Trees

A *forest* is a set of one or more *trees* (two or more domains linked together through a common schema) that do not form a common namespace. Trees share a common set of cross-relationship objects and Kerberos trust relationships known to the member trees in the forest.

Windows 2000 and Sites

A *site* is a place in a network that contains Active Directory servers. Sites are also defined as one or more TCP/IP subnets.

Organizational Units

Organizational units, or OUs, are logical containers in which you can place users, groups, computers, and other OUs. An organizational unit is an "electronic container" that you use in the Active Directory world to organize each domain into a logical grouping for your company. Figure 1-11 shows the creation of a new OU within the Active Directory.

The OU can contain the following familiar objects: users, computers, security groups, printers, applications, security policies, file shares, and more. Active Directory supports the delegation of administration of containers and subtrees to other users and groups. You could decide to create a tree of OUs inside each domain and then delegate authority for certain parts of the OU tree to a user or group of users.

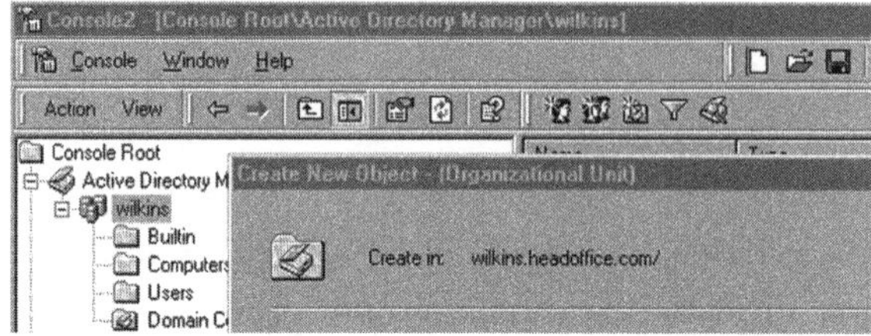

Figure 1-11 Creating an organizational unit in Active Directory.

Global Catalog

The *global catalog* is a new Windows 2000 network service that holds directory information from all domains in your company. It answers queries about objects anywhere on the network, even across domain trees. The global catalog works on an attribute search that is carried out across domains to find the desired object.

A global catalog is created automatically on the initial domain controller in the forest and is stored on specific servers throughout the enterprise on domain controllers that also act as global catalog servers.

Schema

Schema is a hard word to first digest. It is the formal definition of all object classes and the attributes that make up the defined object classes that can be stored in the Active Directory. The object classes that can be defined are users, groups, computers, domains, organizational units, and security policies.

Figure 1-12 shows the choices of objects that can be defined through Active Directory.

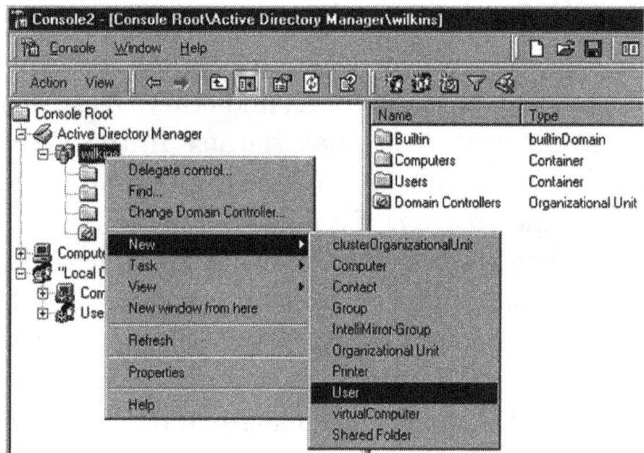

Figure 1-12 Active Directory object class examples.

Scripting

Scripts can be created for the control of the startup and shutdown of the computer system and the user logon and logoff. You can now control any system process or backup procedure you want to mandate for your users via a script file.

The Windows Scripting Host (WSH) was first introduced with Windows 98, and it is now a standard option for creating scripts for Windows 2000. WSH also integrates with VB script and PERL-type scripting, among others. There are five scripts that exist by default in Windows 2000:

- Legacy logon scripts. These are active on the User object; they also support WSH scripting for Windows 2000 and Windows 98 clients by default. Support for WSH can be installed on Windows 98 and NT 4.0 clients.
- Group Policy logon scripts
- Group Policy logoff scripts
- Group Policy startup scripts
- Group Policy shutdown scripts

Group Policy

Group policies are the successor to NT 4.0 system policies and much more. Microsoft's noble goal is to reduce the level of administration. Much greater control can be achieved with Group Policy, because it can be applied at the site level, at a domain level, or at the container level. Group Policy can also be inherited with security groups, another new feature of Windows 2000.

The five main areas of Group Policy are summarized in Table 1-3.

Windows Installer Service

The Windows Installer Service is a key IntelliMirror component for installing software applications. Using a standard package format also called an MSI (Microsoft Software Installer) package, identical to the SMS 2.0 package, the Windows Installer works with the SQL Server database that holds the information needed to install the application.

TABLE 1-3

Windows 2000 and Group Policy.

Group Policy	Description
Folder redirection	Allows folders that are used by a local user to be automatically redirected to a Server location. Upon logout and login, the folders would be resynchronized with no user input.
Logon/logoff scripts	Can be activated by computer name, user name, groups belonged to, and organizations.
Software installation	Involves installation of operating systems and software applications to the user's PC based on their placement in Active Directory objects (site, domain, or organizational unit).
Security settings	Complete security for files, folders, Registry keys, and system services based on group or user objects.
Administrative templates	The new name for system policies. ADM templates control access to the operating system, desktop settings, application menus, and settings.

The Windows Installer will also be able to repair or reinstall applications and perform rollback on installations that run into problems, just like SMS. Another term used with the Windows Installer is *just-in-time installation* (JIT), borrowed from the inventory control buzzword camp. This will allow the installation of software components as they are needed. Microsoft's forward-thinking plan is to utilize this feature for future Windows 2000 service packs, virus updates, and so on.

The administrator will also be able to force the installation of software components. The Windows Installer technology will be implemented on all Windows 2000 servers as a network service, the Application Installation Service. This will allow you to install applications completely even if the users don't have the privileges needed to install the application. Although this is a feature of the current SMS 2.0, the key benefit of Windows 2000 is the integration with Active Directory.

Remote OS Installation Service

This new feature for Windows 2000 takes advantage of a new technology called the *Pre-Boot Execution Environment* (PXE) that is linked to DCHP and allows the installation of an operating system to a remote client's

PC. How much advantage this will actually be in the real world where client-based operating systems are usually preinstalled and where most PCs that want to run Windows 2000 Professional will be new remains to be seen. However, for reinstalling selected clients, this feature could prove to be a great benefit. (In fact, we can already do this with Symantac's Ghost cloning software and other third-party utilities; the benefit, again, may be the integration with Active Directory.)

The remote server that supports the Remote Installation Service (RIS) provides two options:

1. Installation from an RIS network location that mimics the CD-ROM installation of operating systems or software applications. In the current SMS 2.0 world, a package is created that then installs from a distribution server. So this is not new—just repackaged SMS features.
2. Cloning through a process called SysPrep that creates a generic installation image that is replicated to the RIS server for network installation on new or damaged workstations. This is also not a new feature; we can use a software tool called SysDiff to carry out the same task in the NT 4.0 world.

Licensing Requirements for Deploying SMS

Ahhh... licensing. Just the term conjures up the fear of lawsuits and the hassle of just how many darned licenses do you really have to buy this time. Licensing and upgrades are the secrets to Microsoft's success.

With regard to SMS, one site server license is required for each site regardless of the number of site systems that are configured within a site. SMS clients can only use per-seat licensing, not per-server licensing, to access the SMS site. Per-seat licensing costs more than per-server licensing, but when you think about it, there'll be more than one server in your organization running NT or 2000 server. Therefore, in the long run, per-seat licensing will be cheaper for using SMS.

If you purchase Microsoft BackOffice and SMS and SQL Server bundled together, then the SMS site server and SQL Server have to be installed on the same computer system. If you decide that you want SQL Server and SMS to be installed on two different computers, an additional

SQL Server license will be required. SQL Server database client licenses are not necessary if the SQL Server database supports SMS exclusively.

SMS and SQL Server

As you know, SMS is a client/server application that runs primarily on the NT platform working with a Microsoft SQL Server database. The inventory that we've talked about in this chapter with regard to the hardware/software inventory and software metering is stored in two SQL databases.

CHAPTER 2

Concepts and Architecture of Systems Management Server

In this chapter you will learn about:

- Resources and clients of SMS
- The roles that processes, threads, and services play with SMS
- SMS architecture and design
- Primary and secondary site roles

Understanding SMS Concepts

When SMS is first installed, it's as a single primary SMS site on a Windows NT server and preferably a domain controller. If you had just the one SMS server, it would perform all of the management tasks required across your defined site boundaries. The term *SMS site* in the SMS world describes the resources working with the SMS site server that resides within a local subnet or group of subnets bound by a common IP network address or IPX network. (Remember that resources are the computer systems, routers, hubs, and bridges installed across your network.) Another way of looking at this is from the administrative point of view. The site defines the network that your SMS server will manage and control through your defined SMS administrative tasks.

Your SMS site server is configured to discover all of the current resources across the network as defined by your site boundaries, and all of the site-related information is stored in the SMS site SQL database.

The last few sentences may have your head spinning, so we'll look at common SMS concepts in more detail. (After all, the concepts can't be assumed to be familiar to you; otherwise, what would be the point of reading this book?)

Resources and Clients

First of all, a *resource* is an object that can be managed by SMS. You are probably used to hearing the term and concept of the object by now, but if not, think of the term *object* as a single entity, such as, say, an office chair. When you sit down on the chair, you may decide to adjust the height and position of the chair. You have just adjusted the object's *properties*.

Now, if you are sitting in front of any computer running Microsoft Windows, then you will have the Explorer shell desktop with familiar icons such as My Computer, Network Neighborhood, and so on. Each of these icons is also called an object. If you want to change the size or color of a particular icon, you have to adjust its properties by using the mouse to right-click and display a context menu and then selecting the option properties to make the desired changes.

In the world of SMS, the SMS server scans and manages client and server resources, and all resources are defined as objects. Depending on the type of object or objects found, SMS can control the object by modifying and controlling its properties. That is, if the object found is supported by SMS, then SMS can manage it. Supported resources within the architecture of an IP or IPX network include computers, hubs, routers, bridges, gateways, communication servers, and printers.

The process of finding these resources is called *discovery*. The information collected from supported resources is stored in a discovery data record (DDR) that is passed on to the SMS site server, where it is stored in the SMS site SQL database.

SMS uses several methods to perform the process of discovery, and we will step through all of the methods available to deploy in Chapter 7 "Resource Discovery and Client Installation."

SMS can be executed to run on all computer systems across your network, including workstations, where the clients are located, and also on servers. Workstation and Server clients can have SMS client software installed on them either at the time of discovery or as a local installation at the client's PC.

Depending on the size of your network, your dedicated SMS servers will be installed as either a primary SMS site server or as a secondary site system. In addition, you will most definitely have other existing file servers performing other file and print tasks besides SMS management roles. As mentioned, for these servers, SMS client software can also be installed, making them SMS clients; this allows you to manage all file servers through SMS management.

SMS Site Models and Roles

Your complete network can be managed quite well as one SMS site, assuming you don't have more than a few hundred clients. Microsoft recommends that each LAN has at least one SMS site, and no site should span more than one LAN. If your network is connected together through a wide area network, then it would be divided into several SMS sites, and each site will have its own SMS site server—that is, an NT server with SMS installed. The IP address of each site would define the site boundaries used by SMS.

Your total SMS site hierarchy, or chain of command, classifies or defines the roles and relationships of all of the installed SMS sites in your organization.

Starting at the Top

At the top of the tree in your hierarchy, the SMS site found here is known as the *central site*. All management and configuration data move down the SMS tree in a "top-down" manner, from the central site to lower-level sites.

Another way to describe this relationship is as a parent-child relationship. The parent site sends its management instructions down to its child sites for processing and deploying on existing SMS clients. The child site or sites reports on its current situation, and in response to the parent site's queries, it sends status information back up to the parent sites.

The Central Site

As mentioned, the central site is the primary site at the top of the SMS tree or hierarchy. It is the only SMS site that cannot be a child to any other SMS site. It's the top dog in the total chain of command. As a result, it obtains and stores the entire database for the entire SMS tree, including all lower primary and secondary sites that exist. Since all lower-level sites report all SMS information to the central site, you can view all lower sites and discovered resources across your SMS environment.

Primary and Secondary Sites

If your network is small (less than a few hundred clients), your first SMS installation will be a site that is defined as a *primary site*. As your network grows, you can add additional child sites that can be either primary or secondary sites.

A *secondary site* is defined as a site that has SMS client computers to administer but lacks an SMS database or an SMS Administrator console locally. It instead passes its data onto a defined primary site, and all SMS administration needed at the secondary site is performed from the primary site, even across a WAN link.

That is not to say that a child site can't be a primary site; it can, and the proper name would then be a *child primary site*. Child primary sites, in turn, are attached or linked to *parent primary sites*.

Sounds like a good time for a picture right now, so take a look at Figure 2-1, which shows the possible combinations.

Just a few sentences ago I described the parent-child concept. Let's expand that a bit further. A parent site is a primary site that has at least one other site below it in the SMS tree. Only primary sites can have child sites. You can't have a single child site administering a child site below it; it would have to be a parent site with a child site below it.

Child Sites

A child site always reports to a site above it in the SMS tree. In a large network, at the child site, SMS copies all of the information collected at the child site to the parent site above it. In turn, the parent site could

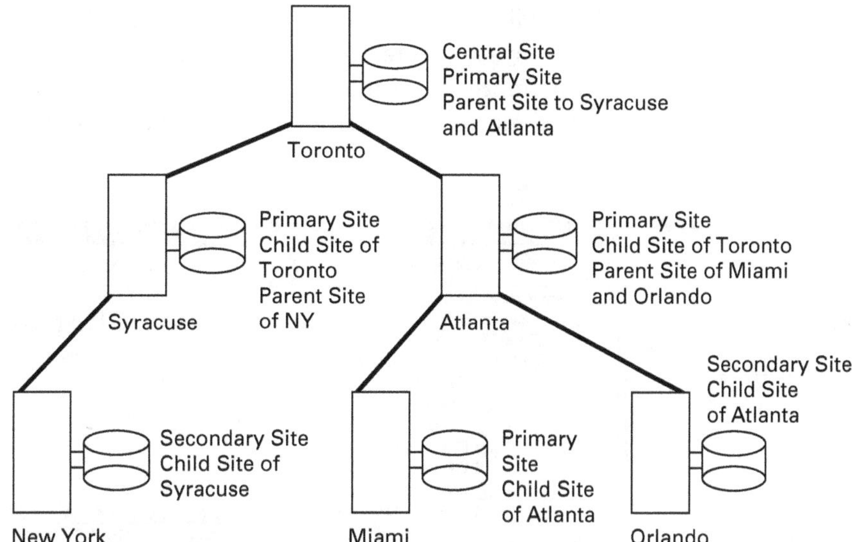

Figure 2-1 SMS site architecture.

also be a child site to another parent site. If this were indeed the case, the parent site would then copy all of the amassed data from the lower child site and the local parent/child site to the parent site above it.

A primary site can have one or several child sites below it. However, a secondary site cannot have a child site below it; it can only be a child site.

Using primary and secondary sites combined with the parent-child relationship allows for great flexibility in planning and expanding your SMS deployment. Using the SMS Administrator console, shown in Figure 2-2, you can view and monitor the entire SMS hierarchy. The SMS model can also be greatly expanded to meet your network's needs now and in the future. In addition, it can be made to fit your existing network either locally or across WAN links.

SMS Site Architecture

Hopefully, it's understood that on a small network the initial implementation of SMS will be with one primary site server performing all of the SMS management, access, and database roles. However, if other available NT computer servers in fact exist, you may want to deploy SMS server tasks on those servers rather than on your primary site server. The role of a specific site system would be that particular SMS function that the defined system performs during the day-to-day operations of Systems Management Server.

By adding additional resources to the SMS site and assigning particular site system roles to these resources, system performance can be greatly improved because the SMS load on your network will now be distributed more evenly across your existing servers

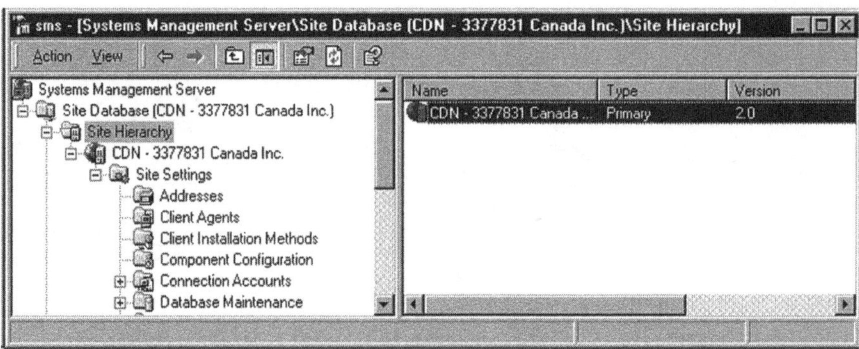

Figure 2-2 SMS Administrator console showing the primary site.

Defining Site Systems

To define your site systems, you will have to do the following:

- Think about which roles to assign to your site systems.
- Make sure that the selected site system computers are up to par with regard to hardware.
- Prepare the site system connection accounts.
- Finally using the SMS Administrator console, create the site systems and assign the site system roles that you have decided on.

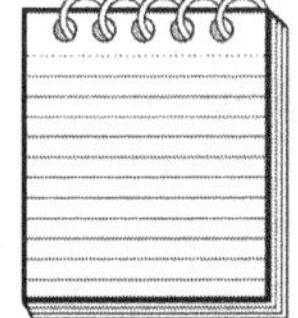

NOTE *Chapter 3 "Planning for the Deployment of Systems Management Server" holds the detailed answers to these design issues.*

Defining Site Systems

The four types of site systems that you can utilize for SMS system roles are as follows:

- *NetWare bindery volumes* Versions 2 and 3.X of NetWare used a hidden database called a *bindery* for control of the server's environment. In the world of SMS, NetWare 3.X is extremely limited, as we will see in the next section.
- *NetWare NDS volumes* Versions 4 and 5.X of NetWare support NDS. In the future, as Active Directory is implemented with Windows 2000 Server, the NetWare NDS environment will become seamless with the Active Directory world.
- *Windows NT servers* This includes primary and backup domain controllers as well as any standalone (member servers) in the domain.
- *Windows NT shares* Using the existing technology available in NT networks, network shares can be used to create what are called "site systems within a site" by combining servers and network shares to provide support to the SMS site server. This can be a network share on any NT server or workstation share. The workstation share is usually not going to be a valid option, since the NT workstation PC isn't usually on all the time and the point of SMS management is 24/7 coverage. However, in theory, it would work.

The SMS roles that you can delegate to these site system and installed components are described below.

Client Access Point (CAP)

The client access point, or CAP, is responsible for communicating with SMS client computers and the site server. You must have at least one CAP in each site. You should plan on having additional CAPs in order to distribute the workload and also to act as a backup if the other CAPs are unavailable.

Once the client is a registered SMS client, during every logon, a client access point is contacted for any relevant SMS management tasks that are to be performed on the client computer. All hardware and software inventory collection, plus any additional changes in the client's current circumstance, are sent to the CAP. The CAP is also responsible for the initial setup of SMS agents at the client's PC. If you have just one primary site server, then it will automatically be assigned the role of client access point.

To check your site system for its current role in SMS, start by selecting *Start | Programs | System Management Server*, and then select *SMS Administrator Console*. Next:

1. Select and highlight the desired site hierarchy.
2. Click on and open your primary or secondary site server.
3. Click on and open *Site Settings*.
4. Highlight the *Site Systems* icon.
5. Double-click on the site server or site servers that are displayed to show the current site system properties assigned.
6. Select the *Client Access Point* tab; the checkbox that reads "Use this site system as a client access point" should be checked, as shown in Figure 2-3.

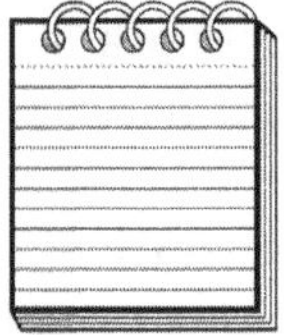

NOTE *The larger the network, the heavier the load at the client access point. If you have multiple backup domain controllers backing up your primary domain controller, then multiple CAPs are probably needed.*

On your CAP server you must have at least one NTFS (NT File System) partition available. SMS does not support CAPs on FAT (file

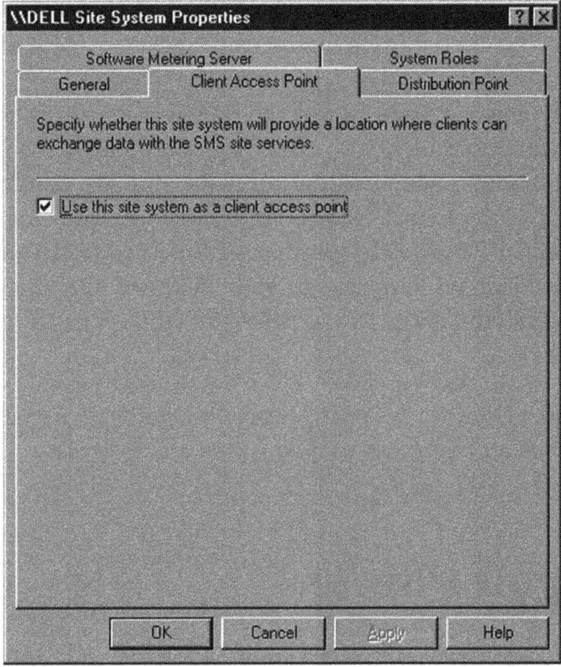

Figure 2-3 Site system properties as viewed with the SMS Administrator console.

allocation table) partitions, and the rationale goes like this: Files stored on FAT partitions are not secure. I think you would have to agree that in the server environment, this is good thinking.

Distribution Point

The role of the distribution point is to store the files and software application programs that will be used for automatic software distribution to client computers. When the client computer accesses a CAP, it may receive a *software distribution advertisement*, which will in turn direct the client PC to the appropriate distribution point to begin the defined process. A distribution point is always associated with a specific package; in addition, a package may have several distribution points.

Either an NT share, a Windows NT server, or a NetWare volume can be designated a distribution point. Each distribution point has the potential to be quite busy. Think of being on the Internet and trying to connect to a popular site to download software, and you get the idea of how overloaded the distribution point could become, depending on the software being installed.

The most common use of the distribution point in day-to-day network operations will be in providing an operating system patch or virus software updates, which can occur daily but are usually weekly, and that's enough to deal with. You have to keep in mind the size of the update as well. Good long-term planning will dictate that your distribution points will not just be assigned to your primary site server but to other computer systems within your SMS site (if they are available, of course).

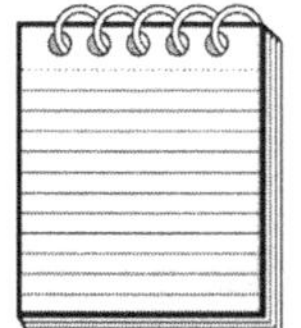

NOTE *The Site systems properties shown in Figure 2-3 also show the distribution point role played by your site server.*

Logon Point

One of the first points of contact between an SMS system and a client computer is at the logon point. The primary and backup domain controllers on an NT network act as the default logon points across the domain. SMS installs the needed logon software onto the domain servers within the domain. When the client logs on to the NT domain, the logon script points the client to the correct client access point, which would then take over the SMS discovery and management role.

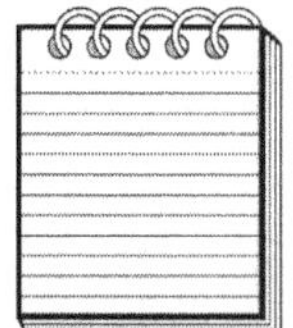

NOTE *If NetWare were the primary network environment, then the NetWare NDS or bindery volume would carry out the logon point task.*

SMS Site Database Server

The system that stores the SMS site database for the primary site carries out the SMS site database server job. SQL Server must be installed on this computer system. SQL can be installed on the actual primary site server, or you can move the SQL server to another network location. There can even be several SQL databases in use within an SMS site. For example, the software-metering feature of SMS uses a separate database for the storage of this information.

SMS Provider

This is another internal function of SMS. The SMS Provider must be located on the computer system that is the site server or that functions as the site database server. Its internal role is linking the SMS Administrator console and the site database server.

Software Metering Server

Only NT servers can provide this role in an SMS environment. Server-located software metering is performed when the Software Metering Client Agent initiates direct communication with the software-metering server. An example would be the software-metering server responding to a client request for licensing for a particular software program. The software-metering data is then passed to the SQL database server that handles and stores this unique separate database.

Software-Metering Database Server

The software-metering database server is again an SQL server. The SQL database for the software-metering task can be installed on the primary site computer system, or it can be installed on another site server within the SMS site.

Understanding Site-to-Site Communication in the SMS Hierarchy

Every SMS site continually communicates with its parent sites and its child sites, if available. These communications take the form of packages, advertisements, queries, and software collections. The management information and SMS depend on travels from parent to child sites and back to the parent throughout the SMS hierarchy. If you had a central site connected to several primary sites, which in turn were connected to primary or secondary sites, the design model used by SMS means that any direct contact from a lower secondary site back to the central site is not required.

For example, let's trace the communication paths in Figure 2-3. This example uses a central site in New York linked to sites in Boston and Washington, D.C. These sites in turn are linked to Philadelphia and Pittsburgh. The SMS design in Figure 2-4 has three primary sites. The New York site has been configured as the central site and it is also a primary site. The locations New York, Boston, and Washington, D.C. are all primary sites. Sites in Philadelphia and Pittsburgh can be either primary or secondary sites.

The central site, New York, needs to communicate with all sites only if there is a need to distribute software or send any other data directly to the Philadelphia or Pittsburgh sites without channeling it through the other primary sites in Boston or Washington, D.C. For most day-to-day SMS operations, the central and primary site in New York only needs to communicate with the primary sites in Boston and Washington, D.C.

Moving down to the other sites and their communication roles within the SMS organization, both sites in Boston and Washington, D.C. are the important links in the entire chain. Follow the communication paths that each site must maintain:

- The Boston site needs to communicate with sites in New York and Philadelphia.

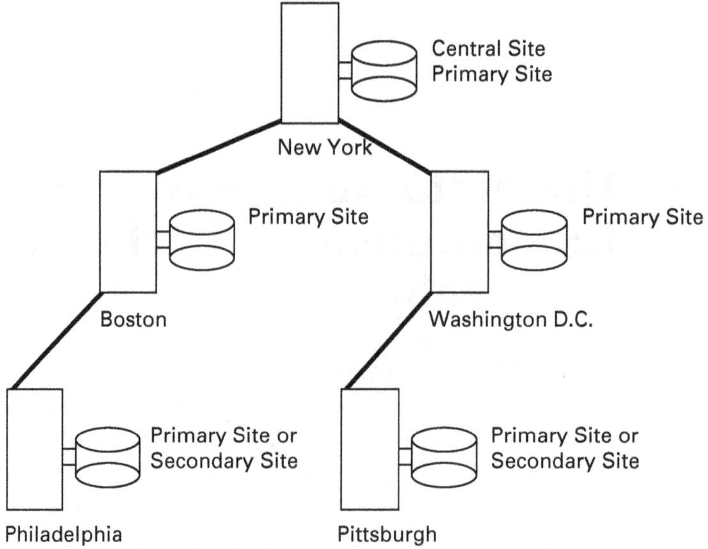

Figure 2-4 Site-to-site communications.

- The Washington, D.C. site needs to communicate with the Pittsburgh site and the New York site.
- Philadelphia in turn must only communicate with the Boston site.
- Pittsburgh must only communicate with the Washington, D.C. site.

Under the hood, in order to communicate, these sites must have installed a communications manager called a *sender*. Typically, one or more senders will have been installed by default. The sender does not provide the actual connections from site to site. What the sender does do is provide "connection management" by making sure that the data transfer between sites is free from errors, by fixing errors when they do occur, and by closing all connections when they're not needed.

An analogy could be made between the management tasks carried out by the Transmission Control Protocol (TCP) used in TCP/IP and Windows networks and Sequential Packet Interchange (SPX) used in IPX/SPX and NetWare networks. Both TCP/IP and IPX/SPX control the order of packets, packet errors, and overall synchronization of data flow across the network. In the SMS world, the sender assumes this task.

When a primary site is first installed, two senders are installed and configured by default: Standard Sender and Courier Sender.

Checking out Standard Sender

To look at Standard Sender, open up the SMS Administrator console, which is found by selecting Start | Programs | System Management Server, and then selecting SMS Administrator Console.

1. Now select and highlight the desired site hierarchy.
2. Click on and open your primary or secondary site server.
3. Click on and open *Site Settings*.
4. Highlight the folder called *Sender*.
5. On the right-hand side of the screen, Standard Sender will be visible.
6. Double-click on *Standard Sender* to see the defined properties.

Figure 2-5 shows the properties of Standard Sender on a primary site server.

When SMS is installed on a local area network using either TCP/IP or IPX, you do not have to install any additional senders. However, you can

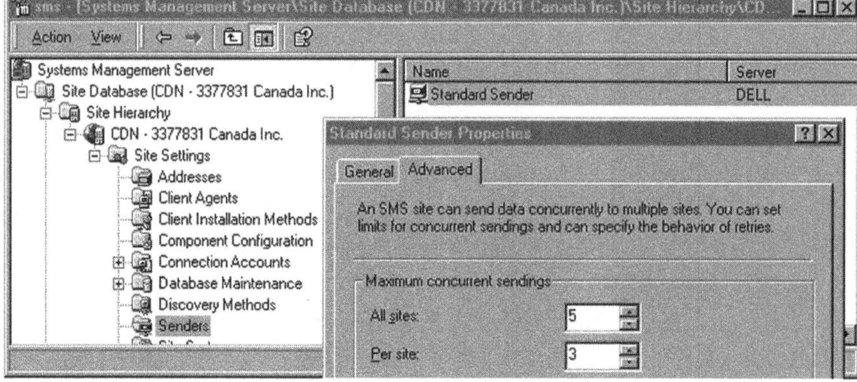

Figure 2-5 Looking at the Standard Sender properties using the SMS Administrator console.

tweak the number of concurrent sendings or the number-of-retry settings for the Standard Sender. There are no system settings that can be changed for the Courier Sender.

Courier Sender is located and started by selecting Start | Programs | System Management Server, and then selecting Courier Sender. Details on using Courier Sender are found in Chapter 12 "Using the SMS Installer." All senders do their work as an internal part of a site server called a *component server*.

Component Server

Any site system or computer system that uses a sender is using a *component server*. The component server is a hidden system thread that ensures accurate communications with other SMS primary and secondary sites using senders. The *sender* is the manager of the installed network protocols, such as TCP/IP and IPX, and supported remote protocols, such as RAS, ISDN, X.25, and SNA.

Your choice in choosing additional senders really depends on how reliable and fast your WAN connections currently are between your existing SMS sites. If speed or reliability is not a problem, you can use the default Standard Sender. If you're using RAS to communicate between sites remotely, there are several RAS options for your remote connection.

The default senders installed and configured for SMS sites are as follows:

- Standard Sender and Courier Sender for primary sites

- Courier Sender, then the choices of either Standard Sender or Asynchronous for secondary sites

When a secondary site is first created, one of your tasks will be to create an address that links the new secondary site you are installing to the existing parent site. Choices will be either a Standard Sender address or an Asynchronous RAS Sender address. When you select one of the address choices, the corresponding sender is automatically installed to the new secondary site.

There are six possible types of senders that can be installed to support the existing protocol environment. Windows NT 4.0 must be the server of choice for installing senders. NetWare servers cannot carry out this role.

- *Standard Sender* Installed by default for every primary site installed, the Standard Sender is utilized for LAN and WAN communications when sites and segments are interconnected by routers.
- *Asynchronous Sender* This sender is used for communicating remotely using RAS over an asynchronous link. It is not installed by default.
- *ISDN RAS Sender* This sender is used for communicating remotely using RAS over an ISDN link. It is not installed by default.
- *X.25 RAS Sender* This sender is used for communicating remotely using RAS over an X.25 link. It is not installed by default.
- *SNA RAS Sender* This sender is used for communicating remotely using RAS over an SNA link. It is not installed by default.
- *Courier Sender* Installed by default for every primary site, Courier Sender is used to transfer package data used in software distribution using a compact disc or tape as the medium. Microsoft is merely facing reality here; sometimes a custom package you create will be much too large to send across the network. An example could be a package containing Office 2000 to be sent across a slow network. You could then decide to use the Courier Sender Manager at the SMS site to create what is called a *parcel*. A parcel is a collection of software files to be transferred from one site to another using Courier Sender. The parcel can be written to tape, CD-ROM, or a Zip drive. Then you would physically overnight or snail-mail your package to the destination site where the support people could then use the Courier Sender Manager to accept the parcel and then import the package into the destination site.

Courier Sender can be only used for sending package data. In order to create a package, you would use the Courier Sender Manager to create and receive parcels. More details on configuring and the deploying senders can be found in Chapter 5 "Configuring SMS Sites."

Configuring Address for SMS Sites

All sites in an SMS hierarchy use a defined address for parent and child sites. Much like a data packet, each site that sends data must have an address for the site that will receive it. However, addresses in the SMS world contain sets of information about how to actually contact a destination site, so there's a little more detail than just sending and receiving addresses. The address information will detail how to contact a destination site, what site to contact, and which server needs to be contacted and connected to.

Depending on the sender you've chosen to use, you will create the address type that coincides to the sender used for communication. Both the address and sender must be properly configured before communication can be enabled between SMS sites.

When you install a secondary site through the SMS Administrator console, the Installation Wizard prompts you for the type of address to create; the default is Standard Sender.

As a further example: To establish communications to another site using Standard Sender, you must first create a Standard Sender address to that site. To contact the site using Courier Sender, you must create a Courier Sender address to that site, and so on. This task is carried out through the SMS Administrator console by selecting the Senders folder, then right-clicking and selecting New. This will present the five sender types that SMS supports for communication.

SMS Architecture

In order to properly troubleshoot and understand SMS when things don't work as planned, having a solid background in the architecture and design of SMS is vital. Knowing how both the server and client architecture work and deploy together can really help you in understanding troubleshooting problems and bandwidth issues as you roll out SMS.

First, let's start with the SMS server architecture. The architecture of the SMS server is broken down into two separate sections: the installed SMS components and the WBEM interface.

SMS Components

Keep in mind that this architecture is closely linked to the NT operating system architecture, since your SMS site server is an NT server and SMS is indeed a Microsoft product. Any change that you make through the SMS Administrator console involves accessing SMS software services. All installed SMS components found on your NT server can be viewed through the Services icon in the Control Panel.

The services are actually the SMS subroutines that work together to carry out your SMS tasks. Depending on what SMS features you have installed, there could be services for software distribution, hardware inventory, software metering, and any other scheduled SMS management task or utility. See Figure 2-6.

WBEM Interface

The WBEM interface (WBEM stands for "Web-Based Enterprise Management") works in conjunction with two fairly new technologies through two Microsoft initiatives called Windows Management Instrumentation (WMI) and Dynamic Component Object Model (DCOM).

WBEM is an initiative supported across the computer industry, establishing a standard for accessing management information from potentially diverse hardware and software manufacturers and systems. In English, this means WBEM is the middle interface to raw data from various sources that can be used by the Windows Management Instrumentation front end. WBEM is based on the Common Information Model (CIM), another standard being pushed by the Desktop Management Task Force (DMTF).

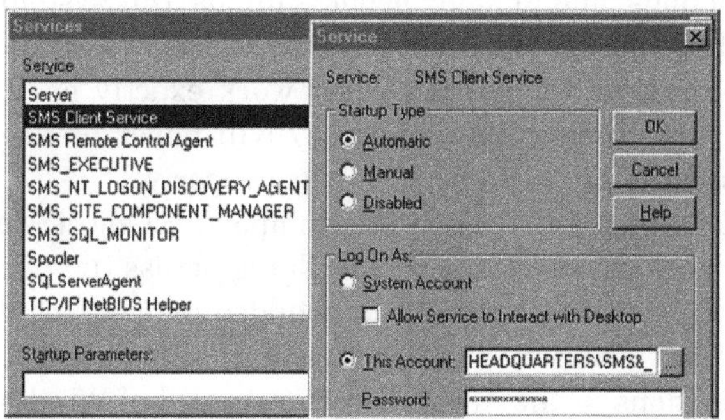

Figure 2-6 SMS services installed on the primary site server.

The standards are as follows:

1. Define the structures and conventions necessary to access information about the objects that are to be managed.
2. Support the centralization of information so that different clients and management tools can provide, retrieve, and analyze data.
3. Support authorized access to managed objects from anywhere in the network so that these objects can be analyzed and manipulated.

So, WBEM is not a user interface or a database, Registry, directory, or file replacement. It is merely an initiative that proposes a set of standards for managing networks that both Microsoft and SMS fully support.

Dynamic Component Object Model (DCOM)

DCOM began life as Dynamic Data Exchange (DDE) and OLE for the object linking and embedding of data records across a network between clients and server locations. The classic example is the manager who doesn't know how to use computers that well yet and who needs to know how his company is doing. A spreadsheet could be created for the manager so he can view a spreadsheet with summarized data pulled from different departments, along with network locations throughout the company.

Using OLE and DDE, a master spreadsheet could be linked with several other spreadsheets stored in different locations around the network. When the manager started up his spreadsheet, in the background his computer queried the other linked spreadsheets and provided an updated view of the company's data for the different departments for the hapless manager. DDE and OLE in the real world had problems due to memory restrictions, and in many people's minds, this system was never deployed.

What you should realize about Microsoft is that once they roll out a product, even though it doesn't work exactly as promised, this doesn't mean the underlying technology will never be used. They will merely rename the product once it works properly.

OLE and DDE became the Component Object Model (COM), allowing us to perform linking and embedding across the network, and across the Internet, with security features added in. COM then became DCOM, for Dynamic Component Object Model, which will allow for distributed applications in the Active Directory world of Windows 2000.

Today, the choices of objects that we can link with are much more than just spreadsheets or documents. Since everything in our 32-bit world is a defined object, we can link and embed with most anything using DCOM as a communication tool. And using SMS, we're using it distributed application that is used to control clients and resources across LANs and WANs

DCOM is a current component of Windows NT 4.0, Windows 98, and Windows 2000, and it can be installed for Windows 95. A free update can be downloaded from http://www.microsoft.com/win95.

Microsoft's Implementation of WBEM Using WMI

Microsoft is using the Windows Management Instrumentation standard for their deployment of WBEM. Other supporting management tools in the NT world include Active Directory (AD), the Microsoft Management Console, and the Windows Scripting Host (WSH).

On NT 4.0 systems, with the installation of Service Pack 4, the WMI components are also installed on your NT system. If you are a developer, the WMI components are available through the Software Development Kit (SDK). The components provide you with:

- A COM API that provides a single point of access for all management information on your NT network. This API is the interface for data retrieval from primary and secondary sites.
- Event architecture that allows any changes in management information to be reported or analyzed and forwarded to either a local or remote management location. SMS uses this architecture for network analysis through the Event Viewer and the more robust version of Network Monitor found in SMS.
- A query language for reporting that interfaces with SQL Server.
- A new scriptable API that allows developers and administrators to use either the new Windows Scripting Host or Visual Basic, Microsoft JScript, or Perl for developing custom deployment, installation, or logon scripts.

So how does it all work together? When SMS needs to review or manipulate any supported object, a request is made to the CIM Object Manager through the COM interface. In English, this means you are using the SMS Administrator console.

The SMS site database is used to store all object data. Figure 2-7 shows the relationship between WBEM and SMS.

Threads and Services

Threads, services, and applications are all part of the "under the hood" world of an SMS site server or client. Site-to-site communication, resource discovery, client installation, database maintenance, and reporting are but a few of the SMS tasks that must be deployed and maintained across your SMS site. Threads and services are the components that the SMS Executive employs to carry out its management tasks.

Think of a thread as a miniature task that is running in the background in parallel with other tasks. The thread's overall status and overall job progress is being monitored by the boss at all times. And, as mentioned, the SMS boss is the SMS Executive that monitors and controls all installed and functioning services. If you press the keys Ctrl-Shift-Esc at

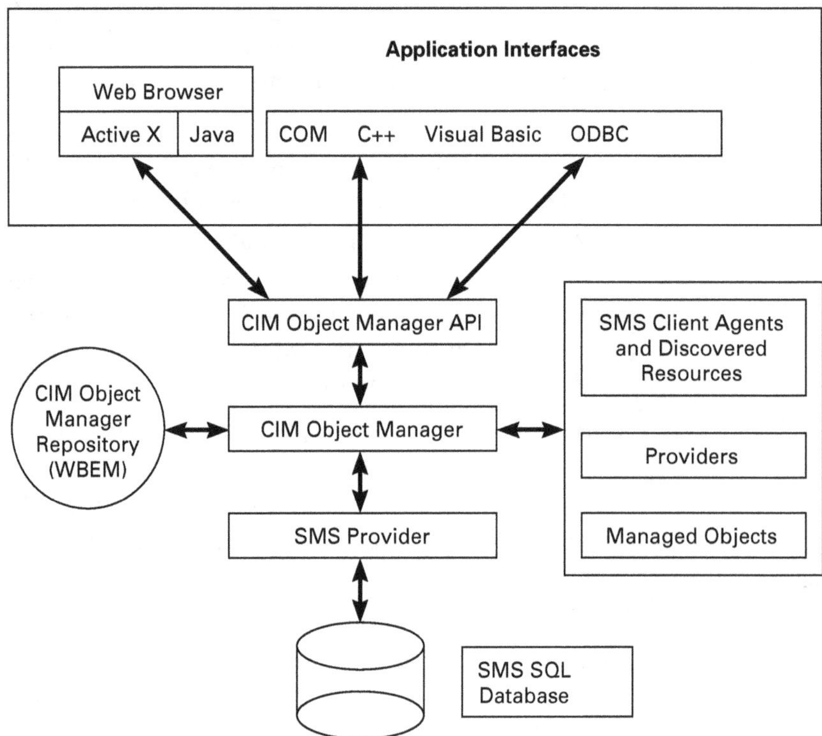

Figure 2-7 How SMS and WBEM fit together.

the same time, you can view the running processes on your NT workstation and server through the Task Manager, as Figure 2-8 shows you. Notice the EXE processes running on my primary site server and the number of threads assigned to each process. The more responsibility the process has, the more threads you will see assigned to the task.

To check out the actual performance of SMS in real time, we can use Performance Monitor, or Health Monitor. Details are found in Chapter 15 "Troubleshooting with SMS." If you install another SMS service, for example, Software Inventory, the required software services and thread components will be installed and then started. A collection of DLLs, EXE files, and Registry settings are the very real pieces that are installed for every SMS software component running.

If you take a few minutes to look at the relationship between the installed SMS services and the thread components of the SMS Executive using the Services icon in Control Panel shown in Figure 2-9 and Task Manager shown in Figure 2-8, you will get an excellent feel for the service and thread components.

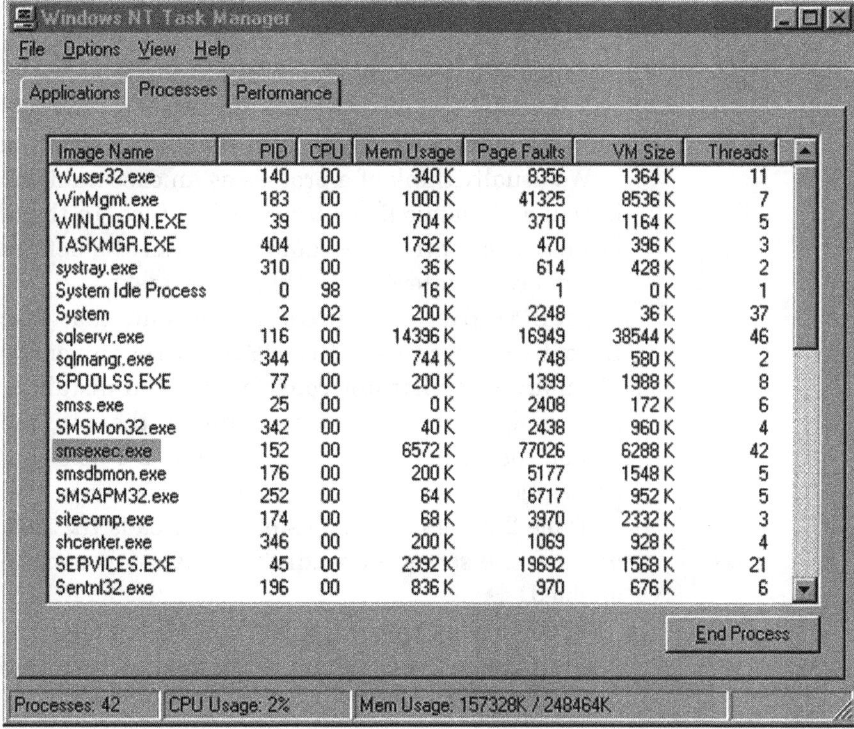

Image Name	PID	CPU	Mem Usage	Page Faults	VM Size	Threads
Wuser32.exe	140	00	340 K	8356	1364 K	11
WinMgmt.exe	183	00	1000 K	41325	8536 K	7
WINLOGON.EXE	39	00	704 K	3710	1164 K	5
TASKMGR.EXE	404	00	1792 K	470	396 K	3
systray.exe	310	00	36 K	614	428 K	2
System Idle Process	0	98	16 K	1	0 K	1
System	2	02	200 K	2248	36 K	37
sqlservr.exe	116	00	14396 K	16949	38544 K	46
sqlmangr.exe	344	00	744 K	748	580 K	2
SPOOLSS.EXE	77	00	200 K	1399	1988 K	8
smss.exe	25	00	0 K	2408	172 K	6
SMSMon32.exe	342	00	40 K	2438	960 K	4
smsexec.exe	152	00	6572 K	77026	6288 K	42
smsdbmon.exe	176	00	200 K	5177	1548 K	5
SMSAPM32.exe	252	00	64 K	6717	952 K	5
sitecomp.exe	174	00	68 K	3970	2332 K	3
shcenter.exe	346	00	200 K	1069	928 K	4
SERVICES.EXE	45	00	2392 K	19692	1568 K	21
Sentnl32.exe	196	00	836 K	970	676 K	6

Figure 2-8 Processes and threads viewed through the Task Manager.

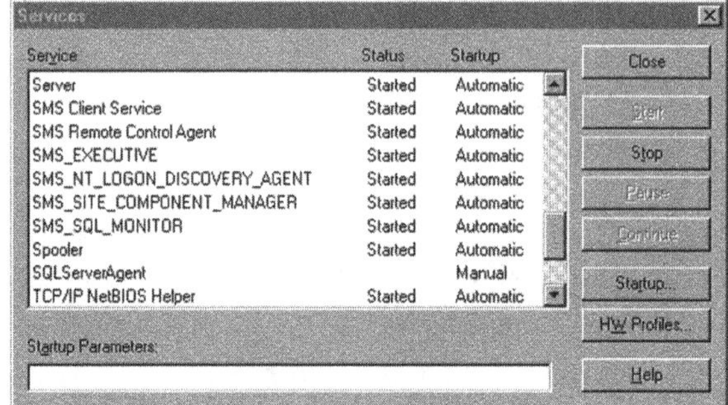

Figure 2-9
SMS Server Service components.

Services, Processes, and Threads

The design of SMS is a very complicated client/server system made up of many integrated components, network services, dedicated processes, and threads. Each installed SMS feature relies on a defined set of services, processes, and threads to do its job.

Practically all SMS processes run as a Windows NT service on the installed primary and secondary site servers, as well as the other installed site systems. The SMS Executive service runs as a NT service, and it is the primary "worker process" in the SMS world. This process contains many threads, each in charge of a different SMS task.

We usually think of a process as an executable file working with a collection of dynamic link library (DLL) files. In the SMS world, think of a process as a control program that works at a defined address space managing a set of interrelated threads or tasks.

An SMS Executive thread is a module that executes below the SMS Executive service. Certain SMS processes run only site systems or where the SMS Administrator console has been installed. If an SMS task has been assigned to another computer in the site, these defined processes run on the assigned site system. Table 2-1 lists the SMS services, its job description, and where it resides on the server.

Table 2-2 lists the names of the threads that are, or can be, executed on your site server, depending on the components and features that are enabled.

The types of processes that can be running on your site server are listed in Table 2-3 as an aid in troubleshooting SMS problems.

TABLE 2-1 SMS services, location, and job description.

Name of SMS Service	Server Location	Job Description
Info Agent	SMS site server	Create reports from the data.
Info Aps	SMS site server	Manages Crystal components.
Info Sentinel	SMS Administrator console computer	Uses the Crystal snap-in and Crystal services to manage communication between the SMS Administrator console and the Crystal services.
Monitor Control Service	SMS Administrator console computer	Executes Network Monitor collection of data.
NT Logon Discovery Agent	Defined logon point	Sends all Logon Discovery DDRs to the sites with Logon Discovery enabled.
SMS Executive	SMS site server, CAP, SMS Sender server	Is the main SMS component managing and controls all SMS operations with threads.
SMS License Server	Software metering server	Is responsible for the granting and denying of client registration of licensed and metered software applications.
SMS Site Component Manager	SMS site server	Responsible for the monitoring and working condition of all other SMS services.
SQL Monitor	SMS SQL server	Responsible for examining and maintaining SMS/SQL operations.

TABLE 2-2 SMS server threads executing on the site server.

Thread Name	Location Executed	Startup Method	Job Description
Asynchronous RAS	SMS sender server	Automatic	Controls communications between sites using RAS.
Client Configuration Manager	SMS site server	Automatic	Starts the SMS client software installation after notification from the Discovery Data Manager.
Client Installation Data Manager	SMS site server	Automatic	Monitors all client installation files on the SMS site server.
Collection Evaluator	SMS site server	Automatic	Continually evaluates collections as per the schedule.

TABLE 2-2 SMS server threads executing on the site server. (Continued)

Thread Name	Location Executed	Startup Method	Job Description
SMS Component Status Summarizer	SMS site server	Automatic	Keeps track of each component status.
Courier Sender Confirmation	SMS site server	Automatic	Oversees confirmation messages that are sent from subsites when courier packages are deployed in.
Despooler	SMS site server	Automatic	Uncompresses files received from parent and child sites, then delivers them into the component's inbox.
Discovery Data Manager	SMS site server	Automatic	Reads DDR files, creates CCR files, and manages existing site boundaries.
Distribution Manager	SMS site server	Automatic	Controls and oversees the packet distribution across the site.
Hierarchy Manager	SMS site server	Automatic	Responsible for changes and updates and processing of the database image of the site control file. Also manages installations for secondary sites.
Inbox Manager	SMS site server	Automatic	Synchronizes all client access points defined within an SMS site.
Inbox Manager Assistant	CAP	Automatic	Transfers files from CAP inboxes to component inboxes on site servers.
Inventory Data Manager	SMS site server	Automatic	Reviews hardware inventory files and uploads data to the SMS site database.
Inventory Processor	SMS site server	Automatic	Creates inventory header information for 16- and 32-bit clients.
ISDN RAS Sender	SMS sender server	Automatic	Controls communications using the ISDN RAS connection.
LAN Sender	SMS sender server	Automatic	Controls communications between sites using the existing LAN or WAN.
License Metering	SMS site server	Automatic	Manages software application licenses.
License Server Manager	SMS site server	Automatic	Installs, uninstalls, and oversees all metering services.
NDS Logon Discovery Manager	SMS site server	Automatic	Manages the NDS logon discovery settings.
NDS Logon Installation Manager	SMS site server	Automatic	Manages the NDS client logon installation settings.
NDS Logon Server Manager	SMS site server	Automatic	Performs synchronization between NetWare NDS servers and clients.

TABLE 2-2 SMS server threads executing on the site server. (Continued)

Thread Name	Location Executed	Startup Method	Job Description
NetWare Bindery Logon Discovery Manager	SMS site server	Automatic	Manages all NetWare bindery Logon Discovery settings.
NetWare Bindery Logon Installation Manager	SMS site server	Automatic	Manages all NetWare bindery logon client installation settings.
NetWare Bindery Logon Server Manager	SMS site server	Automatic	Performers synchronization between NetWare bindery servers and clients.
NetWare Bindery Server Discovery Agent	SMS site server	Scheduled	Builds DDR files for NetWare bindery site systems.
Network Discovery	SMS site server	Scheduled	Builds DDR files from the collected information gathered from the network scan.
NT Logon Discovery Manager	SMS site server	Scheduled	Oversees the Windows Logon Client Discovery.
NT Logon Installation Manager	SMS site server	Automatic	Oversees the Windows Logon Client Installation.
NT Logon Server Manager	SMS site server	Automatic	Performs and synchronizes all domain controllers involved in the discovery and logon installation.
NT User Discovery Agent	SMS site server	Scheduled	Builds a user's DDR file from the SAM Registry database of the primary domain controller.
NT User Group Discovery Agent	SMS site server	Scheduled	Builds user group discovery records from the SAM Registry database of the primary domain controller.
Offer Manager (The Advertisement Manager)	SMS site server	Automatic	Builds a software distribution instructions files based on the advertised software applications.
Offer Status Summarizer (The Advertisement Status Summarizer)	SMS site server	Automatic	Reports on the end results of software distribution.
Replication Manager	SMS site server	Automatic	Stores and manages files for sending to and from parent and child sites.
Scheduler	SMS site server	Automatic	Compresses files stored in inboxes for the Replication Manager, also schedules delivery for packages sent between sites.

TABLE 2-2 SMS server threads executing on the site server. (Continued)

Thread Name	Location Executed	Startup Method	Job Description
Site Control Manager	SMS site server	Automatic	Updates changes to the site control file, also creates heartbeat site control files.
Site System Status Summarizer	SMS site server	Automatic	Reports on the real-time status of all site systems in the SMS site.
SNA RAS Sender	SMS sender server	Automatic	Oversees site communications using RAS over SNA.
Software Inventory Processor	SMS site server	Automatic	Processes all software inventory files.
Status Manager	SMS site server	Automatic	Responds to all status messages.
Windows NT Server Discovery Manager	SMS site server	Scheduled	Builds DDRs for all and the SMS site systems.
X.25 RAS Sender	SMS sender server	Automatic	Oversees communications between sites using X.25 RAS.

TABLE 2-3

System processes and location executed from.

Name of Process	Location	Job Description
Reports Agent	SMS site server	Started from the SMS Administrator console to create reports.
Info Report Designer	SMS Administrator console machine	Started from the SMS Administrator console to design and also to modify existing reports.
Courier Sender Manager	SMS Administrator console machine	Creates and receives Courier Sender packages for distribution.
Remote Tools Console	SMS Administrator console machine	Started from the SMS Administrator console for the remote control of client machines.
Software Metering Console	SMS Administrator console machine	Oversees licensed and metered software applications; also started from the SMS Administrator console.
SMS Service Manager	SMS Administrator console machine	Started from the SMS Administrator console, this service is used to show details of active SMS service and threads.

TABLE 2-3

System processes and location executed from. (Continued)

Name of Process	Location	Job Description
Network Monitor	SMS Administrator console machine	Started from the SMS Administrator console, this service is used to monitor and analyze network traffic.
Network Monitor Control Tool	SMS Administrator console machine	Started from the SMS Administrator console, this service is used to start and configure real-time network monitor agents.
SMS Setup	SMS Administrator console machine	Started from the Start | Programs menu, this service is used to change the current SMS installation.
Event-to-Trap Translator	SMS Administrator console machine	Started from the SMS Administrator console Action menu, this service allows you to select the NT events that then are translated into SNMP traps.

Trace and Log Files

Every component that executes on an SMS site system for SMS clients can be directed to report all of its activities to an ASCII text file called a *trace* or *log file*. By default, generally most of the SMS logs on the server are disabled using the SMS Service Manager. You can enable or disable tracing here by component, or you can have multiple selected components detail all other activities to a single log file. To activate all activities to one log file, you enable the Use Same File for All Selected Components option, if available in the SMS Service Manager. Some logs do not permit this option. See Figure 2-10.

SMS Service Manager

Using a single SMS Service Manager, you can control multiple SMS sites and also create and modify all tracing activities from this one location. The site system logs that can be generated by different SMS site system components are listed in Table 2-4. Although there are many log files you can enable, increasing the log files that are actively running and reporting their progress to the site server consumes more bandwidth.

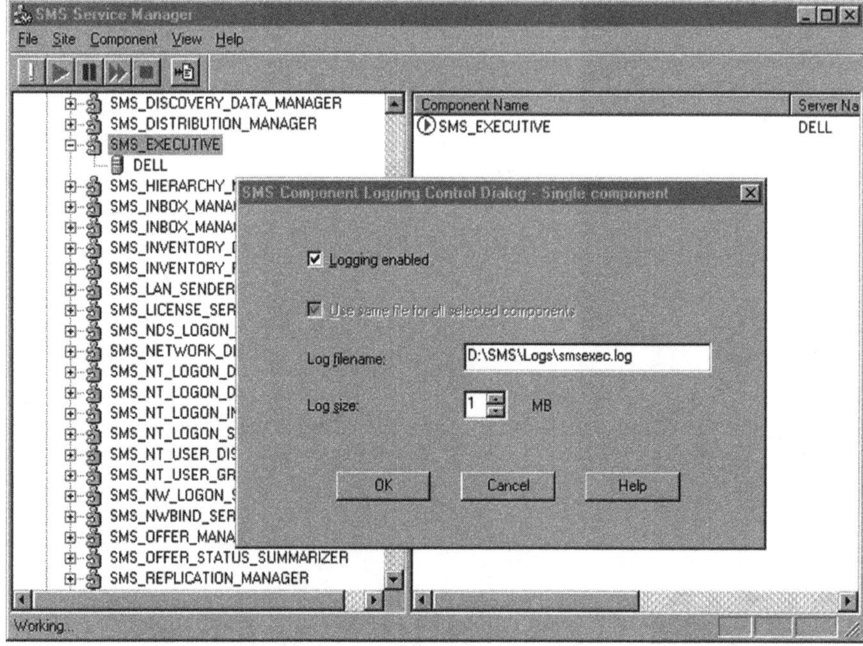

Figure 2-10 Displaying component logging choices with the SMS Service Manager.

Look at these log files listed in Table 2-4 as a great tool for troubleshooting all SMS server components that are not working properly. The log file allows us to view the workings of the SMS site at the component level in an English format.

SMS Data Storage

Obviously, data storage, retrieval, and manipulation is the heart of SMS. Clients must report their current or changed status at every logon to the SMS environment. The data needed falls into two main categories: system data and configuration data.

System data is collected from all of the various SMS resources across your site. This data will change on a day-to-day or monthly basis as you upgrade current software and hardware, add new computer systems your network, and retire older computer systems, bringing them offline.

TABLE 2-4

Log files can track the complete workings of SMS server components.

Log Filename	SMS Component that Produces the Log File.
CCM.LOG	Client Configuration Manager
CIDM.LOG	Client Installation Data Manager
COLLEVAL.LOG	Collection Evaluator
COMPSUMM.LOG	Component Status Summarizer
COURSEND.LOG	Courier Sender Manager
CSCNFSVC.LOG	Courier Sender Confirmation
DATALDR.LOG	Inventory Data Loader
DDM.LOG	Discovery Data Manager (DDM)
DESPOOL.LOG	Despooler
DISTMGR.LOG	Distribution Manager
HMAN.LOG	Hierarchy Manager
INBOXAST.LOG	Inbox Manager Assistant
INBOXMGR.LOG	Inbox Manager
INVPROC.LOG	Inventory Processor
LICSRV.LOG	License Metering
CONLICSVCFG.LOG	License Server Manager
ND_LOGON.LOG	NDS Logon Server Manager
NDLGDSCM.LOG	NDS Logon Discovery Manager
NDLGINST.LOG	NDS Logon Installation Manager
NETDISC.LOG	Network Discovery
NT_LOGON.LOG	NT Logon Server Manager
NTLGDSCA.LOG	NT Logon Discovery Agent
NTLGDSCM.LOG	NT Logon Discovery Manager
NTLGINST.LOG	NT Logon Installation Manager
NTSVRDIS.LOG	Windows NT Server Discovery Agent
NTUG_DIS.LOG	NT User Discovery Agent
NTUSRDIS.LOG	NT User Group Discovery Agent
NW_LOGON.LOG	NetWare Bindery Logon Server Manager
NWLGDSCM.LOG	NetWare Bindery Logon Discovery Manager
NWLGINST.LOG	NetWare Bindery Logon Installation Manager

TABLE 2-4

Log files can track the complete workings of SMS server components. (Continued)

Log Filename	SMS Component that Produces the Log File.
NWSVRDIS.LOG	NetWare Bindery Server Discovery Agent
OFFERMGR.LOG	Offer Manager (Advertisement Manager)
OFFERSUM.LOG	Offer Status Summarizer (Advertisement Status Summarizer)
REPLMGR.LOG	Replication Manager
SCHED.LOG	Scheduler
SENDER.LOG	LAN Sender, Asynchronous RAS Sender, ISDN RAS Sender, SNA RAS Sender, X.25 RAS Sender
SINVPROC.LOG	Software Inventory Processor
SITECOMP.LOG	SMS Site Component Manager
SITECTRL.LOG	Site Control Manager
SITESTAT.LOG	Site System Status Summarizer
SMSDBMON.LOG	SMS SQL Monitor
SMSEXEC.LOG	SMS Exclusive
SMSPROV.LOG	SMS Provider
SRVACCT.LOG	Used when SMS setup or any SMS component modifies the NT account or database
STATMGR.LOG	States Manager
APASETUP.LOG	Details the available programs in a manager installation.
CCIM32.LOG	Details the processes linked to client configuration and synchronization.
CLICORE.LOG	Details the installation of SMS client core components.
CLINST.LOG	Details the installation of the License Metering Client Agent.
CLISVC.LOG (CLISV95.LOG)	Details the current status of all SMS components. Note the separate Windows 95/98 log file.
CQMGREG.LOG	Reports the communication at client access point (CAP) events.
HINV32.LOG	Details the Hardware Inventory Agent's progress.
INHINV32.LOG	Details the progress of the hardware inventory agent installation.
LAUNCH32.LOG	This lot is for NT users only, providing details on the installed SMS components, their work schedules, and how they impact specific NT workstation users. This log is for NT users only.

TABLE 2-4

Log files can track the complete workings of SMS server components. (Continued)

Log Filename	SMS Component that Produces the Log File.
LICCLI.LOG (LICCLI95.LOG)	Details the License Metering Agent's progress. Note the separate Windows 95/98 log file.
ODPSYS32.LOG	Details the progress of the Systems Offer Data Provider.
LICCILOG (LICCLI95.LOG)	Details the License and Metering Agent's progress. Note the separate Windows 95/98 log file
ODPYS32.LOG	Details the activities of the Systems Offer Data Provider.
ODPUSR32.LOG (ODPUSR9X.LOG)	Provides details on the activities of the Users Offer Data Provider. Note the separate Windows 95/98 log file.
ODPWNT32.LOG (ODPWNT9X.LOG)	Provides details on the activities of the User Groups Offer Data Provider. Note the separate Windows 95/98 log file.
PEA32.LOG	Details the advertised programs that have executed for the user. This log is for NT users only.
REMCTR.LOG	Details the installation of the Remote Tools Client Agent.
SINV32.LOG	Details of the progress of the Software Inventory Agent.
SMSAPM32.LOG	Details the progress and activities linked to the scheduling and deep line of distributed software. Also provides administrative details on the software advertisements and distribution.
SMSCLI.LOG	Details the activities of the Advertised Programs Control Panel Agent.
SMSCLREG.LOG	Details of the Registry cleanup performed during the component's uninstall progress.
SMSMON32.LOG	Details the progress of the Advertised Programs Monitor.
SMSWIZ32.LOG	Details the activities linked to an advertised software application started by a user.
STSINSTL.LOG	Details the installation of the NT Event to SNMP Trap Translator Agent.
SWDIST.LOG	Details the installation of the Available Programs Manager, Available Programs Monitor, and all Offer Data Providers.
WN_LOGON.LOG	Provides details on the progress of the installation of the logon client.
WNMANUAL.LOG	Provided details on the progress of the installation of the manual client.
WNREMOTE.LOG	Provides details on the progress of the installation of the remote clients. This log is for NT users only.

All of this information is stored in the SMS site database in the following formats:

- DDR—Discovery data records
- MIF—Management Information Format
- Network discovery data
- Site configuration data
- Software-metering database
- Product compliance database

Configuration data will change as you make changes through the SMS Administrator console and any changes SMS services make. These configuration changes will be recognized by SMS, which in turn updates the site control file and other Registry on the site server. The site control file holds the configuration for an SMS site. With regard to the SMS components that operate on a defined schedule, such as the Windows Network Logon Discovery service, the active service and thread components will query the site control file for any changes in their configuration and schedule as they continue to do their work.

SMS Client Architecture

The SMS client on your network can be any computer system that has SMS client software installed. Remember, in order to completely manage all your clients and servers, the computer servers serving as SMS site servers and site systems can also be installed as SMS clients.

Client software executes as a service, processes, or as an application that starts after the SMS client agents have been installed. SMS client software also runs from the client computer locally and not across the network. The history information for most client SMS functions will be stored and maintained at the client computer, for example, software and hardware inventory and configuration information used by remote tools.

SMS client computers have the following client components installed:

- *Windows Management* This service component is limited to running on 32-bit client computers such as Windows 95/98 and Windows NT

4.0 clients. It contains the Microsoft WBEM implementation that is only supported by 32-bit clients. Windows Management provides the data for hardware inventory. This inventory can also be used by other management applications if they support the WBEM initiative.

- *SMS Client User Interface* Once software distribution has been enabled at the SMS site, this client application installs its needed DLL files, the Advertised Programs Monitor, and the Advertised Programs Wizard on the client PC. The internal client infrastructure for the SMS client user interface can be broken down into three main elements:
  - *Available Programs Manager (APM)* Any SMS programs that are available to be executed on this client are managed by this component. If APM is informed through SMS, or concludes that a particular program needs to be run, it in turn launches the Program Execution Agent to start the program.
  - *Program Execution Agent (PEA)* This client component runs programs as directed by the APM. It also monitors the progress of a program execution and reports back to the Available Programs Manager.
  - *Program Information Provider (PIP)* As the name of this component suggests, its responsibility is providing information with regard to distribution points for software to be installed on decline computer. Its job is to query existing CAPs, returning the needed information to the APM.
- *Optional Components for SMS clients* Optional client components that you wish to install to your client computers are selected at the SMS Administrator console. The choices are as follows:
  - Hardware Inventory
  - Software Inventory
  - Software Distribution
  - Remote Control
  - Software Metering
  - Windows NT Event to SNMP Trap Translator

Table 2-5 lists the 32-bit client components that are installed on the client's PC.

TABLE 2-5

32-Bit operating system components.

SMS Client Component Name	Method of Startup	Job Description
Client Configuration Installation Manager	Scheduled	Every 23 hours or when the system restart or logon occurs, the Client Configuration Installation Manager synchronizes all SMS client files.
Available Programs Manager	Automatic	Controls all software advertisements and the agent installation by monitoring the schedule and the success and failure of the installation.
Advertised Programs Monitor	Automatic	Started by the SMS application launcher, this component is used to observe the advertised programs.
Advertised Programs Wizard	Manual	This wizard is used to run the advertised software.
Copy Queue	Automatic	Copies all client data to the client access point.
Hardware Inventory Agent	Scheduled	Collects hardware inventory by querying the Common Inventory Model (CIM).
License Metering Client	Automatic	Analyzes all started software application processes and in turn passes the captured information to the metering server, which then allows or disallows the application to run.
NT Event to SNMP Trap	Automatic	Changes Windows NT Translator Agents to SNMP traps.
SMS Application Launcher	Automatic	Starts the SMS client components on schedule or when failure occurs.
SMS Client Service	Automatic	Executes as the main service on Windows NT computer systems.

CHAPTER 3

Planning for the Deployment of System Management Server

In this chapter you'll learn how to:

- Plan a successful implementation of SMS
- Design your SMS site structure
- Plan simple and multiple SMS sites

You will also learn about the hardware and software requirements for SMS.

Planning for SMS

The first question to ask yourself before you slide the SMS CD-ROM into your drive and run Setup is this: Just why are you installing SMS? In other words, what's your defined need behind the request for SMS in the first place?

This question may be much harder to honestly answer if the imminent implementation of SMS is primarily due to political reasons. Upper management may have the idea that deploying SMS will allow them to reduce the number of support personnel they have, saving them valuable budget dollars. Well, this may be true, but informing your IT staff of this goal will ensure a lousy implementation and deployment of SMS.

A lot of prospective new clients of mine, along with network administrators that I talk to during my presentation of hands-on seminars about SMS, are asked, "Why SMS?" The consistent top answers for deploying SMS are for automating weekly virus software updates and for software metering.

If you have the same reasons and your network is small, say, less than 100 clients sharing one domain, then your implementation of SMS may be very straightforward. Then again, you may have a huge network spanning multiple WAN links with all sorts of different types of networking equipment and client software.

The bottom line is this: Plan before implementing. Proper planning must be carried out for a successful SMS rollout. We all know that elusive quantity we are all searching for—more time. So, it's very, very tempting to start the installation of any eagerly awaited software application without doing the proper planning. My advice: Take the time to go through this chapter, do the planning properly, and you will end up saving lots of time. OK, end of lecture.

Define How SMS Will Help Your Company

First identify your goals for SMS from a business standpoint. These could be items such as:

- We need to start tracking licenses on software to make sure it's legal.
- We want to centrally carry out the weekly updates for McAfee's virus software.
- We must install Office 2000 to all clients with new Pentium III desktops by the end of the year.

You should define your goals in this manner to help you sell the implementation of SMS to your company, to upper management, and to yourself. The final cost of deploying SMS is not going to be cheap; it's going to be very expensive.

Having some plain-English "sound bites" to use during your presentation can help you tap into some of the goals that management may be thinking about but have no real idea how to achieve (Boy, do I remember the time I mistakenly went in to sell a company on a network. Instead of starting at the management level, I talked at the technical level, losing my audience—and the sale—completely.)

Make sure that your audience is aware of the basic features of SMS 2.0. Again, these are Software Metering, Hardware Inventory, Software Inventory, Remote Control, Automatic Software Installation and Distribution, and Network Diagnostics.

This doesn't mean that you don't do the needed work of defining your current technical state. You just don't start out with the technical details first when you are selling SMS to your company. In fact, the technical details are the most important, because if your current network infrastructure can't handle the added workload that SMS will generate, then it's best not to start at all.

Now it's time to gather information about your current hardware and software environment, as well as how you and your support staff carry out your day-to-day tasks and duties.

Current Hardware Characteristics

These characteristics include the following:

- *Primary and backup domain controllers, standalone servers, and their network locations* The number of servers available and their location on the network will determine their potential SMS role: site server, logon point, client access point, distribution point, or software-metering server.
- *NetWare bindery and NDS servers to be used (3.X, 4.X)* If you have a mixed NetWare and NT environment, the placement and role of your NetWare servers are very important. NetWare servers cannot carry out some SMS tasks. For example, a NetWare server cannot be installed as an SMS client or perform software metering.
- *Mainframe, microcomputer, and minicomputer hardware and operating systems* These other operating systems and hardware may not be involved with SMS, but they can generate significant amounts of network traffic depending on their role in the current network. Never underestimate the amount of network traffic that may be generated by another server sharing the same network infrastructure.
- *The location of your network client's PC* If all your clients are on the local network within one domain, as opposed to a multiple master domain structure, then software installations, hardware and software metering, license monitoring may generate significant traffic you hadn't planned on. Remote clients at a secondary site will have to be considered as well.
- *Hubs, switches, routers, bridges, and network printers* All network devices should be checked for speed, for future growth potential, and for any current design bottlenecks you haven't contemplated. For example, can your current switches and hubs run at 100 MB, and can your routers' firmware be upgraded to TCP/IP version 6, IPng (IPnext generation)?
- *Current cabling* Determine the cabling used, such as twisted-pair CAT 3, CAT 5, or RG 58 coaxial cable. Old or slow cables could pose the biggest problem of all. The weakest cable is also the most important. Check the twisted-pair cable color code to make sure that what you think is CAT 5 is really CAT 5. The early days of twisted-pair cabling used some very interesting color combinations, because everyone assumed that twisted-pair cabling was just that, basic twisted-

pair. If your network environment is one that you were parachuted into, a cable verification check is an essential system task.

- *T1, 56 K lines, leased lines* Regardless of your WAN link, what free line access is left over for SMS to use? These lines will have to be monitored for their current bandwidth and future capacity needs.
- *WAN reliability and speeds* The reliability and availability of your WAN links are very important to consider. Although some SMS tasks can function adequately across a WAN link, other features such as deploying software and advertised packages will not provide acceptable performance.
- *Current traffic patterns on each segment/subnet of the network* The boundaries of your local subnets are the site boundaries for your SMS site. Where do your users load their software? Is it installed locally or executed from a network location? Is there a great deal of Internet traffic on certain segments? What about dedicated print servers? This monitoring of network traffic at the human level can tell you more about the workings of your network than any other performance tool can.
- *Future expansion plans* Your network may be about to undergo some additional expansion—in other words, more clients and servers. If they will be active within the next two years, these additions should be drawn on your network map as if they were actually present. The reasoning is that the computer rollout and successful deployment of SMS will take a substantial amount of time.

  If you don't add in your network expansion before it happens, you probably will forget to properly include it in your SMS rollout. Since SMS can automatically discover newly installed clients and network devices, planning before the clients and devices are actually deployed can help you in deciding what logon scripts could be prepared and what user groups the new users could be added to before they actually arrive.

Current File Server Characteristics

What is each current files server's function?

- File and print services
- Database

- Internet server
- Intranet services
- Client/server software.
- Data storage location
- Where users log in and gain access to the network

Network Client Characteristics

Each type of client should be grouped as 16-bit (Windows 3.X) or 32-bit (Windows 95/98/2000; Windows NT 3.51/4.0/2000 Professional). SMS supports both 16- and 32-bit clients; however, every SMS feature is not available for all clients. For example, 16-bit clients cannot participate in Remote Control. Other factors to document:

- Is the client PC shared with other users?
- Are desktop or notebook PC with docking stations used, or both?
- Are dual-boot operating systems installed and used?
- Are FAT partitions or NTFS partitions used?

Security Characteristics for the User

Probably the biggest job to get a handle on is the real security rights your network user actually has. The type of partition on the client's local PC has a large say in the level of security (if any) that has been deployed. With NT workstations, complete local control of all files and folders can be mandated, and this could cause a problem with software distribution if the rights are too restrictive for the software installer to carry out its job. The point is, you have to know this information in the planning stages for a successful deployment of SMS. Document the following security characteristics:

- Logon script usage per user or group
- Local NT user group on local Windows NT Workstation PC
- Local user group on NT domain or NetWare bindery/NDS

- Global group on NT domain
- Current user rights on local Windows NT Workstation PC
- Password restriction
- User profiles—local, roaming, or mandatory
- Logon time restrictions
- System policies or Group Policy enforcement

Current Server and Network Load

How busy are your current servers and your network infrastructure? That is, what current workload are they under? Performance Monitor (PM) can help you to test the current load of all NT servers and workstations currently installed on your network. Figure 3-1 shows a local NT workstation in local Chart mode under normal workstation load running several applications with 128 MB of RAM.

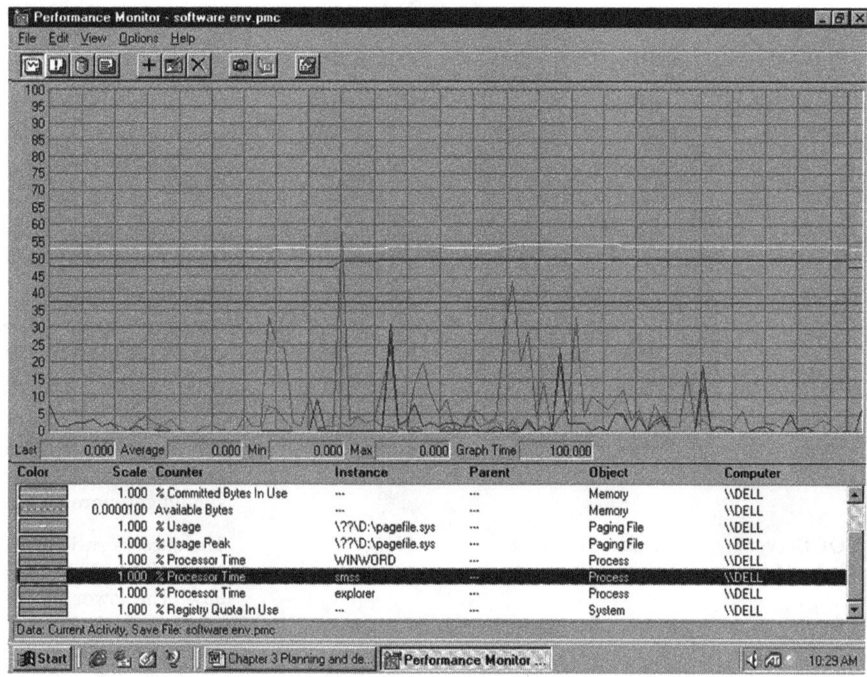

Figure 3-1 Viewing current workstation workload with Performance Monitor.

Some of the objects and counter values that you should monitor on existing systems with Performance Monitor (PM) are listed in Table 3-1. Take note that the physical disk counters are not turned on until you exit to the command prompt and enter `DISKPERF -y` to turn the counters on and `DISKPERF -n` to turn the counters off. A system reboot is also required to enable and disable the counters through PM.

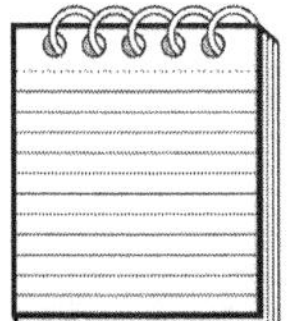

NOTE *Performance Monitor can run in Alert Mode, where the objects report, but only when they exceed a predefined level. You set per object/*

TABLE 3-1 Objects and Counters Performance Monitor Can Track.

Object	Counter	Instance	Details
System	% Total Processor Time	None	Less than 75% is normal; over 85% means overload.
System	Processor Queue Length	None	Two or less means that your CPU is handling its current workload well.
Physical Disk	% Disk Time	Each Hard Drive Platter	The percentage defines the level of hard drive activity. The level of file fragmentation, a full disk, and the number of open files all contribute to a higher percentage.
Physical Disk	Current Disk Queue Length	Each Hard Drive Platter	The count should be less than 2 once you subtract the number of spindles each disk platter has. Greater than 2 indicates the drive is overloaded.
Thread	Context Switches/SEC	_total	The lower the total, the less work that is currently being performed.
Memory	Committed Bytes	None	Shows the amount of virtual memory/paging file that has been reserved. It should not exceed the amount of actual chip memory. If it does, you need more RAM. See Figure 3-2 for clarification.
Memory	Page Reads/Sec	None	How many times virtual memory was accessed to read stored data. Greater than 5 means you should get more memory.
SQL Server Cache Manager	Cache Hit Ratio	None	The success ratio of finding the needed data in the SQL RAM cache should be high, over 95%. The lower the percentage, the lower the success, and the more hard drive page file access is needed to find the requested data.

counter to the Event Log. It can also run in Log Mode, where the defined objects details are logged to a report file for analyzing at a later date.

Network Monitor, another NT 4.0 tool that can be installed through the Network icon in Control Panel, can provide you with details on current network traffic. The Network Tools and Network Agent are installed on the NT server, and the Network Monitor Agent is installed on the NT workstation. See Figure 3-2, Network Tools and Network Agent.

Users and Groups

The users and groups that you have currently set up across your domains must be documented. SMS can install software and discover network clients based on the NT user and group account. Windows 16- and 32-bit clients can be NT user members and group members.

Software Inventory

Compile a complete listing of software applications in use throughout your company. Include MS-DOS, Win16, and Win32 applications. Take note where applicable when custom applications are deployed; the environment that is required may be unique, as in the startup procedure and operating system needed.

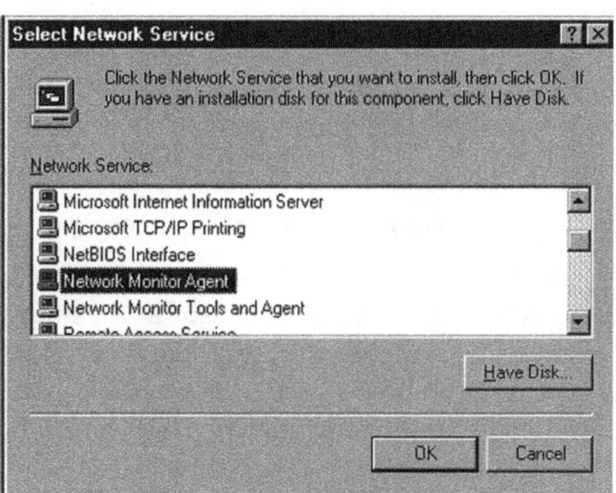

Figure 3-2 Network Monitor and Network Monitor Agent.

All of these details will be needed in order to successfully distribute software applications. And don't forget the security permissions that may be necessary in order to install and execute particular software applications.

Current Logon Script Usage

If you already use login scripts to enforce certain conditions at startup, some existing commands may interfere with SMS management. In addition, Network Discovery of clients for SMS can also be performed through login scripts. If NetWare servers are also installed, they also have their own login script language. All login scripts should be printed out and added to the document pile. Login scripts are usually stored in the NETLOGON share on primary and backup domain controllers.

Current Network Management

Analyze the current methods for managing your network before SMS is deployed. Knowing how current network management is carried out is crucial to tabulate so that any current problems can be recognized and possibly solved with SMS.

Questions to ask include the following:

- Do you currently have remote access to the client's PC?
- Is software installed over the network or locally?
- Do you perform software and hardware inventory every year?
- Is software locally installed or always on a network server?
- Who backs up users' data files?
- How do you rebuild a damaged PC?
- Are virus updates performed monthly or weekly?
- How is software application troubleshooting done?

Once you have all of this information (and I know it takes time, but it's absolutely necessary), you can now see at a glance what structural problems you may be facing for the deployment of SMS. This information also provides a great tool for troubleshooting any problems that come up in the future that are network-related. Most people never do this step.

Creating the Network Map

Now that you have all this valuable and relevant information about your network and infrastructure, I recommend that you draw a neat, detailed network map showing all of the network resources that you have discovered. I can't count the times I've arrived at a new client's site to analyze the current network only to have a very embarrassed network administrator admit that "We actually don't have a network map, yet." With an up-to-date network map, you can quickly analyze and solve most any problem much faster and more efficiently.

Current Hardware Specification Check

Now it's time to drill down even further and detail the current state of your primary and backup domain controllers, other servers, and clients across your network. You want to know:

- Make and speed of the CPU
- How much RAM and L2 cache is installed
- What type of hard drive array or subsystem is installed: mirrored or duplexed, or RAID, SCSI, or IDE controllers. IDE disk transfer rates are 4 to 8 MB/sec, while SCSI disk transfer rates are from 50 to 150 MB/sec, depending on the actual controller and hard drive configuration.

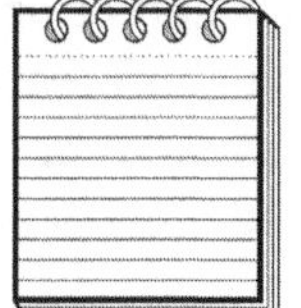

NOTE *Check out www.adaptac.com for lots of SCSI hardware specifications and design details.*

- What type of network adapter is installed and what speed and type: Ethernet 10 to 100 MB/sec or Token Ring 16 MB/sec

This hardware information is especially relevant if you plan on using some of your current servers to carry out and maintain some SMS site tasks. Each server that falls into this category will need memory, hard drive, and possibly more CPU power.

Site Server Hardware Specs

The listed hardware specifications for your site servers are very loosely based upon the Microsoft recommendations found in the *Systems Management Server 2.0 Resource Guide*. However I have greatly increased the minimum hardware requirements, since they are almost obsolete and are much too broad. For example, categories range from 500 to 100,000 clients based on what SMS tasks you choose to deploy in a given work week.

The problem I have with this type of category breakdown is that it really has no value with such a large number of listed clients. The TCP/IP subnet subdivided by routers is probably how your network segments are currently defined; this breakdown also is used by SMS to define the site boundaries that SMS will adhere to. Therefore, the site servers and the jobs that they each perform are the important benchmarks for SMS hardware requirements.

To properly size your hardware, you need to know about the following SMS components:

- The SMS object types
- Network traffic generated by SMS
- The SQL site database size on the site server
- The working memory size on the client
- The working data set size on the client

SMS Objects

These include SMS-generated objects that contain either server or client data that is stored in the SQL database. Each installed SMS feature in turn creates a specific set of objects for monitoring, creating, and storing its data. Table 3-2 lists the most common SMS-generated objects and the data records that they generate.

The SMS Object Creation Cycle

The object types that are used vary depending on what data information is being delivered to the SQL database. During the very first time frame

TABLE 3-2

SMS-Generated Objects and Data Records.

Software Feature	Number of Objects	Data Type Generated
Heartbeat Discovery	1 DDR per heartbeat interval	Discovery data record (DDR) per week
Logon Discovery	1 DDR per user logon	Discovery data record (DDR) per login
Other discoverys method	1 DDR per discovered resource	Discovery data record (DDR)
Hardware inventory	1 status message and 1 MIF file per interval	Management information file (MIF)
Software inventory	1 status message and 1 SIC or SID file per interval	Software inventory files (SIC) and (SID)
Software distribution	3 status messages per new advertisement; 2 status messages per existing advertisement	Status VarFiles (SVF) stored in the \SMS\Inbox folder

(interval) that the SMS inventory process is executed, the objects will be quite large, since they will contain the entire hardware and software discovered. The next interval the inventory process is executed SMS uses an object called a *delta object*, which is smaller and therefore faster to process, since the delta object will only contain changes found to the existing inventory.

However, SMS can also request a resynchronization of the entire inventory. When this takes place, the full object will be used, resulting in increased network traffic.

Network Traffic Generated by SMS

SMS Client

On the client's PC, Heartbeat Discovery creates 1 DDR per week per client, and a check is made for any new advertisements every 60 minutes. If software metering is deployed, a check with the defined software-metering server occurs when the user starts any application.

Client Access Points

At the site server, network traffic is generated at the client access points when the SMS client is first discovered. The CAP is responsible for installing the SMS client software and agents. The other SMS features, hardware and software inventory, and software distribution also generate network traffic and load on the node performing as a CAP.

Distribution Points

If distribution points are enabled for software distribution, then a significant load will be placed on the node that is acting as the distribution point. The amount of traffic will depend on the number of clients that are advertised to via software distribution and how large the software install is. A small virus update will obviously be faster than deploying Office 2000.

Software Metering

The number of users that you have, the number of logon and logoff sessions during a typical workday, and the number of application requests will determine the amount of network traffic this feature will generate. This is the one time that tracking logons and logoffs through an audit trail is recommended.

If your organization is quite large, with clients in excess of 50,000, the recommended hardware is just that, a recommendation. A full pilot project should be carried out to test your actual network topology.

SQL Database Sizing

The database used for SMS is all SQL data. The best starting point is to have a dedicated SQL database for SMS only installed on the same computer system where SMS is installed. Then the factors to consider are in the following order of priority:

1. *Hard drive space* The Microsoft-supplied formula for sizing your SQL database is as follows:

$$7.4 \text{ MB} + C \times 70 \text{ KB}$$

Where *C* is the number of clients per SMS site

This formula takes into account the following defaults:

- Weekly hardware and software inventory
- Automatic deletion of aged discovery and inventory records every 90 days, and aged status messages every 7 days
- 20 status messages generated per week per client

2. *Hard drive I/O* SCSI is the only hard drive solution for SQL data. As your needs increase, you will have to consider RAID solutions. At a minimum, deploy duplexed hard drives (that's two identical hard drive controllers connected to two identical hard drive platters, plus a third-party SCSI hard drive controller kit for NT Server).
3. *RAM* You can never have too much RAM for SQL Server. Start at 256 MB RAM minimum for the SQL Server software database component only. If you don't have a strict budget, get 512 MB.
4. *CPU* Even if you don't initially start with two CPUs, I recommend that the site server have the provision for two CPUs.

Client Hard Drive and RAM Usage

Tables 3-3 and 3-4 list the hard disk space and RAM space used for an SMS client PC. The hard drive space required is not large by today's standards; however, considering that SMS is supposed to be a hidden background process that the end user is unaware of, you want to make sure that SMS does not overwhelm your users' memory space. Also plan for a minimum of 10 MB of virtual memory/swap file size available for SMS.

Hardware Pressure Points

What's a hardware pressure point? It's a term I use to describe the bottleneck in a system created by an inadequate level of hardware attempting to support a large software application. SMS in this case is the software, and the hardware must be up to or exceeding par.

TABLE 3-3

SMS Client Hard Drive Space Required.

SMS Client Feature	Windows NT	Windows 96/98	Windows 3.X
Infrastructure	8.0 MB	8 MB	5.0 MB
Hardware inventory	0.5 MB	1.0 MB	2.5 MB
Software inventory	0.5 MB	0.5 MB	0.5 MB
Software distribution	1.0 MB	1.0 MB	1.0 MB
Software metering	2.0 MB	2.0 MB	0.5 MB
Remote tools	2.0 MB	2.0 MB	1.2 MB
SNMP	0.3 MB	Not available	Not available
All features installed	14.0 MB	13.0 MB	11.0 MB

TABLE 3-4

RAM Usage.

SMS Client Feature Installed and Executing	Total RAM
Infrastructure	10 MB
Hardware inventory	5 MB
Software inventory	3.6 MB
Software distribution	3 MB
Software metering	3.5 MB
Remote tools	2.0 MB
All features installed	26 MB

Hardware that is to be used for deploying SMS should be broken down into two main categories:

1. The primary site server located on your local subnet
2. The secondary site server (if present) located on another subnet connected by routers or through a WAN connection

Your network map will quickly show you your existing and future subnets, your WAN connections, and remote sites and users. (You did draw a network map, didn't you?)

You now can plan your SMS site boundaries, as well as any potential bottlenecks that you may have briefly considered but forgot about because they were not easy to visualize. Remember, your subnets will be your SMS site boundaries.

Analyzing Your Hardware Requirements

Now let's break down our network even further. The hardware components you need to analyze for any hardware pressure points are listed below. Remember that any server that is called upon to do extra duty, as part of the SMS hardware team, will need two upgrades for sure, RAM and hard drive space, and possibly more CPU power (that means multiple CPUs and speed). The primary site server with SMS and SQL Database installed locally with up to 500; 5,000; 10,000; and 20,000 clients is the model used for Table 3-5.

Analyzing your current network environment and comparing against the eight common scenarios listed below will help you start your network analysis.

1. *The primary site server with SMS is on one computer system, but the SQL Database is installed on another computer system within the same subnet.*

   This arrangement's success is dependent on the weakest link—the bandwidth of the network. If you are using 10 MB/sec Ethernet, I strongly suggest rethinking this scenario. Ethernet bandwidth, once error checking and basic overload is factored into the equation, is around 5 to 6 MB/sec. A bandwidth of 100 MB/sec would be acceptable, but you first want to talk yourself out of this equation, unless the system where you have to install SMS is not powerful enough for SQL as well. If this is the case, you have to accept the pitfalls that occur. This would not be a long-term solution.

2. *Primary domain controllers are also performing the SMS role of a client access point.*

   Consider adding a backup domain controller to take the load off the PDC. Make the BDC a client access point as well. Add 128 MB of RAM, and allocate a 5 GB NTFS hard drive partition at a minimum for the workspace needed to the execute SMS tasks. All hardware and software inventory data is passed to the CAP before it is sent to the site server for storage in the SQL database, so the extra RAM is needed.

3. *Backup domain controllers are also performing the SMS role as a client access point.*

   Add 128 MB of RAM and allocate a 5 GB NTFS hard drive partition at a minimum for the workspace needed to execute the SMS tasks. And just like Scenario 2, all hardware and software inventory data is passed to the CAP before it is sent to the site server for storage in the SQL database. Therefore, the extra RAM is needed here as well, since you don't know what domain controllers your users will be authenticated from.

4. *An NT or NetWare server is assigned the role of a distribution point.*
   Add 128 MB of RAM and, for a starting point, allocate a 10 GB NTFS hard drive partition at a minimum for the workspace needed to hold the advertisement and package information. The

TABLE 3-5

Hardware Recommendations for SMS Servers.

Up to 500 Clients

Suggested SMS Features Enabled	Minimum Site Server Hardware for 2 Years
Logon Discovery enabled Heartbeat Discovery weekly 5 advertisements per week Software inventory Hardware inventory	Pentium 450 MHz or K6-450 MHz with 512 K L2 cache, 128 MB RAM, SCSI 10 GB hard drive platter

500 to 5,000 Clients

Suggested SMS Features Enabled	Minimum Site Server Hardware for 2 Years
Logon Discovery enabled Heartbeat Discovery weekly 5 advertisements per week Software inventory Hardware inventory	Pentium 450 MHz or K6-450 MHz with 512 K L2 cache, 512 MB RAM, SCSI 15 GB hard drive platter

5,000 to 10,000 Clients

Suggested SMS Features Enabled	Minimum Site Server Hardware for 2 Years
Logon Discovery enabled Heartbeat Discovery weekly 5 advertisements per week Software inventory Hardware inventory	Pentium 450 MHz or K6-450 MHz with 512 K L2 cache, 512 MB RAM, SCSI 20 GB hard drive platter

TABLE 3-5

Hardware Recommendations for SMS Servers. (Continued)

10,000 to 20,000 Clients

Suggested SMS Features Enabled	Minimum Site Server Hardware for 2 Years
Logon Discovery enabled Heartbeat Discovery weekly 5 advertisements per week Software inventory Hardware inventory	Pentium 450 MHz or K6-450 MHz with 1 MB L2 cache, 1 GB RAM, SCSI 25 GB hard drive platter

real size depends on the number of software installations and distributions you will ramp up to in the coming years. Office 2000 requires two CD-ROMs for a complete install and 1.2 GB is needed.

The space required can explode in size, especially if the software is large (and what isn't?) and will be stored on the distribution point for the next year or two. Standardization on Office 2000 for two years would require at least 2 GB when you factor in the basic size of the product plus the updates and service packs that will inevitably appear.

5. *An NT server is assigned the role of software metering.*

   The software-metering database talks directly to its own SQL Server database, usually located on the site server where the primary SQL site database is stored. RAM is the most important resource for this SMS feature, since data is stored that is received from all software-metering clients. Add 128 MB RAM for this feature. Remember, NetWare servers cannot provide this service.

6. *A wide area network connection exists between secondary or primary site.*

   T1 lines should be acceptable for SMS, with the exception of software distribution. You can't take my word, though; proper testing must be carried out. In the very near future, cable modems and faster bandwidths will change the meaning of "slow." For now, remember any WAN link is at best a couple of MB per second.

7. *There is a wide area network connection to a remote user.*

   Test with a real-life scenario that matches your work reality. Although remote users can attach to an SMS environment using a modem, X.25, ISDN, or SNA, that's all they can really do—attach.

8. *There is a secondary site server.*

   The secondary server does not have any database responsibilities, so its roles are limited to software metering and remote tools, plus CAP and distribution point roles. The bottleneck for a site server is the communication link to the primary site server, usually the WAN link. Add 128 MB of RAM and allocate a 5 GB NTFS hard drive partition at a minimum for the workspace needed to execute SMS tasks.

9. *Requirements for the SMS client.*

   The clients' computer environment should have 32 MB and 1 GB of local hard drive space for supporting the SMS agents. This is pretty basic for today's client.

Planning Your SMS Support Team

Table 3-6 details the team members that a large SMS deployment might actually have. I use the word *might* because we both know the reality that you may be wearing all of these hats or several of them.

The other reality might be that you will be deploying SMS for one task only for the time being, and those other features may happen or may never happen, depending on the ever-present budget. Therefore, this next section will quickly list the SMS features and then quickly detail where the task will need to be carried out for the installation and support of each feature. By checking off the features you are going to install and by using your network map, you can now begin to plan your client access points, distribution points, and resources needed by SMS for proper execution.

Client Access Points

If you have installed your primary site in an NT domain, both primary and backup domain controllers are automatically made client access points. The number of users that you have will determine the number of additional CAPs to install. Hardware inventory, software inventory, status messages, and advertisements can cause an excessive load to a CAP server, depending on the frequency that the installed SMS features perform and the size of the installed client base. At least one client access point per network segment is recommended.

TABLE 3-6

SMS Support Roles for Deploying and Supporting SMS.

SMS Job Titles	Description
Technical Designer	Plans and designs SMS hierarchy and layout, interfaces with current and future network design staff, or may do both jobs.
Network Administrator	Keeps the network running, providing basic and advanced server and network infrastructure support and troubleshooting. Schedules, performs, and maintains all data backups.
SQL Server Administrator	Handles the installation, tuning, and troubleshooting chores. Schedules and performs SQL data backup.
SMS Server Administrator	Installs and configures all primary and secondary SMS sites. CAP, distribution, and software metering roles require communication and planning with the network administrator and staff.
SMS Client Administrator	Installs, designs, and monitors all SMS client tasks and procedures, including collections, advertisements, software metering, and hardware and software inventory. Oversees the 7-day/24-hour client monitoring and report status using Crystal Report tools.
Help Desk	Performs end-user support using the Remote tools.
SMS User Support Provider	Provides tier 2 and tier 3 support at the local desktop.
Scripting/Programmer	Creates and maintains logon scripts, batch processes, system policy, and user profile setup and maintenance. Responsible for the backup of all customization procedures out in place.

By using the SMS Administrator console and selecting the properties of any site system and then selecting New, you can add a CAP to a NetWare server, NT server, or NT share.

Distribution Points

The number of users that you have will help determine the number of additional distribution points to install. If you are planning for regular installation of software applications and updates, the number of clients will determine the number of distribution points to have active. Windows NT and NetWare servers and NT network shares can all be defined as distribution points. The only job of a distribution point is for storage of software that will be installed by SMS. Multiple distribution points should be configured for large-scale rollouts of software applications per network segment.

By using the SMS Administrator console and selecting the properties of any site system and then selecting New, you can add a distribution point to a NetWare server, NT server, or NT share.

Windows Networking Resource Discovery

This method is automatically installed when Express Setup is chosen; if Custom Setup is chosen, this discovery method must be selected during the Installation Wizard.

Windows Networking Resource Discovery is driven by commands in the logon scripts; in fact, you can configure it to automatically update existing logon scripts, or you can choose to perform this task manually.

In addition, you may choose to install the SMS client files from the CD-ROM at the client's PC rather than have them automatically installed at the time of discovery.

NetWare Bindery Logon Discovery/NDS Logon Discovery

This method is automatically installed when Express Setup is chosen; if Custom Setup is chosen, this discovery method must be selected during the Installation Wizard.

Either NDS or bindery servers can be used for client logon points, and it can be configured to automatically update the NetWare bindery system or NDS container logon script.

Windows NT User Account Discovery

This method is automatically installed when Express Setup is chosen; if Custom Setup is chosen, this discovery method must be selected during the Installation Wizard. During a regular polling cycle, the domain controller is queried for any new user accounts that may have been added. There is no setup at the user's PC.

Windows NT User Group Discovery

This method is automatically installed when Express Setup is chosen; if Custom Setup is chosen, this discovery method must be selected during the Installation Wizard.

During a regular polling cycle, the domain controller is queried for any new global group accounts that may have been added; local groups are not supported.

Heartbeat Discovery

This method is installed when either Express Setup or Custom Setup is chosen and relies on an installed client agent. The enabling, disabling, and scheduling is carried out at the SMS Administrator console by configuring the properties of Heartbeat Discovery. Execution will not start until the client agent has been installed at the client either manually or automatically by one of the three Windows Logon Discovery methods. Then once a week, like a guilty son or daughter, the client phones up the site server and says, "OK, I'm alive...bye."

Server Discovery

This method is installed automatically when either Express or Custom Setup is chosen. There are no settings to configure and change.

Network Discovery

This method is automatically installed when Express Setup is chosen; if Custom Setup is chosen, this discovery method must be selected during the Installation Wizard.

The desired configuration of Network Discovery is carried out at the SMS Administrator console. Discovery can be enabled through subnets, using DCHP, SNMP triggers, the existing topology, and other options. There is no user configuration required.

Software Distribution

At least one distribution point and client access point must be available to the SMS clients across your network for software distribution. If the software distribution is to be started based on a particular type of hardware device or software application, then either hardware or software inventory must also be enabled. If you want to use users and global groups (or both users and groups) as the trigger for software installation, then user account or group account must also be enabled.

Software distribution will not begin until the advertised program's client agent has been enabled and configured through the client Agent properties in the SMS Administrator console.

Hardware Inventory

Hardware inventory is automatically installed when Express Setup is chosen; if Custom Setup is chosen, it must be selected during the Installation Wizard. Hardware inventory is enabled on a site server by accessing its properties through the SMS Administrator console and selecting Client Agents. The client agent for hardware inventory is automatically installed when the client is discovered through one of the three client discovery processes. Once you enable hardware inventory through the SMS Administrator console, the inventorying process begins.

Software Inventory

Software inventory is automatically installed when Express Setup is chosen; if Custom Setup is chosen, it must be selected during the Installation Wizard.

Software inventory is enabled on a site server by accessing its properties through the SMS Administrator console and selecting Client Agents. The client agent for software inventory is automatically installed when the client is discovered through one of the three client discovery processes. Once you enable software inventory through the SMS Administrator console, the inventorying process begins.

Software Metering

This method is automatically installed when Express Setup is chosen; if Custom Setup is chosen, this discovery method must be selected during the Installation Wizard. A separate SQL database is required for storage of the software-metering data. Both a primary and secondary server location can support software metering, except the secondary site server will pass the metering data it collects to its parent site. Configuration of software metering is carried out at the SMS Administrator console by opening the properties of the site server.

SQL Server

According to Microsoft, the following guidelines should be followed for properly defining the size of your database components and devices.

SMS database device—A minimum of 50 MB

SMS database device size per client—100 KB

SMS transaction log device—20% of the SMS site database

Software-metering device—A minimum of 10 MB, plus an additional 200 KB per client

Software-metering transaction log device—15% of the software-metering database

Tempdb data device—20% of the sum total of the SMS site and software metering database

Tempdb transaction log device—20% of the Tempdb database

Designing the SMS Infrastructure

The overall design of your SMS sites and layout requires that you include the network site boundaries each site server will belong to and the type of site server that you are implementing. Obviously, if your initial SMS endeavor is to simply deploy one SMS primary site server, then your planning will be much simpler than a multiple SMS site installation. Taking time to plan properly before doing the actual physical installation work is the key to your success. Decisions that you make should be based on the following criteria.

Site Boundaries

Your existing network will probably use the TCP/IP protocol for server/client/Internet communication. If you are a NetWare 3.X 4.X shop, however, you will be using the IPX/SPX protocol. Network numbers are used for identifying your groupings of NetWare servers and clients. Using TCP/IP on your existing network will have already defined your site boundaries for SMS, since the use of subnets and IP addresses are the parameters SMS requires. Document the number of users, servers, and IP subnets, or IPX network numbers. If you have multiple domains and they are linked by trusts, they should also be documented. The entire subnet must be included in an SMS site, It cannot be used or split between two site servers.

Site Connections

Your site connections and their relative speed—that is, the amount of bandwidth that will be available for SMS—should be determined. Performing a bulk copying of 20 MB of files across the site connection to one and then multiple locations will provide you with a good idea of your actual network performance under load conditions. If the LAN or WAN connection is very slow, then multiple SMS sites should be created.

Site Senders

In Chapter 2 the concept of a sender was discussed. If your sites are linked together by LAN connections, then the subnets will be running the same network protocol; in this case, the standard sender should be used. Table 3-7 lists the sender choices that SMS can use; your WAN links will determine which additional senders to deploy.

TABLE 3-7

SMS Senders That Can Be Deployed to Manage SMS Communications.

Type of Sender	Descriptions
Standard Sender	Communication on the same line connected by routers, switches, or bridges
Courier Sender	Copying a package to an offline remote location
Asynchronous RAS Sender	RAS across an asynchronous line
ISDN RAS Sender	RAS across ISDN
X.25 RAS Sender	RAS across an X.25 line
RAS over SNA Sender	RAS accessing an SNA link

All senders other than Standard Sender will have to be tested with SMS tasks in mind. Even an ISDN line can become overloaded.

Types of SMS Sites

The very first SMS site must be a primary site. All other SMS sites can either be primary or secondary sites. The primary site will house the SQL database for the SMS data generated by the primary and secondary site resources. There are no administrative tasks that can be performed at an SMS secondary site, and there is no SQL database storage at a secondary site. You can, however, install an SMS Administrator console at any NT workstation or server location, allowing you to remotely administrate a primary site.

If your SMS deployment will grow in size, increasing from one site to several child sites, consider making the site a primary site, since a secondary site cannot be upgraded to a primary site and child sites cannot be added to a secondary site.

Site Hierarchy

The hierarchy is the primary/secondary and child site topology. The first primary site will also be the central site, with possible primary and secondary sites below the primary site. The administrators in the central site manage all the computers (servers and clients), as well as all connected sites below it. The headquarters of your company would be the logical location for the central site.

Backup and Maintenance

All SMS site servers and SQL data must be backed up; this includes custom installation/advertised packages and the SQL database that SMS creates. The database devices can be many MB in size, so sizing your backups is important. Certainly, the customized scripting and advertisements are the most important data types to back up. If you lose any SMS licensing data history or hardware and software inventory, this data can be re-created. The basic SQL databases for the site server should be backed up separately after SMS is installed and fully deployed and stored off-site; however, the most important component is the database devices.

Running an SMS Pilot Project

The pilot project for every Microsoft operating system is usually highly recommended by all of the resource kits for Windows 95/98 or NT systems. And most of us don't have time to carry out a realistic pilot project or test deployment of a new version of Windows, because by the time we are aware of the new version, it's already coming in through the door preinstalled on a new notebook, and the user that is on the receiving end is higher up in the company. And on it goes.

Well, for SMS, the rules are different. If you don't test your network and carry out all the suggestions in this chapter, you lose big time. So a pilot project is a must.

The Mobile SMS Testing Site

The coolest suggestion I have for your SMS pilot project is to use a collection of four notebooks to create a roaming SMS pilot project. A Pentium notebook with 64 MB of RAM and adequate hard drive space, say, 3 to 5 GB, would be perfect for deploying all of your SMS sites. At a minimum, one notebook computer could be a primary SMS site.

The beauty of using laptops is that they are moveable, powerful enough, and don't require a lot of space. Of course, any spare PC could be used, but a notebook could be rented for a 1-month term and used solely for SMS testing purposes.

Now, if you are thinking, "Hey, Mark, I've got several laptops, but they're not really powerful; they are Pentium 120s with 96 MB of RAM. Could I really use these?" I will now let you in on a little secret: The specifications earlier in this chapter for hardware were slightly inflated by yours truly, because after much testing and real deployments of SMS in different environments, Microsoft's recommendations were found to be much too conservative. In other words, the marketing department, rather than the technology department, defines the hardware recommendations.

So, the earlier hardware recommendations in this chapter *are* for a real network environment, and the following are Microsoft's minimum specs for an SMS site for 500 clients.

- CPU—Pentium 166 MHz
- RAM—96 MB
- Free hard drive space—1 GB NTFS partition
- Operating system—NT Server 4.0 with Service Pack 4, Internet Explorer 4.0 with Service Pack 1

Therefore, these hardware specs are just fine for a pilot project, as long as you keep in mind that you might have some processing limitations. However, that's the reason for a pilot project in the first place; to evaluate a project or a process using the manufacturer's recommendations to see how they actually hold up under scrutiny.

Creating your Test Lab and Roaming SMS Pilot Site

Use the following hardware specifications for desktop PCs first in an isolated testing lab and then as a roaming SMS test lab. Your actual testing decisions only you can make, since I don't know how much time you really have. And it's important to ask yourself, "Do I have the time for this?" If the answer is positive, then my recommendation is the following:

First do a test lab SMS deployment, and then do a roaming lab deployment. The testing results will provide you with two environments to compare and contrast. The minimum hardware required is as follows:

- Desktop/Notebook 1—Backup domain controller CAP/Distribution point
- Desktop/Notebook 2—SQL server for SMS data

- Desktop/Notebook 3—SMS primary site server
- Desktop/Notebook 4—SMS client

In the Lab

Try to mimic a real SMS/SQL server environment. The network traffic on your actual network will be missing, so you will have to mimic some network traffic from client to client.

Deploy a primary site server with SQL also installed, a primary domain controller also acting as a CAP and distribution point, and several SMS clients that mirror your actual network clients. Test each SMS feature separately, and time the login/logout of your users and the increased network traffic with Performance Monitor.

Test Installation Notes

Following are a few helpful guidelines:

1. Install your primary site servers first.
2. Install your secondary sites, and then connect them to their parent site.
3. Connect all primary sites together, and verify connections with the SMS Administrator console.
4. Add clients to your sites using the preferred Logon Discovery procedure.
5. Deploy logon scripts to your test users and groups.
6. Add SMS features one at a time.
7. Implement and test your backup and restore procedures.
8. Document your pilot installation.

Real-Mode Testing

For your first real-time testing, use a single subnet for your first SMS testing phase. If you know that SQL will be on a separate server within the subnet, then of course add a separate notebook with SQL installed. SQL Server should be installed and at the ready before the installation of SMS. Deploy your second laptop as a primary site server with SQL Server also installed.

For your client access point within the subnet, next add the third notebook as a backup domain controller. This notebook will have to be installed on the subnet where the Primary Domain Controller is.

Add your fourth notebook as an SMS test client. Test each SMS feature separately and time the login/logout of your users and the increased network traffic with Performance Monitor.

SMS Deployment

Obviously, you will be using the entire contents of this book for a successful deployment of SMS, and this chapter is concentrating on the testing and proper deployment of SMS. So, here's a final list for a successful deployment:

1. Install your primary site servers first, but do not activate any clients.
2. Install your secondary sites and then connect them to their parent site.
3. Connect all primary sites together and verify connections with the SMS Administrator console.
4. Add and configure any other senders for remote site communications.
5. Train your users for the deployment of SMS.
6. Add clients to your sites using the preferred Logon Discovery procedure.
7. Deploy logon scripts to users and groups.
8. Add SMS features one at a time.
9. Implement your backup and restore procedures.
10. Document your installation.

CHAPTER 4

Installing Systems Management Server

In this chapter you'll learn how to:

- Plan a successful upgrade from SMS 1.2 to 2.0
- Set up SQL Server
- Install a primary site
- Install a secondary site

Upgrading from SMS 1.2 to SMS 2.0

There are several SMS versions still present in the marketplace. The latest version, SMS 2.0, has made many major changes to the architecture, as well as the overall functionality. Chapter 1 of this book detailed the feature set of SMS 2.0; the purpose of this section is to provide some basic notes for planning your upgrade to SMS 2.0 for both servers and clients.

Although there are earlier versions of SMS (1.0 and 1.1), we will not discuss those versions here, as only 1.2 can be directly upgraded to SMS 2.0. For details on these versions, refer to the *Systems Management Server 2.0 Resource Guide* and to www.microsoft.com/smsmgmt for additional white papers on upgrading.

Upgrading 1.2 Site Systems

Before you perform any upgrade, it is best to first take a good long look at your entire site hierarchy. Some of the potential problems you may face are as follows:

- An SMS 2.0 site can't be a child site to an SMS 1.2 primary site, so the first upgrade rule is this: All of your SMS 1.2 primary sites must be upgraded to SMS 2.0.
- Upgrading an SMS 1.2 parent site does not automatically upgrade any existing SMS 1.2 child sites; each child site upgrade must be manually performed.
- Any SMS 1.2 primary sites that you may have just upgraded can only administer SMS 1.2 child sites; this is also a task that SMS 2.0 primary sites can't perform.

Finally, once you upgrade SMS 1.2 site to SMS 2.0, certain data is converted and some data types are discarded. The converted data types are as follows:

- Hardware inventory data (with the exception of hard drive size)
- Machine groups
- Software packages
- Programs
- SQL Server views

The data types that are not converted are as follows:

- Hard drive sizes
- PDF files
- Software inventory
- Queries
- Jobs
- Alerts
- Events
- Site system settings

The reality is that all of your SMS 1.2 primary and secondary sites should be upgraded at the same time. Now this is just my opinion, but a mixed site is a big mess to administrate and manage. Other companion software versions to be running or upgraded to before performing any SMS 1.2 to 2.0 upgrade are listed in Table 4-1.

TABLE 4-1

Software versions you must be running before installing SMS 2.0.

Software	Version Required by SMS 2.0
Windows NT	4.0 with Service Pack 4
MDAC (Microsoft Data Access Components)	2.0
Y2K Components	Bundled with Service Pack 4
SQL Server	SQL 6.5 with Service Pack 5 or SQL 7.0
Internet Explorer	4.0 with Service Pack 1

Upgrading SMS 1.2 Clients to SMS 2.0

The first issue to contend with is the type of clients you are still supporting with SMS 1.2. SMS 2.0 does not support the following clients:

- MS-DOS 5.0 or later
- IBM OS/2 2.11
- Macintosh clients using System 7.X

You probably don't support in a substantial way any of these three older legacy clients, but if you do, there is a potential problem. You could reserve one SMS 1.2 primary site for the management and control of your older clients, but perhaps they all won't be in the same network location. The reality, however, is that the majority of your client base will be Microsoft 95/98 with NT Workstation clients; otherwise, you wouldn't have an interest in SMS.

If you are preparing an SMS 1.2 site location to upgrade, make sure that you confirm the following minimum list of "gotchas."

Upgrade Checklist for All SMS Sites

1. Make sure the current version you are upgrading is SMS 1.2.
2. Make sure the computer hardware that is to be upgraded can support SMS 2.0.
3. Copy all MIF-generated package definition files at your primary site to a safe location. The SMS 2.0 upgrade will remove these files.
4. Copy all collected files at your 1.2 primary site to a safe location. The SMS 2.0 upgrade removes these files.
5. Make backup copies of your current logon scripts.

Primary Site Checklist

1. Make sure that SMS 2.0 supports the version of SQL Server you are currently running. At a minimum, you must be running SQL Server version 6.5 with Service Pack 5; the preferred version is SQL version 7.0.
2. Software metering uses a separate SQL database from the SMS site database. If you are planning to install this feature, make sure

that your current SQL server install can handle the extra database required by software metering.

3. Increase the size of your temporary database (tempdb) to 80 MB for the installation procedure.

Upgrade Steps for Your 1.2 Primary Site Servers

To upgrade your primary site server:

1. Make sure that your supporting SMS software mix is the correct version. (Check Table 4-1 to make sure.)
2. Execute SETUP.EXE from the SMS CD-ROM on your SMS 1.2 primary site server. SMS 2.0 Setup will start and automatically locate your current SMS 1.2 installation. See Figure 4-1.
3. Click on *Next* to accept the license agreement and start the upgrade.
4. If your primary SQL Server database is not installed on the site server, the SMS Provider Information screen will be displayed. Choices are to install the SMS Provider as recommended, on the current SQL Server, or on the SMS site server.
5. The installation and data conversion will then complete. You will not have any option to stop the database conversion once it begins.

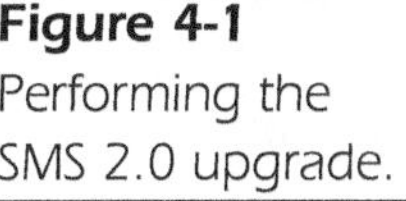

Figure 4-1
Performing the SMS 2.0 upgrade.

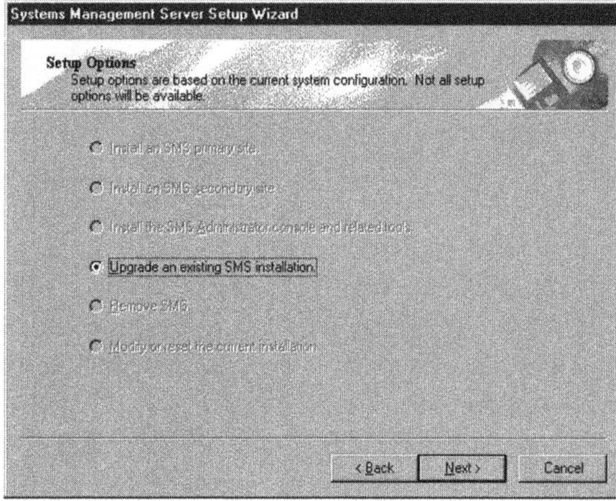

Installing New SMS 2.0 Components

To add any SMS 2.0 components to an upgraded site server:

1. Run the SMS Setup once again from the SMS 2.0 CD-ROM, and select the option *Modify or reset the current installation.*
2. From the Setup Installation Options, select the software options that you want to install and click on *Next.*
3. Accept the default names presented for the SQL Server database, the service account, and the SQL database name, then click on *Next.*
4. If you chose to install the Software Metering option, you will have to specify where SQL Server is installed. Then select the type of security required for the database—SQL or integrated security. (Further details can be found later in this chapter under "SMS Installation: Step-by-Step.")
5. The SQL Server Device for the Software Metering Database screen will allow you to use preexisting database devices or create your own devices through these installation steps.
6. The installation information will be summarized on the Completing the Systems Management Server Setup Wizard. Click on *Finish* to complete the installation of the software components.

Upgrading Secondary Site Servers

You have two choices: An existing secondary site server can be upgraded from the parent site using the SMS Administrator console or by using the SMS 2.0 Server CD-ROM directly at the secondary site server. The recommended method is to perform the upgrade at the local site server.

Once you have started the SMS installation, the secondary site will be found and you will be given the choice to upgrade. Merely starting the process is the only choice you have, whether you perform the upgrade from the primary site server through the SMS Administrative console or directly at the secondary site.

After the upgrade, you can use the following notes on the installation of SMS 2.0 primary and secondary site servers to tune your upgraded sites.

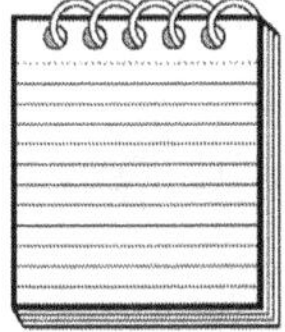

NOTE *These notes are an overview of the complicated process of upgrading existing SMS 1.2 site primary and secondary servers to SMS 2.0. The scope of this book is SMS 2.0, so a cursory walk-through the basic steps is illustrated briefly. Complete notes can be found in the* Systems Management Server 2.0 Administrator's Guide, *which is bundled with SMS 2.0 and can be found under the Systems Management Server option off the Start | Programs menu.*

Installing SMS 2.0 Sites

Your choices when installing SMS 2.0 primary or secondary sites are by the Express or Custom installation procedure. Choosing the Express option results in the installation of the complete list of SMS features. The Custom installation deploys a core set of SMS features but leaves most setup and configuration choices to be decided on by the installer or administrator.

The Installation Wizard steps through all the available choices, controlling both modes of the entire installation. At the end of the decision-making section of the installation, you're given the opportunity to review the selected selections before the actual install, file copying, and registry additions are carried out.

Finally, you complete the installation by manually defining your site boundaries and other site settings through the SMS Administrator console on the primary site server.

At all primary sites, SMS 2.0 must interact with SQL Server. The supported versions are SQL Server version 6.5 with Service Pack 5 installed or with SQL version 7.0 as the SMS site database.

The SMS setup can also install a dedicated copy of SQL Server if you want to maintain the SMS site database on the site server. In most cases, this is the preferred option, since the potential database traffic could be enormous if the database and SMS server were located at separate network locations.

Installing SQL Server Manually

You will have to manually install and tweak SQL Server 6.5 with Service Pack 5 or SQL version 7.0 if you decide to have:

- SQL execute on a different computer than the one you installed for your site server
- SMS use an existing installation of SQL Server 6.5 with Service Pack 5 or SQL version 7.0

Choosing to maintain the SMS site database on the same computer as your site server directs Setup to create all the necessary databases and data devices that SMS requires. This is called a *local SQL Server installation*, because the database engine is installed on the same computer as SMS. If you had chosen to install SQL Server on a separate computer system, it would then be called a *remote SQL Server installation*.

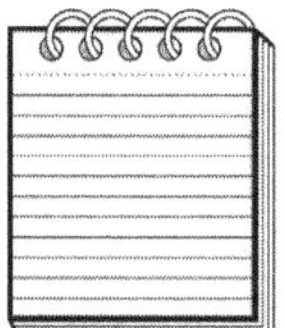

NOTE *The choices of Custom and Express for your SMS installation will only be presented if SQL Server is not already installed on the site server computer. However, if SQL Server is presently installed on the site server PC, the Express option will not be available.*

Choosing Express Setup over Custom

In a nutshell, the Express Setup should be chosen when:

- You are installing your test environment.
- Your SMS installation is a small single-site hierarchy.
- All of the SMS optional components are to be installed.
- SQL Server 6.5 with Service Pack 5 or SQL version 7.0 is to be installed on the site server.
- All discovery and installation methods need to be installed.

Choosing Custom Setup over Express

The Custom Setup should be chosen when you:

- Are installing a large site with several primary and secondary sites.
- Wish to make all of the decisions about what SMS components are installed.

- Don't want any of the discovery installation methods to be enabled after installation.
- Want the choice for either installing SMS SQL Server 6.5 with Service Pack 5 or SQL version 7.0 on the site server.
- Want to use an existing installation of SQL Server on either primary site server, earning other remote location.

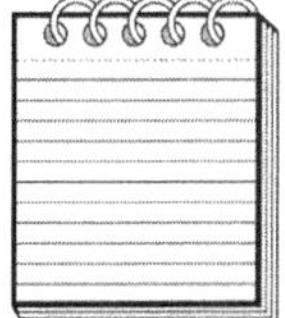

NOTE *This is a great time to consider creating and maintaining an SMS network logbook that will hold the very important installation information that you may have to refer to during a reinstall or just for day-to-day reference. As you make changes to your SMS environment, logging them on paper is the best way to remember your changes. It may feel old-fashioned, but it works.*

Minimum SMS 2.0 Specs: Hardware and Software Check

The absolute minimum hardware and software specs were quite detailed in Chapter 3 "Planning for the Deployment of System Management Server," so here's a short summary for a quick reference. These specs are for a site server that is supporting 100 computers maximum and all of the core SMS functions. If you have not read Chapter 3, take the time to do your planning first.

Remember that in the NT world, the hardware compatibility list (HCL) has the final say. You can view the current HCL by visiting www.microsoft.com and searching for the current list. Absolute minimum SMS 2.0 site server specs are as follows:

- 100 MB of hard drive space, either FAT or NTFS on the system drive
- 500 MB of free space on an NTFS partition
- A Windows NT 4.0 server configured as either a primary or backup domain controller with a minimum of Service Pack 4 installed
- Internet Explorer 4.01 with Service Pack 1
- Data Tools version 2.0
- Y2K patches

- Pentium 450 MHz CPU
- 128 MB of RAM

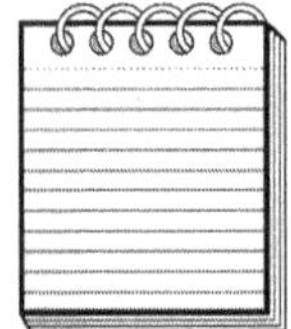

NOTE As with all of Microsoft products, doubling or even tripling the minimum requirements can't hurt in the slightest. Remember, they want to sell first.

SMS/SQL Boot Camp

SQL Server is an absolute necessity; it must be available in order for you to install SMS, so let's have a crash course in SQL Server concepts, deployment, and tuning methods. You may not have even considered the need for any SQL Server background when you started considering SMS. (Funny, isn't it, how Microsoft always seems to get us to use all of their products?)

First of all, SQL Server is the only database engine that will support and store SMS data. SQL can be installed during the installation of SMS 2.0, or it can already have been installed as a standalone. During the installation of SMS, the Installation Wizard can create the required database device files in SQL Server automatically if you choose.

A device file is made up of tables, stored procedures, indexes, and views—in effect, the guts of the SMS database. Tables are used to store the data collected by SMS services; stored procedures allow SQL Server to manipulate the SMS data; indexes help search for data quickly; and views give options for presenting the data.

The site database is created during the installation of the primary site server. In addition, another, separate database specifically for software metering is created if software metering is chosen for installation.

Both the site database and the software-metering database each require two device files: one, called a primary data file, stores the SMS data; the other, called a transaction log file, records in the changes made to the database. In addition, each database will have its own primary data file and transaction log file, which makes sense when you consider they are totally separate databases. The following default names are used for the two devices:

Database Device Names

- SMSData_ <sitecode> is the default name of the SMS data device.
- Loc_Data is the default name of the software-metering data device.

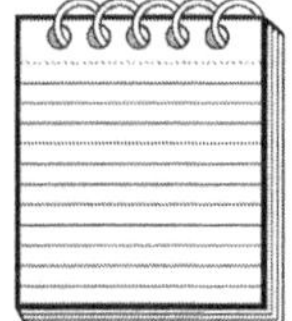

NOTE <sitecode> refers to the three-letter site code of your primary site that you entered during installation of SMS.

Transaction Log Names

- SMSLog_<sitecode> is the default name of the SMS log device.
- Lic_Log_<sitecode> is the default name of the software-metering log device.

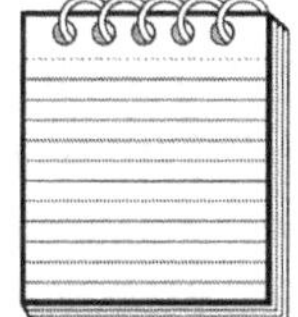

NOTE If you chose Express Setup, the default names for the SMS data device and log device are always SMSDATA and SMSLOG.

SQL Server Accounts

During the installation of SMS, the Installation Wizard must actually log on to SQL Server in order to create the needed databases. You'll be prompted to specify the account that will be used to create these databases during the installation and during the execution of SMS on a day-to-day basis. These accounts are called *SQL Server accounts*. SQL Server Security defines how SMS logs on and interacts with the database.

If you choose standard SQL Server security, by default, *sa* (the default administrator account for SQL) is suggested. However, you can use any SQL account that has the following three permissions: Create Database, Dump Database, or Dump Transaction Log. The other option for security is to use integrated Windows NT security. SQL security may have been used in the path if SQL Server was being used as an application server. If you are moving toward or already use NT domain security, integrated security allows you central control of all your user and group accounts at the primary domain controller.

NOTE If you plan to use integrated Windows NT security, SMS will need to use an NT local administrators group account that also has the same permissions: Create Database, Dump Database, or Dump Transaction Log. The account also must have the advanced user right "Log on as a service" *at the computer where SQL is installed. Details on user rights are discussed later in this chapter.*

SQL Database Access Methods

The three common database access methods that are used by SMS are as follows:

- *WBEM application access* Using the SMS Administrator console, access to the SQL database is provided through the WBEM and SMS Provider layers.
- *SMS Service account access* The installed SMS services manage and maintain data from the site systems using the defined SMS Service account. This account has equivalent Administrator permissions.
- *Software-Metering Service account access* The SQL Server manages and updates the software-metering database as directed by the Software Metering Service account.

Sizing the Data and Log Devices

Once the data and log devices have been created, you will have to make sure that the devices are set to a realistic size for the number of SMS clients that will be using the database. As you may expect, these settings will have to be adjusted as your client base grows. The SQL Server Resource Kit, part of the BackOffice Suite of Microsoft products, is packed with lots of details on continued maintenance and tuning of the database server; but don't worry, tuning settings are coming right up.

The SMS site database will grow larger as more hardware and software detail is collected from the client and as the use of software distribution is increased through advertised packages and software programs. Network and resource discovery will also increase the size of the database.

Microsoft recommends at a minimum that the SMS data device should be 50 MB per 100 clients; however, I'd recommend 75 MB as the standard benchmark per 100 clients. Continuing this train of thought, a site with 1,000 clients should have a data device of 750 MB. The size of the SMS database log device should also be sized at 20 percent of the size of the site database device.

Using the SQL Server Enterprise Manager found in the SQL Server 7.0 Programs group, we can view and set the server and the database properties. Right-clicking on the installed SQL Server and selecting Properties brings up the available choices for tuning. See Figure 4-2.

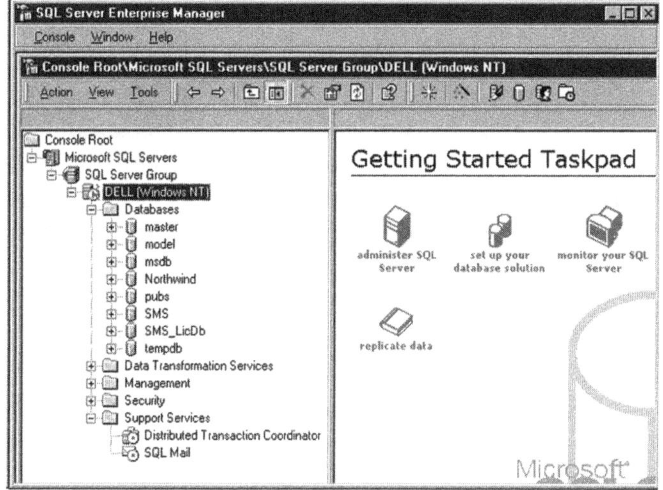

Figure 4-2 Viewing the SQL Server Enterprise Manager.

This sizing math is very important in SQL 6.5, but in SQL 7.0 these settings can be configured to grow automatically. In fact, setting maximum values for all configuration parameters in version 7.0 allows SQL to dynamically allocate needed resources when required and decrease the resources when they are no longer required. I've included the sizes to remind you how large the database requirements can become.

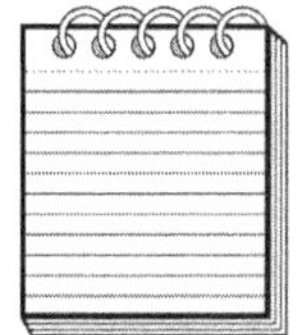

NOTE *If at all possible, upgrade to SQL Server 7.0 before installing SMS 2.0. The autotuning features are worth the upgrade work.*

Other components and their recommended settings to be aware of when setting up SQL Server are detailed in the following sections.

Temporary Database (tempdb) Size

SQL Server uses a system database called tempdb for holding temporary tables and temporary stored procedures during real-time processing. The file size for tempdb should be 20 percent of all device files on the SQL system, with the exception of the master database device files. If SQL is holding the site database and software-metering database data only, and the database size is 400 MB, then the size of the tempdb should be set to a minimum of 70 MB.

User Connections

A user connection allows software application access to the SQL Server database. SMS uses these connections for software installations, SMS service calls, and for access to the SMS Administrator console. The primary site server will need a minimum of 40 user connections to perform installations and perform the essential operations. Two more connections will be needed for the next five concurrent SMS Administrator consoles.

Each active user connection uses 40 KB of RAM on the SQL Server PC. Set user connections at the maximum allowed, since memory will not be committed until the user connection has been established. (See Figure 4-3.) Once the user connection becomes inactive, SQL Server 7.0 automatically returns the preallocated RAM back to the memory pool.

Open Objects

In the Windows 32-bit world, everything is defined as an object, and SQL Server is no exception. As the number of tables, views, rules, traders, and stored procedures that SQL is using is increased, the number of objects deployed also increases. Fortunately, there's no need to adjust this set-

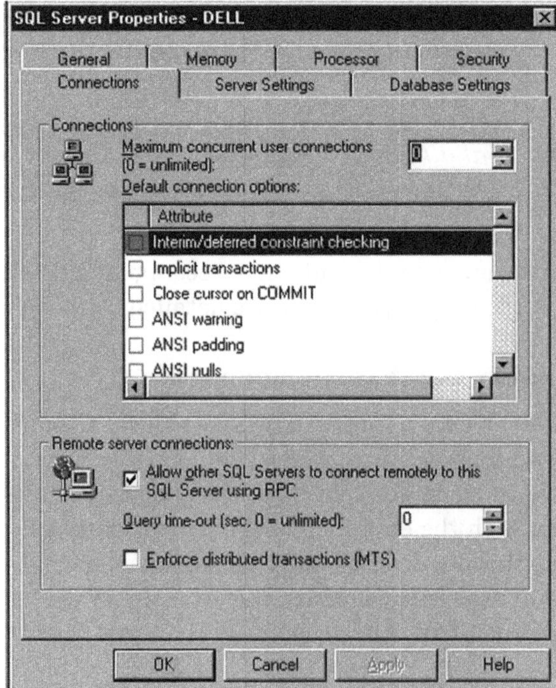

Figure 4-3
Setting user connections through the Enterprise Manager.

ting, since it is increased automatically. Using the new SMS Performance Monitor counters, we can view the number of open objects; it will be in the hundreds or thousands depending on the size of the active SMS environment.

RAM

All SQL operations require real chip memory, and SQL functions are allocated in memory units: a 2-KB slice of RAM. Setting the option "Dynamically configure SQL Server memory" under SQL Server Properties' total memory allocation is autoconfiguring. The maximum allocated ramp for an SQL Server is 2 GB, the same size that you can also set the size of virtual memory for SQL Server. SQL Server attempts to keep its free physical RAM available at approximately 5 MB in an attempt to stop excessive swaps to virtual memory.

Locks

SQL can also use a feature called *locking* to allow multiple-process access of the database. The requested task determines the level of blocking that is applied; either by table-, page-, or row-level locking. These locks are objects managed in RAM and are automatically set in SQL Server 7.0. SQL Server 6.5 requires a minimum of 1,500 locks in order for normal database processing.

Performing the Installation of SMS 2.0

As we know, AutoRun will take over once the SMS 2.0 CD-ROM has been slipped into your CD-ROM drive. The standard SETUP.EXE can also be started from the \SMSSETUP\BIN folder. Standard command-line SMS syntax that you also can choose from at the command prompt is listed in Table 4-2.

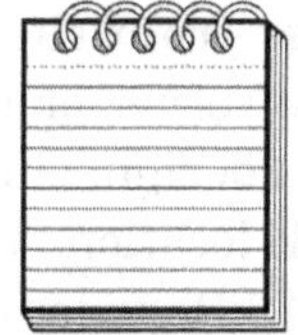

NOTE *Internet Explorer 4.01 with Service Pack 1, Microsoft Data Access Components (MDAC), and the Y2K components must be currently available or installed in order to complete SMS 2.0 installations. In addition, NT 4.0 with Service Pack 4 must also be installed. There may be no need to move up to Service Pack 5 or 6. I have had the best success with Service Pack 4. However, this is due to change over time.*

TABLE 4-2

Command-Line Syntax for SMS Installation.

Install Syntax	When to Use
/SCRIPT	Points to the path of the script file.
/UPGRADE	Carries out an unintended upgrade.
/NODISKCHECK	Does not check on the available disk space.
NOACCTCHECK	Does not check if the service account you specify ensuring installation has administrative permissions.

As noted previously in this chapter, SQL is required for SMS to function, but the SQL Server source files are not included on the SMS CD-ROM. The SMS installation will prompt you for the location of the SQL CD-ROM if the SQL Server installation is to be performed as well.

The only installation of SQL Server that can be performed during the actual SMS installation is a dedicated local installation of SQL Server on the SMS primary site server. Tasks also performed during the combination installation of SMS and SQL are as follows:

- The creation of a central site server
- Setup of SQL Server for dedicated use by the SMS site server

SQL Database Security and Location

The SQL installation requires an SQL Server account and password that will be used to set up the database engine and for database management after installation. If SQL Server is already installed on the domain controller, the SMS installation can create the needed database device files, or you can identify the existing device files that will be used.

If you have a remote SQL Server location presently installed on your network, you may decide to use that remote location for your SMS database. The SMS installation will then ask you for the location of the SMS Provider. This agent is used for SQL data access from the SMS Administrator console. It can be installed on the site server or on the remote SQL Server, but be careful with your long-term design, since the SMS Provider cannot be moved to any other network location without removing and reinstalling SMS. Installation of the SMS Provider on the SMS site provides the best performance.

SMS Installation: Step-by-Step

The very first screen that presents itself is the System Management Server 2.0 Setup Wizard. You can choose to install SMS 2.0, install NT 4.0 SP4, or read the release notes. SMS requires Windows NT with Service Pack 4 in order to function properly, so make sure that's what you have running. The easiest way to check is to use the Windows NT Diagnostics found in the Administrator Tools (Common), as shown in Figure 4-4.

> The Service Pack 4 CD-ROM also includes several key components that SMS requires that are not usually installed when Service Pack 4 is normally installed. These components are Internet Explorer 4.01 with Service Pack 1, Microsoft Data Access Components, and the Y2K components. By installing the Service Pack 4 option from this splash screen, the correct IE4 version, and Service Pack 1, the Microsoft Data Access Components, and the Y2K components will be all installed.

Selecting the installation of SMS 2.0, the Installation Wizard first checks the computer system for any previous installations of an SMS site server, secondary site server, client access point component server, or SMS Administrator console. If it finds no such history through the local hard drive and Registry check, it proceeds to the next screen, shown in Figure 4-5, which allows you to install:

- An SMS primary site
- An SMS secondary site
- The SMS Administrator console and related SMS tools

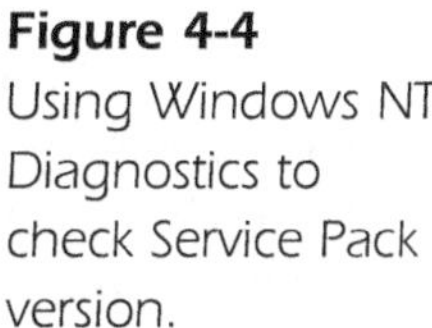

Figure 4-4
Using Windows NT Diagnostics to check Service Pack version.

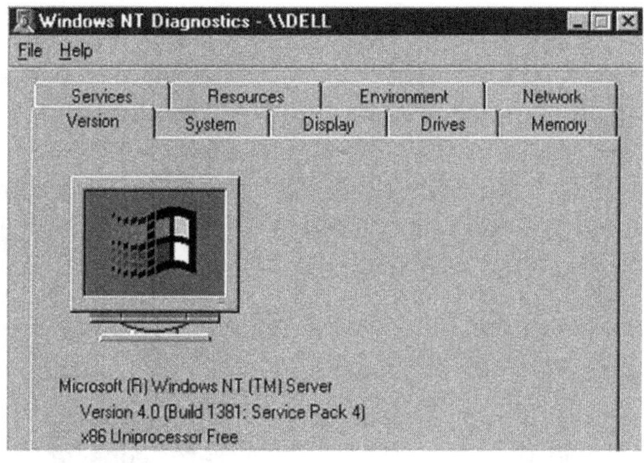

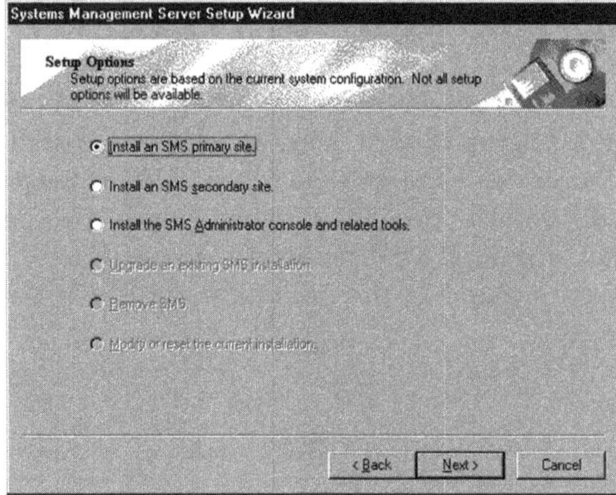

Figure 4-5 Choices for SMS 2.0 installation.

If a past SMS history is indeed found, it will prompt you for the decision to continue with the following options:

- Upgrade an existing 1.2 SMS installation to SMS 2.0
- Remove SMS
- Modify or reset the current installation

After you agree to the SMS license agreement, the actual installation begins.

NOTE *Does anyone really read this agreement completely? Did you know that if you are using an evaluation copy of SMS for evaluation and testing purposes, you can't benchmark your SMS installation and report the results to a third party without telling Microsoft first? Does this really mean that you inform Microsoft about all SMS problems before your own company?*

Your choices at this point in the installation are either Express or Custom. As discussed earlier, each install method performs much differently. Table 4-3 details the SMS component and choices that occur when installing the Custom or Express method for primary or secondary sites.

Either method of installation requires the following information:

- *A unique three-character site code.* Choices are from 000 to ZZZ, a total of over 46,000 choices.
- *The site name.* The name is used to identify the site that appears when you run the SMS Administrator console.

TABLE 4-3 Component Options for SMS 2.0.

	Express Primary Site Installation	Custom Primary Site Installation	Secondary Site Installation	SMS Administrator Console Installation
Site Server	Installed	Installed	Installed	Not available
SMS Administrator Console	Installed	Installed	Not available	Installed
Software Metering	Installed	Optional	Optional	Not available
Software Metering Console	Installed	Optional	Not available	Optional
Remote Tools	Installed	Optional	Optional	Not available
SMS Installer	Installed	Optional	Not available	Not available
Network Monitor	Installed	Optional	Not available	Optional
Package Automation Scripts	Installed	Optional	Not available	Not available
Crystal Info	Installed	Optional	Not available	Optional
NetWare Bindery Support	Installed	Optional	Optional	Not available
NetWare NNDS Support	Installed	Optional	Optional	Not available
Product Compliance Database	Installed	Optional	Not available	Not available

- *The domain controller where SMS will be installed.* It must be a domain controller; a standalone (member server) Windows NT server cannot run SMS. SMS relies on global groups and domain user accounts.
- *SMS Service account information.* This account can be created for you, or you can specify an existing domain account.
- *The number of clients that are to be supported.* SQL Server uses this information to size the SMS database. If you're using SQL Server 6.5, this is very important information, since configuration of the database size is a manual process. Using SQL 7.0, the database can be expanded automatically, as discussed earlier in this chapter.
- *The number of SMS administrative consoles to create.* SQL Server also uses this information in the preset number of connections to be created for SQL Server. Each instance of the SMS Administrator console running requires the default number of connections. The Express install sets the minimum number of connections required; a Custom install allows you to define the connections that will be created.

Regardless of the installation method chosen, the Installation Wizard presents the entire installation in screens. First we'll look at the Express Setup screens, along with detailed notes.

Product Registration

To start the SMS installation, first enter your name, your organization's name, and the CD key number found on the back of the jewel case for the SMS 2.0 product.

SMS Site Information

The next decisions are the unique site code name, your site name for the SMS site (this will identify the site later in the SMS Administrator console), and the domain that the site server resides in or will reside in.

SMS Server Account Information

Next, you will be asked to specify the SMS Service account information, as shown in Figure 4-6. The account name that is entered must have the following permissions granted:

- Be a current member of the Domain Admin global group
- Be a member of the Local Administrator group
- Have the right to log on as a service on the SMS site

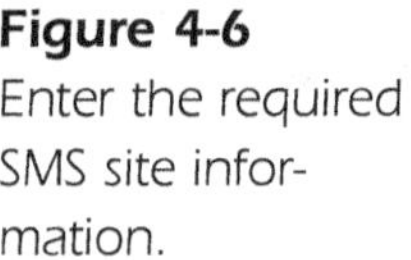

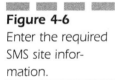

Figure 4-6
Enter the required SMS site information.

SMS Server Account Permissions

You grant the SMS Server account permissions by opening the administrative tool User Managers for Domains on the primary domain controller for the selected domain. Then select the drop-down menu option *Policies* and then *User Rights*, and choose the user rights policy for the domain. In order to set the right option "Log on as a service," make sure the Show Advanced User Rights option at the bottom left of the screen is checked. Then by pressing the black triangle drop-down indicator, you can select all standard and advanced rights, one at a time.

Once you have highlighted the right "Log on as a service" option, you will see that the local group Administrator is already selected to perform this system function, as shown in Figure 4-7. Clicking the Add button allows you to specify the specific user or local/global group you wish to also grant this user the right to.

SMS Primary Site Client Load

The next information that you enter is the number of nodes that will be clients. This number is the total of actual client *and* server computers that will be in the primary site and all child sites. Make sure that the number entered considers all of these current and future parameters, since SMS uses this number to calculate the size of the SQL database. I would add a factor of 25 percent to your entered number as a buffer zone.

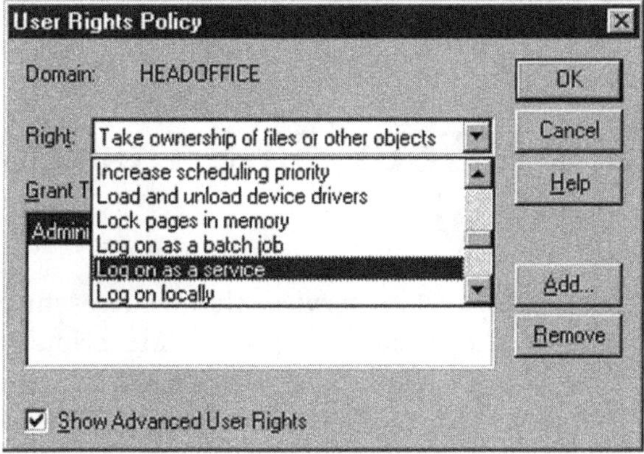

Figure 4-7 Selecting advanced user rights using User Manager for Domains.

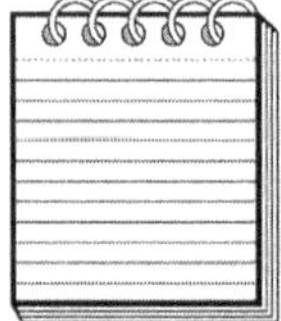

NOTE *You can increase this number by rerunning the SMS installation and selecting the option "Modify or Reset the current installation."*

SQL Server Administrative Account

Now the SQL Server setup information is required. The default SQL Administrator account name is *sa*. At this point in the installation, the wizard is informing you that the sa account for administering the SQL database will be created with a NULL password, meaning the SQL administration is carried out with the default account sa with no password. You can, and should, change this password. Make sure, however, that you are documenting all of this installation information as you perform the installation.

Concurrent SMS Administrator Consoles

Enter the number of SMS Administrator consoles that will be running in this site you are installing. Accept the default of 5; this will set the number of connections that SQL can concurrently support. The SMS Administrator console can be installed at the desired domain locations after this installation is completed using the SMS Server CD-ROM.

Completing the Systems Management Server

At this point you will be informed that you have successfully completed the SMS installation. When you click on OK, the Installation Wizard checks the information that you have entered to make sure the user accounts that you have chosen for SQL and SMS administrative tasks are correct. If all of your choices are verified, the SMS installation continues with the copying and installation of SMS files and components.

Check If Your SMS Installation Was Successful

There are several system services that a successful SMS installation will have installed and initiated. On your SMS primary site server, open up *Control Panel* and select the *Services* icon. By using Table 4-4, you can verify the correct Status and Startup values for each service that SMS installed.

TABLE 4-4

Services Installed by SMS 2.0.

SMS	Correct Status	Startup
SMS_Executive	Started	Automatic
SMS_SITE COMPONENT_MANAGER	Started	Automatic
SMS_SQL_MONITOR	Started	Automatic
Windows Management	Started	Automatic
SQL Server	**Correct Status**	**Startup**
MSSQL_Server	Started	Automatic
MSDTC	None	Manual
SQL_ServerAgent	None	Manual
Crystal Report Services	**Correct Status**	**Startup**
Info Agent	Started	Automatic
Info APS	Started	Automatic
Info Sentinel	Started	Automatic

Next, check the status of your SQL Server database. Click on *Start* and open *Programs*, and then select *Microsoft SQL Server Enterprise Manager*. The MMC should open, showing you Microsoft SQL Servers. Expand *SQL Server Group*, and select your domain controller.

Scroll down until you find the three SMS databases that should have been created: SMS, SMS_LicDb, and tempdb. By selecting either General, Tables and Indexes, or Space Allocated, as shown in Figure 4-8, you can verify the default properties of the SQL databases created for SMS.

Express installation also enables and disables the SMS system settings shown in Table 4-5. If you choose to perform a custom SMS installation and setup, you can use the table to define configuration settings that you may wish to change.

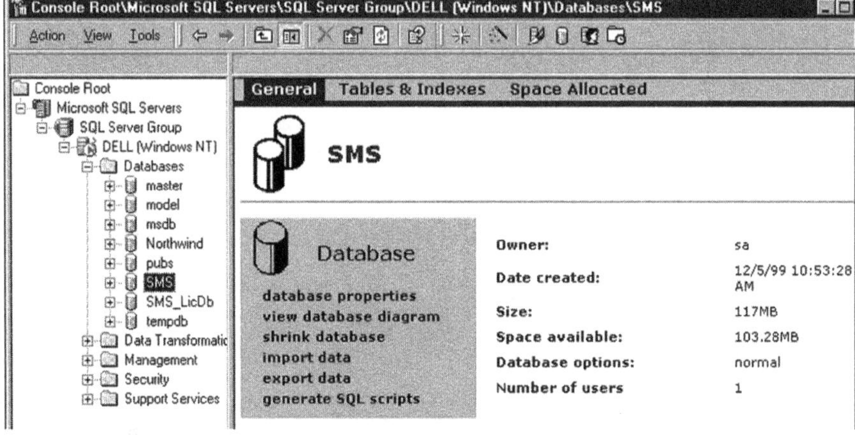

Figure 4-8 SQL Databases installed for SMS Server.

TABLE 4-5 Default Settings for SMS Express Installation.

SMS Optional Component	Enabled/ Disabled	Timing Interval
Network Discovery	Disabled	
Windows NT User Group Discovery	Enabled	1 day
NetWare NDS Logon Discovery	Enabled	25 hours
Modify Logon Scripts	Disabled	
NetWare Bindery Discovery	Enabled	1 day
Modify Logon Scripts	Disabled	
Windows Networking User Account Discovery	Enabled	1 day
Heartbeat Discovery	Enabled	1 day—Express 1 week—Custom
Windows Networking Logon Discovery	Enabled	Every logon
Modify Logon Scripts	Disabled	
Windows NT Remote Client Installation	Enabled	N/A
NetWare Bindery Logon Client Installation	Enabled	N/A
NetWare NDS	Enabled	N/A

SMS Utilities

The SMS installation installs seven shortcuts into the Systems Management Server program group found on all primary site servers, as shown in Figure 4-9. They are as follows:

- *SMS Administrator Console* This shortcut starts the Microsoft Management Console (MMC) that holds the main SMS utility used to administer Systems Management Server.
- *SMS Administrator's Guide* This is the abridged version of the *SMS Administrators Guide*. The complete guide is found in the *BackOffice Server Resource Guide* or on the Web at www.microsoft.com/technet.
- *SMS Courier Sender* This shortcut launches the SMS Courier Sender, which checks for the current status for any created parcels typically created by a removable media type such as a CD-R.
- *SMS Release Notes* You should read the release notes; they contain late-breaking information that was not included in any paper documentation.
- *Network Monitor* You may have seen a version of this software tool before; a somewhat limited version could be installed on NT Server 4.0, or the full version may have been used if you're familiar with Microsoft BackOffice Server. This utility can be used for network analysis at the data packet or frame level. We will use the network monitor in Chapter 15 "Troubleshooting with SMS."
- *Network Monitor Control Tool* This software tool works with Network Monitor as an extra level of security, continually analyzing the network for network events or suspicious network activity.
- *SMS Setup* This shortcut allows you to modify the currently selected wizard selections that were used for the installation for your SMS site

Figure 4-9 SQL icons found in the Systems Management Server program group.

server. You can remove, change, or reset the site server installation, but you cannot install new SMS software components from this icon. In this case, you must use the SMS 2.0 CD-ROM setup program SETUP.EXE.

Registry Keys Used by SMS 2.0

After a successful SMS site server installation, four main Registry locations will hold the bulk of the SMS Registry keys for storing configuration changes. The two system hives that will be used are SOFTWARE and SYSTEM. Both are found under HKEY_LOCAL_MACHINE (HLKM).

- *HKEY_LOCAL_MACHINE\SOFTWARE\Microsoft\NAL* This location is where the client access point data and hard drive information is stored and retrieved by the Client Install Data Manager.
- *HKEY_LOCAL_MACHINE\SOFTWARE\Microsoft\SMS* This location stores essential data for the SMS site that is updated from the SMS Administrator console. Categories found here include essential SMS site information, SMS database locations, and SQL triggers. You may on occasion have to strip values from the Registry for future SMS upgrades or for interfacing with Windows 2000.
- *HKEY_LOCAL_MACHINE\SOFTWARE\Microsoft\WBEM* All WBEM applications use this location for a central storage of DCOM and ODBC system information.
- *HKEY_LOCAL_MACHINE\SYSTEM\Current Control Set\Services* This folder holds subfolders for each installed SMS service and their startup parameters.

SMS Shares

NT Network shares are used for communication links with the installed site systems and for communication within the defined SMS site boundaries. The following shares are added by the SMS installation:

- *CAP_ site code* This share is created on all client access point on all site systems and directly links to the \CAP_ site code folder.

Administrators have Full Control permission to this folder. This folder is used as the communication link between the SMS client and the site server when client software is being installed.

- *Cinfo* This share is used as the installation share for the Seagate Crystal Info service. The global group Everyone Has Full Control permissions to this folder.
- *SMS_site code* This folder is where you installed SMS.
- *SMS_SITE* This share points to the path SMS\INBOXES\DESPOOLER.BOX\RECEIVE. When SMS data is updated to the SMS site server from a remote SMS client, this folder is used as the temporary storage location until it is passed to the SQL database.
- *SMS_PKGx$* This share is a hidden administrative share that points to the local location on the site server that initially has the most free hard drive space. It is used as a storage space for the SMS site server that performs as a distribution point.

Windows NT Users and Group Accounts

After the SMS installation has successfully completed, three Windows NT user accounts and two Windows NT group accounts will have been created for running and administering the SMS site. These include:

- *SMS Service Account* This account is used to execute SMS services, processes, and threads in the background across the SMS hierarchy.
- *SMSClient <site code>* This user account is used by the SMS client components for the continued updating and maintenance of client access points and distribution points.
- *SMSServer <site code>* This user account is created and used as a backup account if the SMS Server account fails.
- *SMS <Admins>* This local group was created during the SMS installation with the addition of the user that carried out the actual install. This local user account is used for securing local access to the SMS site database.
- *SMSInternalCliGrp* This global group is used to carry out local SMS internal operations.

Performing a Custom SMS Site Installation

As mentioned several times (because it's so darned important), the Custom Setup of SMS disables by default most SMS features, assuming that you know what features you are going to use. To install an SMS primary site with Custom Setup, follow these steps.

First run SMS Setup using the SMS CD-ROM. However, this time choose *Custom Setup* from the initial choices presented with the install splash screen. Accept the licensing agreement, fill in the CD key value, and click on *OK*.

For a custom setup, you will be presented with the following screens:

Product Registration

To continue the custom installation, enter your name, your organization's name, and the CD key.

SMS Site Information

For a custom setup, you will be presented with the following screens:

The next entries are the same as the Express Setup: your unique site code name, your site name for the SMS site (this will identify the site in the SMS Administrator console), and the domain that the site server resides in.

SMS Server Account Information

Next, you will be asked to specify the SMS Service account information. The account name that is entered must have the following permissions granted:

1. Must be a current member of the Domain Admin global group.
2. Must be a member of the Local Administrator group.
3. Must have the right to log on as a service on the SMS site.

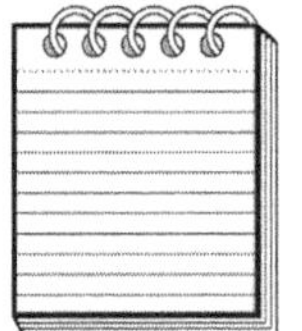

NOTE *Details on setting up the advanced rights for the SMS Service account are covered earlier in this chapter under the heading "SMS Server Account Permissions."*

SMS Primary Site Client Nodes

The next information that you enter is the number of nodes that will be clients. This number is the total of actual client *and* server computers that will be in the primary site and all child sites. Make sure that the number entered considers all of these current and future parameters, since SMS uses this number to calculate the size of the SQL database. Again, I would add a 25 percent factor to the current number to allow for future growth.

NOTE *You can increase this number by rerunning the SMS installation and selecting the option "Modify or Reset the current installation."*

Setup Installation Options

Since the installation is being run in Custom mode, the selection of the SMS components to be installed are chosen from Options screen. Options checked are installed; options unchecked are not installed. The directory that will be the storage location for the SMS components must be formatted as an NTFS volume. Also note that you can change the chosen location from this screen.

Using a Dedicated Copy of SQL Server

At this point in the installation, you must make a decision as to where and how to install SQL Server. If SQL Server is to be installed on the local primary site server, choose *Yes, install a dedicated local copy of SQL Server for SMS*; you will then be shown the SQL Server Administrator Account screen.

If SQL Server is installed on another server remote to this SMS primary site, choose *No, do not install a dedicated local copy of SQL Server for SMS*. If you click on Next, the Installation Wizard presents you with the Using an Existing SQL Server Database screen.

For this example, we'll assume you want to install a dedicated local copy. The following screens will appear:

SQL Server Administrative Account

Now the SQL Server setup information is required. The default SQL Administrator account name is *sa*. At this point in the installation, the wizard is informing you that the sa account for administering the SQL database will be created with a NULL password, which, again, means no password. You can, and should, change this password. However, make sure that you are documenting all of this installation information as you perform the installation.

SQL Server Installation

Choose the location where SQL Server is to be installed by accepting the default location, or change the location presented to the path you wish to use.

Concurrent SMS Administrator Consoles

Enter the number of SMS Administrator consoles that will be running in this site that you are installing. Accept the default of 5; this will set the number of connections that SQL Server can concurrently support across the entire SMS site. You can install the SMS Administrator console at any desired domain location after this installation is completed by using the SMS Server CD-ROM on any Windows NT 4.0 PC.

Completing the Systems Management Server Setup Wizard

At this point you will be informed that you have successfully completed the SMS installation. When you click on OK, the Installation Wizard checks the information that you have entered to make sure the user accounts that you have chosen for SMS administrative tasks are correct. It will also prompt you for the location of SETUP.EXE for SQL Server and the CD key value that will be used to install SQL Server. Once this information is entered and verified by the Installation Wizard, SQL Server is installed and then the SMS installation continues with the copying and installation of SMS files and components.

Using an Existing SQL Server Database

If you have chosen to use an existing SQL Server installation, the SQL Server Information for SMS Site Database screen is now presented. Enter the computer name of the system where SQL Server is presently installed and specify the current version, 6.5 or 7.0.

You also must choose how security is handled between SMS and SQL Server when they communicate with each other, either by the NT domain security or exclusively by SQL Server. The choice of "integrated security" means "Do you wish SQL Server to verify all logons to its database through the NT security system?"

Choosing Yes allows you to create, and later on maintain, the SQL Server database using the currently logged-on user; the standard SQL logon will not used. The rights that must be given to this user for system administration access to the master database are Create Database, Backup Database, and Backup Log privileges.

Choosing No means integrated security is not implemented and all SMS logons to SQL Server must first enter an SQL login ID and password. The SQL Server Devices for the SMS Site Database screen is now presented.

The default SQL server login ID for the SQL Server Account is *sa*. Accepting this logon ID and entering the chosen password defines the user account that has the required system administrator rights to the SQL database. If you choose another login name, you will have to make sure that this user has the proper database operator rights to the database. The rights that must be given for administrative access to the master database are Create Database, Backup Database, and Backup Log privileges.

You will now be presented with the following screens:

SQL Server Devices for the SMS Site Database

This screen allows you to define any SQL devices already created or to specify that you want the SMS Installation Wizard to create them for you. If you selected Yes, you want the devices created for you now, the "SMS Site Database Device and Device Names" screen is presented.

SMS Site Database Device and Device Names

The default names for the database, database device name, and the log device name are now shown. You can choose to accept these names or choose your own naming conventions. Again, make careful notes in your network log.

If you are using SQL Server 6.5, when you select Next, the SMS Server Device Directory Path for SMS Site Database screen is presented. Enter the path to the existing SMS data device path location.

If you are using SQL Server 7.0, the SMS Site Database Name screen is presented. Select the SMS site database that you want to use.

If you selected No, you want to create or define your own devices, then the devices must be created right now, before the installation can proceed. The Installation Wizard must check that the devices and logs actually exist so it can update the Registry. The next screen that is presented is SMS Site Database Device Sizes.

SMS Site Database Device Sizes

The size of your SMS database and log devices are presented. The number of SMS clients that you entered earlier in the installation calculated these values.

SMS Site Database Device and Device Names

The default names for the database, the database device name, and the log device name are now shown. You can choose to accept these names or choose your own naming conventions.

If you are installing the SMS software-metering feature, the separate SQL database for this option must now be setup. The SQL Server Information for Software Metering Database screen now appears.

SQL Server Information for Software Metering Database

Enter the name of the computer system where SQL Server is installed. It will most likely be the same location as your site database server. You also choose the type of security that will control access to the software-metering database. The choices are, again, integrated security or SQL security. If you want to use integrated security, this option must have been selected previously for the site server SQL database security.

If integrated security is not selected, the SQL Server Account for Software Metering Database screen appears. Enter the SQL Server login ID and password that will be used for access to the software-metering database.

SQL Server Devices for Software Metering Database

If you select No on this screen, you can create your own data devices and log names. Selecting Yes informs the Installation Wizard to create the database devices automatically. If you choose No, the Software Metering Device Size and the Software Metering Database and Device Name screens are displayed sequentially.

Software Metering Device Size

The calculated sizes for the database and log devices based on the number of clients you entered previously are displayed.

Software Metering Database and Device Name

Enter the names for the database, the data devices, and the log devices that you have created for software metering.

If you choose Yes, you want the Installation Wizard to create the data devices, the Software Metering Database and Device Names screen is displayed.

Software Metering Database and Device Names

Define the names you wish to use for the database, the log, and data devices. If you are using SQL Server 6.5, you will be prompted for the SMS data device path. If you are using SQL Server 7.0, you will be prompted to enter the SQL Server database name for software metering.

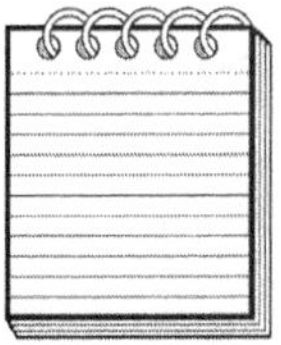

NOTE *The names for your database and log names must contain only alphanumeric characters, or the setup/installation will fail.*

Concurrent SMS Administrator Consoles

Enter the number of SMS Administrator consoles that will be running in this site you are installing. Accepting the default number will also set the number of connections that SQL can concurrently support. The SMS Administrator console can be installed at the desired domain locations after this installation is completed using the SMS Server CD-ROM.

SMS Provider Information

If your SQL database is not located on your primary site server, then the SMS Provider Information screen will be presented. The SMS Provider is the communication interface or link from the SMS Administrator console to the SMS site database. For the best performance, the SMS Provider should be installed on the computer system where SQL Server is installed. This will probably be the primary site server where SMS and the SQL database are both installed. This choice cannot be changed without reinstalling SMS.

Completing the Systems Management Server Setup

At this point you will be informed that you have successfully completed the SMS installation. When you click on OK, the Installation Wizard checks the information that you have entered to make sure the user accounts that you have chosen for SMS administrative tasks are correct. Then the SMS 2.0 installation is completed.

Installing a Secondary Site

The installation of a secondary site can only be successful if a parent primary site has first been created. SQL Server can't be installed on a secondary site; it must reside on the primary site or at a defined remote location within the defined site boundaries.

Although the SMS Administrator console cannot be installed on the secondary site during the actual installation of the secondary site, it can be installed later. The secondary site can be installed by two methods:

1. From the primary site server using the SMS Administrator console
2. From the SMS 2.0 CD-ROM

Installing a Secondary Site Server from the SMS 2.0 CD-ROM

Select *Install an SMS Secondary Site* from the screen that presents the installation choices. You will be presented with the following screens:

- *Product Registration* Enter the CD key from the SMS 2.0 CD-ROM and product registration.
- *SMS Site Server Information* Enter the three-digit site code, the site name, and the site domain that are currently used by the existing site.

SMS Service Account Information

You will probably already have a current service account that was created during the installation of the SMS primary site, and if so, use this account information again.

If a different account is entered, it must have the proper administrative rights for proper SMS system access.

You will now be presented with the following screens.

SMS Installation Options

Next, choose the SMS components that you want to install on the secondary site.

Parent Site Information/Identification

Enter the site code of the current parent site and the name of the primary site server that will interface with the secondary site you are installing. Also enter the type of network connection that will be used to link the secondary site to the parent site. The default connection type is Local Area Network; however, this may be a remote site not on the local network infrastructure. In this case, RAS (Remote Access Service) could be chosen. The best idea is to go to the remote location and install from the SMS 2.0 CD-ROM.

Connection Account Information

The account name and password should be entered to allow access to the parent site.

Completing the Systems Management Server Setup Wizard

The choices you have made for the secondary site will be summarized on this screen. If you accept the choices, the installation of the secondary site server is carried out and completed.

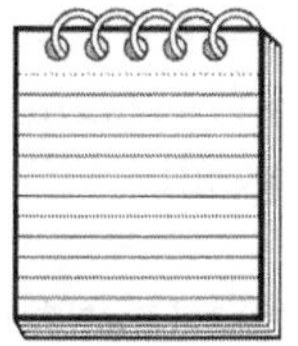

NOTE *Even though you can perform the installation of the secondary site server successfully, it is not complete until the primary site creates and issues a connection address from the primary site to the secondary site. This task is performed through the SMS Administrator console at the primary site. This information is found in Chapter 6 "Using the SMS Administrator Console."*

Installing a Secondary Site Using the Secondary Site Wizard

By using the SMS Administrator console, you can completely install a secondary site from the primary server site without physically going to the remote site location. The success of this feature depends greatly on the local bandwidth available. If your network is always busy, then use the installation from the SMS 2.0 CD-ROM. The package sent from the primary to the secondary site can exceed 50 MB.

The lucky computer that is to be made a secondary site must have the following minimum characteristics:

- Free space of 55 MB formatted as NTFS
- A minimum of 100 MB of free disk space on the boot partition
- NT Server with Service Pack 4 installed as the operating system
- A trusted domain user account on the primary site
- A local domain user account belonging to the Domain Admins global group with the "Log on as a service" advanced user right

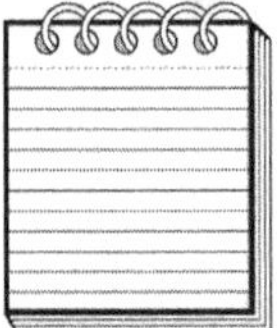

NOTE *You may want to test the ability of the primary and site server to talk to each other at the proper permission levels. Use a* `NET` *command test to specify that the user account can communicate each way by attaching to the root of drive C: through the Administrative share C$.*

The syntax to verify communication at the command prompt is as follows:

```
NET USE\\SERVER\C$/USERNAME:SMSACCOUNT PASSWORD
```

To install a secondary site using the SMS Administrator console, first log on to your primary site server as Administrator. Open up the SMS Administrator console and highlight the <site code - site name > of your primary site server. Right-click, and select *New* and then *Secondary Site*. The Welcome screen informs you of where the secondary site will be created in your hierarchy. See Figure 4-10.

The following information summarizes the screens that the Site Creation Wizard presents in order to collect the necessary information to install your secondary site server.

Site Identity

The information that is needed is your unique site code and site name. In addition, a free-form comment field is presented. I suggest entering a comment that identifies the type of the site you are creating; this can be helpful for troubleshooting.

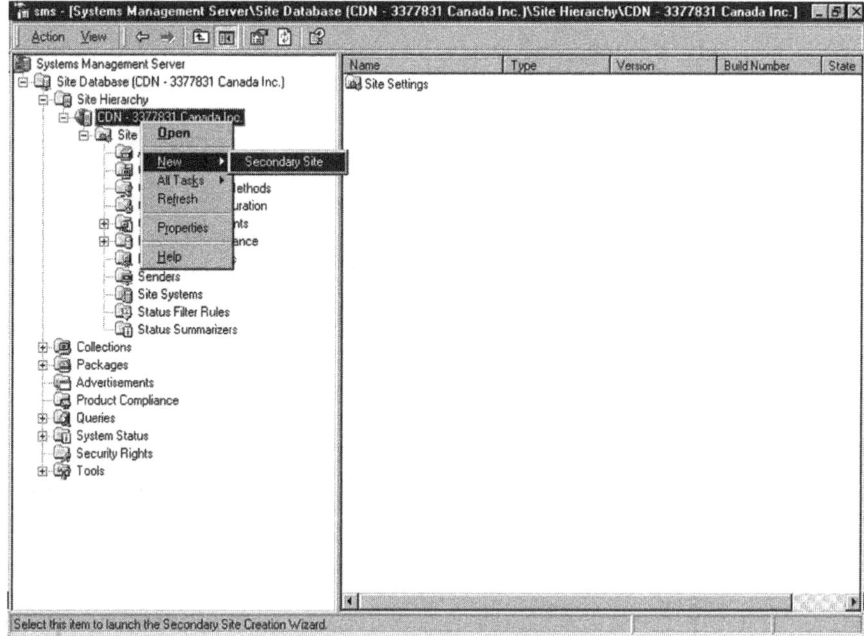

Figure 4-10 Installing a secondary site using SMS Administrator console.

Secondary Site Creation

Enter the name of the Windows NT domain where the site server is located, along with the name of the site server. The processor platform defaults to Intel X86 and compatible; this is probably your platform, but if not, you can switch to Alpha. (This platform will not be around much longer in my opinion.) Be careful to spell the name of the server correctly. This installation procedure does not check that the server named actually exists. The purpose of this methodology is to allow you to create a secondary site on a server that you're not currently attached to.

Installation Source Files

The location of the SMS installation files can be from the parent site to the server that you're installing, or you can choose to install the source files directly from the local SMS CD-ROM at the secondary site server location.

SMS Service Account

You will probably already have a current service account that was created during the installation of the SMS primary site, and if so, use this account information again. If a different account is entered, it must have the proper administrative rights for proper SMS system access.

Addresses to Secondary Site

Select one of the preset addresses that are configured for this site. The options will be either the Standard Sender address or the RAS Sender address. These senders are deployed for the purpose of managing the communications during the installation of the secondary site software files from the primary site. You will also have to specify the user account and password that will be used when a secondary site attaches to the primary site.

Completing of the Create Secondary Site

At the final wizard screen, check to make sure the defined secondary site characteristics are correct. Note the disclaimer on the screen indicating that the installation could take several hours.

Once the secondary site installation has finished and the site control file has been copied to the parent site, open the SMS Administrator console to verify the new secondary site was installed.

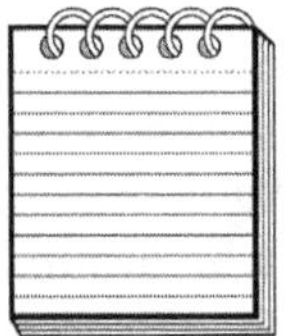

NOTE *Now that we have finished the basic installation of primary and secondary sites, the site boundaries and other site settings must be defined using the SMS Administrator console. For a detailed discussion of these settings, see Chapter 5 "Configuring SMS Site Systems." For information on installing additional SMS Administrator consoles, refer to Chapter 6.*

Secondary Site Server Services

Since the secondary site does not have access to a local SQL database, there will be less local system activity; however, there are still SMS processes that will be installed on a secondary site server. These include:

- *The SMS Executive* After installation, this service automatically starts.
- *The SMS Component Manager* After installation, this service automatically starts as well. Its job is to monitor and control the local installed SMS processes and threads.

- *The Windows NT Logon Discovery Agent* If the secondary server is a domain controller, this process is also automatically started.

Secondary Site Server Shares

Communication from the parent site to the secondary site is controlled through Windows NT network shares. The following shares are created on a secondary site server:

- *CAP <site code>* This share is used for communication with client access point site systems.
- *SMS Logon Share* If the secondary site server has been installed on a domain controller, this share is created to support the site systems that function as logon points.
- *SMS_SITE share* This share is used for essential communication between the primary and secondary site server.
- *SMS <site code>* This share holds information used for collections, along with inventory information, that is then passed on to the primary site.

SMS Service Pack 1

The first service pack for SMS 2.0 has been released and should be applied to all primary and secondary site servers that are installed in your company before you have added any SMS clients locally or through logon scripts. When a SMS 2.0 site is upgraded to Service Pack 1, all existing SMS clients, CAPs, and distribution points will be automatically upgraded with the new SMS components. The size of the upgrade per client is 8 MB minimum and can be up to 24 MB depending on the software applets installed at the client.

NOTE *Disable logon scripts for all clients connecting with RAS. The bandwidth will not be sufficient to handle the upgrade. The remote client will have to be upgraded at the local site. The best solution is to apply the service pack at night. Have the users leave their computers on. After the site servers have been upgraded, they will be automatically upgraded as well.*

You can also choose to install Service Pack 1 silently using Setup.exe/Upgrade/NoUserInput from the \SMSSetup\Bin\%platform% directory on the Systems Management Server SP1 CD-ROM.

To find out what is fixed by this service pack update, print out and read the Readme.txt file that is included with the service pack, or download and read Knowledge Base document Q235991—SMS: Systems Management Server 2.0 Service Pack 1 Fixlist.

A sampling of Service Pack 1 fixes with corresponding Knowledge Base (KB) number is listed below.

Q214979 SMS: Service Manager Does Not Connect to Secondary Site Servers

Q215018 SMS: Cannot Add Local Groups in Manage User Wizard

Q215123 SMS: SMS_LOGON_SERVER_MANAGER Fails to Enumerate Shares

Q223044 SMS: Remote Control Agent Not Found

Q223755 SMS: SMS Executive Crashes When Enumerating Non-Microsoft Server

Q224574 SMS: Remote Control Installation Fails to Recognize LANDesk 6.x

Q225514 SMS: WinNT Logon Server Manager Replicates Files When It Should Not

Q226114 SMS: Advertisement Fails When Sent to Win95 & Win98 Users in More than 10 Groups

Q228276 SMS: Software Inventory Processing Degrades Foreground Performance on Win95 & Win98 Clients

Q229950 SMS: Provider Deletes Collection When Computer Name Starts with Number

Q232240 SMS: Specifying Long File Name for Status MIF Causes Error

Q234257 SMS: Secondary Site Server Processor Utilization Always High

Q235735 SMS: Site Backup Only Occurs Once a Week and Does Not Adhere to Schedule

Q235746 SMS: URLs Listed in Product Compliance Database Are Incorrect

Q235772 SMS: If DHCP Server Has "Unlimited" Leases, NetDisc Fails to Retrieve Client Information within that scope

Q235788 SMS: Distribution Manager Fails to Process PKG File and Update Distribution Point

Q235792 SMSINST: Long File Name File Installed With Version Checking Gets Truncated at Destination

Q235835 SMS: Users with Restricted Collection Viewing Rights May See All Resources

CHAPTER 5

Configuring SMS Site Systems

In this chapter you will learn about:

- SMS site security settings
- Site system connection accounts
- Site systems configuration
- Sender configuration
- Address configuration
- Client connection accounts

Configuring Site Systems

After the initial installation of an SMS site, you may think that your installation has finished, when in fact, just like a Windows NT Server installation, it has only just begun. Administration tasks that define the site system's characteristics and security of your site server tidy up and finish your SMS installation. Of course, these tasks will change somewhat depending on the type of site server you are deploying and setting up.

Implementing SMS Site Security

Security should be planned and implemented for the SMS structure: the SMS software files, the SQL database files, and any software distributions you have defined. The file partition that should be used is NTFS (NT File System) rather than FAT (file allocation table). Additionally, security must be defined for the use of SMS and its features. Just because you are a member of the Domain Admins group does not give you rights to administer an SMS system.

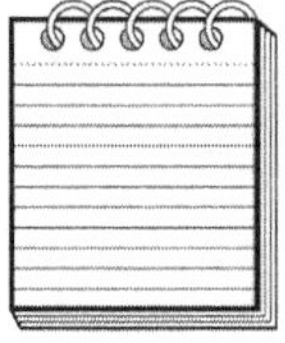

NOTE *You may be new to NT security as well as SMS. The entire NT security world, including NTFS and file and directory permissions, is a very large book in itself. I would recommend < McGraw-Hill / Osborne addition here > We are dealing with two sets of rights: SMS site servers and NTFS. The overlapping permissions must be set properly for both SMS and NT for the proper level of assumed permissions.*

The entry point for deploying SMS and its features is the SMS Administration console, and in most cases, through a remote installation of the SMS console on another NT workstation or server located within the defined SMS site subnet boundaries. Unless the administrator must have access to the SMS site server, all SMS administration should be performed using a remote SMS Administrative console.

The size of the support team or personnel that will use SMS as a support tool across your network will determine how many additional remote Administrator consoles to create and what groups or users should have access. Also, NTFS security levels on the SMS folders and files, as well as SMS object and class security must be deployed.

Windows NT File and Directory Security

As you know by now, the SMS file structure must be installed on an NTFS partition so that the SMS system files and folder structure are properly protected. The default security level for the SMS site share and directory structure is accessible only by Administrators; however, the CAP and Logon shares are readable and accessible by all users. Table 5-1 lists the default security levels for SMS.

NT File Security

If you are not familiar with security permissions used by NT, the Administrator has full rights to the local domain and the Domain Admin is a global group of administrators that have rights across the domain, including domains linked by trusts. The Everyone group is a global group created by the NT operating system that you belong to by default.

In NT, file and folder security is set through the Explorer applet using the Security tab, as shown in Figure 5-1. File and folder security can only be enabled when the file partition chosen is NTFS. The Fat16 partition and the 8/3 file system has no real security and should not be used for NT systems if a secure environment is needed.

TABLE 5-1 Shares and folders and assigned permissions.

Name of Share	Share Permissions	Folder	Folder Permissions	Details
SMS <site code>	Everyone—Full Control	\SMS	Administrators—Full Control	Root folder located on site servers.
CINFO	Everyone—Full Control	\SMS\Cinfo	Administrators—Full Control	Report info stored on the site server, created by users.
SMS_SITE	Everyone—Full Control	\SMS\Inboxes\Desplooer.box\Receive	Administrators—Full Control	The transfer point for data between a child and parent site.
\CAP <site code>	Everyone—Full Control	\CAP <site code>	Domain Admin—Full Control Domain Users—Read	Found on all CAPs, it holds inventory data and software distribution data.
SMSLOGON	Everyone—Full Control	\SMSLOGON	Administrators—Full Control Everyone—Read	Found on all logon points within a site.
LICMTR	Everyone—Full Control		Administrators—Full Control Everyone—Change	Found on all license servers, it stores software-metering data and license info.

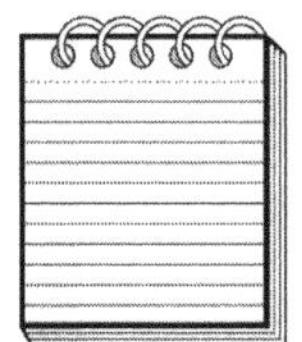

NOTE *Windows 2000 can use FAT16 or FAT32, but there is no security advantage by using either choice.*

Setting Directory and File Permissions on NTFS Partitions

The choices for setting file permissions are varied and must be set correctly for a secure network. Usually this is the weak point of most networks. Don't make the mistake of assigning an excessive number of permissions before you test them out in the real world. Directory permissions are cumulative, since they build on previous rights from a

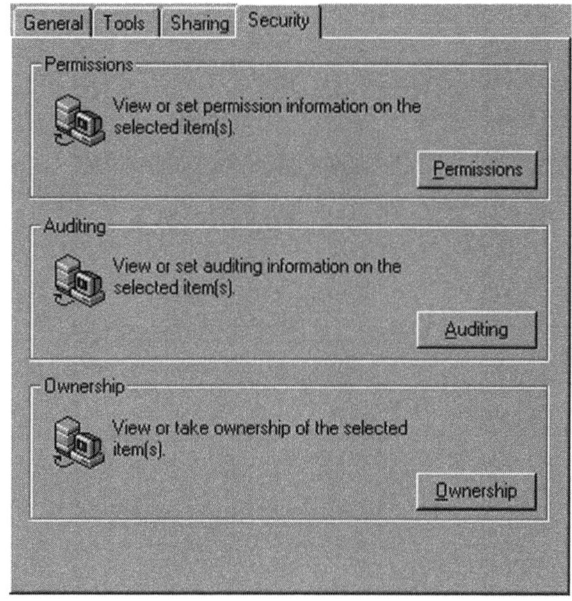

Figure 5-1 The Security tab is only available with NTFS.

higher directory level. Permissions should not be assigned at the root level for files unless the user is an Administrator.

Directory/Folder Permissions

Directory/folder permissions actually apply to the named directory/folders and the files in these directories, as detailed in Figure 5-2.

The options are as follows:

- *No Access* The user has no access.
- *List* The user can view all files and subdirectories and can change to shown subdirectories.
- *Read* The user can read all files shown in the directory/folder and can run the shown applications.
- *Add* The user can add files to the directory/folder but cannot read or change the shown files in the directory/folder.
- *Add & Read* The user has Add and Change permissions for the directory/folder.

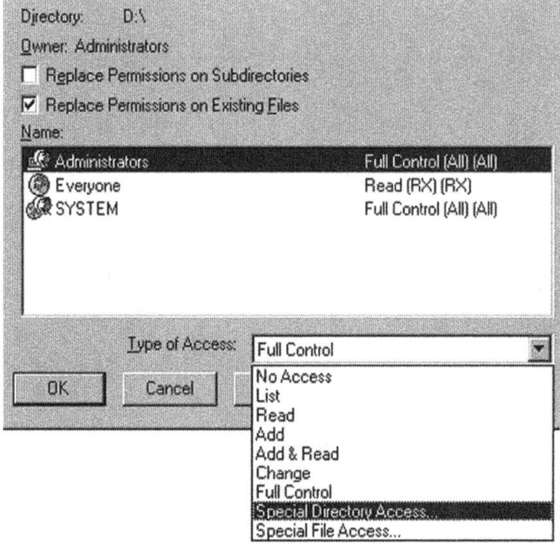

Figure 5-2 Directory/folder permissions for NTFS partitions.

- *Change* The user has Read and Add permissions, plus the user can change the contents of files and also delete files.
- *Full Control* The user has Add, Read, and Change permissions and can also change file permissions and take ownership of files.

File Permissions

File permissions are to be applied sparingly, if at all. These permissions apply to each individually selected file or files within the folder/directory, as shown in Figure 5-3.

The options are as follows:

- *Read* The user can read all files shown in the directory and can run the shown applications.
- *Change* The user has Read and Add permissions, plus the user can change the contents of files and also delete files.
- *Full Control* The user has Add, Read, and Change permissions and can also change file permissions and take ownership of files.

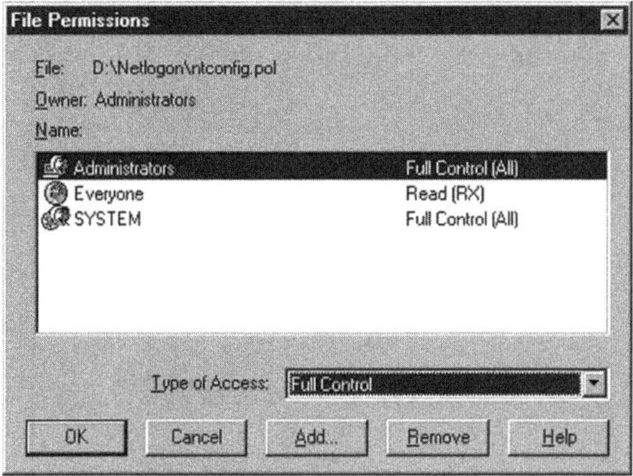

Figure 5-3 File permissions for NTFS partitions.

Users and Groups for NT Domains

User Profiles and System Polices are designed to function in a primary and backup domain environment. However, both users and groups are defined for both the global and group environment. SMS uses both local and global groups.

Local Groups

NT uses groups to define users and groups that can be granted permissions to resources such as printers, files, and folders. Local groups are created in both NT domains at the primary domain controller and on local NT workstations. A local group has rights only in the domain or workstation where it was created. The confusing aspect of local groups is that a local group can contain global groups and users; however, global groups can only contain users; no nesting of groups is allowed.

Global Groups

Global groups are the only types of groups that system policies can be created for. A global group contains users that have user accounts in the domain where the global group was created. If you have trusts linking your primary domain controllers, then global groups from the other linked domains can be included in SMS security settings.

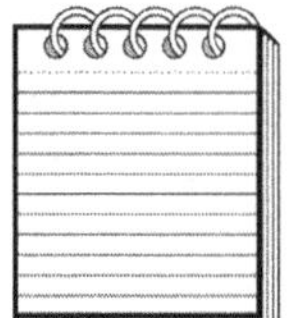

NOTE *Windows 2000 has both local and global groups, plus a new group type called* universal groups.

SMS System Accounts

SMS creates several system accounts to perform both site and client tasks. The most widely used account is the SMS Service account (SMSService). It is used in the background for both local and remote SMS site communications that use the following SMS services:

- SMS Executive Services
- SMS Site Component Manager
- SMS SQL Monitor
- Crystal Info Services
- SMS Client Configuration Manager

The SMS Service account must be granted the advanced user right "Log on as a service" on all site servers. This allows the SMS services listed to start up and execute automatically across your network. By default the SMS Service account is added to the Domain Administrators global group in the domain where SMS has been deployed. This is discussed in detail in Chapter 4 "Installing SMS." Table 5-2 summarizes the SMS Service accounts that are created and used by SMS.

SMS Client Accounts

The only required client account necessary for Windows NT clients is the SMS Client Network Connection account. This account is automatically created during the SMS installation. For software installation, initial client access, and remote installation, certain client security rights are required, as detailed in Table 5-3.

TABLE 5-2

SMS System accounts.

SMS Account	Default Rights Required	Details
SMSService (SMS Service account)	Local Administrator. "Log on as a service" right on all site servers.	Executes on all site servers.
SMSLogonSvc (SMS Logon Service account)	Local Administrator. "Log on as a service" right on all domain controllers.	Needed by the Logon Discovery Agent, is found on all logon points and is installed automatically when Windows Networking Logon Discovery/Installation is enabled.
SMSSvc_sitecode_XXXX (SMS Remote Service account)	Local Administrator on the CAP server. "Log on as a service" right on the CAP server.	An SMS Remote Service account is created automatically when the CAP role is assigned to a site system that is not a site server.
SMSServer_sitecode (SMS Server Network. Connection account)	"Read" permission to the SMS folder. "Full Control" to the SMS_SITE share. Permission to write DDRs.	Required by the NT Logon Discovery Agent for accessing inventory data from CAPs and site system services communicating with the site server.
SWMA Account (Software Metering account)	Not required.	Runs on license servers and executes the Software Metering Service. Created when a software metering server is activated.
SMS Site Address account	"Read," "Write," "Delete," and "Execute" permissions granted to the SMS\Inboxes\Despoolr.box on each site server.	Maintains site-to-site and parent-child site communications. It is also used to transfer status messages between primary and secondary site servers.

Setting Security on SMS Objects

In order to manage and support SMS and deploy its features, a support person needs access to specific SMS objects. These are grouped together into six objects types:

- Sites
- Queries

TABLE 5-3 Security requirements for SMS client accounts.

Account Name	SMS Role	Assigned Permissions	Details
SMSClient_site code	The SMS Client Network Account is required by clients to access CAPs and distribution points.	"Read" for CAPs and distribution points; "Write" for CAP inboxes and logon points.	This account is created during SMS setup and is mandatory.
SMS Windows NT Client Software Installation account	Used for unattended software distribution.	The permissions that will be required depend on the needs of the installation.	This account is enabled when software distribution is enabled.
SMS Client Remote Installation account	Used to install software on Windows NT clients. Allows access when user is not logged on, or when the logged-on user does not have administrative permissions.	Must be a domain user.	This account works for both NetWare and NT.

- Collections
- Status Messages
- Packages
- Advertisements

Notice that all of these objects are defined with the ability of being plural. In other words, there could be multiple instances of each object—for example, more than one status message or SMS site. SMS Security can be defined for the entire object or for a single instance—for example, a single site or package. When you add an administrator to only one instance of an SMS object, this is called an *instance security right*.

Obviously, you would define all status messages to be read by the administrators that support and troubleshoot your SMS environment; however, you may define security individually when it extends to software distribution and advertisements.

When you add an administrator to an entire object, you are defining a *class security right*.

By default, after the initial installation there are just two administrators that are provided with full access to the SMS site and its objects. These are the local administrator DOMAIN\Administrator (probably you) and NT AUTHORITY\SYSTEM (the SMS service account created

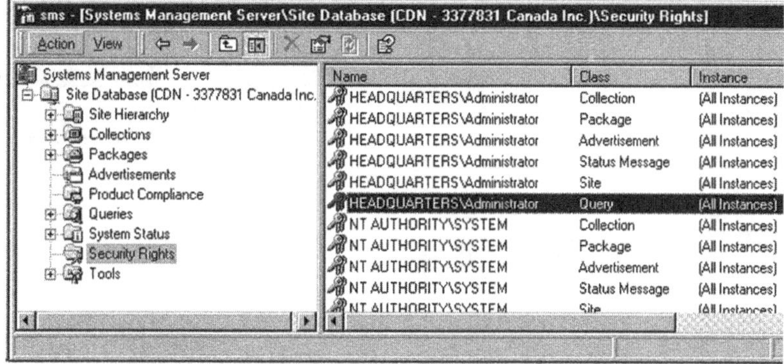

Figure 5-4 Security rights viewed through the SMS Administrator console.

during installation). Refer to Figure 5-4 to see how the initial or current security levels are displayed.

One of the first security tasks you will have to do is to add a backup administrator even if you are the only person assigned to SMS. A primary and backup administrator account without the default NT security name of "Administrator" should always be set up. Remember the user account "Administrator" can be renamed but not deleted.

SMS Task: Adding an NT User to the SMS Administrator Team

Following are the steps necessary to add an NT user:

1. First create the user by using the User Manager for Domains administrative tool on the primary domain controller for the domain or on the SMS site server itself.
2. Open up the SMS Administrator console, and from the Explorer-like tree listing of your SMS site, highlight the *Site Database* folder. Right-click on the *Security Settings* folder and select *All Tasks* and *Manage SMS Users*; this will launch the SMS User Wizard, as shown in Figure 5-5. Click on the *Next* button to continue.
3. The Wizard User Name tab screen shown next allows you to add a new user or modify or delete an existing SMS user. Adding a new

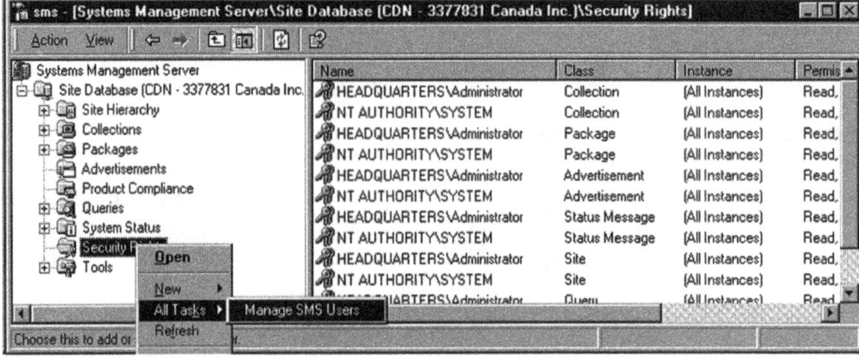

Figure 5-5 Launching the SMS User Wizard from the SMS Administrative console.

user is made simpler by using the Browse button to display the Add Users and Groups and selecting the desired user that you wish to assign to SMS. Select *OK* to continue.

4. The Rights tab screen will appear next, allowing you to accept the existing listed rights or add or modify additional rights. The third option allows you to highlight an existing user or group and copy their rights to the newly created user or group. Selecting this option shows you the rights that will be copied; clicking on Next will redisplay the rights screen.
5. Click on *Finish* to add the user to the system.

The Security Rights folder should now show the user that you just added. The user has also been added to the SMS Admins group; this can be verified through User Manager for Domains.

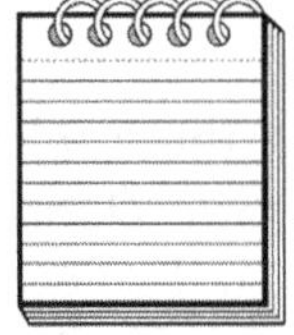

NOTE *The wizard allows you to add rights to the SMS Admin group and to the SMS objects at the same time. You could also choose to highlight and right-click on the Security Rights folder and select New to select the context menu Class Security Right or Instance Security Rights if you just want to modify the rights of an existing user.*

The permissions for each object that you assign to a user will vary depending on the amount of SMS administration performed. Table 5-4 lists the permissions assigned to the SMS objects.

TABLE 5-4 SMS objects and permissions.

SMS Objects and Permissions	Advertisement	Collection	Package	Query	Site	Status Message
Administer	X	X	X	X	X	X
Advertise		X				
Create	X	X	X	X	X	X
Delete	X	X	X	X	X	X
Delete Resource		X				
Distribute			X			
Modify	X	X	X	X	X	X
Modify Resource		X				
Read	X	X	X	X	X	X
Use Remote Tools		X				

SQL Server Account Security

As you know, the SQL database holds the SMS site database. The SQL data that you access is presented through the SMS Administrator console.

The default account that is automatically created for you during the installation of SQL for database administration is the *sa* account, and it can't be removed. If you choose the option of standard security, then this account is used automatically by SMS to access both the site server and software-metering database.

If you defined a specific user account during installation for SQL Server access through SMS, this account can be changed through the SMS Administrator console using the Accounts tab found in Site Properties.

SMS has two types of security: standard and integrated. If standard security is used, every time you connect to the SQL Server database through SMS, you must enter a valid user account and password. The SMS Express Setup assumes that you will use the *sa* username to access the database rather than entering a username and password every time.

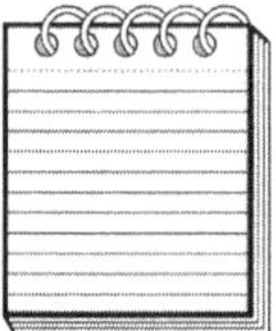

NOTE If you are at all concerned with security, a password containing upper- and lowercase characters along with numbers should be set on the SQL sa *user account.*

The second choice for SQL Server security is integrated security. A current NT user account can be associated with the SQL database, typically the SMS administrator. When the administrator accesses the SQL database, no user account or password is requested. However, if the user has not been granted permission to the SQL database, access will be denied. Be aware if you use NT group access to the SMS site database: only the current user's assigned to the NT user group has access; any new users added to the group will need their SMS rights added manually.

Security and SMS Recommendations

If you are the sole administrator of SMS and you have but one site server, then security can be very straightforward. In fact (and you have probably noticed this), Microsoft starts with a minimal level of security.

Let's face it. How important are hardware and software inventory records anyway, compared to other sensitive data records such as payroll or legal pleadings? I'd bet most users wouldn't be targeting SMS data records to see if they really have the best video adapter. And most SMS data, with the exception of advertisements and custom programming batch files, can be easily re-created when the user logs on to the network again.

However, sloppiness with regard to security is not a commendable administrative trait, so the following notes are some realistic suggestions on the level of security to deploy.

1. The site server should always be installed (if possible) on an NT server that is not a primary domain controller. For Windows 2000 networks, this is not possible, since all servers are domain controllers. The premise here is that you limit the access to your PDC and BDC user accounts and groups when at all possible.
2. Use only local domain Administrators for all SMS administration and maintenance.

3. Assign only the local Administrators to the SMS Service account for the site server, SQL server, client access points, and logon points.

Configuring SMS Site Security

Once SMS 2.0 is installed, the security rights will have been assigned to the Windows NT operating system and to the user that installed SMS, typically an administrator. Both of these accounts will have complete access to the SMS site system. Granting additional security rights for SMS objects or other administrators requires that you log in as the user that installed SMS.

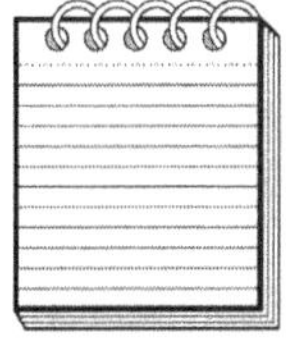

NOTE *I'm assuming that you installed the SMS with an administrator account; otherwise, you won't get far, because you won't have a complete set of security permissions that allow you to access the complete SMS site.*

The administrative tasks that you must perform are the following:

- Setting site boundaries
- Configuring site systems
- Determining site system roles
- Setting up client connection accounts
- Configuring senders
- Configuring addresses
- Attaching primary sites

Setting Site Boundaries

Your SMS site boundaries are used for assigning clients to a particular SMS site. The client access point, or points, will then be accessed by the client to report their current hardware and software inventory status and to check for any software distributions.

Defining either an IP subnet or IPX network numbers configures your site boundaries; these numbers should also be local variables to the specific site server. In order to successfully set your site boundaries, you must have the Modify permission assigned for the Site object class or instance.

SMS Administrative Task: Set Your Site Boundaries

To set site boundaries:

1. Open up the SMS Administrative console, and select the site code-site name.
2. Right-click the site code-site name, and select *Properties*.
3. Select the *Boundaries* tab, and right-click on the white space within the tab screen to activate the New menu.
4. Click the *New* icon.
5. Define the type and ID of the subnet you want to include in the site, as shown in Figure 5-6.

Configuring Site Systems

First, a reminder as to what a site system can be. A Windows NT server, a Windows NT share, or a NetWare NDS or bindery volume can be site systems; NetWare, however, cannot be a software-metering server.

The *site system role* is a particular SMS function needed by the entire SMS site. The most common example is the site server where SMS is installed; this is called the primary site server, and NT must be the operating system. The computer where the SQL Server database is installed is called the *site database server*, and it must also be an NT server.

By adding additional site systems to your network, you can reduce any pressure points that SMS could generate if one computer system is performing, or attempting to perform, too many SMS roles at one time. NetWare can only play a supporting role intertwined with NT networks as a client access point or as a software distribution server.

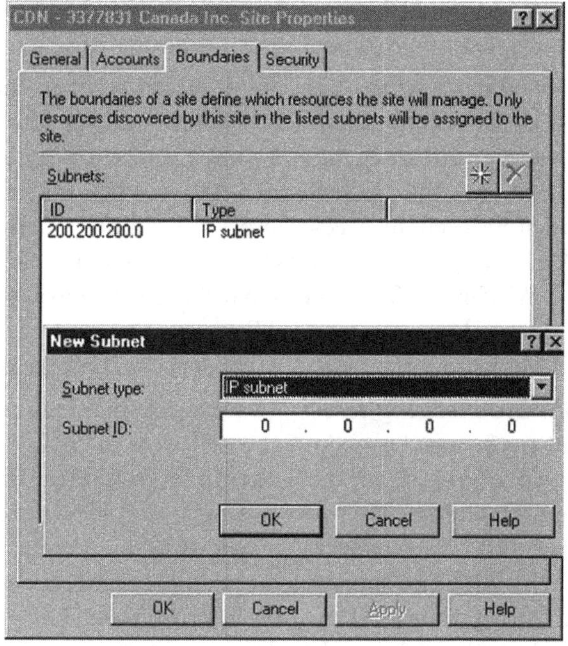

Figure 5-6 Setting site boundaries using the SMS Administrative console.

The site server and SQL database server can be the same NT Server computer system; however, if the SMS site server and SQL are to be separate computer systems, at a minimum, they must be part of the same local subnet. The same rules apply to the designated software-metering server and the location of the software-metering database; they must have a common shared computer location, or at the very least, the computers must belong to the same subnet.

Additional Site System Roles

The following roles can be assigned to site systems:

- *Distribution point* Its primary role is in storing package files that SMS clients can access and deploy through the software distribution process. As you increase the use of custom installations, your network traffic and number of users will inevitably force you to add additional distribution points.

A Windows NT server, a Windows NT share, or a NetWare NDS or bindery volume can be a distribution point.

- *Client access point* The client access point is the prime communication location common to SMS clients and the site server. Although the site server automatically assumes the role of a CAP, and you need one CAP in each site, additional CAPs can be created to spread the workload of SMS client access across the subnet; it can also act as a backup CAP if the primary CAP is unavailable due to failure or maintenance.

  A Windows NT server, a Windows NT share, or a NetWare NDS or bindery volume can be a CAP server. The type of network environment will determine the type of CAP servers that are deployed.
- *Software-metering server* A software-metering server is a site system that performs the task of the software metering, along with the real-time checking of currently available software application licenses for the SMS clients. The software-metering server must be a Windows NT server; NetWare cannot perform this role.

  Why not? The software-metering server component works only with an SQL database. This is a Microsoft marketing decision and not a purely technical decision; having massive market share allows them to make this decision.

SMS Task: Creating a Distribution Point, Software-Metering Server, or Client Access Point

To create a distribution point, software-metering server, or CAP, you must have been assigned the Modify permission to the SMS site. To start assigning a site system role:

1. Open up the SMS Administrative console, and select the site code-site name.
2. Highlight the *Site Hierarchy* folder; this will display the Site Settings folder.
3. Scroll down the displayed tree. At the bottom of the tree, the Site Systems folder will be displayed.

4. Right-click on the site system that you want to assign an SMS role and select *Properties*, as shown in Figure 5-7.
5. If you wish to add a site server, right-click on the white space within the windows to display the new context menu.
6. From the menu, select the desired NT or NetWare resource you want to add as a site system.
   - To activate the CAP role, select the *Client Access Point* tab and check *Use this site system as a client access point.*
   - To activate the distribution point role, select the *Distribution Point* tab and check *Use this site system as a distribution point.* You can also set up the distribution point groups.
   - To activate the software-metering point role, select the *Software Metering* tab and check *Use this site system as a software-metering server.* You also must configure the software-metering server stats as shown in Figure 5-8.

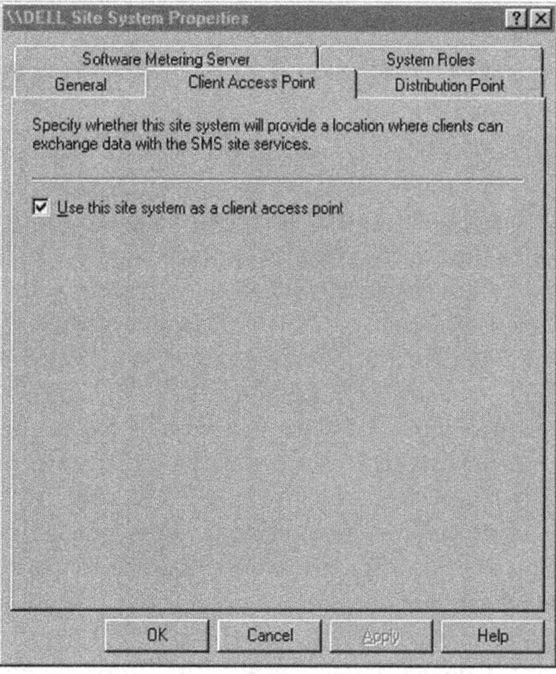

Figure 5-7
Site system properties displayed though the SMS Administrator console.

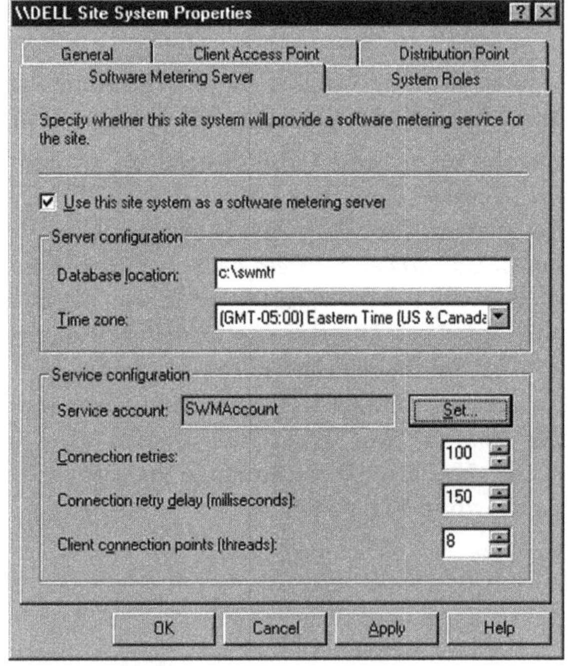

Figure 5-8 Defining software-metering server properties at the SMS Administration console.

Client Connection Accounts

Once SMS has been installed on the client computer, the Client Connection account is used to communicate with the subnet's active client access point(s) and distribution point(s), if they exist. Although this sounds quite complicated, in fact what I am describing is the standard NT user account created on a primary domain controller, or a NetWare user account created on NetWare servers.

When SMS is first installed on the designated site server, one client connection account is automatically created called SMSClient_sitecode, as shown in Figure 5-9. This is used as a backup account, allowing SMS to connect even in the event that the client's own user account does not work.

Obviously, in order to access the client access and distribution points, the user must have the proper permissions to attach to these site servers or network shares.

After your user accounts have been created in either Windows NT or NetWare, Client Connection accounts must be created using the SMS Administrator console. The creation of the connection accounts notifies

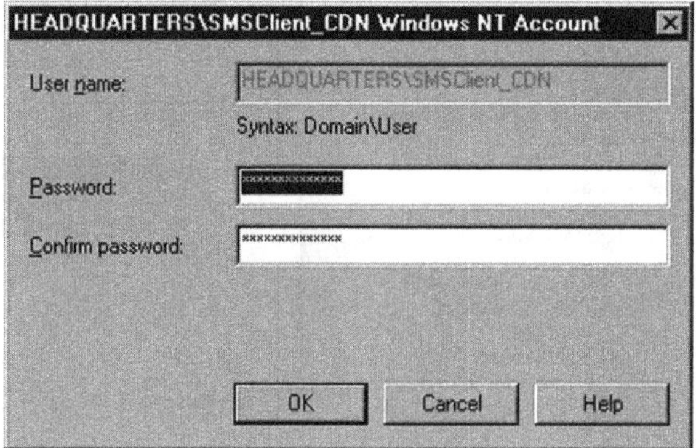

Figure 5-9 The default client connection account added during SMS installation.

SMS that active clients will begin using these accounts for communication with the client access points and any available distribution points.

SMS Task: Creating a Client Connection Account Using the SMS Administrator Console

To be able to create a client connection account, you must have been assigned the Modify permissions for the actual SMS site.

1. Open up the SMS Administrative console, and select the site code-site name.
2. Next, highlight and select the site hierarchy, and open up and highlight the *Site Settings* folder.
3. Navigate down the tree, and open the *Connection Accounts* folder.
4. Select *Client*, then right-click and select *New*.
5. Choose the account type to create, as shown in Figure 5-10, and enter the name and the password of the new account.

Configuring Your Site Hierarchy

If you have more than one SMS site, then you will have to set up communications between your multiple sites. Remember that SMS information containing collections, package, and queries moves from the primary

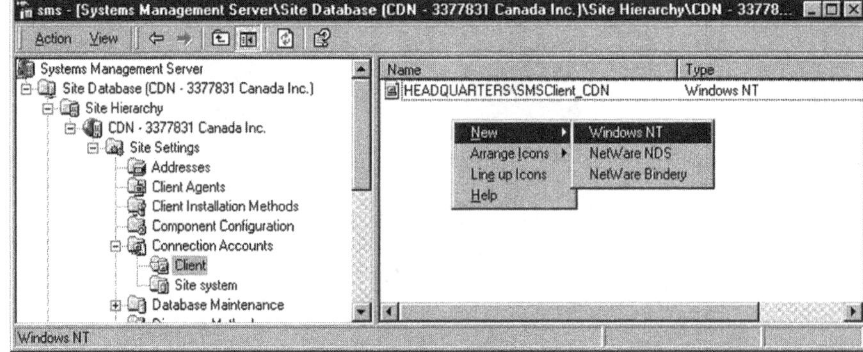

Figure 5-10 Creating a Client Connection account using the SMS Administrator console.

site to the secondary site or from the secondary site up to the primary site. The only reason a central primary site would communicate directly with a lower-level secondary site is when software distribution or remote troubleshooting needs to be controlled *from* a specific location *to* a specific location.

In order to configure inter-site communications, senders must be installed and configured on each site. A *sender* is an internal SMS component that manages an existing communication up protocol shared between the sites either locally or remotely.

The addresses must then be enabled, linking all of the sites together with which you wish to communicate. An address is like our phonebook; it contains information on how to contact the destination site and which server to attach to.

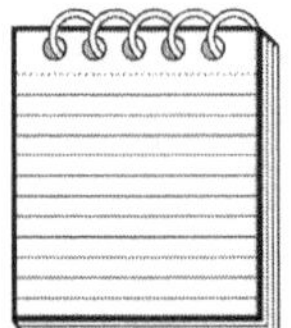

NOTE *In order for sites to communicate, the proper LAN protocols, such as TCP/IP or IPX/SPX, or the Remote Access Service must be installed. Both sites must also have the same senders installed and a valid configured address.*

Configuring Senders

For sites to communicate with each other, each site must have one or more senders installed, along with a supported LAN (TCP/IP, NetBEUI, IPX/SPX) or WAN protocol (Windows NT RAS, X.25, ISDN, or Windows NT SNA).

There are six types of senders that can be installed:

- Asynchronous RAS Sender
- ISDN RAS Sender
- ISDN RAS Sender
- SNA RAS Sender
- Courier Sender
- Standard Sender

At all primary sites, the senders installed are Standard Sender and Courier Sender. At all secondary sites, both Courier Sender and, depending on what address selection you make during the SMS secondary site installation, either the Standard Sender or Asynchronous RAS Sender will be installed. Standard Sender is used for local area network communications and also for wide area communications for networks connected with routers.

SMS Task: Installing or Changing Senders

To install, change, or delete a sender, you must have been assigned the Modify permission for the site object type or at the local site server where the changes or additions are to be made.

1. Open up the SMS Administrator console, and highlight *Site Database*.
2. Open the *Site Hierarchy* folder. Now scroll down and open the *Site Settings* and finally the *Senders* folder.
3. If you want to modify an existing sender, select from the installed senders shown in the right value pane and detailed in Figure 5-11.
4. To install a new sender, right-click on the *Senders* folder and select *New*. The senders you can install will be shown. Selecting a sender will start the installation.
5. From the General Properties tab, enter the name of the site server you are installing the sender on.
6. From the Advanced Properties shown in Figure 5-12, define how many sites this site will communicate with; you can also modify the number of retries and the retry delay.

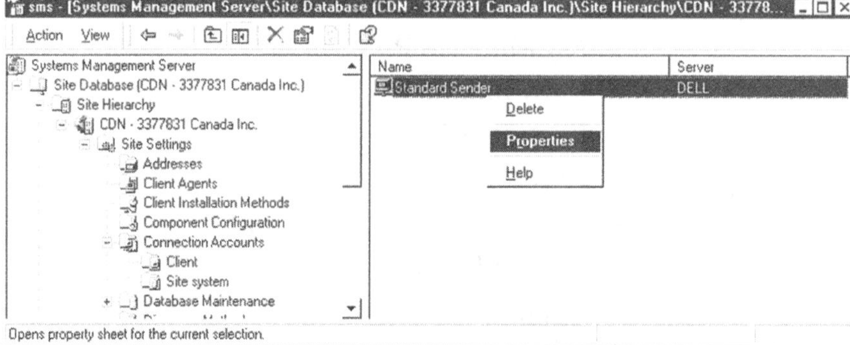

Figure 5-11 Installed senders found on this site server.

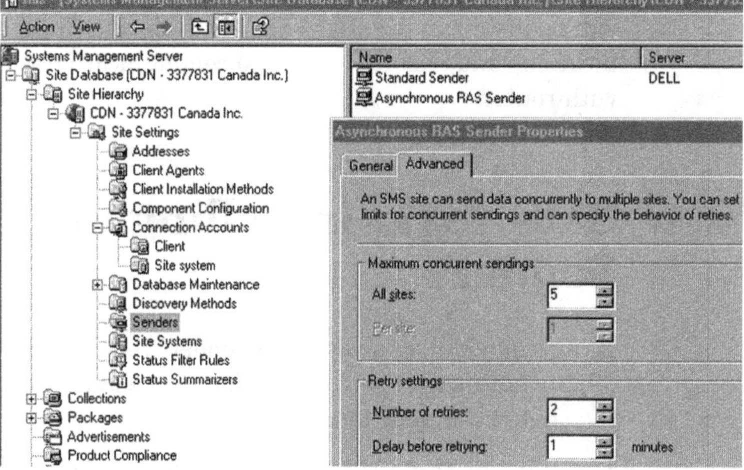

Figure 5-12 Advanced properties for a new sender on a site server.

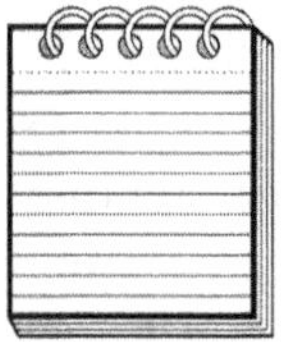

NOTE *Courier Sender is configured by logging on locally to the site server, and from the Start Menu selecting Programs | Systems Management Server | SMS Courier Sender.*

Configuring Addresses

First of all, addresses are actually a collection of information used by SMS sites across your network that define how to contact each destination site, the site server names, and the senders that are installed. Each address when it is created is automatically linked to a specific type of sender.

The SMS site that sends data must know the receiving site's address. The address will contain structure information about the type of server, the server's name, and the types of senders installed at that site. Each SMS site in a hierarchy will contain addresses for the parent site and each child site.

If you were using Standard Sender and Asynchronous RAS Sender, you would have to create two addresses, one for each sender, at each site.

Address Creation

The information needed to create an address is as follows:

1. The SMS site code the address will be connecting to
2. The name of the SMS site server at the site
3. The desired type of center you wish to use for the address

You must also have Modify permissions assigned to the site object or at the actual site where the address is to be created.

SMS Task: Creating an Address

To create an address:

1. At the local site server open the SMS Administrator console.
2. Once the site database is active, click on the plus sign to the left of the site code-site name. The Site Systems folder will then be shown.
3. Open the *Site Settings* folder to display the Addresses folder just below.
4. Right-clicking on the *Addresses* folder and select the New option on the context menu to list the six sender addresses that can be installed, as shown in Figure 5-13.
5. Select a sender to install. Properties sheets for the sender will be displayed.

To finish installation of the sender, you must enter the user account that will be used to connect to the destination site server. As shown in Figure 5-14, when this address is available for data transfer, as well as

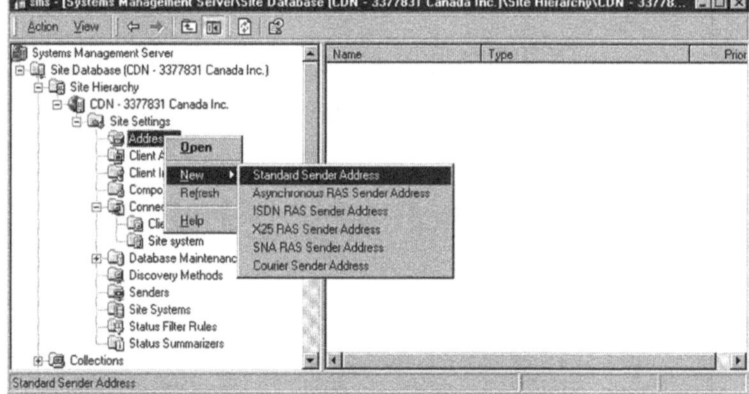

Figure 5-13 Selecting a sender address to install from the SMS Administrator console.

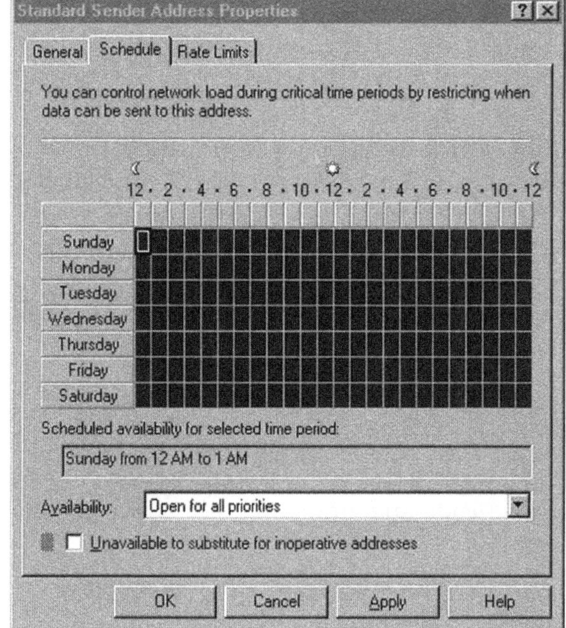

Figure 5-14 Address properties set through the property tabs.

the times during the day when the SMS data transfer bandwidth is to be reined in.

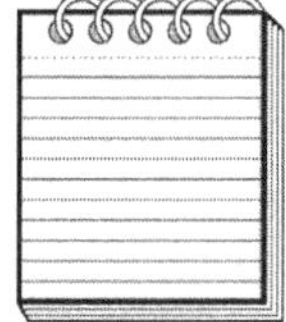

NOTE *Also check to make sure that a valid site system connection account has been created at the Windows NT site. Remember, this is the account used by SMS for connecting to the site server.*

Connecting Primary Sites

If your SMS environment contains multiple SMS sites, you will have to establish the primary sites within your total SMS hierarchy. Next, you will have to set up the communication links between your primary sites by defining the senders and addresses that will be used for SMS data transfer and site-to-site communication.

Looking at your network map and focusing on the primary sites, decide which primary sites will be parent sites. If you only have one SMS site server, then it will be a primary site as well as a parent site, as shown in Figure 5-15, it will also be defined as the central site. Remember that the central site is at the top of the SMS chain, so it will not have a parent site to report and send data.

The parent site of a primary site can be changed at any time, but remember that the flow of data records will be completely changed if you change the order of reporting. Any secondary sites created must first have a primary site to report to, as the secondary site has no database to store information in.

To define a parent site for an installed site, you must have been assigned the Modify permission for the child site. The site code for the parent's site must also be known.

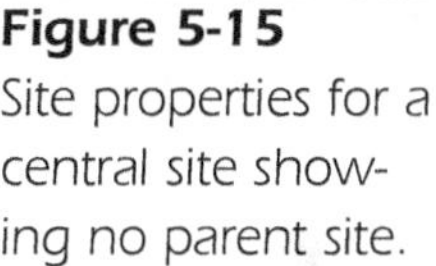

Figure 5-15
Site properties for a central site showing no parent site.

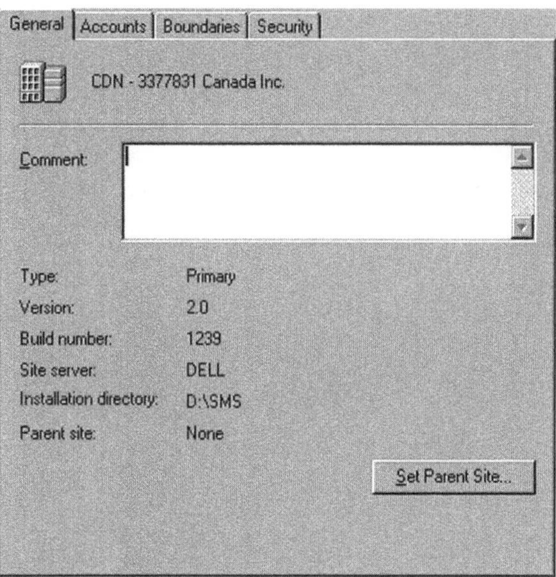

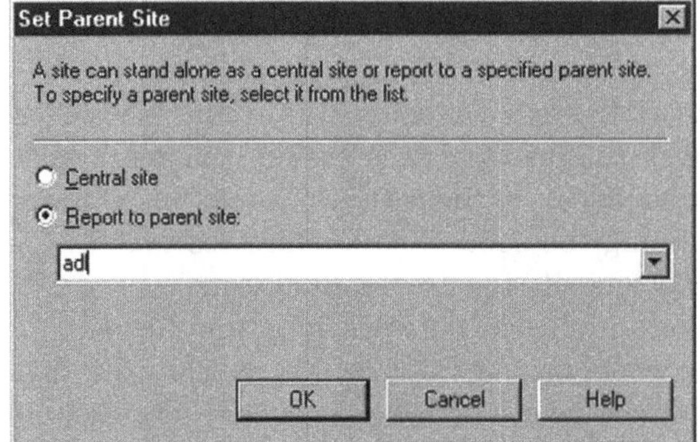

Figure 5-16 Setting parent site options for SMS sites.

SMS Task: Setting the Type of SMS Site

To set the SMS site type:

1. At the local site of the site server, open up the SMS Administrator console.
2. Select the site code–site name, then right-click and select *Properties*.
3. After selecting the *General* tab, click on the *Set Parent Site* button.
4. Define whether the site is to be the central site, or if it is to report to a parent site, enter the site code of the parent site it is to report to, as shown in Figure 5-16.

CHAPTER 6

Using the SMS Administrator Console

In this chapter you will learn about:

- The context menus of the SMS Administrator console
- MMC (Microsoft Management Console) and snap-in creation
- The details of the SMS Administrator console
- Packages and advertisements
- Collections and security rights

The SMS Administrator Console

As mentioned, the SMS Administrator console is "Command Central" as far as SMS administration is concerned. SMS configuration and execution of the troubleshooting and support tools is all carried out through the console.

The SMS Administrator console is contained as a "snap-in" component of a new interface called the Microsoft Management Console (MMC); this interface is used for Windows 2000 and was first used for housing Internet Information Server 4.0 administration.

Although the initial introduction to the MMC with the term *snap-in* can be confusing, it's actually a slick idea. Microsoft provides the empty shell of a utility, called a *tool host* in official development lingo, and by using the mouse, you fill in—that is, "snap in"—the software components provided that you want to use. The current version of MMC is 1.1, and it can be activated by using the Run option from the Start menu and typing in MMC.

After filling up your MMC Console, you can save your electronic toolbox as a console file with the .msc extension. This file can then be sent to other administrators at different locations for their use. Fast-forward to the end of the year 2000, and you will probably find yourself using the MMC and creating your own custom console holding utilities for Microsoft BackOffice, Office 2000, SMS, and Internet Information Server (IIS), to name but a few choices. (Oh, there's one more operating system I forgot to mention, and that's Windows 2000.)

The SMS Administrator console is created when SMS is installed. You can also choose to run the SMS Administrator console in "author mode," which allows you to customize the default SMS console, as shown in Figure 6-2.

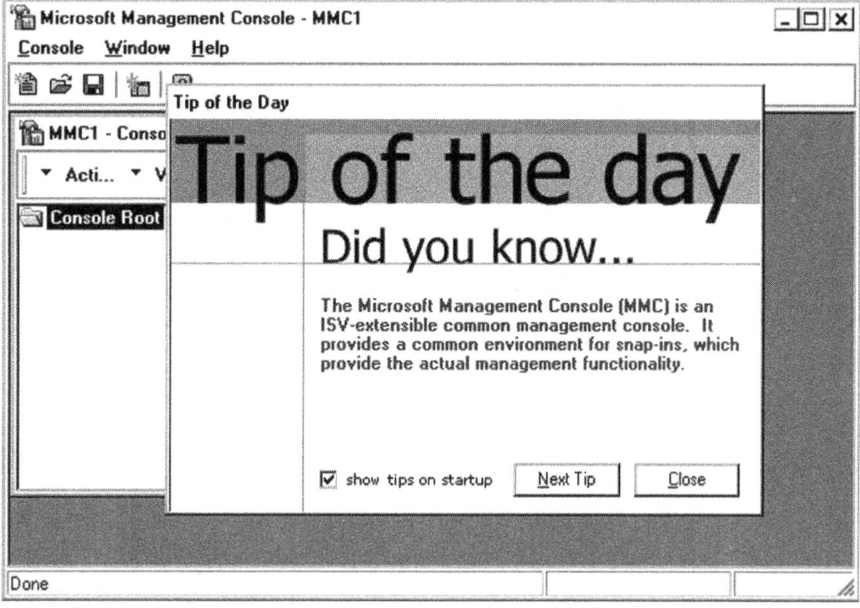

Figure 6-1 Starting the Microsoft Management Console.

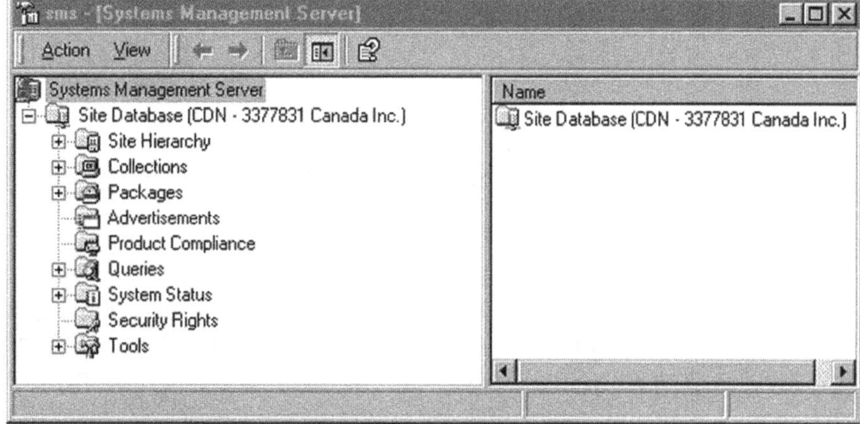

Figure 6-2 The SMS Administrator console as the only installed snap-in.

Using the SMS Administrator Console

Once the console has attached and initialized the SQL database, the console tree can be viewed by opening the Site Database folder at the top of the tree. The items that are shown have numerous subcategories that can be seen by clicking on the plus sign beside the folder, which then expands and shows the hidden choices. If you are used to using the Explorer shell, which is a distinct possibility, you will find it easy to move up and down the console tree. All management work is performed through this console. Every folder and subfolder shown has choices that are activated from the context menu found by right-clicking any folder.

Some folders will have predefined context menu tasks found under the heading All Tasks; for example, the Advertisements folder has a predefined task: Distribute Software. Also on the context menu is a New option for adding new advertisements (software packages and files) that would then be activated by the Distribute Software option.

Site Database

Opening the site database shows the SMS components of the selected site. Although there are many choices, they are not necessarily activated. You must check the properties of each SMS component to find out the current status of each object.

Site Hierarchy

Opening this folder will show you your primary site and any secondary site that has been installed and attached to the primary site. Right-clicking on either a primary or secondary site allows you to view and change the properties of the selected site. As shown in Figure 6-3, the properties include the defined site boundaries, the defined SQL and SMS service accounts, and the current class and/or instance security rights that have been assigned to this particular site.

Site Settings

Expanding any of the available sites further shows us the Site Settings folder, which defines the current setup of the SMS site. If your installation was automatic, more of the choices found under Site Settings will be

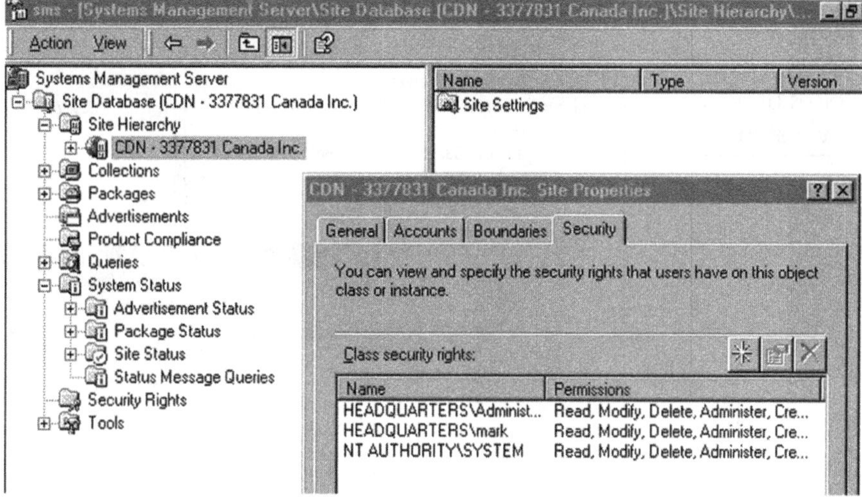

Figure 6-3 Viewing the primary site properties with the SMS Administrator console.

activated. If you chose custom install, this will be your starting point for activating client agents and client installation methods, to name but a few of the administrative tasks you must complete.

Addresses

Highlighting the Addresses folder shows you the currently installed sender addresses. As shown in Figure 6-4, right-clicking on the Addresses folder and selecting New allows you to select from the six possible choices for addresses:

- Standard Sender Address
- Asynchronous RAS Sender Address
- ISDN RAS Sender Address
- X.25 RAS Sender Address
- SNA RAS Sender Address
- Courier Sender Address

Selecting an additional address results in the properties of the address you're installing being displayed. Choices are the Address Schedule, Rate Limits, and General Information.

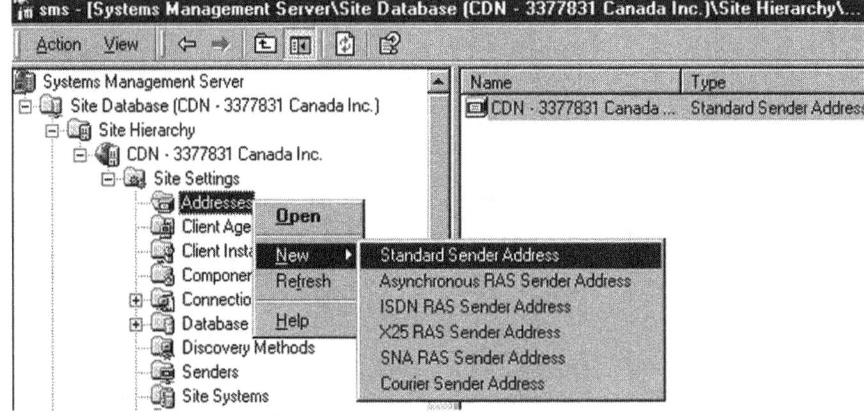

Figure 6-4 Address selection choices using the New option.

Client Agents

The six client agent objects will be shown, but they might not necessarily be activated, as this will depend on the type of installation you have performed. Client agent choices are as follows:

- Hardware Inventory Client Agent
- Software Inventory Client Agent
- Remote Tools Client Agent
- Advertised Programs Client Agent
- Software Metering Client Agent
- Event to Trap Translator Client Agent

Client Installation Methods

There are four client installation methods supported by SMS. You may have no need for the NetWare NDS and bindery logon clients, but they are available if needed. The choices are as follows:

- Windows Networking Logon Client Installation
- NetWare NDS Logon Client Installation
- NetWare Bindery Logon Client Installation
- Windows NT Remote Client Installation

The first three choices allow you, through the General tab, to enable each selected logon method and specify whether to keep the logon point lists for both discovery and installation synchronized at all times. The logon settings allow you to insert the SMS client software into an existing client logon script either at the very top or at the bottom.

Selecting the Windows NT Remote Client Installation allows you to enable the installation of SMS client software onto NT servers that are not domain controllers, NT workstations, and domain controllers (which are, of course, NT servers). The NT servers are nodes that are performing a site server role but were installed as *standalone* or member servers within a domain.

Component Configuration

The operation procedures of both software distribution and software-metering components can be set and adjusted by selecting the properties of each respective component. Software-metering options include how you're going to handle versions of software products, schedule setting of license balancing and overall site management, and when to summarize all software-metering data from one source or several intersite sources.

Client and server component reporting levels can be adjusted from the default of All Milestones (when something significant happens SMS- and component-wise), to showing only Error Milestones and Warning Milestones, to the bandwidth-limiting All Milestones and All Details.

Selecting the data processing and storage object shown in Figure 6-5 defines if spacing is tight you can remove the word "the" on the next line before SQL when the SQL database reports will be updated. The default is that after processing 500 management information format files and 1,500 discovery data records, the statistics will be updated automatically. If your SMS site is small—say, for 50 clients—you may want to adjust the database statistics to a lower threshold so your reports will be more up-to-date.

Client Connection Accounts

The client connection accounts allow both SMS and SQL Server and SMS clients to access the installed client access points and distribution points.

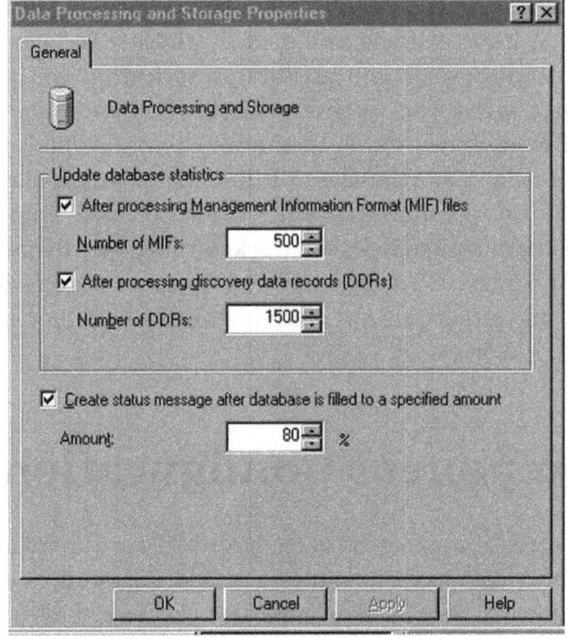

Figure 6-5 Data processing and storage properties.

A separate account is needed for Windows NT and NetWare clients. Selecting the New option from the context menu, as shown in Figure 6-6, allows you to define a new client or site system account.

The site system access is carried out via a service account. The mandatory service accounts that are set up during installation are listed in Table 6-1. The currently installed service accounts can be viewed through User Manager for Domains on the selected site server.

Database Maintenance

Selecting the New option from the context menu of SQL Commands allows you to add any SQL command to execute at any time on a prescribed schedule. The Tasks option allows you to execute the predefined SQL database maintenance tasks. By double-clicking on the Tasks folder, the following task list is displayed:

- Back Up SMS Site Server
- Delete Aged Collected Files
- Delete Aged Discovery Data
- Delete Aged Inventory History

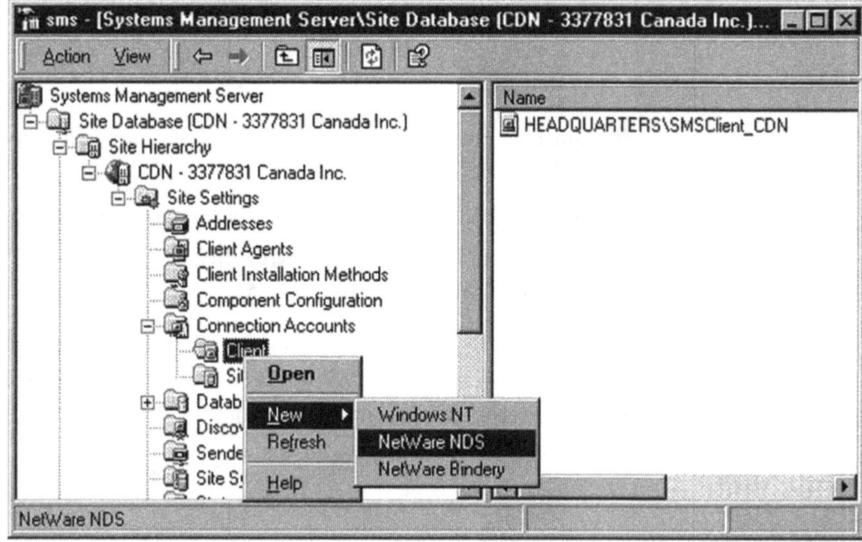

Figure 6-6 Adding a new client connection account.

- Delete Aged Status Messages
- Export Site Database
- Export Site Database Transaction Log
- Export Software Metering Database
- Export Software Metering Transaction Log
- Monitor Keys and Re-create Views
- Rebuild Indexes
- Update Statistics

TABLE 6-1 Required service accounts for SMS sites.

Required Site System Account	Details
SMS_Service	Gives the site server access to the installed SMS services.
SQL_Server	Allows the installed services access to the site server database.
SMS_Server_Network Connection	Provides installed SMS services access to the site server and any other installed site systems.
SMS_Remote_Service	Allows the installed SMS services to communicated with the installed logon points and client access points.

By default, the only tasks that are enabled are as follows:

- Delete Aged Status Messages Every Day between 12:00 AM and 5:00 AM.
- Monitor Keys and Re-create Views Every Sunday between 12:00 AM and 5:00 AM.
- Rebuild Indexes Every Sunday between 12:00 AM and 5:00 AM.
- Update Statistics every Monday, Wednesday, Friday, and Saturday between 12:00 AM and 5:00 AM.

Certainly the task "Back Up SMS Site Server" should be enabled immediately, and the tasks that are enabled should be checked to make sure that the processing time does not conflict with any other currently planned network maintenance.

Discovery Methods

The seven discovery options available for discovering SMS resources are shown in this folder; however, depending on the type of installation, some of the displayed objects will be either enabled or disabled. Choices for SMS resource discovery are as follows:

- Heartbeat Discovery
- NetWare Bindery Logon Discovery
- NetWare NDS Logon Discovery
- Network Discovery
- Windows Network Logon Discovery
- Windows NT User Account Discovery
- Windows NT User Group Discovery

Double-clicking on each shown object displays the current properties, as shown in Figure 6-7.

Each discovery method's schedule of when it performs its job can be modified through the Polling Schedule tab. Network Discovery has the most options to define, as here you are defining a networkwide search for SMS resources. Network hardware and software resources to enable can be chosen from the following tab options:

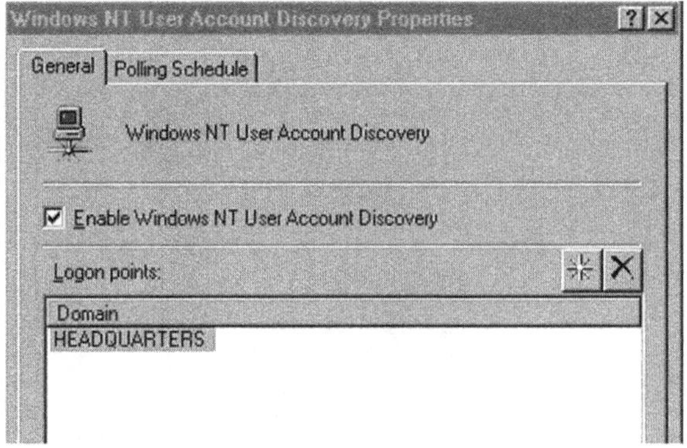

Figure 6-7 Properties of the Windows NT User Account Discovery method.

- Subnets
- Domains
- SNMP
- SNMP Devices
- DHCP
- Schedule

Selecting either the Windows NT User Account and User Group Discovery properties allows you to define and add additional logon points for your SMS sites.

Selecting Windows Networking Logon Discovery, NetWare Bindery, or NDS Logon Discovery and selecting the Logon Settings tab allows you to define if and how your users' logon scripts should be modified.

Senders

Senders are a software component that manages the network connections between SMS sites, as well as verifies the error-free transmission of the data stream. The senders that can be installed are shown in Figure 6-8. The Standard Sender is installed by default in a local area network SMS installation. If you have routers connecting your existing subnets, the Standard Sender is also used for WAN communications.

Note that Courier Sender does not show up on the context menu shown in Figure 6-8; the setup and access of Courier Sender is found in

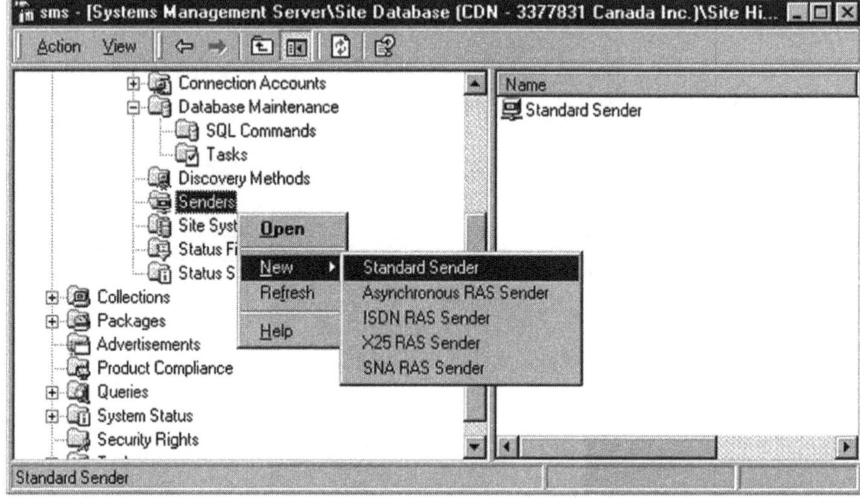

Figure 6-8 Sender choices are selected from the context menu.

the Systems Management Server program group off the Start menu of the primary or secondary site server.

Courier Sender is installed on all primary and secondary sites; it allows you to create software packages called *parcels*. A parcel is an actual CD-ROM or tape holding a large amount of data or software program. Courier Sender can be configured to send outgoing or receive incoming parcels.

Site Systems

A site system is usually thought of as the installed SMS site server, and that's true. However, one of the following network resources can be manually configured and used as an SMS resource:

- NetWare Bindery Volume
- NetWare NDS Volume
- Windows NT Server
- Windows NT Share

Additional SMS resource choices will depend on the actual network resources that are available and can include both NetWare and Windows NT servers.

A client access point can be assigned to a Windows NT server for Windows-based clients, or to a NetWare bindery or NDS server for NetWare clients.

A distribution point can be assigned to any server found within the SMS site boundaries, however, the same rule applies: A distribution point can be assigned to a Windows NT server for Windows-based clients, or to a NetWare bindery or NDS server for NetWare clients.

Any Windows NT server can be assigned the role of a software-metering server. NetWare servers, however, cannot perform this role.

Right-clicking the Site System folder and selecting the New option from the context menu, as shown in Figure 6-9, starts the installation process. From the displayed property sheets shown, you select the role you wish to assign to the available network resource.

Selecting the primary site server within the Site System folder, then right-clicking and selecting the All Tasks context menu option provides you with the SMS Administrative options shown in Figure 6-10.

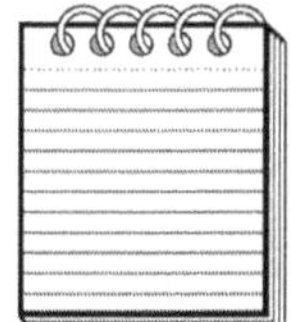

NOTE *Further details on executing these tools are found in Chapter 15 "Troubleshooting with SMS."*

Figure 6-9 Assigning additional site system roles.

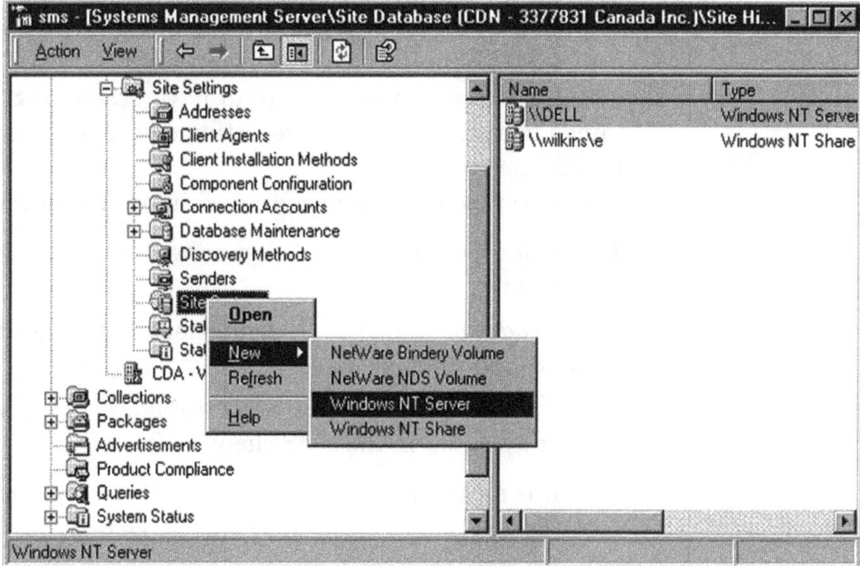

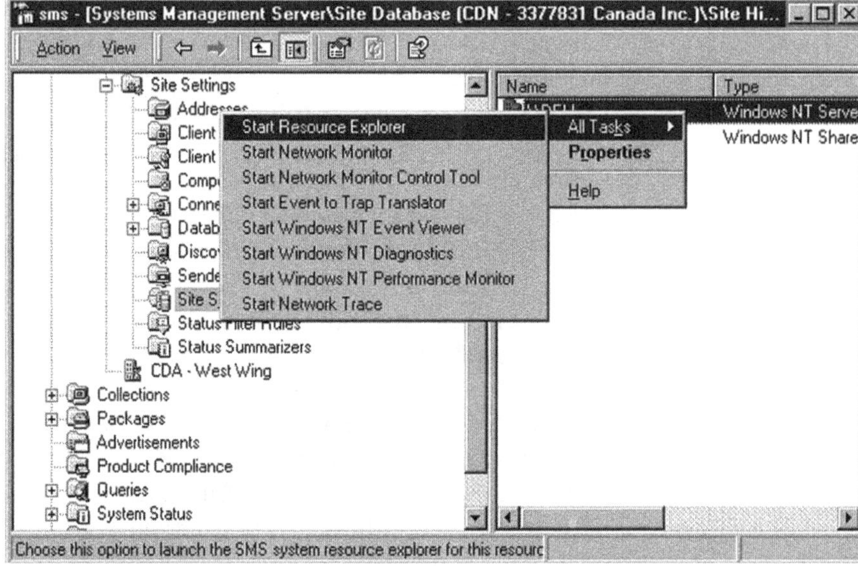

Figure 6-10 Site system administrative tasks that can be performed.

Status Filter Rules

A *status filter rule* automatically "filters" or tracks some of the regular SMS status messages that occur during the normal day-to-day operation of an SMS site. These status messages show us a real-time inside view of actual SMS activity within and across the SMS site. Enabling the status message rules provides a way to have essential SMS information contained in a status message reporting on the progress, or lack of progress, of SMS components.

SMS components can be grouped into three primary types:

1. *Service Components* A component executed as a Windows NT service
2. *Thread Components* A component that executes as part of the SMS Executive service
3. *Client Components* An SMS thread, service, or software utility that executes on the SMS client's PC.

Status messages are subgrouped by three types of status message and by three levels of severity, shown in Table 6-2.

TABLE 6-2

Status message types and levels of severity.

Status Message Types	**Audit**	Contains details on SMS creation and deletion tasks.
	Detail	Holds details on SMS system actions that are carried out.
	Milestone	Extra details are provided on each phase of a system task.
Status Message Severity Levels	**Error**	Indicates a serious situation such as data loss or system failure.
	Warning	Indicates a situation that is degrading system performance.
	Informational	SMS "for your information" messages.

There is no limit on the number of status filter rules that can be defined; each will display information on the component that generated the status message and the severity of the message itself. Following are the four predefined status filter rules after SMS is installed:

1. Write audit messages to the site database and keep them for 180 days.
2. Write all other messages to the site database and keep them for 30 days.
3. Replicate all SMS client messages at low priority.
4. Replicate all other messages at medium priority.

By double-clicking on a defined status filter rule, you can view and change its currently defined properties, as shown in Figure 6-11.

You can also dictate what happens when an active filter rule matches a status message by selecting the Actions tab. Choices include:

- Writing the status message to the SMS database for X number of days
- Updating the NT Event Log
- Executing a program

By first highlighting the Status Filter folder and then right-clicking and selecting New from the displayed context menu, new status filter rules can be added to track and troubleshoot your SMS site.

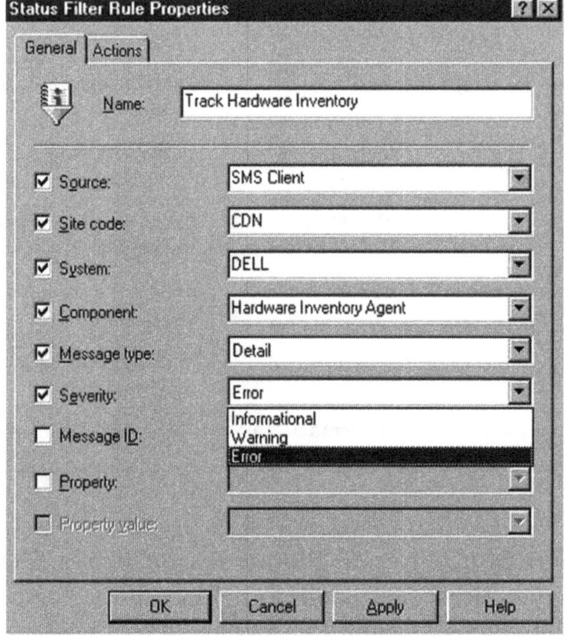

Figure 6-11 Properties of a status filter rule.

Status Summarizers

Unlike a status filter, which focuses on a specific SMS task, a status summarizer is a real-time summary view of the condition of your SMS site. Four status summarizers, shown in Table 6-3, are enabled after installing SMS.

TABLE 6-3 Status Summarizer details.

	Status Summarizers			
Details	**Component**	**Site System**	**Advertisement**	**Package**
Define Specs	Yes	Yes	Yes	No
Set Thresholds	Yes	Yes		
Counts Messages	Yes	No	Yes	No
Track Current State	No	Yes	No	Yes
Schedule Activated	No	Yes	No	Yes
Event Activated	Yes	No	Yes	No

The first three summarizers can be modified through their properties by changing the threshold and critical trigger point. The fourth summarizer, the package summarizer, however, cannot be changed.

Once a status summarizer has been enabled, it will display an OK status. However, when it reaches its defined threshold (the default is 2,000 status messages), a warning will be generated in the component status summarizer folder.

When 5,000 status messages have been generated, the message severity is upgraded to Critical. These default values can be changed by editing the summarizer's property sheet values, as shown in Figure 6-12.

Collections

Selecting the Collection folder lists the SMS supported grouping of discovered network resources. SMS uses these collections for the distribution of software.

Highlighting and right-clicking the Collection folder displays the context menu options New and All Tasks. The New menu option is used to

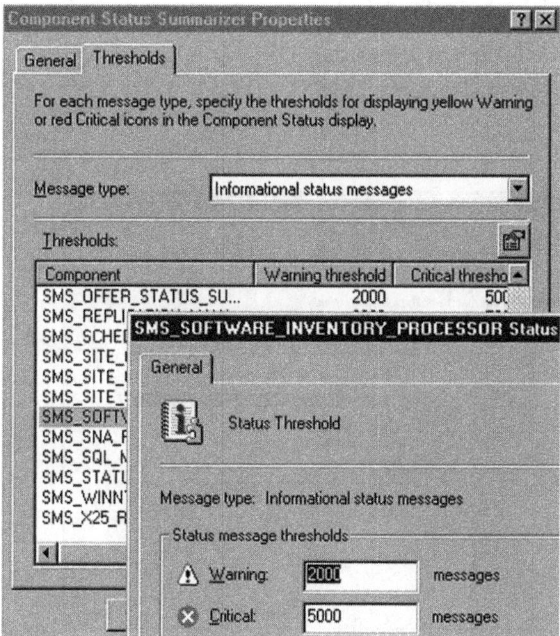

Figure 6-12 Setting thresholds for a component status summarizer.

define a new collection (you must first name your collection before continuing). Then using the Membership Rules tab, you can select either Direct Membership or Query-Based Membership.

Direct Membership allows you to define a collection based on User, Group, or System Resource, complemented by a defining attribute like IP Address or Last Logon User Name, as shown in Figure 6-13.

The Query-Based Collection option uses an SQL query and searches the SMS site database for any objects that match the query's criteria.

When you are selecting an already-defined collection, the Task context menu option allows you to distribute software or to update the existing collection membership. If you have both primary and secondary sites, you can also create subcollections at the secondary site that link to a defined collection at the primary site. The defined collections found on a fresh install of SMS are as follows:

- All Systems
- All User Groups
- All Users
- All Windows 3.1 Systems
- All Windows 95 Systems
- All Windows 98 Systems
- All Windows for Workgroups Systems
- All NT Server Systems
- All NT Systems

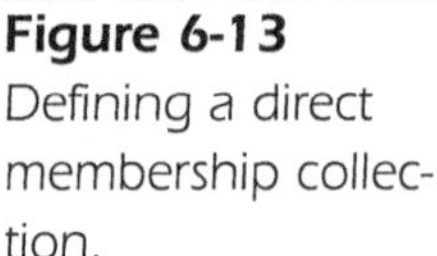

Figure 6-13 Defining a direct membership collection.

- All NT Workstation 3.51 Systems
- All NT Workstation 4.0 Systems
- All NT Workstation Systems

Depending on your active client base, some of the choices may not be needed and can be removed. For example, Windows 3.1 or Windows NT 3.51 systems may just be a fond (or less than fond) memory in your company. Right-clicking the collection you wish to remove and selecting Delete from the displayed context menu will remove the collection.

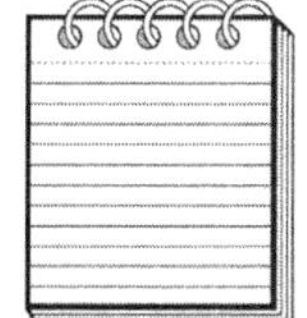

NOTE *You must have been assigned the Delete permission for the collection security object in order to delete any collections.*

Packages

A *package* contains the files and commands that SMS uses to perform software distribution to SMS clients. By default, there are no packages created. To create a package, highlight and right-click the Package folder. Selecting New from the context menu opens the empty properties of the new undefined package you are creating. Figure 6-14 shows an already-created package; tab choices allow you to define the distribution, reporting, security, data source, and data access settings.

Once the package has been created, you can then use the context menu item to distribute software to the distribution points. Other menu items allow you to remove older distribution points or set up the distribution cycle to a specific client base with mandatory rules. The full details on software distribution can be found in Chapter 11 “Distributing Software with SMS.”

Advertisements

An *advertisement* is just like the TV ads you inevitably see: you turn the TV on, an ad appears—then you change the channel. You don’t have that option in SMS land. Here, the advertisement may be mandatory or, you may get choices to accept or reject the software product being offered to you. An advertisement executes a predefined package that we just dis-

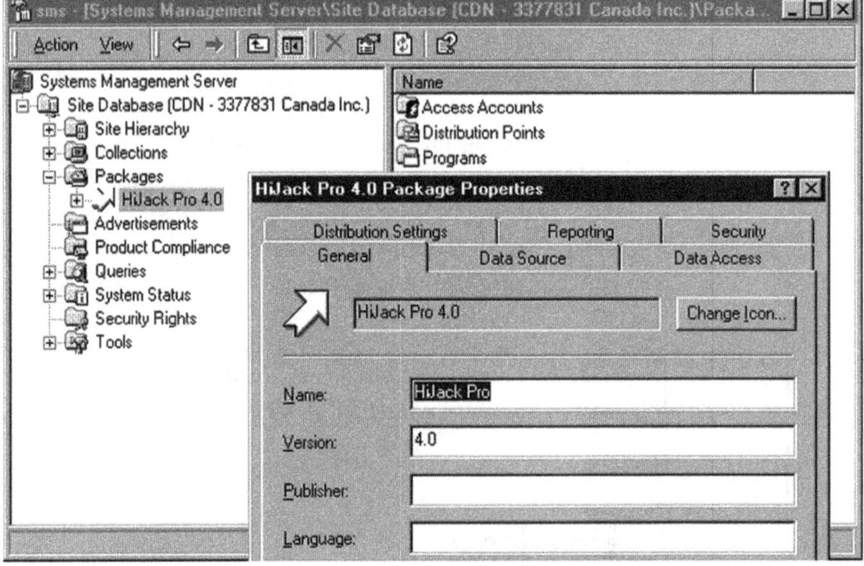

Figure 6-14 Package properties viewed through the SMS Administrator console.

cussed in the last section. Choices for defining the start of a new advertisement are shown in Figure 6-15. Selecting an advertisement and modifying its properties can change these settings. By default, no advertisements are created by just installing SMS.

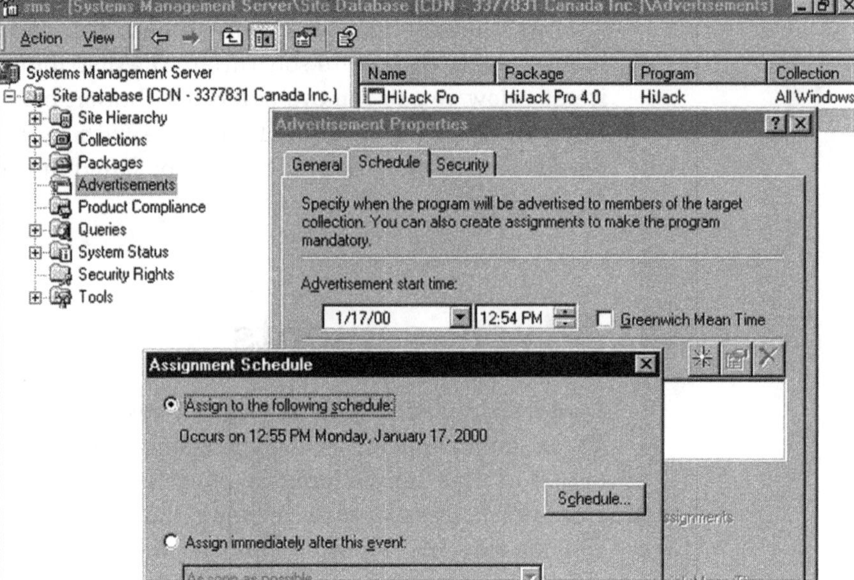

Figure 6-15 Defining an advertisement's start cycle.

Product Compliance

This option is strictly for Y2K issues, so the fact that I'm writing this book in January 2000 means we survived. If this section could measure compliance against other benchmarks, then it may have been useful.

Queries

Since the SMS site database is an SQL database, most SMS data can be searched by using either the defined lists of queries (another name for a query is a customizable search, which you probably do every day on the Net) or your own custom query. A query searches an existing collection or a defined user, system, group, or SMS site resource in order to match a search request, such as "All Windows 98 systems with 2 GB hard drives and 32 MB of RAM."

The query extracts all information found in the SQL database that matches your request. The results are shown in the right-hand windows pane, as shown in Figure 6-16.

A query can find and return the following SMS data objects:

- Hardware Inventory
- Software Inventory
- Advertisements
- Site Information
- Discovery Data
- Any User, Group, or System Resource

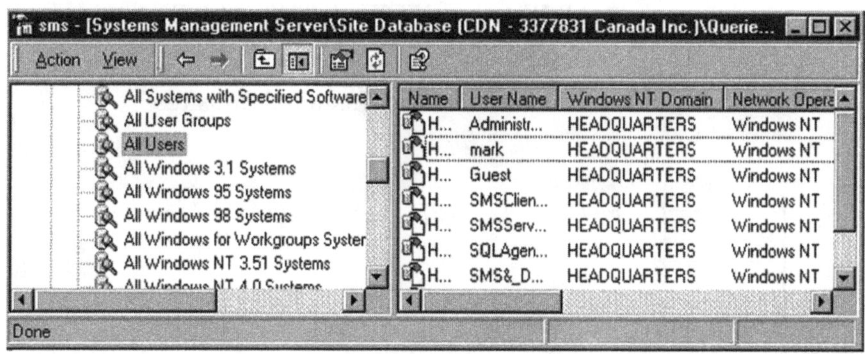

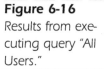

Figure 6-16 Results from executing query "All Users."

All queries are started from the context menu. To start a query, highlight the query that you want to execute, then right-click and select the *Run Query* menu choice. To create a new query, highlight the *Queries* folder, then right-click and select the *New* menu option. You then define the WQL query statement and specify whether the search is based on a defined collection or other SMS object type.

The defined queries that you can execute from the context menu are as follows:

- All Client Systems
- All Non-Client Systems
- All Systems
- All Systems with Hardware Inventory Collected
- All Systems with Microsoft Word
- All Systems with Specified Software File Name and File Size
- All Systems with Specified Software Product Name and Version
- All User Groups
- All Users
- All Windows 3.1 Systems
- All Windows 95 Systems
- All Windows 98 Systems
- All Windows for Workgroups Systems
- All Windows NT 3.51 Systems
- All Windows NT 4.0 Systems
- All Windows NT 4.0 Systems
- All Windows NT Systems with Service Pack 3
- All Windows NT Server 4.0 Systems
- All Windows NT Workstation 4.0 Systems
- Systems by Last Logged On User
- This Site and Any Installed Subsites

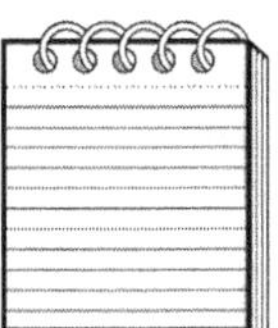

NOTE *The Y2K queries have not been listed due to their obsolescence.*

System Status

The System Status folder at this level of the SMS Administrator console is where you'll find the monitoring and reporting information for details on the current real-life state of all the sites servers installed in the SMS hierarchy. The folder contains the following status summaries:

- *Advertisement Status* A summary of all advertisements deployed across the SMS hierarchy, as shown in Table 6-4.
- *Package Status* Displays a summary of all of the packages that have been distributed by SMS, as shown in Table 6-5.
- *Site Status* The site status folder displays the preset thresholds shown by three status indicators, as shown in Table 6-6. The Status Threshold Properties displays the current states for executing SMS services, threads, and client components, and the Free Space Threshold Properties is concerned with the relative size of any SMS device that has been defined for storing SMS data, including the SQL

TABLE 6-4

Advertisement summary details.

Advertisement Summary Information	Details
Name	The advertisement name.
Failures	The number of clients that failed in processing the advertisement and/or package successfully.
Programs Started	The number of clients that started executing the advertised program.
Program Errors	The number of clients that had errors while running the advertised program.
Program Success	The number of clients that successfully ran the advertised program.
Program	The program type.
Target Collection	What collection this advertisement was sent to.
Available After	The time limit that this advertisement is available to the targeted collection.
Expires After	The time limit when this advertisement is no longer available to the targeted collection.
Advertisement ID	The advertisement ID.

TABLE 6-5

Package summary details.

Package Summary Information	Details
Name	The package name.
Source Version	How many times an existing package has been updated and reset to the distribution points in the site hierarchy.
Version Date	The last time an existing package has been updated and reset to the distribution points in the site hierarchy.
Targeted	How many distribution points were sent the package.
Installed	How many distribution points actually received the package.
Retrying	How many distribution points are having problems receiving, but SMS is still attempting to deliver the package.
Failed	The number of distribution points that failed to receive the package.
Source Site	The site server where the package was created.
Size	The total size in bytes of the uncompressed package.
Compressed Size	The total size in bytes of the compressed package.
Package ID	The ID number that was assigned to the package.

Server database, the SQL Server Transaction Log, all Windows NT shares, and any NetWare NDS volumes.

Security Rights

The complete security rights for the SMS site are displayed in the Security Rights folder. Security is set based on a permission such as read, create, or delete that is then assigned to a security object. The secu-

TABLE 6-6

Site status details.

Status Indicator	Details
OK	No metrics have exceeded the Warning or Critical threshold.
Warning	One or more metrics has crossed the Warning threshold.
Critical	One or more metrics have crossed the Critical threshold.

rity objects can be either a complete class object, such as a Collection, Advertisement, Package, Query, Site, or Status Message, or an instance, which is a singular instance of the listed class objects. The current security rights for a selected site system are shown in Figure 6-17.

If you wish to assign a new Class Security Right or Instance Security Right, display the context menu choices by right-clicking the Security Rights folder and select *New*. If you wish to assign a user to a new instance security right, select the *All Tasks* context menu option; this will start the SMS User Wizard, which will step you through the process.

Tools

The Tools folder allows you to use the following four tools, provided you selected them as installation options when you installed SMS.

- Network Monitor
- SMS Service Manager
- Crystal Reports
- Software Metering

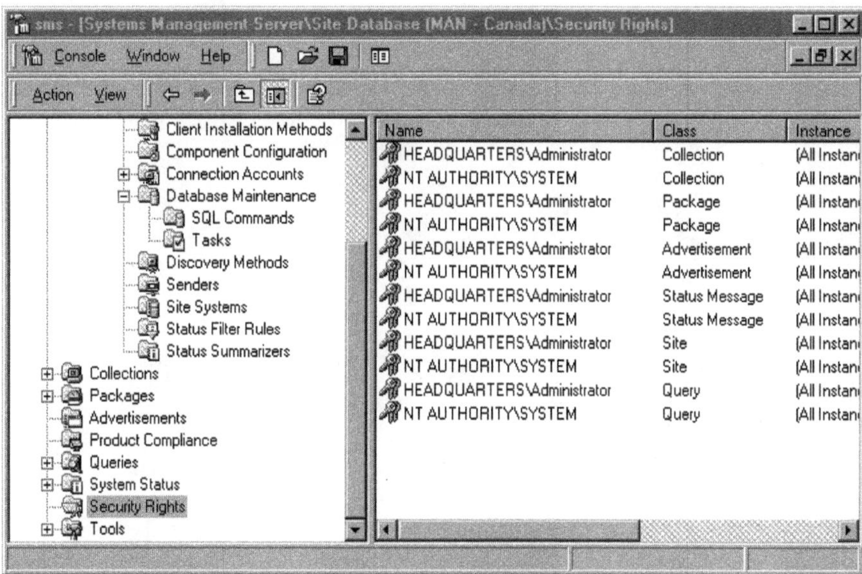

Figure 6-17 Current security rights viewed at the Security Rights folder.

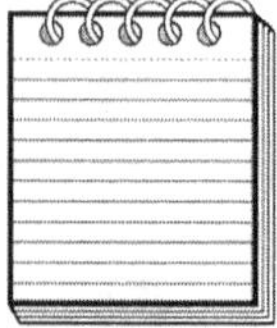

NOTE *If the tools have not been installed, you will need the SMS 2.0 CD-ROM. Start the SMS setup once again, and select* Set Up SMS 2.0. *Now navigate through the splash screens until the Set Up Installation Options screen is displayed. From here select the SMS tools that you wish to install.*

CHAPTER 7

Resource Discovery and Client Installation

In this chapter you'll learn about:

- Resource discovery and the available methods
- How the resource discovery process works
- Discovery data records and their use
- Client installation and configuration
- EXE and DLL components installed for 16- and 32-bit clients

Discovering Resources and SMS Client Installation Methods

One of the first decisions you'll make in actually setting up SMS across and throughout your organization will be which features to start at the SMS site server and at the network client, in order to discover the existing network and computer resources installed across your network. For the discovery of your network users, the detection process is automated from the SMS server and typically happens when the user first successfully logs on to the network after a successful authentication by NT Server, the primary domain controller, or a NetWare server.

Installation of the SMS Client Agent can also be performed during the actual process of discovery; however, you can choose to manually install the SMS client software and agents at the local computer, depending on the method of discovery enabled at the SMS server.

Resource discovery and the installation of SMS client software has to be carried out before you can continue with the deployment of the other SMS management tasks, including hardware and software inventory, using the remote rules for troubleshooting, software metering, and distributing software applications. This makes sense; each client agent has to be active before SMS can start its job of network management.

The Resource Discovery Process

The process of resource discovery and client installation is usually a dual process that fills the SMS site database with the current knowledge of installed computer systems in your company and also installs the SMS client software for further SMS management.

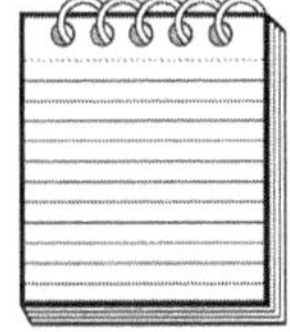

NOTE Remember that a resource is the object that can be recognized and supported by the SMS software, such as computers, printers, users, and so on.

Once the client software has been installed, the computer is then a recognized SMS client. The complete process of resource discovery and the client installation occurs in three related processes: the discovery, site assignment, and client installation of SMS software and agents.

Step 1: Discovery

As you know, this discovery process locates computer resources across your network. After the discovery process, the information in your site database will contain details about the discovered resource. Details can include computer name, IP address, and operating system version, to name but a few items that can be tracked and stored in the discovery data record.

Step 2: Site Assignment

Next, the assignment process determines which actual SMS site is responsible for managing the particular client computer. During the configuration of the SMS site, you must specify the boundaries of the site; these boundaries are actually the subnets that you've selected to be managed by the SMS site. See Figure 7-1.

Step 3: Client Installation

The last of the three bundled processes is the actual software client installation. SMS client software and software client agents, such as the advertised programs client for the Remote Tools client, will be installed on the discovered computer. The agents remain dormant until the SMS feature is enabled at the server location.

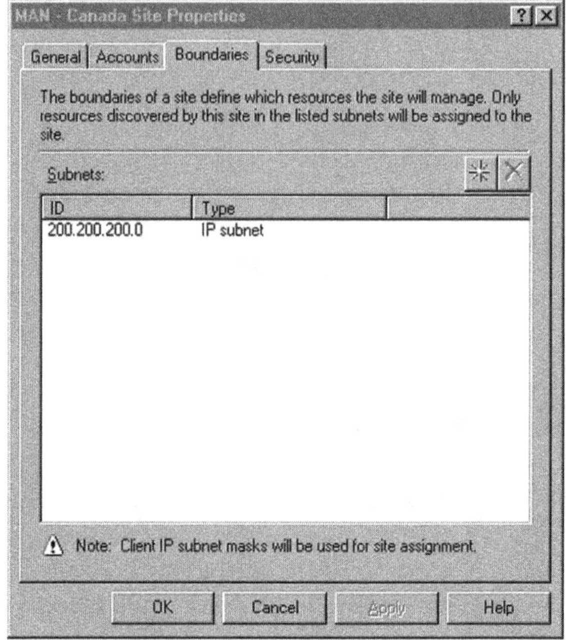

Figure 7-1 The defined site boundaries of an SMS site.

NOTE *During the client installation, the IP address or the current IPX network number of each discovered computer is examined to determine the site server that is responsible for the particular computer being discovered. If the IP address or IPX network number is not within the confines of the currently defined SMS sites, the software installation process will fail and the computer will not become an SMS client.*

SMS Discovery Methods

There are six discovery methods that you can choose to deploy. In reality, the discovery method you'll use the most is Logon Discovery. Logon Discovery is activated when the user logs on through a predefined logon point.

Your decisions as to which additional discovery methods to use will be based on the additional installed network resources your network currently has installed and how you actually want to deploy SMS.

Realistically, I'll bet that the user is the main resource you want to control and manage with SMS.

The six discovery methods are as follows:

- Logon Discovery (Windows 3.11, 95/98/2000 networking, NetWare NDS, NetWare bindery)
- Windows NT User Account Discovery
- Windows NT User Group Discovery
- Network Discovery
- Heartbeat Discovery
- SMS Server Discovery

Table 7-1 briefly summarizes the SMS resource discovery methods you can choose to deploy, along with what is discovered and how each discovery process begins.

The last two options in Table 7-1 indicate that the SMS Server Discovery of all servers that are performing a site system role is an automatic background process. SMS Server Discovery is always installed and active regardless of whether you choose the Custom or Express option for installing SMS, and there are no parameters to configure.

As just noted, you can choose to install SMS by two methods; through either Express or Custom Setup. Be careful! If you choose to install SMS using the Custom Setup procedure, all of the discovery and installation methods are disabled by default, with the exception of SMS Server Discovery. Since you chose Custom Setup, it is assumed that you know which discovery methods you will want to deploy. By choosing Express Setup, all discovery and installation methods are enabled by default, with the exception of Network Discovery.

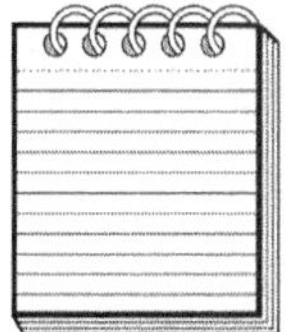

NOTE *Even if you chose to use the Express option for installation and SMS actually installed all discovery installation methods, the actual discovering of user resources will not start until you modify the current logon scripts, enabling the discovery process for the user.*

The setup and configuration of these discovery methods is performed under Site Settings at the SMS Administrator console, as shown in Figure 7-2. Here you can choose to enable the methods you want to use and disable the methods that you do not want to use at this time.

TABLE 7-1 SMS Discovery Methods.

Discovery Method	Discovered Resources	Begins	Works with
Windows Networking Logon Discovery	Computer systems	Logon scripts Systems Management Installation Wizard	Windows Networking Logon Client Installation
NetWare NDS Logon Discovery	Computer systems	Logon scripts Systems Management Installation Wizard	NetWare NDS Logon Client Installation
NetWare Bindery Logon Discovery	Computer systems	Logon scripts (NetWare bindery)	NetWare Bindery Logon Client Installation
Windows NT User Account Discovery	Windows NT Domain user accounts	The SMS site server polls the domain controller.	No method
Windows NT User Group Discovery	Windows NT Global user accounts	The SMS site server polls the domain controller.	No method
Network Discovery	System resources	The SMS servers poll all network devices and watch existing network traffic.	No method
Heartbeat Discovery	Computer systems	By the agent living inside the installed SMS client's PC	Only applicable for computer systems that already are SMS clients
SMS Server Discovery (NT only)	NT servers that are site systems	Automatic	Windows NT Remote Client Installation
SMS Server Discovery (NetWare only)	NetWare bindery servers that are site systems	Automatic	None

Discovery Data Records (DDR)

The discovery of a supported SMS resource results in the creation of a discovery data record that is then forwarded to the SMS site database. It is usually located at the primary site; however, the SQL database could be located elsewhere. The DDR is a detailed record of information about the resources that have been discovered.

The internal information stored in the DDR will vary depending on the type of resource that has been discovered. The DDR resource properties will contain certain information, depending on the resource discovered shown in Table 7-2.

Using the query section in the SMS Administrator console, as shown in Figure 7-3, you can review the DDR properties for your discovered users and systems resources under the "All systems and all users"

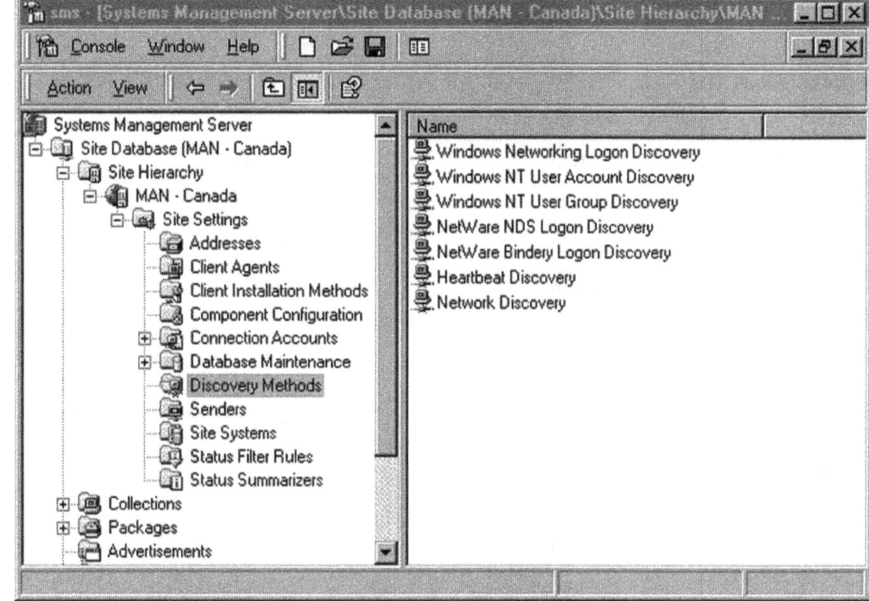

Figure 7-2 The SMS Administrator console and discovery methods.

queries. Remember, a system resource includes computers, routers, printers, and other discovered nonuser components.

Logon Discovery

This method of discovery is the process of discovering clients when the user logs on to the network. This will be the usual method, since most of your clients will be running either Windows NT or NetWare and logging on to the server of choice through a system or user logon script.

Although there are three types of Logon Discovery, the two NetWare Logon Discovery methods will only be available if you chose to include NetWare support when you installed SMS.

The three methods of Logon Discovery are as follows:

- *Windows Networking Logon Discovery* This is used for discovering computers that belonged to an NT domain.
- *Network NDS Logon Discovery* This is used for discovering computers that belong to a NetWare version 3.X/4.X network.

TABLE 7-2

Discovery Data Record Details.

Discovered Resource	Discovery Record Property
System	SMS unique identifier
System	NetBIOS name
System	IP address
System	IP subnets
System	IPX addresses
System	IPX network numbers
System	Media Access Control (MAC) addresses
System	Resource domain or workgroup
System	Operating system and name and version
System	Last logon user name
System	Last logon user domain
System	Client version
System, User Group, User	Discovery agent name
System, User Group, User	Discovery agent site
System, User Group, User	Discovery agent time
System	SMS client
System, User Group, User	Name
System, User Group, User	SMS assigned sites
System	SMS installed sites
System	System roles
System	Resource ID
System, User Group, User	Resource name
System	Resource type
User Group	Unique user group name
User Group, User	Windows NT domain
User Group	User group name
User Group, User	Network operating system
User	Full user name
User	Unique user name
User	User name

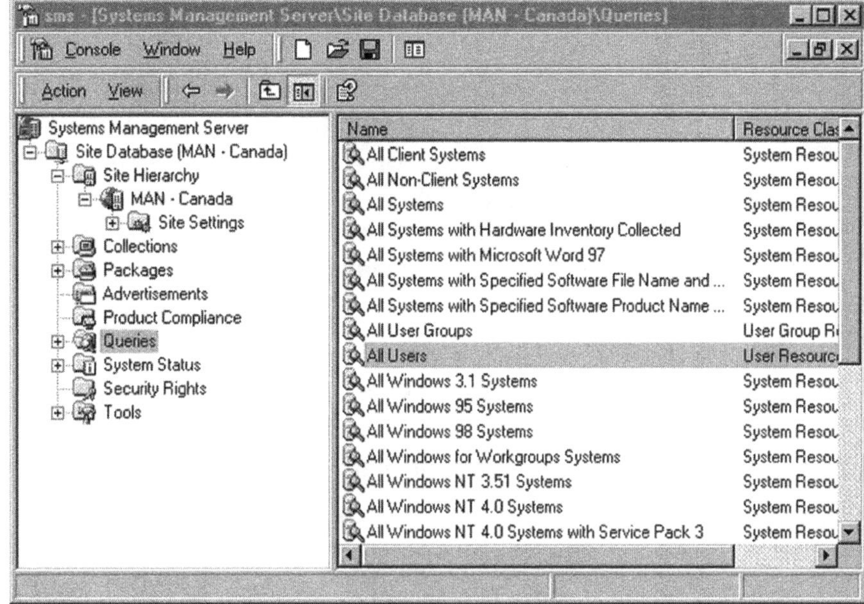

Figure 7-3 DDR properties viewed at the SMS Administrator console.

- *NetWare Bindery Logon Discovery* This is used for discovering computers that belong to a NetWare NDS environment.

When either of the three Logon Discovery methods is enabled, SMS directs the Windows NT Logon Manager to copy the discovery files that will be used for installation of the client agent and other client software components to either the domain controller or NetWare server that was specified. These discovery files will then be available on the network for manual installation or by automatic setup through logon scripts.

The Windows NT Logon Manager will perform the following tasks:

- Create an SMSLOGON share
- Create and start a Windows NT Logon Discovery service
- Copy SMS logon scripts and discovery initialization files to the NETLOGON folder of each domain controller.

Setting up Logon Discovery involves the first step of defining your logon points and then creating and modifying your existing system logon scripts, or running the Systems Management Installation Wizard.

Setting Up SMS Logon Points

A logon point can be a Windows NT domain controller (both primary or backup domain controllers are allowed), a NetWare NDS container and volume, or a NetWare bindery server. You would modify the current logon scripts at these defined logon points. These changes, in turn, will initiate the discovery process the next time your clients log on through these defined logon points and execute their logon scripts.

SMS Task: Set Up Your Logon Points

To actually enable or set up your logon points for your Windows clients:

1. Open up your SMS Administrator console, and select the desired site server.
2. On the Details pane, select the discovery method you want to configure and then right-click and select *Properties*.
3. Choose the *General* tab and click on *New*.
4. In the New Logon Point dialog box, specify the name of the domain, container, and volume, or the bindery server to use as the logon point, as shown in Figure 7-4.

The selection of a particular Windows NT domain means that all domain controllers in the domain will be chosen to be logon points for SMS. NT servers that are standalone servers (i.e., member servers) cannot be included as a login point, since they do not deal with logon requests from users. Only a primary or backup domain controller handles the logon and authentication process. When a server or volume becomes a logon point, it will also become a site system with the logon point role.

When you choose a Logon Discovery method, the equivalent client installation method is also automatically chosen and prepared. Choices are shown in Table 7-3.

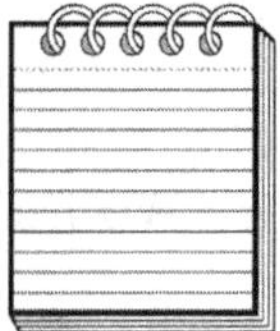

NOTE *Once you have enabled both of the installation and discovery methods, you can choose to synchronize the lists of the logon points used for the discovery and installation of clients. Then in the future, when you change any installation methods or logon point information, these*

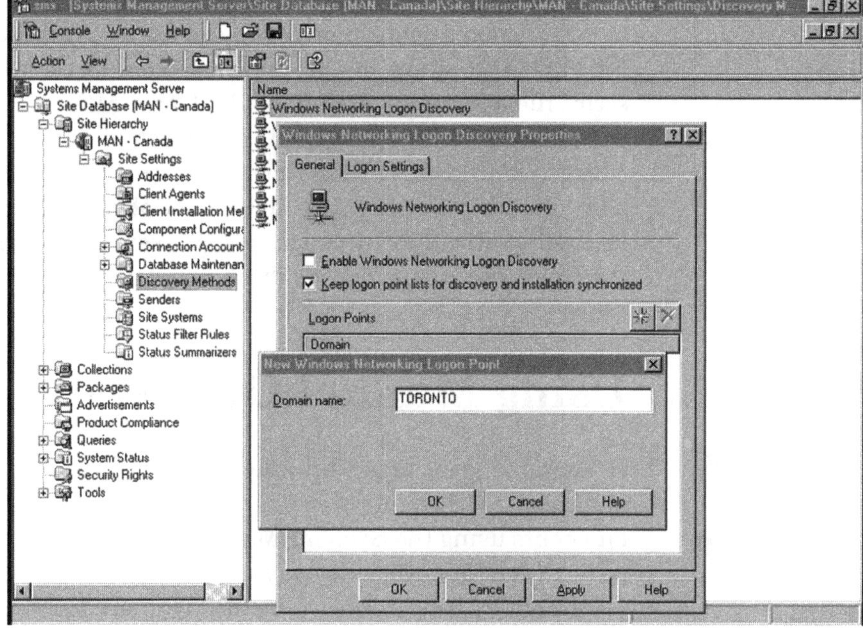

Figure 7-4 Property tab options for Windows Networking Discovery.

TABLE 7-3 SMS Logon Choices and the Installed Components.

If You Choose	SMS Will Install
Windows Networking Logon Client	Windows Networking Logon Discovery files
Network NDS Logon Client	Network NDS Logon Discovery files
NetWare Bindery Logon Client	Network NDS Logon Discovery files

changes will be reflected in all logon and discovery locations automatically. This ensures that you're using the same logon points for both the discovery of clients and the installation of software.

Logon Scripts

SMS will automatically modify your logon script if you desire; however, I would make this a manual task, since the logon script affects all users. By selecting the Logon Settings tab of the discovery method properties dialog box, you can specify if SMS should modify your current logon scripts.

For NetWare users, SMS can also change either the NetWare bindery or NDS logon scripts. For NT users all login scripts are located in the NETLOGON share of the primary domain controller, and the logon script file extensions are either .BAT or .CMD.

The logon script change is the addition of a line that will call and execute the SMSLS.BAT file, which starts the discovery process. Both Guest and Administrator user accounts will not have their logon scripts modified automatically if this option is chosen, although you won't be using the Guest account, since it's disabled by default.

Using Manual Discovery

If you don't wish to use an automated discovery process for finding and installing SMS clients, you can choose to manually discover 16- and 32-bit clients using the Systems Management Installation Wizard. You must have Logon Discovery already enabled for your SMS site and one logon point defined before performing the manual discovery process.

Although the normal process would be to use the logon script method just described to discover and install SMS client software, you may have several or many clients that are not using logon scripts. In this case, the Installation Wizard, shown in Figure 7-5, can be used to discover these computers. If the wizard discovers any computers, it will then install the SMS client software on the discovered computer system.

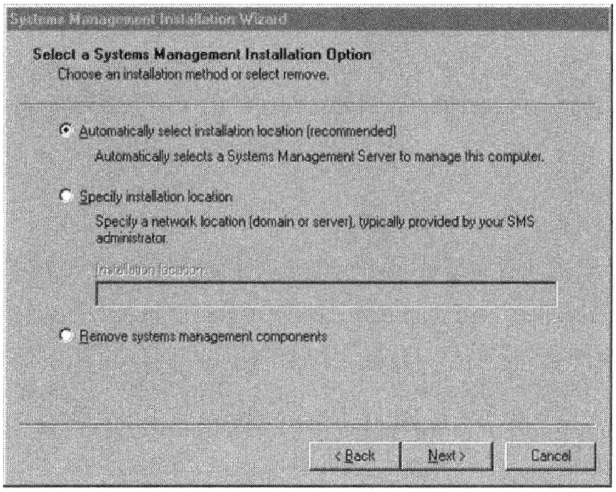

Figure 7-5 Using the Systems Management Installation Wizard.

Running the appropriate executive file from the local computer starts the Installation Wizard. Choices for starting the wizard are from the local hard drive or a defined network share.

Each version of Windows 3.X, 95/98, or NT uses a specific executive file; for 32-bit Windows clients, SMSman.exe starts the wizard; for 16-bit Windows clients, use SMSman16.exe. If you have some DOS clients still hanging in there, the DOS Wizard is started with Manboot.exe.

When the wizard is started, it connects to a specified logon point or performs a search for a logon point in the domain. Both SMSman.exe and SMSman16.exe support unattended installations by using command-line syntax as detailed in Table 7-4.

Using Windows NT User Account Discovery

As the name suggests, this method of discovery uses existing NT user accounts found in the domain. Once you specify a domain or a set of

TABLE 7-4

Systems Management Installation Wizard Syntax.

Command-Line Options	Details
/S <Server_Name>	The Windows NT server discovery/installation directory.
/D <domain_name>	The Windows NT domain discovery/installation directory.
/B <\\server\volume>	The NetWare bindery discovery/installation directory.
/C <tree.org.orgunit>	The NetWare NDS context of discovery/installation directory.
/A	Automatically picks the discovery/installation location.
/U	Uninstalls every SMS client component.
/Q	Silent discovery/installation.
/T	This is the test mode where all discovery results will be displayed.
/V	Sets the level of logging information 0-3 (3 is the highest detail).
/H or /?	Either option displays the Help screen.

domains, SMS can then query the domain controllers of the specified domains and discover all current domain user accounts.

A DDR will be created by the discovery agent, which then will send the record to the SMS database defined by the site. This type of discovery does not perform any client installation of SMS agent software, since user accounts are being discovered, not computer systems.

The SMS discovery must have administrator rights for each defined domain. This is carried out by granting the SMS service account administrator rights to the desired domains. This type of discovery could be handy for defining a list of users before installing a new software update or a new software program. You could advertise the software to a specific collection of users. The permission of Administrator must be given to SMS so it can discover all user accounts.

Windows NT User Group Discovery

This method uses existing NT global groups for the discovery process. To start this discovery method, you must first specify a set of domains indicating where to perform the discovery process. SMS will then query the domain controllers and discover all of the known global groups. Note that the local groups will not be discovered. Local groups on an NT server/domain is really a dying breed. Both system policies and SMS do not support local groups. It's a really good practice to always create global groups when creating new groups in an NT environment. The permission of Administrator must also be given to SMS so it can discover all group accounts.

Group discovery can be very useful if you manage your users by global groups. Usually you'll have groups of users that require the same software or the same virus software update; in a large company, this would be much easier to deploy per group rather than per user. However, deploying or updating your users' software at a local PC would be better served by using user account discovery. By the same token, however, software distribution could be better served using the user group process.

You can schedule how often SMS should query the domain controllers to update the SMS database through the group and user account discovery properties using the SMS Administrator console, as shown in Figure 7-6.

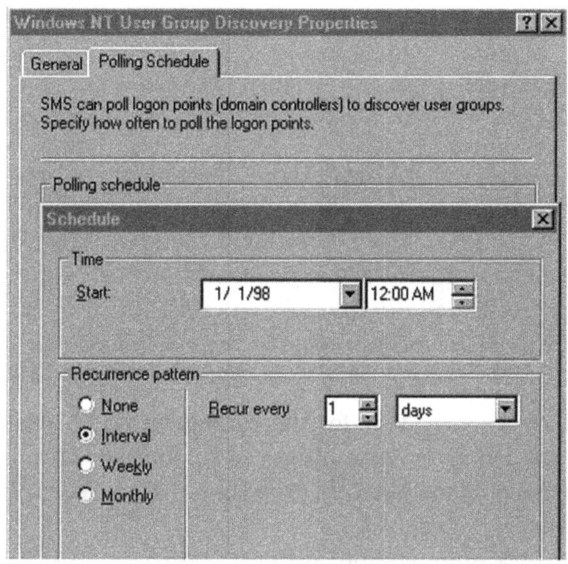

Figure 7-6 Group Discovery Properties.

NOTE *Because SMS version 2.0 software distribution no longer supports distribution to the older clients, 16-bit clients cannot take advantage of the user groups and user accounts distribution and discovery.*

Network Discovery

The process of Network Discovery finds any object across your network that uses an IP (Internet protocol) address. Network Discovery will find any routers, printers, computers, Simple Network Management Protocol (SNMP) devices, defined subnets, any Windows NT Dynamic Host Configuration Protocol (DHCP) servers, or any other network devices.

Your existing site boundaries do not confine Network Discovery. Network Discovery searches and finds resources across your entire network. Each discovered network device found will have a DDR created for each resource. Then the information will be forwarded to the SMS site database act of the site location that ran the discovery.

Discovery can be also initiated without performing the actual installation of the SMS client agents and software. You could choose to use a Network Discovery process just to see what clients are actually installed. So the Network Discovery process could be used just to gather the current information about the number of computers and their current location. The process of Network Discovery can also discover UNIX workstations, mainframes, or other resources that can't become SMS clients. However, this information could still be valuable in the planning stages.

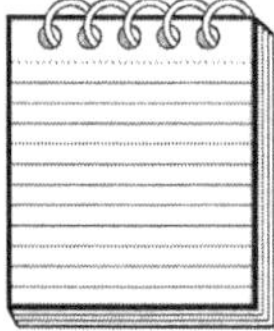

NOTE *You may also use Network Discovery to help create your network map. If Network Discovery is then paired with Windows NT Remote Client Installation, you could then also silently install SMS client software on all your Windows NT 4.0 Workstation clients. This installation can happen whether or not the user is logged in.*

There are two steps for the configuration of Network Discovery. First, Network Discovery is configured to find specific information about the resources on your network. You then define the range of where the actual discovery will occur.

Network management is defined through the SMS Administrator console as shown in Figure 7-7, by selecting the discovery method properties. Once you have set up the parameters for your Network Discovery, you will then need to schedule a timeline for each discovery.

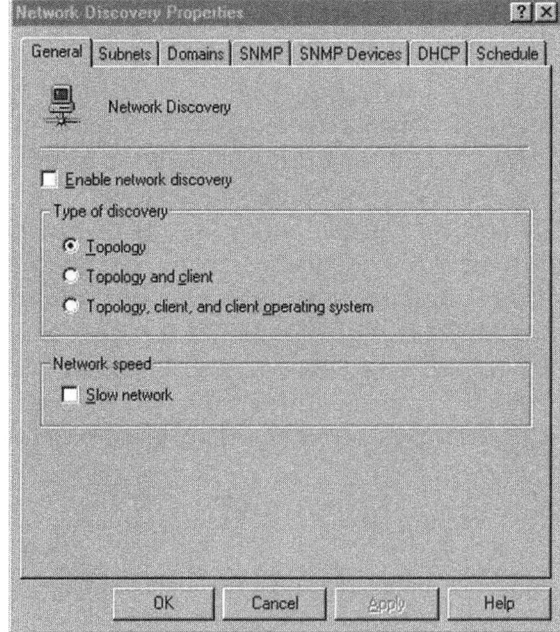

Figure 7-7 Network Discovery choices.

Network Discovery Details

There are three types of Network Discovery supported by SMS 2.0:

1. Topology Discovery
2. Topology and Client Discovery
3. Topology, Client, and Client Operating System Discovery

Topology Discovery

This choice will return information on the subnets and routers found on your network. It will also detail how the discovery objects are connected, for example, by using DCHP or a fixed IP address. The protocol for communication using Network Topology Discovery can be SNMP.

Topology and Client Discovery

Selecting this level of discovery uses DHCP, SNMP, and the NT Browser service to query and identify subnets, routers, clients, gateways, and printers within the defined network area.

Topology, Client, and Client Operating System Discovery

When you select this level, Network Discovery uses every trick it has at its disposal: DHCP, SNMP, the NT Browser service, and installed Windows Networking calls to identify subnets, routers, clients, gateways, printers, and the discovered clients' operating systems currently installed.

NOTE *If your clients are Windows 95 or Windows 98, Network Discovery can only discover client operating system versions if the computer system has been configured for file and print sharing.*

Since Network Discovery dramatically increases network traffic across your network, it is not enabled by default. Scheduling of network discovery should be done at off-peak times when clients are not busy doing actual work.

The other remaining tabs shown in the Network Discovery Properties allow you to further define Network Discovery.

Subnets

Add in the subnets that you want Network Discovery to search for as it searches for resources. Subnet information that must be added is the subnet's IP network ID and subnet mask.

Domains

Add in the domains that Network Discovery can use to find resources.

SNMP

List the community names of the SNMP devices that Network Management will use to gather information. You can also define the maximum hop count that Network Discovery should use. The larger the hop count, the more routers Network Discovery will attempt to query and "hop through." The maximum number of hops is 10.

SNMP Devices

This tab allows you to provide a little more SNMP detail for a more accurate search. Here you can enter in the SNMP devices that Network Discovery can use for querying for discovery data. SNMP community names must be entered, as well as the hop count.

DHCP

This tab, as shown in Figure 7-8, is used to define the Windows NT DHCP servers that can be used for gathering network data from. If your client is a DHCP client, then your DHCP server will be queried by default.

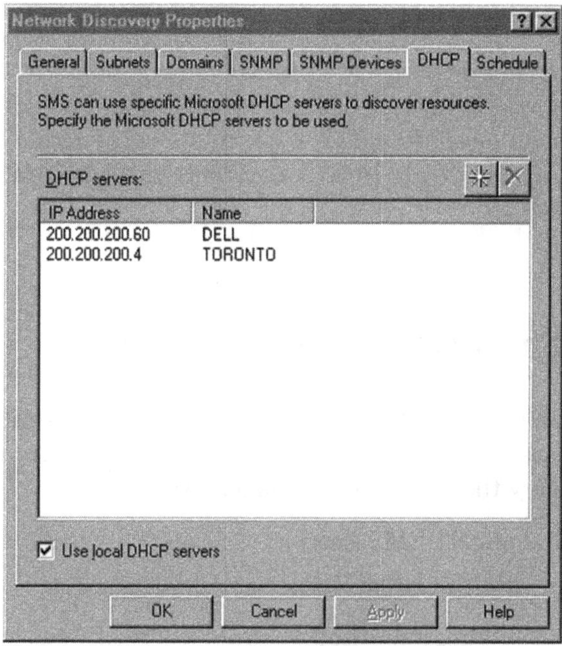

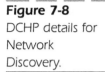

Figure 7-8 DCHP details for Network Discovery.

Schedule

This tab is used to define the date, time, and frequency at which Network Discovery will run. You can also define the line of time that the Network Discovery will actually take.

Heartbeat Discovery

This method of discovery is always enabled by default and depends on the already installed client agents in order to perform its job of rediscovering and updating DDRs for the respective client in the discovery database. Once a resource has been initially configured as a client computer, the Heartbeat Discovery process keeps tabs on all active clients by creating and updating DDRs on a set schedule. The default is every 7 days.

There are only two choices to configure for Heartbeat Discovery:

1. Enable Heartbeat Discovery.
2. Define the time lag until the next refresh.

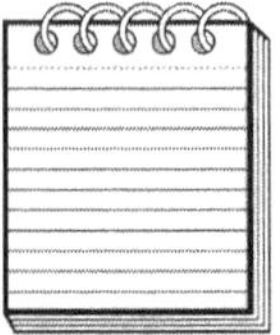

NOTE All records are automatically removed from the database that have aged more than 90 days due to the automatic SMS task Delete Aged Discovery Data. You can choose to increase or decrease the timeline somewhat depending on the size and change across your network. You certainly don't want to have a current database with a lot of old, obsolete data DDRs.

SMS Server Discovery

The job of Server Discovery is to maintain up-to-date discovery data for all installed site systems in the SMS site. The two types of Server Discovery that are used are as follows:

1. Windows NT SMS Server Discovery
2. NetWare Bindery SMS Server Discovery

Both of these methods cannot be modified. They are enabled by default when a site system is first created. Both methods also work on a prescribed schedule that can't be changed or modified.

By using one of the above discovery methods, all site systems will be discovered. All discovered servers that are Windows NT servers that are performing a site system role and are on a defined subnet with the site boundary will then have SMS client software installed. They can then report their availability and status back to SMS Management.

NetWare Limitations

There are limitations with SMS 2.0 if you have a NetWare environment; SMS can discover a NetWare bindery server but not NetWare NDS servers. And even though the NetWare bindery server can be discovered, SMS can't install SMS client software on the NetWare servers, since they are not supported as SMS clients. Perhaps NetWare will receive more support when Windows 2000 is released and NetWare 5.0 is entrenched as running native IP rather than IPX.

Installing Clients

There are several methods available for installing clients across your SMS site once the client computer has been discovered. The types of client installation are grouped into:

- Logon installation methods for NetWare and NT environments
- Windows NT Remote Client Installation

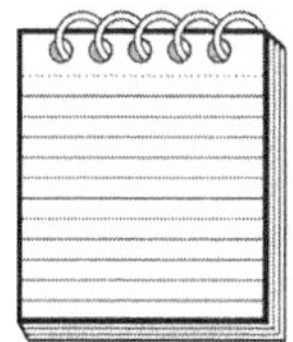

NOTE *Although we usually think of the client as being an actual user at a client PC, remember that the client can also be a supported SMS client even if it is a Windows NT SMS site system discovered by the automatic Server Discovery process.*

Logon Installation

There are three logon client installation methods provided by SMS:

1. Windows Networking Logon
2. NetWare NDS Logon
3. NetWare Bindery Logon

The logon method that you choose depends on the type of networking systems you support. Windows NT networks will use a domain controller for the first point of contact. For NetWare the choices are bindery or NDS container objects and volumes.

Using the logon client installation, client computers don't have to be discovered before SMS client software can be installed; however, the Remote Client Installation method requires that the computers have previously been discovered.

If the SMS client software is installed on the client without being discovered, during Heartbeat Discovery or when software or hardware inventory is collected from the client, a DDR will be created and sent to the site server. Additionally, the client or server computer where the install is being performed must also be within the site boundaries that have been defined. The computer's IP or IPX address will be compared against the site boundary data maintained on the site server, the client access point, or the logon point.

If your SMS installation is on a large network with multiple domains, logon installation can be configured at different sites. If your users log on to a single master domain or a few master domains, it will be simpler for you to have the same master domain shared by all of your SMS sites for Logon Discovery and installation. If you have a large multiple master domain structure, you can and should choose multiple locations for performing the client installation for all of your clients.

Certainly, the most common method you will use is the Windows Networking Logon Installation. You can also mandate that your list of logon points for discovery and installation remain synchronized at all times. Using the same set of logon points for both discovery and installation makes sense when you consider the discovery of a client could determine whether or not a particular installation of an advertised package is carried out.

SMS Task: Windows Networking Client Installation

At the site server open up the SMS Administrator console. Then:

1. Selecting the SMS console tree, look in the Details pane and select the *Client Installations Methods* node.
2. Select *Windows Networking Logon Client Installation*.
3. Now from the Action menu, select *Properties*; the Properties dialog box for the selected method appears.
4. Add the domains that you wish to use for your client installations.
5. Now check *Enable Windows Networking Logon Client Installation*.

Be careful that the "Keep logon points list for discovery and installation synchronized" checkbox is checked off by default, as detailed in Figure 7-9. This option should be left in this state.

NetWare Logon Client Installation

Installing this option allows NetWare clients to attach to NetWare servers and get SMS client software installed. There are two versions of the NetWare Logon Client Installation depending on whether or not your environment is bindery or NDS. If your servers are bindery—that is, NetWare 3.X or earlier—you'll have to enter the name of each bindery server used in the SMS domain. For an NDS environment, you'll have to enter the NDS tree, container, and volume that will be used by the NDS Logon Client Installation.

The logon script is SSMSLS.SCR for both NetWare environments. For bindery servers, you'll be appending or adding to the system logon script; for the NDS environment, you'll be appending the container logon script.

Windows NT Remote Client Installation

In the background, SMS version 2.0 can quietly install SMS client software on all supported Windows NT computers and configure the SMS

Figure 7-9 Windows Networking Logon Properties

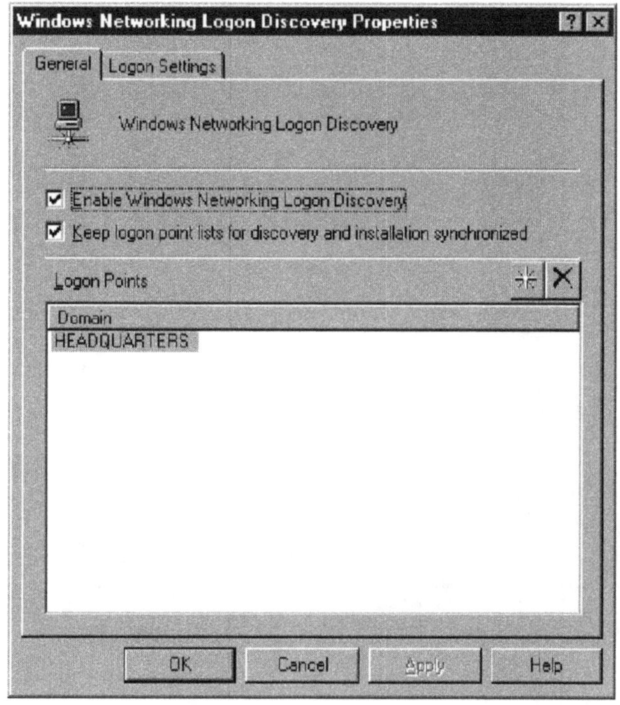

client with no help from the user. This method of installation is configured from the Client Installation Method found in the SMS Administrator console, as shown in Figure 7-10; at this location, you can select whether Windows NT servers, NT workstations, or domain controllers are to be automatically set up as SMS clients.

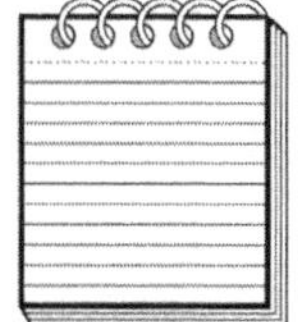

NOTE *Once the Windows NT Remote Client Installation is enabled, any discovered Windows NT resource is automatically installed as an SMS client if its IP address has been defined within the site boundaries of the SMS site.*

This method could be useful for installing the SMS client software onto systems that rarely if ever log on to the network, for users that do not run the logon script at startup, or for network servers.

The Remote Client Installation uses existing Windows NT security and client DDRs in order to make a connection and start the installation. If the SMS Service account or the SMS Client Remote Installation account has Administrative permissions to the discovered NT computer, the Client Configuration Manager (CCM) attaches to it over the network,

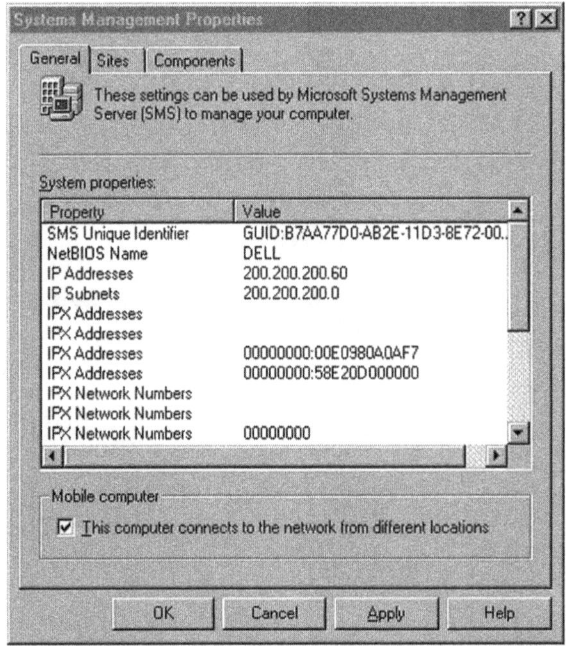

Figure 7-10 Configuring the Windows NT Remote Client Installation (PCX).

copies the necessary SMS installation files, and finishes off the installation process.

Any combination of domain name\user name, any domain name, the name of the NT computer, or the user name is used to attempt to attach to the remote PC. The Client Configuration Manager uses the Client Remote Installation account and a combination of variables to attempt to make a successful remote connection to the client.

1. `Domain_name\user_name`.
2. `Domain_name` is now replaced with the name of the domain that the user is currently logged in with.
3. If there is a machine account domain name, then this name replaces `Domain_name`.
4. If there are any open and current connections to any other domains, the domain's name replaces `Domain_name`.
5. The name of the NT computer system now replaces `Domain_name`.
6. As a last resort, the user's user_name replaces `Domain_name`.

This method of access control is designed for successful SMS client installation in master domain environments where the computer accounts are created in the resource domain, and users log on through the master domain. Check your NT security permissions; they can cause problems if they are not carefully considered. You must have Administrative permissions to install the client software on an NT client computer system. However, during the install, if the needed rights are not present at the local workstation, SMS will attempt to start the needed DLLs with an active system account that has the necessary administrative rights.

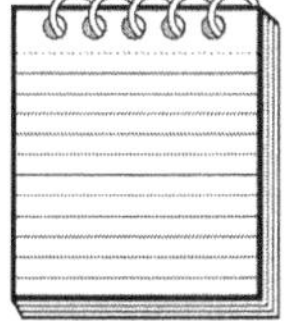

NOTE *If you are searching through untrusted domains, you will have to create identical accounts and passwords in all linked domains for the remote installation to work. The end result is that you will have to give Administrative permissions on all client computers to either the SMS Service account or to the Windows NT Remote Installation account.*

Installing Client Agents

The client agents are background services and applications that execute at the SMS local client. There are six client agents that are installed as SMS workers, but remember this important point: Each client can only be installed and configured for the entire SMS site and not on a per-client basis. Make sure that you install each client with careful consideration for the additional bandwidth each installed SMS feature will generate.

The SMS client agents you can install are as follows:

- Software Inventory Client Agent
- Hardware Inventory Client Agent
- Remote Tools Client Agent
- Advertised Programs Client Agent
- Software Metering Client Agent
- NT Event to SNMP Trap Translator Client Agent

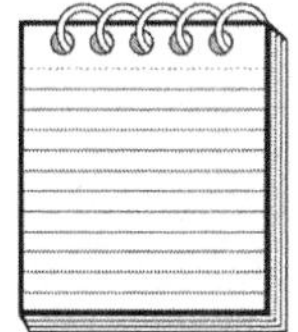

NOTE *The NT Event to SNMP Trap Translator Client Agent is enabled by default.*

Even if all of the client agents have not been installed yet, or you have disabled them at the site server, a core set of SMS software components will be installed on the client computer. The basic SMS components are as follows:

- SMS Client Base Components
- Available Programs Manager
- Windows Management (WMI)

Express Setup installs all of the agents, and Custom Setup expects you to specify which agents to install. After a client agent configuration has been enabled at the SMS site server, the Client Configuration Installation Manager updates the necessary files at the client access point. For details on enabling and setting up the client agents, see Chapter 6 "Using the SMS Administrator Console."

Preparing for Resource Discovery and Client Installation

Defining your site boundaries is one of most important tasks that will challenge you as you plan to deploy SMS in your organization. The rules that determine site assignment resolve whether the computers that are discovered are assigned to a defined SMS site or ignored.

The subnets that make up your network are ultimately the site boundary rules that SMS will use. When a client computer is first installed, it determines which SMS site it belongs to by using the site assignment rules. After installation is complete, the client computer will recheck and confirm the SMS site it belongs to every 23 hours or sooner. This interval cannot be configured and its frequency will depend upon what other SMS events occur.

Where it gets tricky is when you have clients that are assigned to one or many sites. This could happen if the client moves around the network or has more than one connection to the network. For example, say that you, as the administrator, have a laptop that you bring to work occasionally, as well as a desktop PC. You also remote into the network on occasion to perform administrative tasks after hours. Each of these network connections could belong to its own IP subnet, and each subnet could belong to a different SMS site.

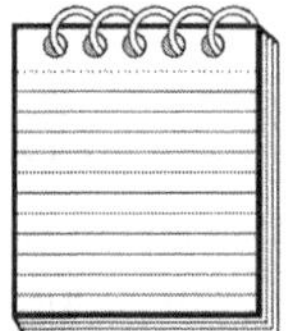

NOTE *Try to keep your site design to a minimum of clutter by assigning clients to one site if possible. Chapter 5 "Configuring SMS Site Systems" covers setting up and configuring site boundaries in detail.*

When you're planning your site boundaries, remember you can also deploy resource discovery to gather information about the current computers that you plan to manage. By totaling up the number of computers in a subnet and taking into account where the servers and clients are located, you will best be able to plan for multiple subnets and multiple sites.

By enabling either Logon Discovery or Network Discovery without enabling Client Installation, you can benefit by receiving up-to-date network information without installing any SMS client software at the present time.

Review the locations of your client access points and distribution points in relation to the clients that will use them. Depending on the tasks you have in mind for SMS, make sure that the client has appropriate bandwidth to access your SMS components in a timely fashion.

Planning your Client Installation and Discovery

Depending on your deployment of SMS, you may want to enable Client Installation but not discovery, or perhaps you prefer the exact opposite.

If Client Installation is turned off when you perform discovery, all of your network resources will be discovered. And on all discovered resources that have Windows 95/98 and Windows NT installed, the Systems Management Control Panel Applet and the Systems Management Installation Wizard will be installed.

Next, you could then enable Client Installation. All clients that have a version of Windows installed will also be installed as SMS clients.

Starting Discovery without Client Installation

For the initial planning process, use Network Discovery to discover any information about the resources on your entire network. No client installation will occur, since installations are not the job of Network Discovery. (Any computer resources that you wished to then install as clients could be discovered and tabulated by Logon Discovery.)

Starting Client Installation without Discovery

In other circumstances the amount of network traffic that could be generated if discovery and the client installation were performed at the same time would be fatal. If your network was designed using a master domain model, all logon points in the authenticating master domain must share the discovery data gathered during the Logon Discovery process with every SMS site server that specified the domain for Logon Discovery.

In this scenario each logon point found in the master domain copies the discovery data to every site server. In a large network this would be a lot of network traffic. One solution would be to start logon installation but disable the Logon Discovery on all of your SMS site servers. This would mean that no discovery data would be replicated to the logon points after the clients executed the logon scripts.

Then, you could enable Heartbeat Discovery, so resources that were installed as SMS clients could send discovery data to each site they were assigned to but on a much looser schedule. Instead of each logon point copying discovery data to every site server at logon, site servers would copy their discovery data up to their parent's site.

The end result is that every site would contain resource discovery data for all clients assigned to that site and any child sites.

SMS Client Agents

For every SMS feature you wish to use on your clients, the corresponding client agent must be installed. Before the actual client agent is installed at the client, make sure to set up the server component of the client agent. The following client agents are available for SMS version 2.0:

- Hardware Inventory (Chapter 10)
- Software Inventory (Chapter 10)
- Software Metering (Chapter 9)
- Advertised Programs (Chapter 11)
- Remote Control (Chapter 13)

Viewing SMS Client Software on the Local PC

Once the SMS client software has been installed, certain SMS services will execute and run on the client, depending on the operating system. (I will assume that you will be running Windows 95/98 or Windows NT 4.0 workstations.)

Certain SMS pieces may show up from time to time depending on the agents installed and tasks that you use SMS for. Some work diligently, hidden deep in the background, and hopefully the client will not be aware that they are even performing their job. Other agents could be available depending on the client agents installed. The control panel applets that can be installed on the SMS client are listed in Table 7-5.

System Management Applet

This applet is found in the Control Panel for all SMS clients that are Windows 95/98 and Windows NT. The three tabs of this applet provide general information, sites that the client is assigned to, and the components that are installed on the client.

On the General tab, the discovery data for the computer is displayed, along with an option to enable Traveling Mode, shown in Figure 7-11. This option stops SMS from collecting information at every site the user connects to.

TABLE 7-5

SMS Control Panel Applets.

Control Panel Applet Name	Control Panel Command File
Systems Management Applet	SMSCFG.CPL
Advertised Programs Applets	SMSCPL32.CPL
Advertised Programs Monitor Applet	
Remote Tools Applet	SMSRC.CPL

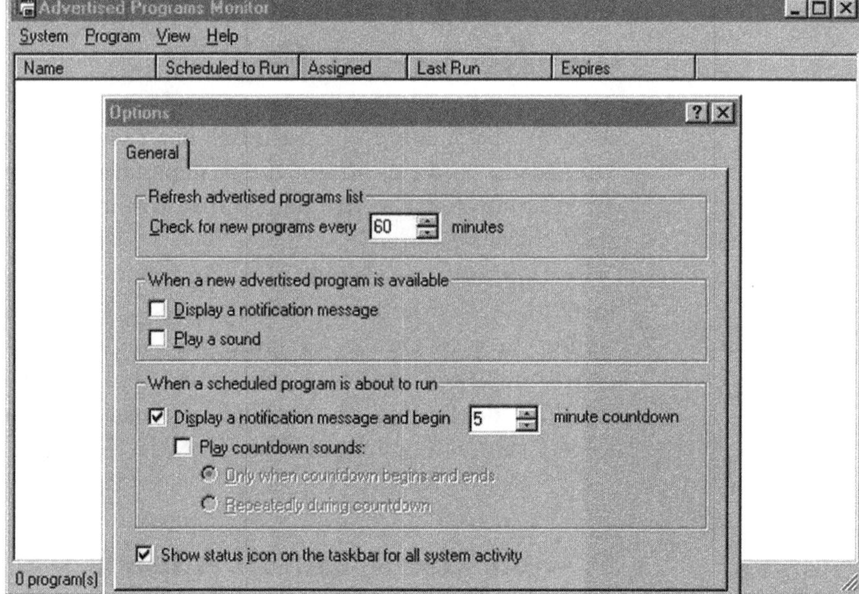

Figure 7-11 Traveling mode options in the Systems Management icon.

Advertised Programs Applet

Once an advertised program is available to be installed on the client, an Advertised Programs indicator will appear on the user's taskbar. The user can then install the software program by right-clicking and selecting Run Advertised Program Wizard. The Advertised Programs Monitor displays the progress of the installation, the Control Panel also has an icon called the Advertised Program Monitor that can be used to view details of the available advertisements as shown in Figure 7-12. Options for advertised programs on the clients PC are also set in this icon as well.

Remote Control Applet

This applet allows the user, if permitted by the Administrator, to change the control of remote access from the default of Full, to Limited, or to None. With full access, the Administrator can execute the following tasks:

- View the user's monitor display in real-time, plus control the keyboard and mouse.

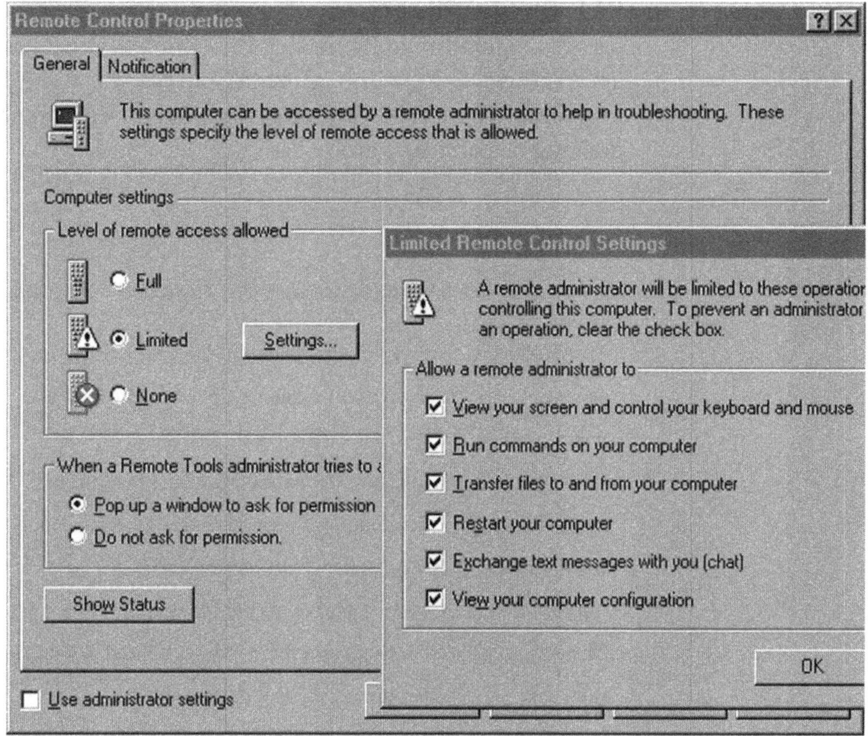

Figure 7-12 Advertised Program Monitor and options set through the Control Panel (PCX).

- Execute commands on the user's PC
- Copy files to the client's PC from the Administrator's PC
- Reboot the user's PC
- Chat via a text chat mode
- Access the user's computers configuration information

The notification options, shown in Figure 7-12, allow the user to define how a remote access session is started and activated.

SMS Client Structure

Once the client software and agents are installed on the user's PC, some of the executables, DLLs, and directory structure listed in Tables 7-6, 7-7, and 7-8 will be deployed on the client's PC. A *dynamic link library*

DLL file is a library of software features that is linked to a specific process depending on whether the client is Windows 95/98, Windows NT, or Windows 3.X. This information can be useful in troubleshooting problems when error messages appear, indicating that a specific file is missing or can't be found.

TABLE 7-6

32-bit Executable Files Installed on SMS Clients.

SMS Executable Files Installed for 32-Bit Clients	
Apasetup.exe	Advertise Programs Client Agent Setup on CAP
Apaunins.exe	Advertised Programs Client Agent Remover
Boot32wn.exe	The Client Bootstrap
Ccmboot.exe	Client Configuration Manager Bootstrap
Ccmbtlr.exe	Client can configure Manager Bootstrap Loader
Chksnmp.exe	SNMP Agent Installation Verifier
Cliore.exe	Court executive all file for clients
Clisvc95.exe	Clients service for Windows 95 and Windows 98
Clisvl.exe	Clients service for Windows NT
Hinv32.exe	Hardware Inventory Agent
Mofcomp.exe	WMI MOF Manager
Nlsmsg32.exe	Client Messages Library
Ntencap.exe	Wrapper for Windows NT operating system upgrade (Intel)
Ntencapa.exe	Wrapper for windows NT operating system upgrade (Intel)
Odpsy32.exe	Offer Data Provider for Windows NT operating system
Odpusr32.exe	Offer Data Provider for User and Group for Windows NT
Odpwin9x.exe	Offer Data Provider for System, User, and Group for Windows 95 and Windows 98
Pea32.exe	Program Execution Agent
Rcclicfg.exe	The Security Manager (reconciler) for Remote Tools
Sinv32.exe	Software Inventory Agent
Smsapm32.exe	Advertised Programs Manager
Smsmam.exe	SMS Client Manual Discovery
Smsmon32.exe	Advertised CAD programs can monitor
Smsnds1.exe	Client Bootstrap for NetWare

TABLE 7-6

(Continued)

SMS Executable Files Installed for 32-Bit Clients	
Smstrav.exe	Travel mode to will
Smswiz32.exe	Advertised Programs can't wizard
Snmptrap.exe	SNMP Event to Trap Translator
Swdist32.exe	Software distribution set up on CAP
Swdunis.exe	Software distribution remover
W95ntug.exe	Windows 95 and Windows 98 to Windows NT upgrade wrapper
Wuser32.exe	Remote Control Listening Agent
Boot16wn.exe	Client bootstrap
Clicor.exe	Core client file
Launch16.exe	Client launcher
Mnlaunch.exe	Installs the base components
QryEdit.exe	Query Editor
Rcclic16.exe	Security Manager (reconciler) for Remote Tools
Smsman16.exe	SMS Client Manual Discovery
Swdist16.exe	Software distribution Setup on CAP
Wuser.exe	Remote Control Listening Agent

TABLE 7-7

Dynamic Link Library Files Installed on the SMS Client.

SMS Dynamic Link Library Files Installed for 32-Bit Clients	
_Osw32rc.dll	Used for operating system setup wrapper programs
Abnwcli.dll	Core library file
Bindcli9.dll	Core library for Windows 95/98 bindery clients
Bindclin.dll	Core library for Windows NT bindery agents
Ccim32.dll	Client Component Installation Manager
Ccm.dll	Client Configuration Manager
CliBase.dll	Core library file
Cliex32.dll	Core library file
Clilog.dll	Core library file
Climsgs.dll	Status message to display stringers
Cqmgr32.dll	Copy Queue Manager
Falcli.dll	Core library file

TABLE 7-7

(Continued)

SMS Dynamic Link Library Files Installed for 32-Bit Clients	
Ismif32.dll	Installation status MIF file
Mlaunch.dll	Installs the base components
Mslmcli9.dll	Core library file
Mslmclin.dll	Court library file
Nalcli.dll	NAL-based library
Ndscli9.dll	Core library file for Windows 95 and Windows 98 NDS clients
Ndsclin.dll	Core library file for Windows NT NDS clients
Pem32.dll	Program Execution Manager
Pipcap32.dll	Program information provider for CAP data
Progrm32.dll	APA program class
Smsclreg.dll	Core library file
Smsdiscv.dll	Core library file
Snmpelea.dll	Event to Trap Translator Service
SMS Dynamic Link Library Files (.DLL) Installed for 16-Bit Clients	
Cliex16.dll	Core library file
Ismif16.dll	Installation status MIF file
Regfile.dll	Client Registry
Smslink.dll	16-bit core components
Smsn116.dll	16-bit core components
Smsnlinf.dll	16-bit core components

TABLE 7-8

SMS Directory Structure.

SMS Directory Structure	Sub-Directories	Description
\Clicompo\Swdist32	APA	Advertised Programs Agent
	Hinv	Hardware Inventory Agent
	Licmtr	Software Metering Client Agent
	Remctrl	Remote Control Client Agent
	Sinv	Software Inventory Agent

TABLE 7-8

(Continued)

SMS Directory Structure	Sub-Directories	Description
	Snmpelea	Windows NT Event to SNMP Trap Translator
\Core\Bin		Local copies of the SMS client core acceptable files are stored here.
\Core\Data		Local copies of DDRs, the SMS GUID, and other configuration files
\Logs		.Log and .lo_files for each SMS client component
\NOIDMIFs		Location for a user-created NOIDMIF files that are sent with hardware inventory data

CHAPTER 8

Network Administration and Management with SMS

In this chapter you will learn about:

- Queries and the SMS site database
- Creating administrative reports
- Using the Info Report Designer to create a new report
- Using SNMP (Simple Network Management Protocol) with SMS 2.0

Understanding Queries

The SMS site server database is populated with a wealth of hardware and software objects. Detailed questions, called *queries*, can be asked of the SMS site database to search against a specific set of objects and criteria. When you create a report, you are, in fact, using a query statement. The report is the detailed answer.

An SMS query uses the SMS Query Builder and the WBEM Query Language (WQL), searching the specific objects that make up the SMS site database. The Query Builder uses certain components and terminology when creating queries.

SMS Object Types

The SMS database is made up of objects, and there are several predefined object types that you can use when building a query. Each of these objects is broken down further into subgroups called *attribute classes* and finally into *attributes* that describe the object types. Each object is described by attributes; one object in particular, System Resource, is broken down into subclasses or attribute classes for a more detailed description. Object types are as follows:

- *Advertisement* An advertisement is used for software distribution. There is only one attribute class for advertisements; it contains attributes that describe the data components in an advertisement. An example of an attribute would be the users or collection to which the advertisement was assigned.
- *Package* A package also has one attribute class, with attributes describing the data components used in a package. A package contains programs and the source files to execute them. An example of an attribute would be the path to the installation program.
- *System Resource* This object type has many attribute classes that describe both the discovery and inventory data of the discovered resource, such as a computer system. The system attribute class describes discovery data, and inventory data uses the remaining classes of the system resource object for its description. An example of an attribute would be the BIOS date of the system BIOS.

- *Program* This object type uses a single attribute class for describing the command lines found in an SMS program. An example of an attribute would be the actual command line and syntax.
- *Site* This is made up of a single attribute class containing attributes describing an SMS site object. An example of an attribute would be the site code.
- *User Resource* This is made up of a single attribute class that details the discovery data for user objects discovered in the SMS site. An example of an attribute would be domain users.
- *User Group Resource* This is made up of a single attribute class describing discovery data for user group objects. An example of an attribute would be a global group.

Optional Query Elements

There are optional query elements that can be deployed to filter the results of a query further, including:

- Criterion types and values
- Relational operators
- Logical operators
- Order of precedence

Criterion Types and Values

Once an object type has been selected, the different attribute classes or attributes are used to acquire the exact data from the site database. However, to refine your query, relational operators and direct comparisons can also be used. These vales are called a *criterion type*—where the attribute is the decisive factor being compared to a constant value (also called a simple value) or a relational operator, for example, `is not equal to`.

Some of the SMS criterion values that can be used in queries are as follows:

- *Simple Value* The query attribute is compared to a constant value. For example, if the `Free Space` attribute is used (part of the

`LogicalDisk` attribute class) with a simple value criterion type, a query could be `LogicalDisk . Free Space is greater than '100'`

- *Prompted Value* When the query is executed, the client is prompted for a value.
- *Attribute Reference* A specific attribute is compared to another attribute.
- *Subselective Values* A specific attribute is compared to the results of another query.
- *List of Values* A list of values is compared to a list of constant values.

Constant Data Values

Constant data values are used in expressions when an attribute is compared to a specific data value. The constant data type must be usable by the attribute it is being compared against. Data values include:

- *Numerical Values* Decimal or hexadecimal values.
- *String Values* String values can be created from alphanumeric characters as a reference. Wildcard values can also be used within the string, for example, using `%` when searching for Pentium CPUs: `%Pentium%`.
- *Date and Time Values* If the attribute uses a date and time data type.

Relational Operators

A relational operator uses the specified value to compare against the attribute in the query. They can be numerical, string, or date and time:

- *Numerical operators*
  Is equal to
  Is not equal to
  Is greater than
  Is less than

Is greater than or equal to
Is less than or equal to

- *String relational operators*
  Is equal to
  Is not equal to
  Is like
  Is not like
  Is less than
  Is greater than
  Is less than or equal to
  Is greater than or equal to
- *Date and time operators*
  Date- Is
  Is not
  Is after
  Is before
  Is on or after
  Year is
  Year is not
  Year is after
  Year is before
  Year is on or after

Logical Operators

A logical operator can be used to join together two expressions within a query. Examples of logical operators are as follows:

- `AND` The two expressions that are joined by this operator are searched by the query to find the objects in the database that satisfy *both of the expressions*. For example, `"Free Space is less than 300"` can be joined with `"Processor Name is like %Pentium%"` to produce:

```
"Free Space is less than 300" AND "Processor Name is like
%Pentium%"
```

- `OR` Two expressions that are joined by this operator are searched by the query to find the objects in the database that satisfy *either of the expressions*. For instance:

```
"Processor Name is like %AMD%" AND "Processor Name is like
%Pentium%"
```

- NOT The two expressions that are joined by this operator are searched by the query to find the objects in the database that *do not satisfy the expression following the* NOT.

Order of Precedence

If logical operators are used, they will be evaluated in a specific order:

1. Expressions set inside parentheses are always evaluated first.
2. Expressions preceded by NOT are second.
3. Expressions joined by AND are third.
4. Expressions joined by OR are evaluated last.

Using Queries to Search the SMS Site Database

SMS comes with several predefined queries that are found in the Queries folder in the SMS Administrator console. Selecting and right-clicking on a query displays the Run Query context menu, as shown in Figure 8-1. The results of the query appear in the details pane.

Modifying an Existing Query

You can modify every predefined query rather than having to start from scratch. To do so:

1. First, select a query, for example, *All Systems*.
2. Next, right-click on the query, and from the context menu, select *Properties*. The All Systems properties will appear. In the properties, the Object Type window shows you the predefined objects that can be used for querying the SMS site database.
3. Choose *Collection Limiting* to select the collection this query will search when it is executed.
4. Click on the *Edit Query Statement* button to see the existing query statement language shown in Figure 8-2.

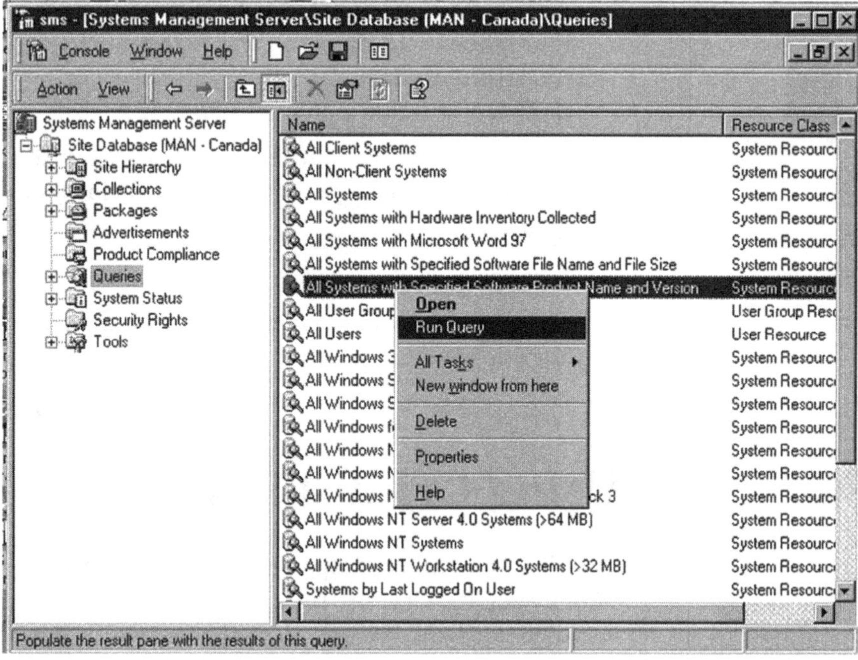

Figure 8-1 Running a predefined query.

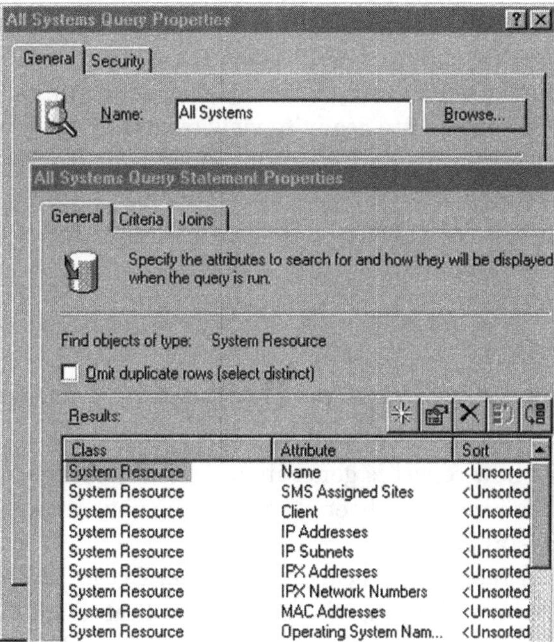

Figure 8-2 Query language for All Systems.

Each class attribute can be double-clicked on to view the class and attribute. Clicking on the Select button allows you to change the attribute selected.

5. Select the *Criteria* tab. This query has no criteria values defined. Right-click on the *Gold Star* icon to view the properties and to select the criterion type, the attribute class, and the logical operator to use.

NOTE. *You could also select Query from the New menu option to display an undefined query that could be built from the start.*

Using Crystal Reports

Creating and running reports in SMS 2.0 is accomplished with a product called Seagate Crystal Info. It is installed automatically if SMS was installed with the Express Installation. With a custom installation, you must select it as one of the installation options.

Crystal Info uses an ODBC driver to communicate with the site server database. Web-Based Enterprise Management (WBEM) data classes are used to both query and manage the database information. Prebuilt reports are included with SMS for general configuration, hardware inventory, product compliance, queries, and status.

These reports are ready to view once they have been scheduled to run and once they run successfully. Once run, the reports can be printed, saved as RPT files to be used on other site server databases, or exported to another data format. The components that drive Crystal Info are listed in Table 8-1.

Generating a Report: Overview

When a new report is generated, Crystal Info executes the Info Designer. Once the report has been designed, the new reports template is stored in the Crystal database.

When reports are scheduled to run, Crystal Info accesses the Crystal API Library, choosing the subroutine that communicates with the Info Server. The report template to be used is loaded from \SMS\CLINFO\

TABLE 8-1

Crystal Info system components.

Component	Details	Filename
Info APS	Is the automated process scheduler service responsible for responding to user requests from queries generating reports	APS32.EXE
Info Agent	Generates the report that can be viewed or printed	CIAGNT32.EXE
Info Sentinel	Is installed on every computer that has a remote SMS Administrator console with Crystal Info installed	SENTNL32.EXE
Crystal Info for SMS	Is the SMS Administrator console snap-in	CISANPIN.DLL
Info Report Designer	Creates or makes changes to the report template files	CRW32.EXE
Info Server	Processes the report template files	CIPE32.DLL
Crystal API Library	Contains components used by Crystal Info	CIAPI32.DLL
Crystal Database	Contains report object details	CRYSTAL.MDB
Crystal Info Viewer	Displays the report data in the SMS Administrator console	CRVIEWER.DLL
WBEM ODBC Driver	Used for accessing data from the SMS site database	WBEMDR32.DLL

SAMPLES\SMS. The report is then processed, creating a new copy of the report containing the queried data that is then saved to \SMS\CLINFO\OUTPUT.

The new report is sent back to the Info APS service, which then sends the report and data to the Crystal Info Viewer. The Info Viewer displays the report in the SMS Administrator console.

To create and generate Crystal reports, you must be using an account that has access to the WBEM data classes; the easiest solution is to be a member of the SMS Admin user group that was assigned the proper permissions when SMS was installed.

Report Server Requirements

If your SMS site is expanding by leaps and bounds, using Crystal Info for generating reports can be a RAM-consuming process. For example, each report that queries the database returning 500 objects will require 25 MB of RAM for processing. The size of your client base and the amount of reports that are generated are the determining factors.

Since reports are generated from collections, and collections increase in size over time on an expanding network, the number of objects in the site server database will increase. Therefore, the amount of processing power and RAM required will increase.

According to Seagate, the manufacturer of Crystal Info, Info APS can support 500 concurrent users if it's running on a Pentium 350 MHz with 128 MB of RAM. The likelihood that you will have 500 users generating reports at one time is remote; however, if you generate a lot of reports, you may want to consider a separate report server. If you're deploying a very large SMS hierarchy, some preplanning as to the number of reports and queries will be necessary.

Crystal Info Preconfigured Reports

Several reports are supplied with SMS to assist you in administering your network. These reports can be used in their present format, or they can be modified using the Info Report Designer. The reports supplied with SMS are detailed in Table 8-2.

Each report is created from objects that inform Crystal Info about the report layout, what information to pull from the database, and the queries to be used each time the report is run. Once a report is scheduled and run, a copy of the object is filled with the results queried from the site database and stored in SMS\CLINFO\OUTPUT.

SMS Task: Scheduling a Preconfigured Report

Crystal Info is built into the SMS Administrator console and is located in the Reports folder. When you select a report, the details pane provides information on each report and its current status. Three icons are used to indicate the status and schedule of each preconfigured report: Unscheduled, Ready to Run, and Failure, as shown in Figure 8-3.

TABLE 8-2 Crystal Info reports.

Report Name	Category	Filename
New Systems Discovered	Configuration	CInfo\samples\sms\config\cf_05.rpt
Servers and Their Roles by Site	Configuration	CInfo\samples\sms\config\cf__04.rpt
Systems Discovered but Not Assigned to a Site	Configuration	CInfo\samples\sms\config\cf__03.rpt
Windows 98 Upgrade Candidates by Site	Hardware Inventory	CInfo\samples\sms\hardware\hi_14.rpt
Windows NT 5 Upgrade Candidates by Site and Role	Hardware Inventory	CInfo\samples\sms\hardware\hi_13.rpt
Windows NT Service Pack by Site	Hardware Inventory	CInfo\samples\sms\hardware\hi_12.rpt
BIOS Versions in Use by Site	Product Compliance	CInfo\samples\sms\prodcomp\pc_02.rpt
Manufacturers by Filename and File Size	Product Compliance	CInfo\samples\sms\prodcomp\pc_01b.rpt
Manufactures by Product Name and Version	Product Compliance	CInfo\samples\sms\prodcomp\pc_01a.rpt
Systems by Filename and File Size	Product Compliance	CInfo\samples\sms\prodcomp\pc_03b.rpt
Systems by Product Name and Version	Product Compliance	CInfo\samples\sms\prodcomp\pc_03a.rpt
All Systems by System Name	Queries	CInfo\samples\sms\queries\q_02.rpt

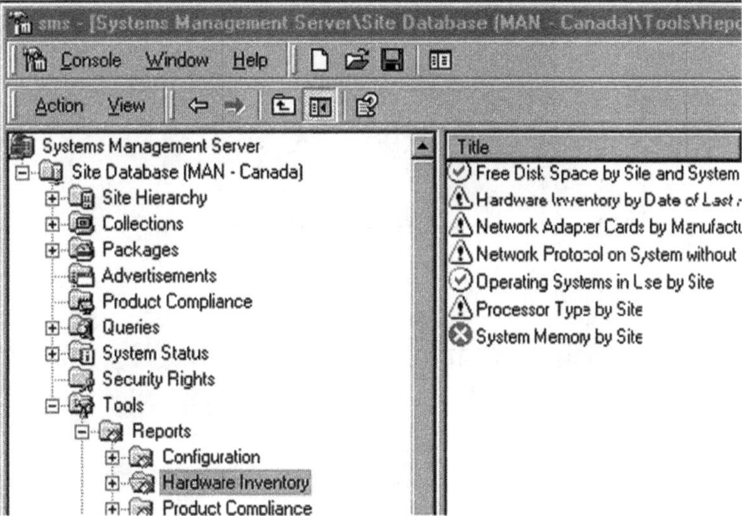

Figure 8-3 Crystal Info report details.

The steps to configure a report with Crystal Info are as follows:

1. Open the SMS Administrator console, and highlight the *Reports* folder.
2. Select the subfolder containing the report you want to schedule, for example, *Windows NT Service Packs by Site*. In the details pane for this report, notice the message that states this report has not been scheduled. (Reports must be scheduled to run and execute before you can view the results.)
3. In the console tree right-click on the report, and from the All Tasks context menu select *Schedule Report* to show the report's properties. In the General tab, the path to the report and the title of the report is shown. Both can be modified.
4. Select the *Schedule* tab. Choose a time to run the report—right now or at a specific time and date. At the bottom of the Schedule tab is the Recurrence option, which defines when and how often the report runs: once right now, or daily, weekly, or monthly at a specified day and time. See Figure 8-4.

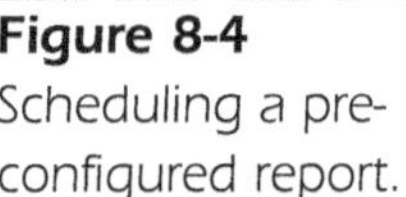

Figure 8-4
Scheduling a pre-configured report.

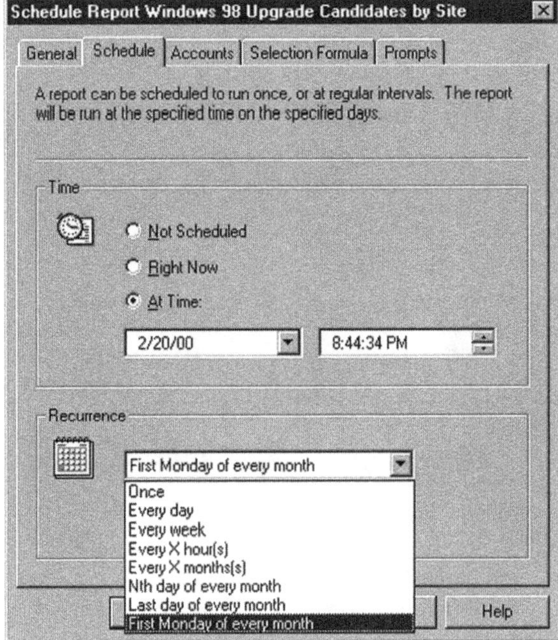

The Account tab is used to enter the required logon account and password that can access the SMS site database. Usually, the administrator will have the required "Log on as a service" right.

The Selection Formula tab is used to change the formula used to select records from the database. The Prompts tab allows you to change any assigned parameter values.

Clicking on OK saves your changes. When the report is run, the results will be displayed in the details pane of the SMS Administrator console.

Once the report is generated, you may also print the report.

SMS Task: Creating a New Report

In order to create a new template for a report, some background programming and database experience is helpful. When a report accesses the SMS site database, the tables of data are WBEM objects defined by resource classes; the same resource classes are used in building queries.

Once selected, each object class can be broken down into many properties of each class. Each property can be chosen for a field in a report created with the Info Report Designer. A summary of available object classes is listed in Table 8-3. For a complete listing of SMS objects, review the appendixes of the *Systems Management Server 2.0 Resource Guide*.

To create a new report:

1. Open the SMS Administrator console and select the *Reports* folder.
2. Right-click on the *Reports* folder, and from the context menu All Tasks, select *Design New Report*. This starts the Info Report Designer.
3. Click on the *New Report* button, and select *Standard* expert, as shown in Figure 8-5.
4. The data source that will be used for generating this report must be specified: Click on the *SQL/ODBC* button, and from the Server Type menu, scroll down and select *ODBC–WBEM Source* as the data source. Click on *OK*.
5. You must now log in to the site database with a valid user name, password, and server name. Click on the *Connect* button to attach to the site server database.

TABLE 8-3 Resource classes for queries and reports.

Object Class	Properties
SMS_Advertisement	AdvertisementID, AdvertisementName, CollectionID
SMS_Collection	CurrentStatus, Name, LastRefreshTime
SMS_CollectionMember	Domain, IsClient, ResourceID, SiteCode, SMSID
SMS_Package	Description, Icon, MIFName, MIFPublisher, Name
SMS_Program	CommandLine, Description, Duration, ProgramName, WorkingDirectory
SMS_SupportedPlatforms	OSName, OSPlatform, OSMaxVersion
SMS_DistributionPoint	ServerNALPath, PackageID, SourceSite, Status
SMS_PDF_Package	Name, PDFFilename, Publisher, Status, Version
SMS_Site	InstallDir, ServerName, SiteCode, Status
SMS_Identification	ServiceAccountName, SMSBuildNumber, SMSSiteServer, ThisSiteCode
SMS_R_System	Client, IPAddresses, IPSubnets, LastLogonUserDomain, LastLogonUserName, OperatingSystemNameandVersion, SystemRole
SMS_R_User	Name, NetworkOperatingSystem, ResourceID, UniqueUserName
SMS_R_UserGroup	Name, NetworkOperatingSystem, ResourceID, UniqueUsergroupName UserGroupName
SMS_R_IPNetwork	SubnetAddress, SubnetMask, SMSAssignedSites
SMS_G_System_Workstation_Status	GroupID, LastHardwareScan, LastSoftwareScan, ResourceID, TimeStamp
SMS_G_System_CollectedFile	CollectionDate, FileName, FilePath, FileSize, LocalFilePath
SMS_ G_System_SoftwareFile	CreationDate, FileCount, FileDescription, FileName, FileSize, ProductID
SMS_G_System_Display_Configuration	Information about the installed display adapter
SMS_ G_System_Network_Client	Information on the installed network client(s)

6. From the Namespace Selection path, scroll down and select the site server database checkbox, as shown in Figure 8-6. Click on *OK*.
7. Successfully logging in to the site server database will display the Choose SQL Table screen. From the SQL Tables box, select the tables you want to include in the report, and then click on *Add*.

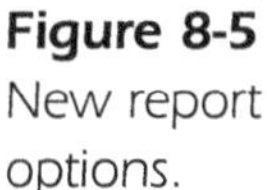

Figure 8-5
New report options.

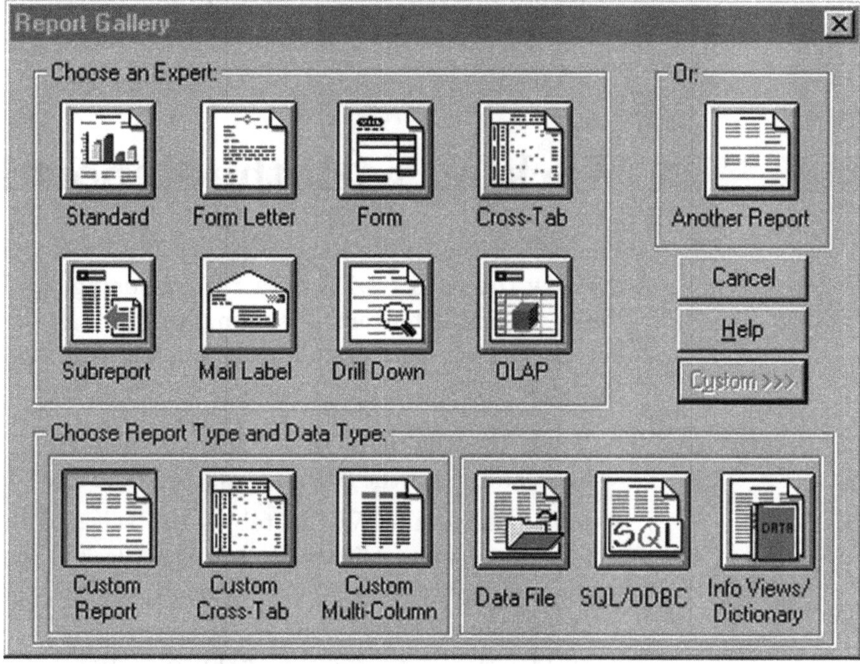

Figure 8-6
Selecting the site server database.

Under the Data tab, the Create Report Expert will then display the selected object classes to build the report from.

Working with the Report Expert

The tab screens of the Report Expert allow you to build your report and preview the report with data records using the Preview Report and Preview Sample buttons. A summary of the tab screens and their use is detailed below; an example of a finished report using the Info Report Designer and the Report Expert is shown in Figure 8-7.

- *Data* Use the SQL/ODBC button to connect to the site server database, and select the SQL tables\objects to add to the report.
- *Link* Shows the WBEM tables you selected through the Data tab, with the common fields to each class linked together. Depending on the complexity of your report, choose the link that is the most useful, and delete the other links.
- *Fields* Select the database fields to include in the report, as shown in Figure 8-8.

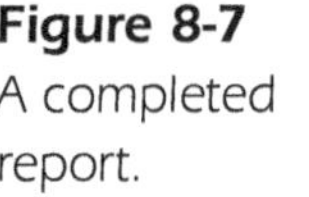

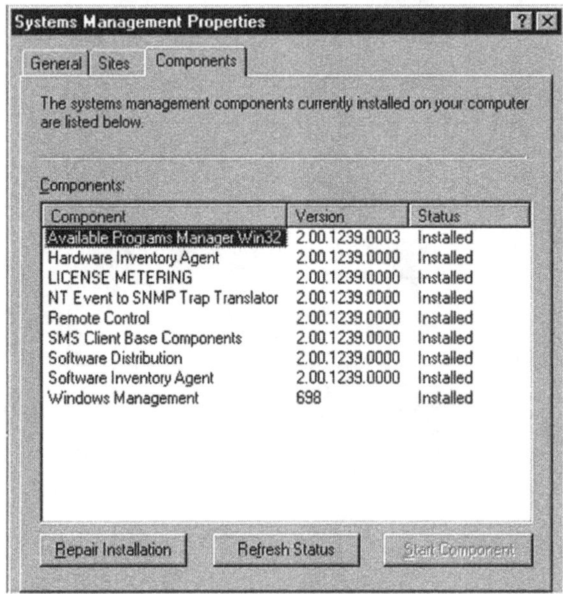

Figure 8-7
A completed report.

User Groups

2/20/00

Name	NetworkOperatingSystem	UniqueUsergroupNan	UsergroupName
HEADQUARTERS\Doi	Windows NT	HEADQUARTERS\Domain Admins	Domain Admins
HEADQUARTERS\Doi	Windows NT	HEADQUARTERS\Domain Guests	Domain Guests
HEADQUARTERS\Doi	Windows NT	HEADQUARTERS\Domain Users	Domain Users
HEADQUARTERS\Hel	Windows NT	HEADQUARTERS\Help Desk	Help Desk
HEADQUARTERS\mar	Windows NT	HEADQUARTERS\managers	managers
HEADQUARTERS\SM	Windows NT	HEADQUARTERS\SMSInternalCliG	SMSInternalCliGrp

Figure 8-8 Select the database fields for the report.

- *Sort* Design how the fields will be grouped and ordered in the report.
- *Total* Select any fields where a subtotal or a count is required.
- *Style* Enter the title of your report and the style to be viewed and printed.

Adding a Report to the SMS Console Tree

To add a report to the Report folders in the SMS Administrator console:

1. First, select an existing subfolder in which to store the report.
2. If you wish to create a new folder for your custom reports, right-click on the subfolder, and from the New context menu, select *Folder*. Then enter the name of the new folder to create.
3. To add a report to the new folder, highlight and right-click on the folder. From the New context menu, select *Report Object*. Search for the report (.RPT) to be added to the selected folder, and enter a name for the report.
4. Click on *OK* to finish the process.

The Set Location Tool

If SMS has been deployed at multiple sites, reports may have been generated and stored at the different locations. Using the Set Location tool, you can define the path for the report or reports that you want to run.

1. At the Site Server's command prompt where SMS is installed execute: SMS\CLINFO\WINNT\SETLOCATION.EXE.
2. Enter the site code into the Set Location dialog box.
3. Enter the site server's name into the Server dialog box, using the UNC path.
4. In the Account dialog box, enter the account that you are using to link to the SMS site database.
5. Now enter the full UNC network path that points to the report you wish to run, and click on the *Update* button.
6. Open the SMS Administrator console, and select the *Reports* folder found under the *Tools* folder.
7. Select and right-click on the report for which the path was defined with the Set Location tool. From the context menu, select *All Tasks* and *Schedule* to schedule the execution of the selected report.

Understanding SNMP

SNMP (Simple Network Management Protocol) is a term that is used but not generally understood in the computer industry. As its name implies, SNMP is a network protocol for network management, and it is supported across any TCP/IP-based network environment.

This does not mean that you have to use this protocol in order to have a functioning network or that SNMP is "simple" to use just because it's part of the name. Still, it's not very complicated; however, like any network protocol, there are some configuration and setup issues.

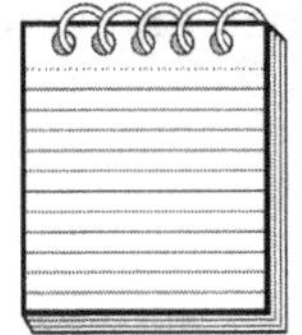

NOTE. *If your company uses Computer Associates' Unicenter, HP's OpenView, or IBM's NetView, then SNMP is being used as the communication protocol.*

Think of any network protocol, SNMP included, as merely the mechanism used to move data from one location to another. On any network, if a particular node wishes to communicate with another node, such as a workstation and a server, a server to another server, or even a workstation to another workstation, both nodes must be able to first talk the same language as they attempt to communicate. Otherwise, the conversation fails.

SNMP provides network management for many hardware types of devices installed across the enterprise network that support this protocol, including bridges, routers, gateways, hubs, workstations, and servers. Implemented at the Application/Presentation layer of the OSI network layers and the Process/Application layer of TCP/IP, an SNMP Software Management Agent, present in each hardware device that is being managed, sends and updates its current status and configuration to a network management station (NMS).

A specific database format called an MIB (Management Information Base) is used to store SNMP information. The MIB is built from hardware objects that each host's SNMP Agent MIB contains and provides to the network management station. The MIB contains information depending on each type of hardware device.

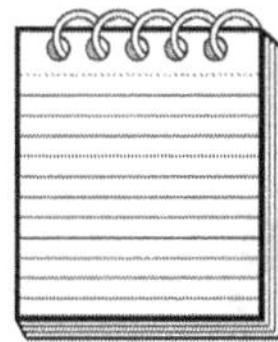

NOTE. *The standard for the MIB database is currently defined as MIB II.*

The network management system uses the following commands for communicating with the SNMP agents for gathering information or resetting the host's MIB:

- *GET* The requested hardware and software data is delivered to the network management system
- *GET-NEXT* The next host's record from the MIB database is delivered to the network management system.
- *SET* The network management system directs an agent to reset the host's data stored in the MIB database.

The only command initiated by the client agent is the `TRAP` command, which is initiated when a failure or a specific event occurs at the host location by the SNMP agent. The data is "trapped" and sent to the network management system console.

NT Server does not have an NMS console; however, if you are using third-party network management software, you can install the SNMP network service on any Windows NT workstation or server, thereby turning it into a SNMP host.

Hardware and operating system objects are then collected and stored in the NT host's MIB, which is then sent to the NMH. WINS, TCP/IP, and IIS (FTP, Gopher, and HTTP) can be monitored using the SNMP protocol; each network service has its own MIB.

Both TCP/IP and IPX/SPX protocols are supported by the NT SNMP Service, as well as Windows 95/98 systems.

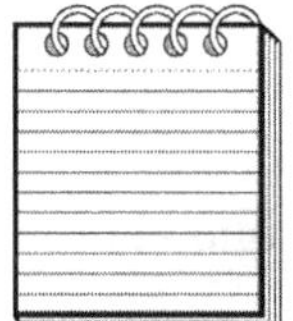

***NOTE**. For the complete list of supported objects, download RFC (Request for Comments) 1213 from www.internic.org.*

If you're seeing a conflict of interest between the services and features provided by SMS and those provided by a third-party SNMP network management system, SMS 2.0 shows Microsoft doing what it does best: extending the operating system at the expense of its competitors.

With regards to SNMP, SMS fits into the picture by accepting NT events destined for the standard event log and converting them into SNMP traps, which are then sent to a third-party network management console.

Installing the SNMP Service

Install the SNMP service:

1. In the Control Panel network applet, select the *Services* tab.
2. Click on the *Add* button and select *SNMP Service* to install the network service from the NT workstation or server CD-ROM. (See Figure 8-9).
3. In the Agent tab, check the Services checkboxes that match the computer system's service. Applications and End-to-End are typically enabled.
4. Select the *Traps* tab; add the community name used and the trap destination IP address of the NMS.
5. Close the SNMP service, and reboot when prompted.
6. Make sure to reapply the service pack currently being used by the NT system.

When the SNMP Agent communicates with the NMS using TCP/IP, it uses the host's IP address and computer name for identification; IPX/SPX identification uses the network address and the MAC (Media Access Control) address.

Each network management system is identified to the SNMP hosts by a community name, and each community can contain multiple SNMP network management systems.

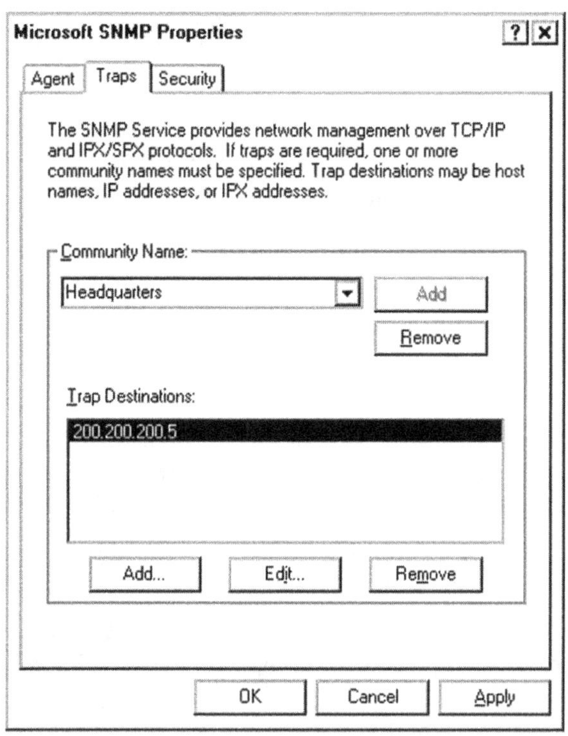

Figure 8-9 SNMP Service properties for NT.

Using SNMP with SMS 2.0

Every Windows NT event that has been captured and stored in the event logs for system, security, or application can be translated into an SNMP event. Each selected event is sent to the Event to Trap Translator, which translates the NT event into an SNMP trap, sending the information to the network management system. In order to use the Event to Trap Translator Client Agent, the following components must be installed:

- Windows 4.0, Windows 95, or Windows 98 client
- The TCP/IP protocol
- The SNMP service

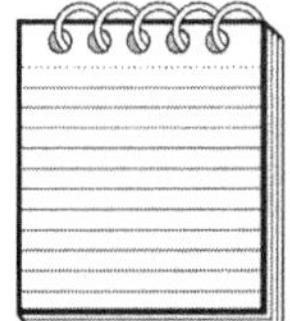

NOTE. *IPX/SPX is not supported by SMS for SNMP support unless TCP/IP is also installed.*

Configuring the Event to Trap Translator

The Event to Trap Translator Client Agent is enabled at the SMS Administrator console in the Client Agents folder.

1. Double-click on the *Event to Trap Translator Client Agent*, as shown in Figure 8-10, to view its properties.
2. Enable the *Enable event to trap translation on clients* option, and click on *OK*.
3. On a client's PC that has the NT SNMP service installed and configured, open the Control Panel and select the *System Management* applet. Make sure that the NT Event to Trap Translator is present and installed, as shown in Figure 8-11.
4. At the SMS Administrative console, select *Collections* and highlight the *All Systems* collection.
5. From the details pane, select and right-click on a client that has the SNMP services installed; from the All Tasks menu, select *Start Event to Trap Translator*. The SNMP Event to Trap translator utility will now load.
6. Click on the *Edit* button to load an event—any application, security, or system log event that will be captured and converted into an SNMP trap.

Other Event to Trap Translator configurations must also be set up through the following buttons:

- *Settings* Set the size of the trap to a small size, such as 1024 KB (the default is 4096 KB) and define the number of traps to be sent.

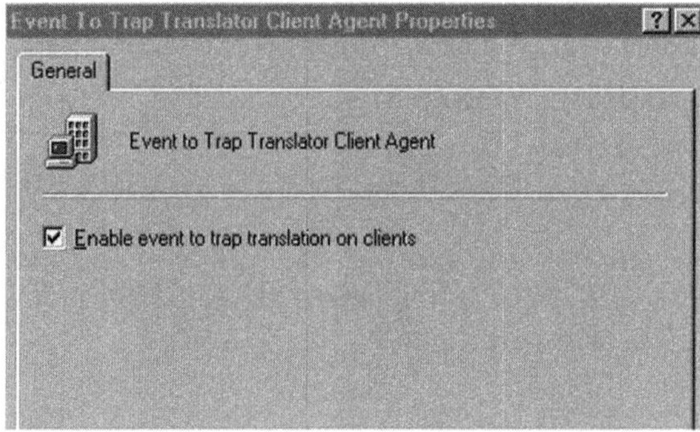

Figure 8-10 Event to Trap Translator Agent properties.

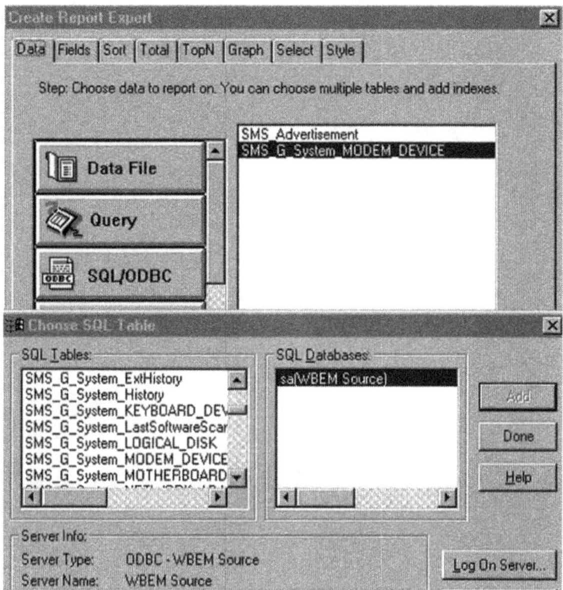

Figure 8-11 Client components installed by SMS.

- *Export* Change the generated traps into TXT format, which is readable by most network management systems.
- *Properties* Set the maximum thresholds limits for when traps are generated

Although SNMP with SMS 2.0 has its benefits, you must have a third-party product to take advantage of this feature. Also, events to be monitored must be added to the Event to Trap Translator utility before any events will be actually trapped and sent to the network management system.

CHAPTER 9

Software Metering

In this chapter you will learn how to:

- Deploy software metering
- Use the Resource Manager to set your user, group, and computer permissions
- Set up the Software Metering Client Agent
- Add both single and suite software products to software metering
- Use the Report and Graph Wizard to generate software-metering reports

Understanding Software Metering

Software metering is an SMS feature that allows you to keep track of software that is used in your organization. If your job is network administrator, in many jurisdictions, you will be found legally responsible if your company uses unlicensed copies of operating system software and application software. The biggest cost in networking is usually the license fees paid to software applications; the cost is always much larger than anticipated.

If you have many network users, software metering can be used to silently monitor all software applications across the SMS hierarchy. Once software-licensing rules have been defined and enabled, software metering can actively enforce the restriction of software usage without a valid license.

Software metering can enforce the defined rules through the user's user name, computer name, group membership, time of day, and available licenses. The benefits of software metering to you and your company are many; however, the most important benefit is that your company's and your own personal legal liability will be limited. Through software metering, detailed reports can be generated showing that proper software-metering practices are carried out as part of regular network maintenance. Other benefits are as follows:

- You can show that enough licenses have been purchased for the software you currently have.
- In a large network environment, software needs can be defined with overall license balancing.
- Users that break licensing rules can be identified.
- The purchase of more software licenses than needed is prevented.

Software metering works in the background, monitoring software applications used by all 32-bit users (Windows 95, Windows 98, and Windows NT clients) across the entire SMS site hierarchy at any location, network, or local hard drive and even on the Internet.

The pieces that make up the software-metering component include the site server, the software-metering server, and the SMS client, which are linked to a separate SQL database called the software-metering database.

Once software metering has been set up and enabled, the Software Metering Client Agent starts its job of monitoring the active SMS clients and their current software usage, sending the collected software-metering data to the SQL database. The software-metering database includes licensing information and executes the License Metering service. Both current and historical software application usage information is sent to the software-metering database from the local SMS client. A memory cache is used to temporarily store the client's current software usage and license requests.

NOTE. *Software metering is not supported for 16-bit Windows and MS-DOS clients, nor can the software-metering server be installed on an Alpha server. The database must also be an SQL database.*

Offline and Online Mode

There are two modes of operation for software metering: offline and online.

Offline mode The default mode is offline mode, where the focus is on tracking the usage of software licenses, not enforcement. Before you can enforce software metering, you first need to find out what software is being used across your network.

The Software Metering Client Agent sends the SMS client's software usage data records for both licensed and unlicensed software applications to a software-metering server on a set schedule. Any user is allowed to use any software application; no user, group, or computer permissions are assigned to any software application limiting its use.

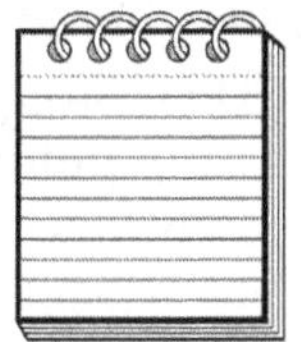

NOTE. *License balancing between software-metering servers does not take place in offline mode, as licenses are not being restricted, just tracked.*

Online mode This mode is enabled by mandating real-time license verification through the Software Metering Client Agent. When an SMS client makes a license request for a particular software application, the request is sent to the software-metering server.

If the user has been assigned permission to use the software that was requested, the number of available licenses is checked. A license is granted if one is available. If no licenses are available, the user can be placed in the callback queue and notified when a license becomes available, and the queue time period can be defined.

If the callback queue has been enabled and a user who has been granted a license for usage of a software application doesn't use the software but simply hoards it, the license is revoked, freeing up the license for another user that has been left waiting in the callback queue. The length of time in which a user can use a software application can also be defined.

License Balancing

License balancing between multiple software-metering servers within the SMS site hierarchy is enabled by default. When a user requests a software license, the primary site server communicates with other existing software-metering servers to see if any spare licenses are available. All software-metering data is sent to and from existing parent and child sites. Any new product license information, plus additions and subtractions from the excluded programs list, moves down through the SMS site structure. All user requests and metering data move up through the existing SMS structure to the parent site.

If your SMS hierarchy contains both child and parent sites, the parent site balances its software licenses with the child sites; however, the child sites do not send any available licenses up to a parent site.

The location where the application software is installed can become important, depending on the number of licensed users you have in your company. Software application licensing information moves in one direction—downward. Metering data about a software application is transferred to the site where the application was registered. Therefore, a software application that is registered at a child site generates software-metering data for the clients located in the child site that remains in the child's site; it will not be transferred to the parent site.

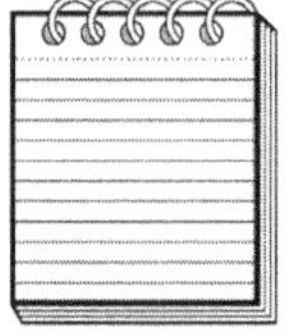

NOTE. *The sharing of licenses assumes that the software installation is network-based rather than local. It's impossible to share a local license for locally installed software with another local user that does not have the software installed; however, if the user goes ahead and installs the software locally, he or she could then be denied access to the software they just installed.*

Setting Up the Software-Metering Server

The primary site server or any other defined site server can perform the role of the software-metering server. If you install the SMS using Express Setup, the software-metering component was installed; a custom installation of SMS required the component to be selected for installation. The computer that performs the software-metering role runs the SMS License service and the SMS Executive threads assigned to this service.

The SMS License service requires a domain user account for performing license service jobs in the background on the software-metering server. It also communicates with any other software-metering components; the default account created at installation is the SWMAccount, with administrative privileges and the advanced user right "Logon as a service."

SMS Task: Defining a Software-Metering Server

To activate a site server as a software-metering server, load the SMS Administrative console on the selected site server. Then:

1. Open the site system's folder and right-click in the details pane; from the context menu, select *New* and *Windows NT Server*. The properties for NT Server appear as shown in Figure 9-1.
2. At the General tab, click on the *Set* button, and enter the name of the NT server that will be assigned the role of software-metering server. (Other roles could be assigned at this time as well.)
3. In the Software Metering Server tab, check the *Use this site system as a software metering server* checkbox.
4. Accept or change the default path to the data cache used, along with the time zone.
5. Check and make sure the service account has been defined as SWMAccount.
6. Click on *OK* to save your changes.
7. In the Control Panel of the selected site server, open the *Services* applet, and make sure the License Metering service has been installed and started successfully.

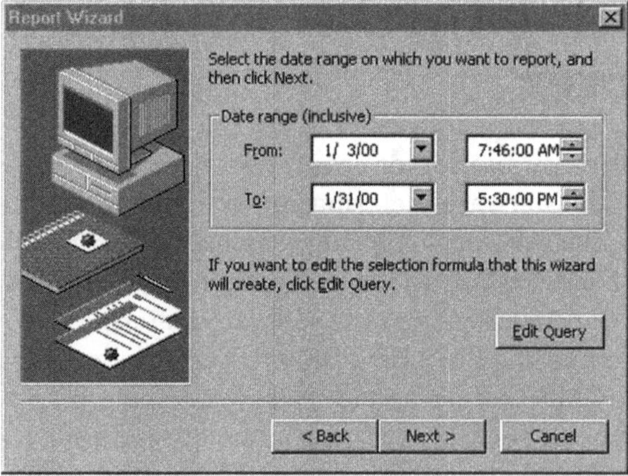

Figure 9-1
Site system properties for NT.

Activating and Defining the Software Metering Client Agent

Once software metering has been activated, the Software Metering Client Agent on the site server must be configured as well.

1. Through the SMS Administrative console, select the *Component Configuration* folder; the Software Metering component should be visible in the details pane.
2. Double-click on the software-metering component to show its current properties, as shown in Figure 9-2.

The properties that are set through this component are in force for the entire SMS site hierarchy. The tabs are as follows.

General

In the General tab, define the policy for the registered versions of the software. Select *Full* for an exact version match. Select *Partial* if the version match can be a number—for example, 8.0—that will apply to all versions of the software application as long as the version number starts with 8.

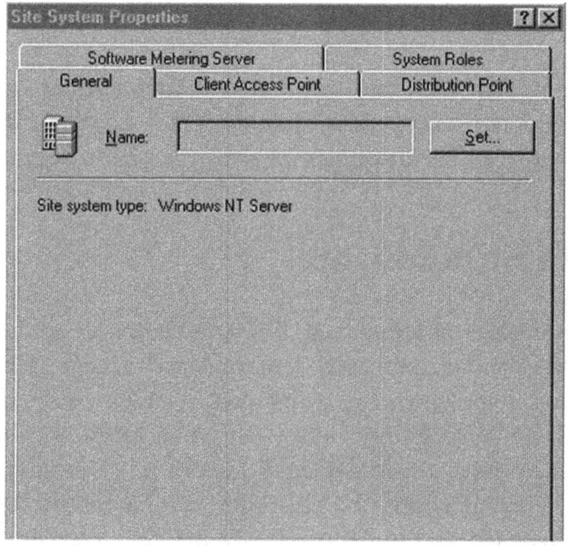

Figure 9-2 Properties of the software-metering component.

Also select how the software-metering service will recognize the program name. Standard defines the software name as the EXE file that starts the application, and Original allows SMS to read the file header information for the application's original name. It is becoming common for 32-bit applications to store this information in the file header.

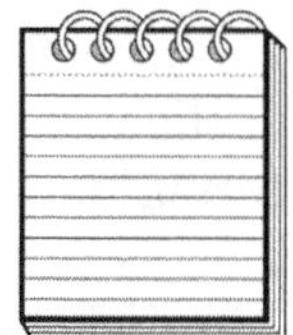

NOTE. *This also means that the end user can't rename a software application to get around being detected by SMS.*

Local

This tab allows you to define the local scheduling for license balancing, site management, and data collation. Site Management specifies the schedule when collected data is sent from a parent site to a child site if multiple software-metering sites are installed and enabled. License Balancing, Site Collation, and Data Collation are set to occur every 4 hours by default; changing these to smaller values can alter your network bandwidth as well, but it might be necessary if software is primarily installed in network locations rather than on local PCs.

Intersite

Through this tab, intersite license management between multiple software-metering servers is enabled. Once enabled, the schedule for sharing license information can be set in minutes, hour, or days.

Data Summation

When data is summarized, a single record is created from the multiple records of each software application's usage. This can save a large amount of storage space over time. As an example, if 10 of your users run Microsoft Word 4 times a day per week, there would be 200 records generated by software metering (10 users × 4 × a day × 5 days in the work week). If you check the checkbox, the schedule for summarization for both licensed and unlicensed data are set together. Therefore, the example for users running Microsoft Word would produce 1 record instead of 200. Individual rules for both licensed and unlicensed data can be individually defined as to the age of the data (hour, day, week, year) and the amount of detail to summarize (day, month, week).

The Software Metering Client Agent

The Software Metering Client Agent provides the intelligence behind the software-metering service, keeping its eyes on what the client is doing and performing research courtesy of the software-metering database. Application software that each SMS client attempts to use is analyzed and either permitted or denied; the software that is used is reported to the software-metering server database.

If the Software Metering Agent cannot find a software-metering server when requesting or sending metering data, it stores the client's software usage on the local hard drive, transferring the data to the software-metering server when communication is reestablished.

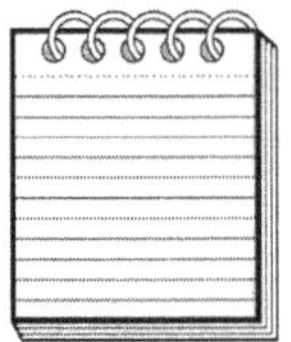

NOTE. *Mobile notebook users can be tracked even when they are not attached to the network. Licensing data and software choices are stored locally until the client reconnects to the network.*

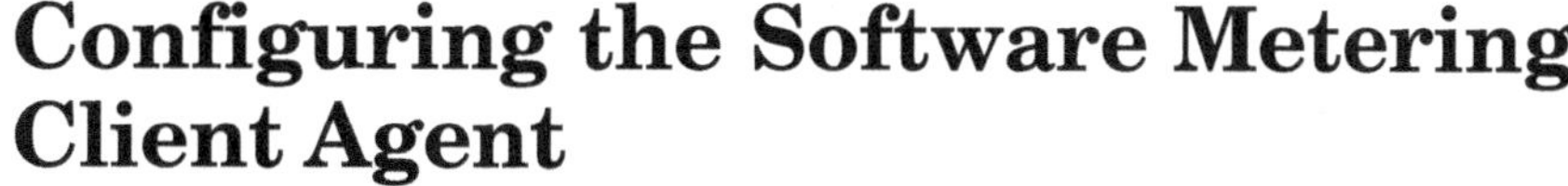

Configuring the Software Metering Client Agent

You define how the Software Metering Client Agent does its job through the SMS Administrative console in the Client Agent folder by double-clicking the Software Metering Client Agent. The properties for the metering agent are shown in Figure 9-3. Tabs are as follows.

General

In the General tab, checking the Enable Software Metering on Clients option starts the software-metering process in the offline, "reporting but not denying" mode. Checking the Force Real-Time License Verification option toggles the system into online, "Big Brother is watching" mode. The number of retries and the delay retrying can also be set here. If the client agent cannot communicate with the software-metering server, it remains in offline mode for the time equal to the defined "delay before retrying." While it is waiting in this imposed delay, it still continues to

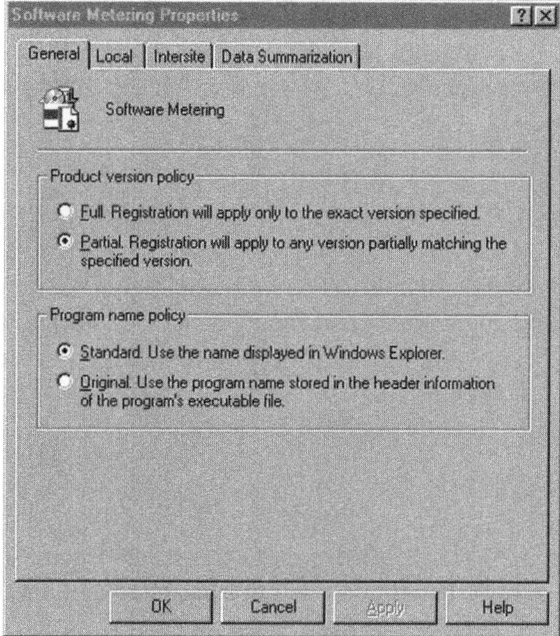

Figure 9-3 Properties of the Software Metering Client Agent.

monitor the client's software usage. The default delay setting is 15 minutes.

Timings

Communication timings between the SMS client and the Software Metering Client Agent are defined here. Settings include the following:

- *Configuration polling* Defines the schedule by which the client agent requests updated licensing information from the License Server service and sends client's data back to the software-metering server.
- *Client time-out settings* Defines when and on what schedule in minutes the SMS client checks in with the metering server, letting it know that it's still active.
- *Callback settings* Defines the length of time a license request is placed in the callback queue when no free licenses are available. Through the Granted callback grace period, you can define the time frame the user has to accept a license that has been freed up and offered to the user.

Checked-out

Here you can customize the message presented in the dialog box to the end user when a software license currently in use is about to expire. See Figure 9-4.

Denials

In this tab you can customize the message presented in the dialog box to the end user when a software license request is denied. The time the denial message is shown on the user's screen can range from 1 second to 24 hours.

Inactivity

The Inactivity tab allows you to customize the message presented in the dialog box to the end user when a software application has not been used for a long period of time.

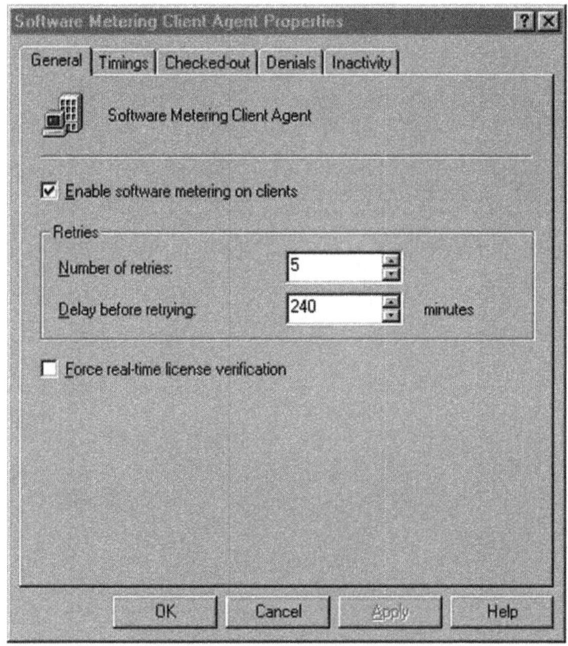

Figure 9-4 Custom messages can be created.

Once the enabling and configuring of software metering and the Software Metering Client Agent is complete, software metering will start on your site after 15 minutes. Now the software applications and licensing restrictions and options must be defined through the setup of the Software Metering tool. Until configuration has been defined and set, all software applications will run without restrictions on the site.

Configuring the Software Metering Tool

The Software Metering tool is opened though the SMS Administrative console from the Tools folder. Right-clicking on Software Metering displays the All Tasks context menu. Select *Start Software Metering* to configure the Software Metering console. The screen shown in Figure 9-5 appears.

Several tasks need to be defined through the Software Metering console to complete the software characteristics.

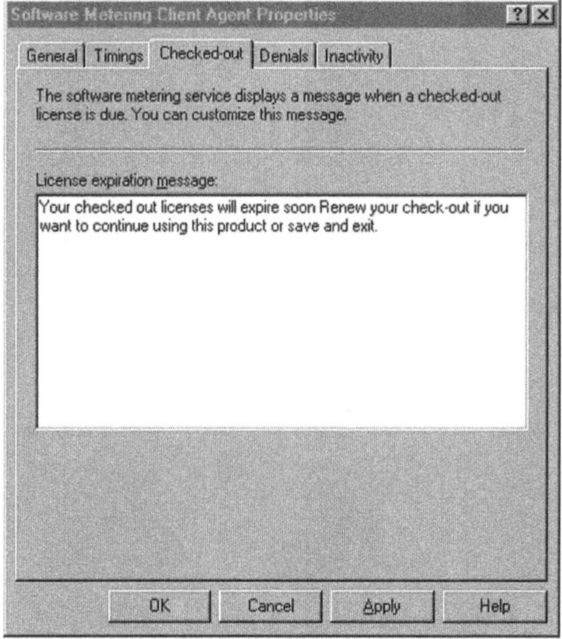
Software Metering Client Agent Properties
General
Timings
Checked-out
Denials
Inactivity
The software metering service displays a message when a checked-out license is due. You can customize this message.
License expiration message:
Your checked out licenses will expire soon Renew your check-out if you want to continue using this product or save and exit.
OK
Cancel
Apply
Help

Figure 9-5 Defining software metering.

Assigning Permissions for Users, Groups, and Computers

A master resource list can be created composed of users, groups, and computer systems to be used by software metering to track the software usage on your network. The only item in the resource list is the user, group, or computer ANY, a global value that tracks the software usage of *any* user or group using *any* computer system during the default offline mode. This specification really depends on your needs and time available to set up software metering.

If you want to track several software programs that every user has access to, then the ALL user object is quite handy. If you have very specific user and group scenarios, then you can use the Resource Manager to import the list of current users and groups or manually add the required permission. The Resource Manager is found in the Tools drop-down menu in the Software Metering console, as shown in Figure 9-6.

- To import users into the Resource Manager, click on the green *User* icon on the *Users* tab.

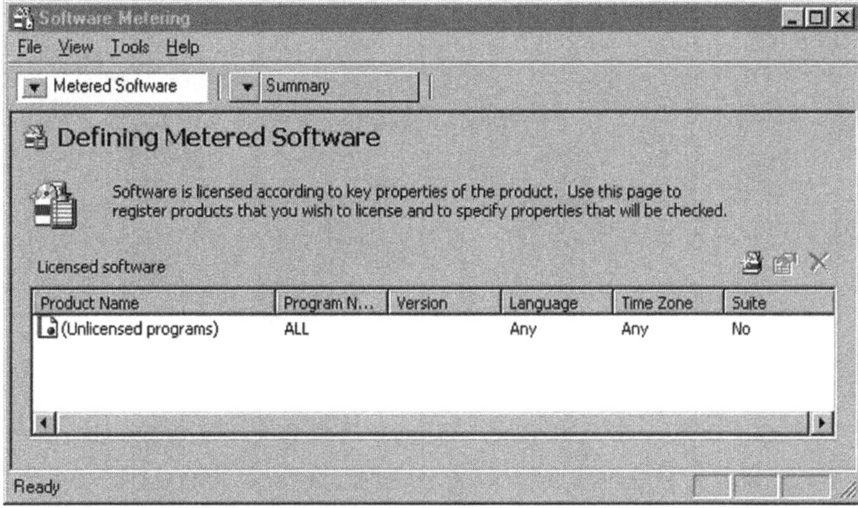

Figure 9-6 The Resource Manager.

- To import groups into the Resource Manager, click on the pink and green icon on the *Groups* tab.
- To import a computer into the Resource Manager, click on the dotted-square *Computer* icon on the *Computer* tab.

All users created with the Resource Manager are started with an initial callback of 5, and the range is from 1 to 9. Callback priority defines the user's level of callback when an available license becomes available for user requests that have been placed in the callback queue.

Registering Individual Software

To register individual software programs, the Software Metering console must be opened to display the Defining Metered Software screen.

1. Click on the blue-and-white *Computer* Icon directly to the right from the Licensed Software title. Select *Create New* from the Add Product dialog; the New Product properties will be displayed, as shown in Figure 9-7.
2. Type the new software application name into the Product Name field. The name for the product should not be the EXE file that starts the program.

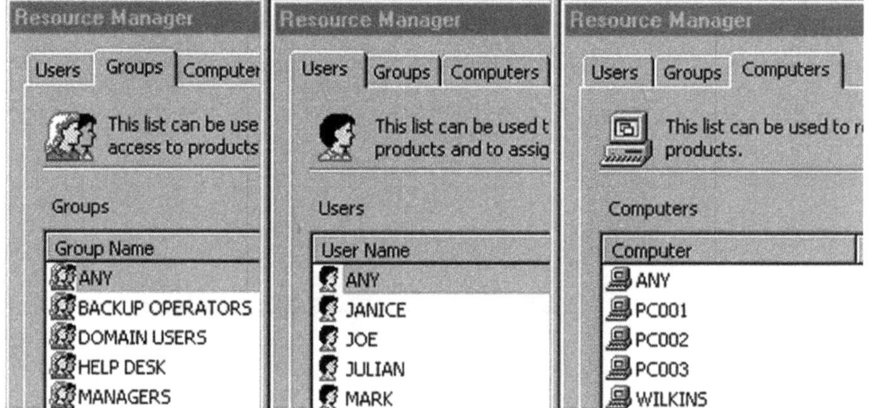

Figure 9-7
New Product properties.

3. Enter the serial number, purchase date (a date must be entered), and the number of purchased licenses if you are going to enable online mode.
4. Enter the name of the program, or browse by clicking on the *Ellipsis* icon [...] to the right of the Program Name group box.

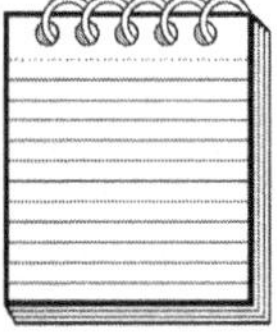

NOTE. *Enter the product name version number only if it is a stand-alone product. When registering a suite, do not enter a version number.*

5. If you want to just monitor the use of this program, clear the *Enforce the license limits for this product* option. For real-time monitoring of this program, check and enable this option.
6. To use a specific language, click on the *Triangle* drop-down icon, and set the desired language. The default setting allows any language to be used.
7. To choose a specific time zone, click on the *Ellipsis* icon, and set as desired. The default setting allows any time zone.
8. If the product is a suite software product—for example, Microsoft 2000—or you are registering a suite program, then check the appropriate checkbox option.
9. Click on *OK* to save and implement your changes.

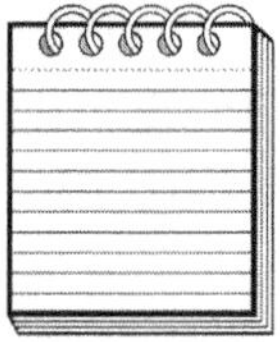

NOTE. *You can use the Load Profile button if your software program supports SMS software metering by including a license profile. The license profile contains all of information just entered in the last example.*

Client Access Permissions for Online Mode

Once software metering has been installed and configured to run in online mode, when a user requests a license with a license profile created, permissions must be available in all six categories, as shown in Table 9-1.

Licensing Software Suites

As you probably know, a software suite is a software product made up of several individual standalone programs that also work together, sharing information. Examples are Microsoft Office 2000 and Corel Office 2000 Professional. Several steps are involved in registering a software suite:

1. Open the Software Metering console from the Tools folder.
2. Register each individual software program contained in the suite; for example, Excel, Word, PowerPoint, and Access are the core components of Microsoft Office.
3. Specify the number of licenses for each individual software program. For example, if you bought a license for 100 clients, set each individual software program to 100 licenses.

TABLE 9-1

These specific access permissions must all be available.

User and group	The specific user or group has permission to use the software applications.
Computer	The software application must be available on the client's computer.
Time	Access must be within the allowable time frame specified for the software application.
Availability	The license for the software application is free.
Time zone	The current time zone is available for the software application.
Language	Only an issue if multiple language versions of the same software application are installed on the network.

4. Next, register the suite itself—for example, Microsoft Office 2000—selecting on the *Product Name* tab the option *This product is a suite product.* Do not enter a version number for the suite on the Product Name tab.
5. Double-click on the product name of the suite product—for example, Microsoft Office 2000—and click on the *Suite Membership* button on the *Identification* tab.
6. Highlight each individual program on the Available Resources list, and move them to the Members list, as shown in Figure 9-8.

The software suite is now completely registered.

Setting the Properties of Licensed Software

Once you have completed the New Product tab screen, the software will be displayed under the Licensed Software listing in Defining Metered Software. Double-clicking a product name will show the properties of the software.

The tabs are as follows.

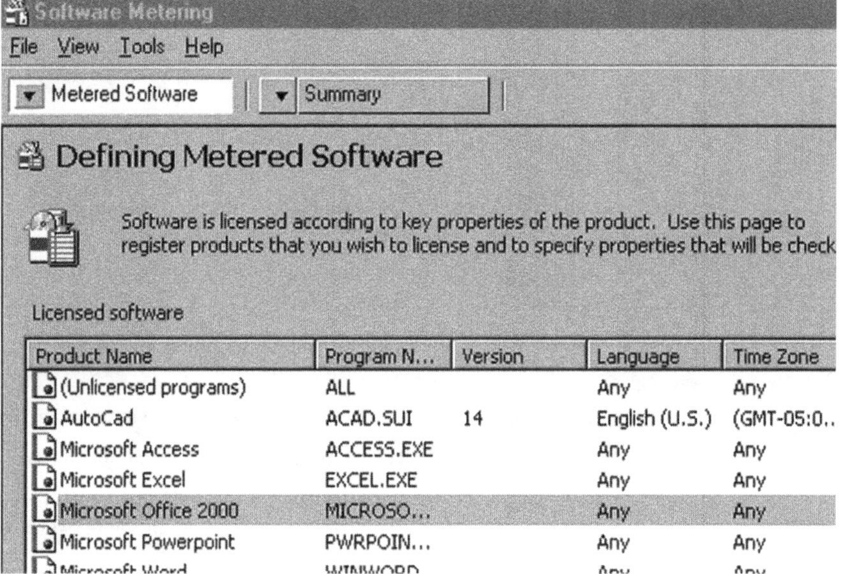

Figure 9-8
Suite registration.

Identification

The Identification tab can be used to change the product name, the number of licenses you have purchased, the serial number, and the purchase date. The properties of the suite master also allow you to add or remove the software applications that are members of the suite. There is also an option to add a product alias, which allows you to monitor a program that depends on or calls another program while it is running. For example, say a user runs Internet Explorer (IEXPLORE.EXE) and checks her mail by clicking on the Mail button to call Outlook (OUTLOOK.EXE), and then downloads and listens to a music file by launching Microsoft Media Player (MPLAYER2.EXE). All these programs could be tracked under the name "Internet Explorer," as shown in Figure 9-9.

Permissions

The Permissions tab is used to select the resources (users and groups, and computers) that will be allowed to use this particular product. Note that the ANY resource is still present in the Has Access choice box. If you

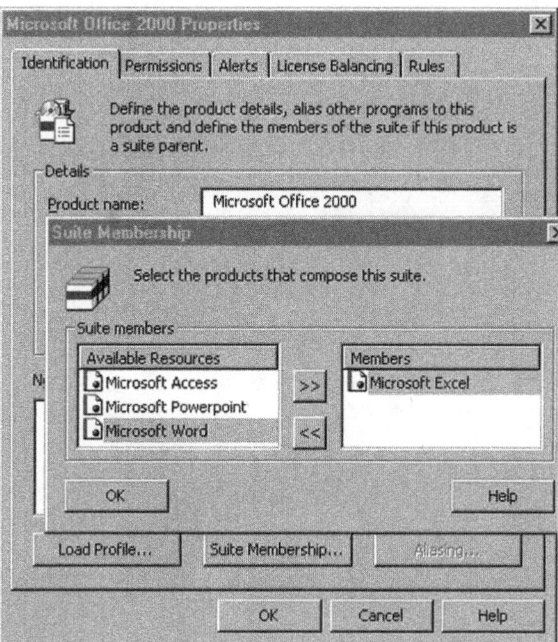

Figure 9-9 Aliased software programs.

really intended to restrict access, move the ANY resource over to the Available Resources, as shown in Figure 9-10.

The access times that the software program is available to the resources in the Has Access choice box is also set through the Permissions tab.

Alerts

Denial to a license, having no licenses available, or having very few licenses left to offer can generate an alert that is sent to the administrator. You can check the computer inactivity checkbox and specify how many minutes of inactivity will pass before an administrator event is generated, a warning dialog box is presented to the end user, or the application is shut down, returning the license to the available license pool.

If the application is to be shut down due to inactivity, a warning is followed by a "wait time period." This allows the user to save his or her files before the application is shut down. Make sure that your applications save their work every minute if this option is selected.

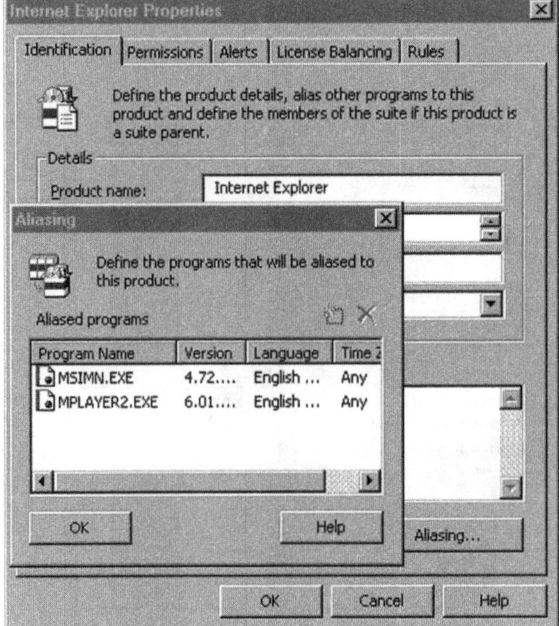

Figure 9-10 Permissions for a software application.

License Balancing

If you have several software-metering servers, license balancing can be defined as a percentage of free licenses and total licenses for each product to be detained at each server. However, there is no real way of knowing sometimes where and when the licenses will be needed.

On a large network with multiple software-metering servers, it is recommended to check the checkbox that reads "Do not enforce the license limits for this product until a trend has been calculated."

Once this feature is enabled, the license metering thread runs for one week for each individual product and two weeks for all listed software suite products. After this time period has passed, the trend analysis is calculated, and then the available licenses are distributed to the software-metering servers.

NOTE. *To be valid, the trend analysis must be carried out under normal working conditions at your company.*

Rules

The Rules tab defines the license restrictions for the software application, as shown in Figure 9-11.

Options are as follows:

- *Offline metering: Reintegrate as a standalone/Reintegrate as suite.* Define how data records are stored in the local data cache when applications are running in offline mode on the client PC.
- *Enable concurrent licensing of this product/Multiple instances count as one.* Define how multiple copies of a program running on a client PC will be tracked
- *Allow license extensions.* A license extension will depend on the software product's licensing rules from the manufacturer. Some software licenses allow you to run the software at work and at home, in effect extending the license.
- *Enable concurrent licensing of the product.* Depends on the license agreement for the software product.
- *License expires.* Defined in the expiration date for software licenses. Usually used for evaluation software or for situations where users are

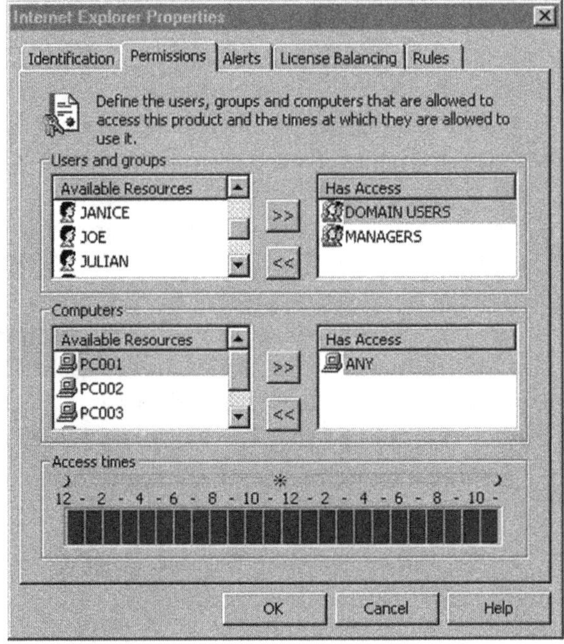

Figure 9-11
Licensing rules.

being migrated to a new version of a software program and there's a cutoff date when the older program will not be available.

- *Enforce the license limits for this product.* Checking this option enables the blocking of licenses for this product once the license limit specified in the Identification tab has been exceeded.
- *Allow licenses to be checked out for this product.* A mobile user can use the SMS user application CHECK32.EXE to check out a software license and use it for specified time while away from the company.

Excluding Software Applications from Being Metered

Software metering monitors processes—in other words, any file with the EXE extension. However, there are many operating system utilities that you do not want to bother with metering—for example, CLOCK.EXE or NOTEPAD.EXE, to name but a few. The operating system runs many executable files in the background, performing many tasks. To exclude a software program from being metered, the Software Metering tool is used.

Start the Software Metering tool from the Tools folder by first selecting *Software Metering* from the *All Tasks | Start Software Metering* menu.

1. From the Tools drop-down menu, select the menu option *Excluded programs.* The Excluded Programs listing is shown alphabetically.
2. To add an EXE file to the excluded programs list, click on the dotted-square icon to the right of the Excluded Programs text. The New Excluded Program dialog box will be shown, as detailed in Figure 9-12.
3. Enter the program you wish to exclude, or browse and search for the program name to include in the exclusion list.
4. To delete an excluded program from the list shown, highlight the program and select the *X* icon beside the dotted-square icon.

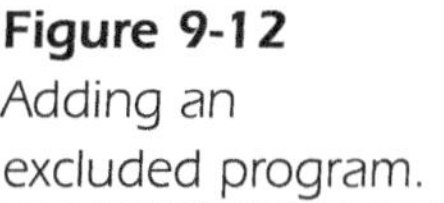

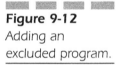

Figure 9-12 *Adding an excluded program.*

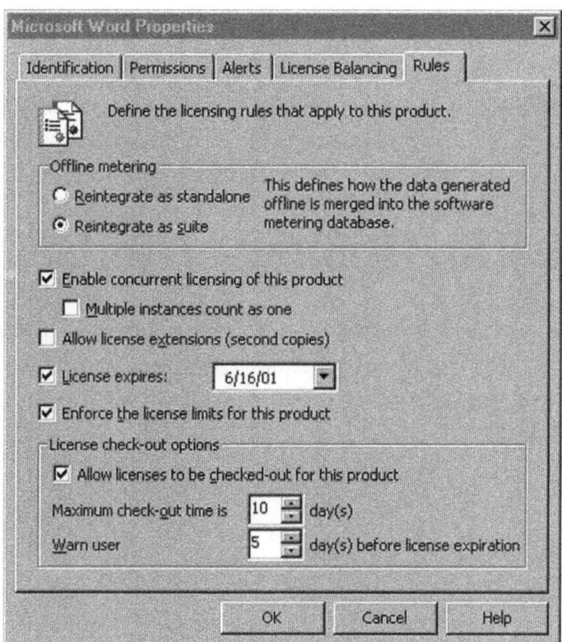

Using Reports

In the Software Metering console, clicking on the Summary tab at the top of the screen displays both Licensed and Unlicensed programs that have been used. Select a program displayed in the Products list; then use the Report icon to view the list of available summary reports that can be created.

The options are as follows:

- *Active summary of license use* Displays all of the registered products being metered across your site, summarized in columns: Server, In Use, and Licenses Available.
- *Details of active license use* Provides details of active software usage at your site, summarized in columns: Server, User, Computer, Started, and Duration.
- *Denials* Lists the product licenses that were denied because no free licenses were available, summarized in columns: Server, User, Computer, and Date.
- *Callbacks* Lists the users who are or were in a callback queue, in columns: Server, User, Computer, Requested, and Granted.
- *Historical license use* The use of the product is shown in summarized or not summarized format, in columns: Server, User, Computer, Started, Duration, and Count.
- *Checked out licenses* Shows the licenses that are currently checked out, in columns: Computer, User, Checked Out, and Reserved Until.

Creating Reports and Graphs

Two wizards, the Report Wizard and the Graph Wizard, can be used to generate reports about your software-metering stats. Using the Software Metering tool, from the Tools drop-down menu, select the Report or Graph Wizard.

Report Wizard

Before formatting and generating the requested reports, the Report Wizard asks you several questions about the type of report you would like to create, the resources that you want a report on, and the range of the dates (from and to). The Report Wizard can create the following software-metering reports based on specific resources on specific year-to-date ranges (see Figure 9-13). Once the report has been displayed on screen, you can choose to use the Printer icon to produce a hardcopy as well.

- *Callback Priority* Lists all users grouped by their callback priority setting.
- *Detailed Product Use (Grouped by Product)* Provides details of each product, what user requested the product, beginning and ending use, and duration.
- *Detailed Product Use (Grouped by User)* Provides details on what products the user requested.
- *Excluded Programs* Lists information about EXE programs that are not being metered.
- *Last Client Runtime Sorted by Age* Tracks the time status of the metering client agents installed at the client.
- *Last Client Runtime Sorted by Computer* Tracks the time status of the metering client agents sorted by computer system.

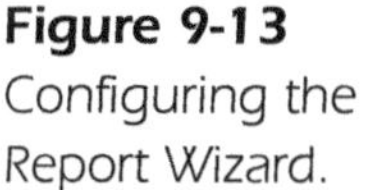

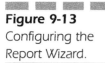

Figure 9-13
Configuring the Report Wizard.

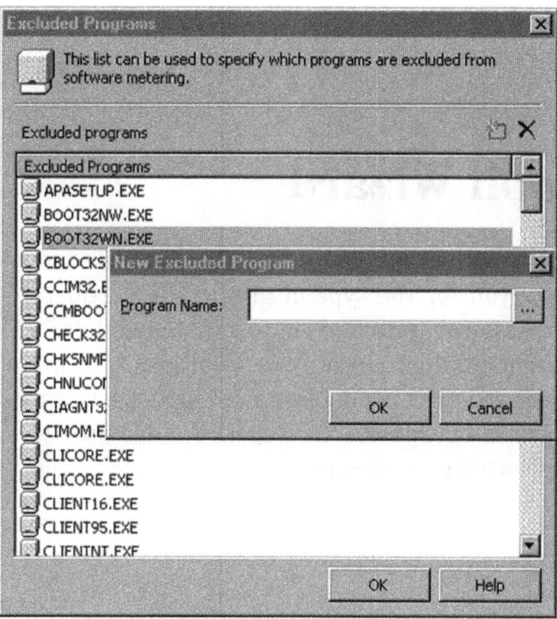

- *Licensed Products* Lists the products that have been registered, providing details on the metered program name, version, and registration date.
- *Multiple Site Summary* Lists the products that have been in use at the multiple sites.
- *Product Denials* Lists the products and users that were denied due to no free licenses being available.
- *Single Site Summary* Lists the products that have been in use at the local site.
- *Software Metering Server Configuration* Provides details on the current software-metering server, listing the server name, server type, time zone, and the path to the software-metering files.
- *Suites* Provides details on the product suites that are registered, including the software programs that make up each suite.
- *Total Use of Product (Grouped by Product)* Calculates the total time each software product was executed by the users and the number of licenses used.
- *Total Use of Product (Grouped by User)* Calculates the total time each user ran the available software products and the number of licenses used.
- *Unlicensed Program Usage* Provides a list showing all of the unlicensed software programs used, providing details on the user, client name, and length of use.

Graph Wizard

Before creating and presenting the requested graph, the Graph Wizard prompts you for the type of graph; the products; sites, users, and computers; starting date and time; and graph detail. This wizard allows you to present product usage in several graph formats: 2D Bar, 3D Bar, 3D Perspective, Area, and Line. Although these graphs may be better for presentation purposes, the Report Wizard provides more details for monitoring software metering.

CHAPTER 10

Hardware and Software Inventory

In this chapter you will learn about:

- The technical details of hardware and software inventory
- Enabling hardware and software inventory collection
- Defining schedules and criteria for hardware and software inventory
- Customizing hardware inventory MIF files with the MOF Manager
- Viewing inventory with the Resource Explorer

Collecting Inventory

The process of collecting hardware and software inventory is essential to collect before SMS features like Remote Control, software distribution, and the Resource Explorer can be used. The hardware portion of inventory collection provides you with data categorized into many hardware properties, including CPU type, hard drive type, RAM size, and monitor type.

Software inventory is split into two services: inventory collection of detailed file statistics and the file collection of specified user files stored at the site server. Both the hardware and software inventory process must be enabled and then defined at the SMS Administrative console, using the Hardware and the Software Client Agents' properties.

Hardware Inventory Process: Overview

Hardware inventory is a global process affecting every discovered SMS client in the SMS hierarchy. Once the Hardware Inventory Agent is enabled at the site server, inventory collection begins at each SMS client, storing the results in an inventory file. The inventory file is then sent to the primary site server, where it is stored in the SMS site database. The hardware inventory process is described in the following steps:

1. Hardware inventory is enabled and scheduled for collection at the primary site server.
2. The SMS client is discovered and client agents, including the Hardware Inventory Agent and the required software components, are installed locally at the client's PC.
3. Hardware inventory starts in minutes after the Hardware Inventory Client Agent is installed, performing a complete hardware inventory and storing the results locally in the folder %WINDIR%\MS\SMS\CLICOMP\HINV\Hinvdat.hic.
4. The inventory file is then sent to the client access point formatted as a desktop management interface file (MIF) and then to the primary site server.

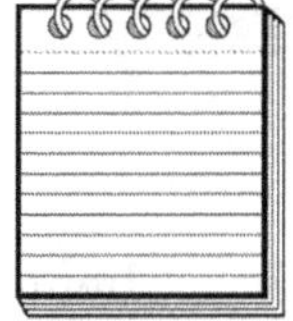

NOTE. The HIC extension for the hardware inventory file stands for "hardware inventory complete."

5. At the primary site server, the Inventory Processor receives the MIF file, adds a binary header to the inventory record, records the history information in the history database, and passes, the file to the Inventory Data Loader process, which stores the file in the SMS site database.

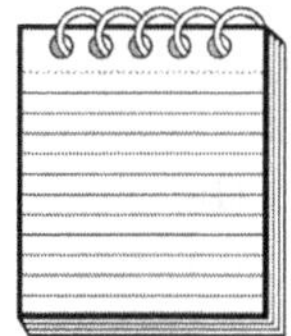

NOTE. If the client agent cannot complete the inventory process, it is attempted again in 24 hours. If the Inventory Data Loader is unable to read the MIF file due to corruption, the bad record is stored in a folder on the site server called SMS\INBOXES\DATALDR.BOX\BADMIFS.

Table 10-1 summarizes the hardware inventory collection process and provides additional details.

TABLE 10-1

The hardware inventory process.

1. Hardware inventory is enabled at the primary site.
2. A schedule for regular hardware inventory collection is deployed.
3. The client's PC is discovered; SMS installs the Hardware Inventory Client Agent.
4. Fifteen minutes pass before hardware inventory starts.
5. Hardware inventory is carried out by the client agent.
6. Hardware history is updated at the client.
7. The client sends the inventory file to the client access point.
8. If the CAP is not the site server, the inventory record is forwarded to the site server.
9. The Inventory Data Loader processes the inventory file, creating a history record.
10. If the data record is corrupted, it is sent to the BADMIFs folder.
11. The Inventory Data Loader stores the inventory record in the site database.
12. If the site server is not the central site, the file is also sent up to the central/primary site server.

The 32-Bit Hardware Inventory Process: Technical Details

After discovery of the client, the Hardware Inventory Client Agent HINV32.EXE is installed on each client, and a default inventory template called SMS_DEF.MOF is stored on the local PC in the folder %WINDIR%\MS\SMS\SITEFILE\<site code >\HINV, as shown in Figure 10-1.

The hardware inventory procedure is a three-step process involving the client, the client access point, and the site server. First, inventory is gathered at the client, and the results are stored in a temporary file. Second, the file is sent to the CAP, where it is transferred to the site server.

However, there may be a custom MIF file stored on the client in the folder %WINDIR%\SMS\NOIDMIFS that adds additional custom hardware inventory settings to be checked and included with the inventory collection. The filename, if present, will have a .MIF extension. The size of the custom file is important, since the maximum allowable size for a third-party MIF is 250 MB.

The Registry key that holds the default value is located at HKEY_LOCAL_MACHINE\SOFTWARE\Microsoft\SMS\Client\Sites

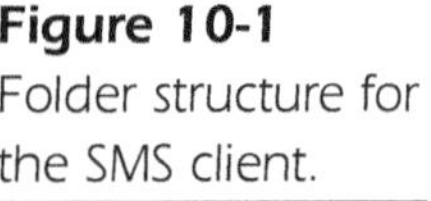

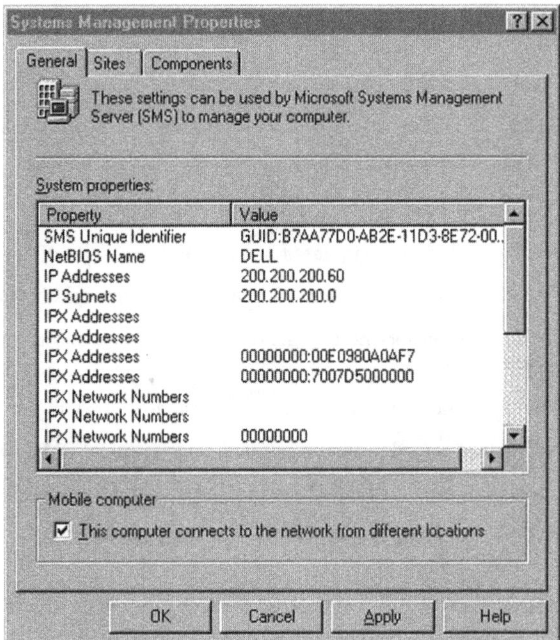

Figure 10-1 Folder structure for the SMS client.

\System\MAN\Client Components\Hardware Inventory Agent, as shown in Figure 10-2.

If the file size is within the allowable limits, the properties of the custom MIF files are merged with the default inventory file, becoming part of the inventory template. If the file cannot be read or is too large, it will be stored on the client in the folder %WINDIR%\SMS\NOIDMIFS\BADMIFS.

Now the hardware inventory process is performed on the client's PC, and the results are written to a temporary file with either the .HIC or .HID extension. A HIC file is created the very first time that a complete hardware inventory is executed and stored on the client's PC in the folder %WINDIR%\MS\SMS\CLICOMP\HINV*.HIC.

A HID file is created if hardware inventory has been performed before. In this case, the file contains only the hardware changes since the last time inventory was carried out. This file is a *delta hardware inventory file* stored on the client's PC in the folder %WINDIR%\MS\SMS\CLICOMP\HINV*.HID.

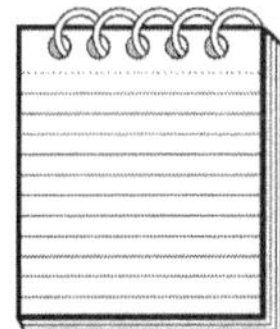

NOTE. *An additional custom MIF file, called an IDMIF file, can be used for completely new architectures. This file will be useful in the future if Windows 2000 Professional clients become SMS clients. An*

Figure 10-2 Registry settings for custom hardware inventory MIF files.

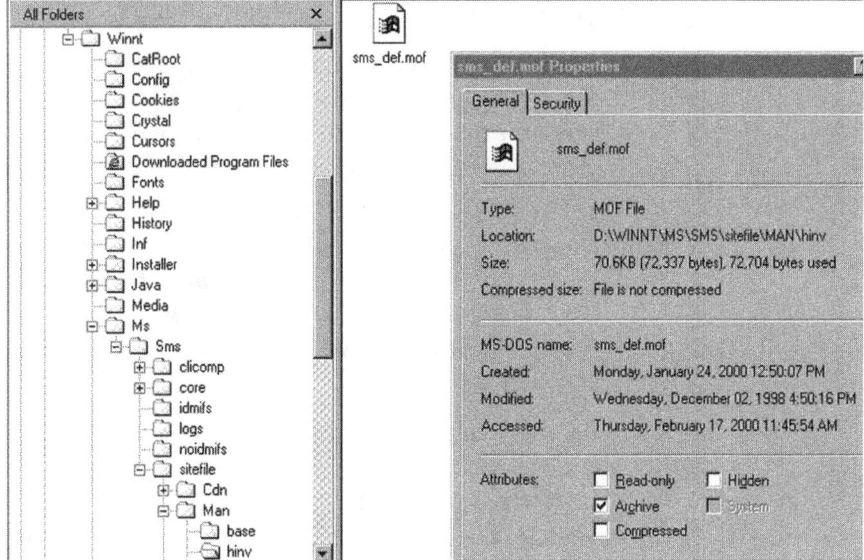

IDMIF file could be created for new hardware devices that are not currently recognized by SMS 2.0.

Hardware Inventory at the Client Access Point (CAP)

The client access point stores the hardware inventory file from the Copy Queue Manager in the folder\\Server Name\CAP <site code>\INVENTORY.BOX. Next, the Inbox Manager Assistant transfers the hardware inventory file to the site server, where the Inventory Processor accepts the MIF file.

The MIF file is the stored in the \\Server Name\SMS <site code>\INBOXES\DATALDR.BOX folder. The Inventory Data Loader wakes up and transfers the inventory data to the \\Server Name\SMS <site code>\INBOXES\DATALDR.BOX\PROCESS folder.

The file is checked for errors and the proper size; it cannot exceed 5 MB. If the file has errors or exceeds the maximum allowable size, it is placed in the \\Server Name\SMS <site code>\INBOXES\DATALDR.BOX\BADMIFS folder. Normally, the file is free from errors and size problems, so the Inventory Data Loader writes the contents of the MIF file to the SMS site database.

If the data written to the SQL database is error-free but still fails, the following occurs:

- If the client does not exist in the SMS site database, the Inventory Data Loader creates a discovery data record (DDR) record for the client and moves the data record for the client to \\Server Name\SMS <site code>\INBOXES\DATALDR.BOX\ORPHANS.
- If the client does exist in the SMS site database, the Inventory Data Loader checks to see if the Discovery Data Manager has read the client's DDR. If not, the Inventory Data Loader creates a discovery data record for the client and moves the data record for the client to \\Server Name\SMS <site code>\INBOXES\DATALDR.BOX\ORPHANS.

At this point, hardware inventory processing at the primary site is complete. If this primary site is not the central site, the Replication Manager sends the MIF files to the parent site in the folder \\Server Name\SMS <site code>\INBOXES\DATALDR.BOX.

Hardware Inventory Schedule

After the initial hardware inventory collection has been collected from an SMS client, the process is repeated every 7 days by a system event that restarts the client agent. Next time, the inventory collection is called a *delta collection*, as the entire inventory is not collected and sent to the site server, only the changes since the last time inventory was performed.

The client agent compares the newly collected data with the previous collection, and if there are any changes, the delta inventory file (HINV-DAT.HID) is created and sent to the CAP and then on to the primary site server.

Hardware Inventory Resynchronization

If the Hardware Inventory Client Agent attempts to update data to the site server database that has no previous history record, or if existing inventory data is found to be corrupted, the Hardware Inventory Client Agent initiates a process called *resynchronization*. This process causes the client agent to perform a complete inventory (just like the first time the inventory process was performed), replacing the client's complete data record at the site server. Resynchronization cannot be manually started; the Hardware Inventory Client Agent is responsible for starting this process.

Management Object Files and Hardware Inventory

SMS provides a default template called SMS_DEF.MOF containing 650 properties that can be collected by the hardware inventory process. Not all of the properties are enabled by default; however, this file can be customized using the MOF Manager to define the class of properties that you wish to collect.

The master MOF file is stored at the site server at the \\Server\SMS\INBOXES\Clifiles.src\Hinv folder location and not at the client.

When the next inventory collection is about to start, the MOF file on the site server is compared with the copy stored at the client.

If the MOF files are not the same, the site server copy is used and is copied to the SMS client.

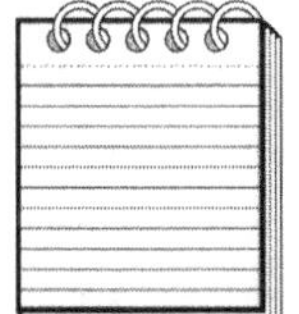

NOTE. The extension .MOF stands for "Management Object File."

Installing and Using the MOF Manager

The MOF Manager is a software utility that comes with the Microsoft BackOffice 4.5 Resource Kit stored in the folder \SMS\i386\MOFman. Running Setup from this folder starts the MOF Manager, as shown in Figure 10-3.

The MOF file displays a huge listing of classes, each with a detailed listing of properties. If the class or individual property is tagged green, it is enabled and used when hardware inventory is gathered. If either the class or individual property is tagged red, then they are disabled. Double-clicking either the class or the property disables or enables each selection, respectively.

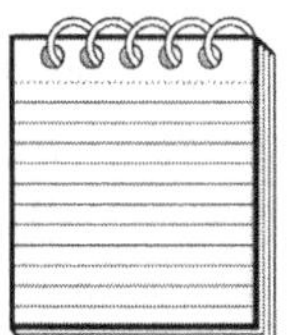

NOTE. The Systems Management Server Resource Kit has devoted an entire chapter to customizing hardware inventory collections.

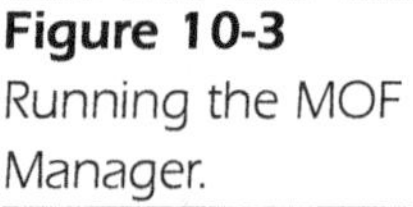

Figure 10-3
Running the MOF Manager.

Enabling Hardware Inventory

Hardware inventory is by default loaded and ready to go, but it may not yet be enabled. If SMS was installed with Express Setup, then hardware inventory will be enabled; if a custom install was performed, then hardware inventory was left in a disabled state.

Open up the SMS Administrator console, and select the *Site Settings* folder to display the available client agents. Double-click on the *Hardware Inventory Client Agent* to view the current properties, as shown in Figure 10-4. To enable hardware inventory, check the *Enable hardware inventory on clients* checkbox.

Setting the Hardware Inventory Schedule

Once enabled, hardware inventory is carried out every 7 days on a default simple schedule. From the General tab, selecting the Full Schedule option allows you to select the date and time that hardware inventory starts and to select the recurrence pattern in minutes, as well as in weekly or monthly stages.

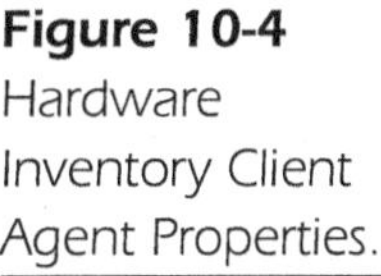

Figure 10-4 Hardware Inventory Client Agent Properties.

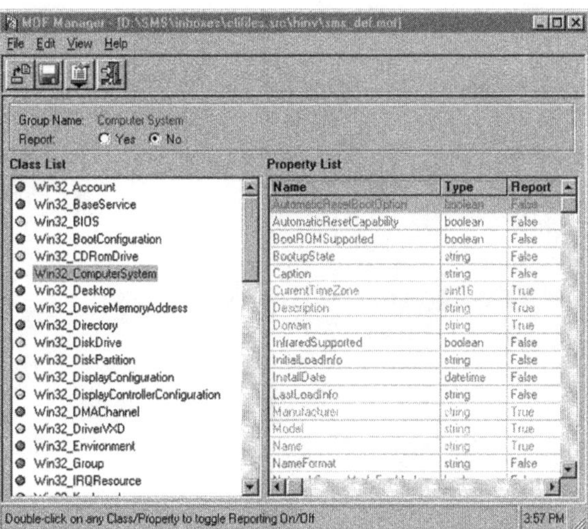

Hardware Inventory at the Client

Any SMS client that is discovered has the Hardware Inventory Agent installed on the local PC. To view the installed agents, select the *System Management* icon in the Control Panel, and then select the *Components* tab. See Figure 10-5.

If your clients have not yet been discovered as SMS clients, then hardware inventory will not take place until the discovery process takes place. Open up the SMS Administrator console, and select the *Client Installation Methods* folder.

Since your client base and servers are probably Windows-based 95/98 or NT clients with NT servers, the Windows Networking Logon Client Installation option would be your best bet. Double-clicking the agent shows its properties; through the logon settings, you can choose to add a line into your user's logon script to enable the installation of SMS client software after a successful discovery.

If you choose to use this method, you will be adding a line to the top or bottom of the logon script to run a batch file called SMSLS.BAT, which is located in the NETLOGON share on the NT server. Login scripts for Windows-based clients are enabled through User Manager for Domains on the primary domain controller.

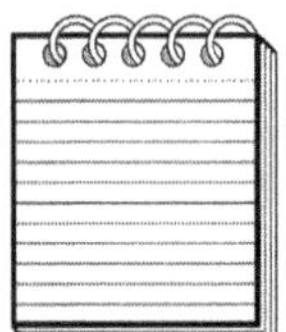

NOTE. *Check out Chapter 7, "Installing SMS Clients and Discovering Resources" for further details on the discovery process.*

Figure 10-5
System management properties at the client.

Understanding Software Inventory

Software files on the client's PC can also be monitored and collected on a defined schedule. Once the SMS client has been discovered, software inventory can proceed.

Once configured, the Software Inventory Client Agent collects file information and can even copy specified client files to the site server for safekeeping and proactive troubleshooting. The file details that are used in software inventory, if present, are as follows:

- Filename, version, and size
- Date and time of creation
- The file author's name
- The software product's name, version, and language

File types recognized by the software inventory process are processed by file extension, and the choices are open-ended; you get to decide what file extensions to inventory. The file extensions to consider inventory collection for are as follows:

.EXE Most software is started by an executable process.

.COM Older MS-DOS programs and utilities use the smaller .COM executable extension.

.REG Software installations in the 32-bit world (Windows 98 and NT) use REG files for installing Registry structure. If a 32-bit software installation is performed at the client's PC, the odds are that the REG files will be left behind on the local hard drive.

When the software files are inventoried on the client's PC, it is considered a *known* file if there are valid entries for company name, product name, version, and language. Checking the file's properties at the Explorer shell can provide a heads-up regarding whether a particular file type will be classified as a known file. All files that are missing these property values are considered *unknown* files. Through the Resource Explorer, files can be viewed through the SMS mandated classes of known and unknown files.

NOTE. *Using this criteria, most MS-DOS and custom software will be defined as unknown by the Resource Explorer.*

Understanding Software Collection

Software collection is a part of the software inventory process allowing you to specify certain files to collect on the client's PC if they exist (or magically appear). Some of the file types to consider collecting are as follows:

AUTOEXEC.BAT You may not use this file, but the user may create it by mistake or copy this file from a location onto his or her PC. The user might also install software that creates this file. The possibilities are endless. You also may require this file.

CONFIG.SYS The same reasons for AUTOEXEC.BAT apply. You also may require this file.

USER.DAT The Windows 95/98 User Profile (the user's Registry).

SYSTEM.DAT The Windows 95/98 System Registry.

NTUSER.DAT The Windows NT/2000 User Profile (the user's registry).

POLEDIT.EXE The System Policy Editor for Windows 95/98 and NT 4.0 clients.

REGEDIT.EXE The Registry Editor that imports REG files for Windows 95/98, NT 4.0, and 2000 systems.

NOTE. *There could be multiple copies of USER.DAT if user profiles have been enabled on your Windows 95/98 clients. Multiple copies of NTUSER.DAT on NT 4.0 and Windows 2000 clients will also be present, since user profiles are enabled in NT by default.*

Software Inventory Process: Overview

When SMS is installed, software inventory is also installed. If Express Setup was chosen, then software inventory is also enabled. However, if a custom installation of SMS was performed, software inventory is left disabled. Once software inventory is enabled, all discovered SMS clients in the SMS site are inventoried by default every 7 days.

Like hardware inventory, the software inventory process executes on the client, passing the results of the process, along with the changes, up to the primary site server. The software inventory process is described in the following steps and also in Table 10-2.

1. Software inventory is enabled and scheduled for collection at the primary site server.
2. The SMS client is discovered, and client agents, including the Software Inventory Agent and the required software components, are installed locally at the client's PC.
3. Software inventory starts in minutes after the Software Client Agent is installed, performing a complete software inventory and storing the results locally in the folder %WINDIR%\MS\SMS\CLICOMP\SINV\.
4. The inventory file is then sent to the client access point and then to the primary site server.
5. At the primary site server, the Inventory Processor receives the inventory file and stores the file in the SMS site database.

TABLE 10-2

The software inventory process.

1. Software inventory is enabled at the primary site.
2. The schedule for regular hardware inventory collection is deployed.
3. The client's PC is discovered; SMS installs the Software Inventory Client Agent.
4. Thirty minutes pass before software inventory starts.
5. Software inventory is carried out by the client agent.
6. Software inventory file capture is carried out by the client agent.
7. The client sends the inventory file and the collected files to the client access point.
8. If the CAP is not the site server, the inventory record is then forwarded to the site server.
9. The Inventory Data Loader processes the collected files, storing them on the site server.
10. If the inventory file is corrupted, it is stored in the BADSINV folder.
11. The Inventory Data Loader stores the inventory record in the site database.
12. If the site server is not the central site, the inventory and the files captured are sent up to the central/primary site server.

The 32-Bit Software Inventory Process: Technical Details

The following outlines the 32-bit software inventory process:

1. Thirty minutes after the Software Inventory Client Agent is enabled, the scanning of every discovered SMS client's local hard drive begins. For every specified file extension, the client agent gathers the following information if present: filename, file version, file size, date and time the file was created, the file description, company name, product name, product version, and product language. The client agent also collects copies of any files listed in the client agent's properties.

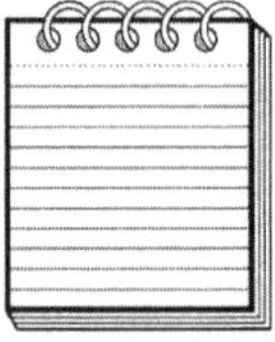

NOTE. *There are no customizable properties to change for software inventory; by specifying the extension at the Software Inventory Client Agent, the listed properties are used.*

2. Once the inventory search has finished, the software inventory file SINVDAT.SIC is created. The collected files (if any are discovered) are attached to the inventory file.
3. The inventory file is then stored in the local folder %WINDIR%\MS\SMS\CLICOMP\SINV.
4. The collected files are removed from the inventory file and stored in the folder %WINDIR%\MS\SMS\CLICOMP\SINV\FILECOL.
5. The collected files and the inventory file are copied to the client access point and stored in the \CAP_<site code>\SINV.BOX folder.
6. The Inbox Manager Assistant sends the software inventory data to the site server in the \\Server Name\SMS_<site code>\INBOXES\SINV.BOX folder.
7. At the site server, the Software Inventory Processor first makes sure a discovery data record for the client PC resides in the site server SQL database.
8. It then checks the incoming software inventory file to make sure it contains newer data than the currently stored records in the site database. If so, the file is error-checked.

9. The collected files are then written to the site server's hard drive folder \\Server Name<site code>\INBOX\SINV.BOX\FILECOL\<resource ID and referenced in the site database for the Resource Explorer utility.
10. The software inventory data is written to the site database.

NOTE *The last five files that have been changed for each defined file type are saved and updated at the site server on the defined software inventory collection schedule.*

Delta Software Inventory Collection

The default interval for software inventory is every 7 days. After the very first software inventory has been performed, the ensuing inventories are called *delta inventories*.

A comparison between what is collected now and what was collected the last collection is compared, creating the delta inventory file that is sent to the CAP and then the site database. This file should be much smaller than the full inventory process. If file collection is also enabled, the collected files are compared with the most recent files, and any files that have been created or changed are tagged onto the delta software inventory file, moving up to the CAP and then the site server.

Software Inventory at the Client Access Point

Once the software inventory is sent to the client access point and received by the inventory agent, it is identified by a unique 8-bit character code attached at the client's PC. Since many clients will be sending software inventory files to the CAP at the same time, this unique character code is essential for identifying the client and the client's operating system version so that the SMS Executive service can assign the correct worker threads to process the inventory file and any attached files.

The following extensions identify the software inventory files that are received by the client access point:

.SIC (Software Inventory Complete) Contains the complete software inventory file

.SID (Software Inventory Delta) Contains only changes to the software inventory

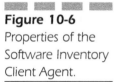

Enabling Software Inventory

Software inventory is enabled through the SMS Administrator console at the Client Agents folder. Remember that all settings affect all discovered SMS clients. To enable software inventory:

1. Double-click on the *Hardware Inventory Client Agent* in the details pane.
2. From the General tab, check the *Enable Software Inventory on Clients* checkbox, as shown in Figure 10-6.

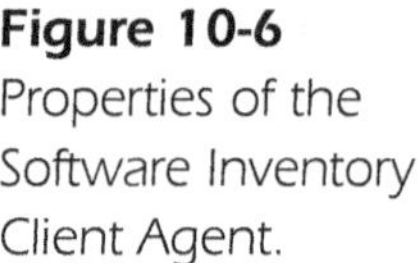

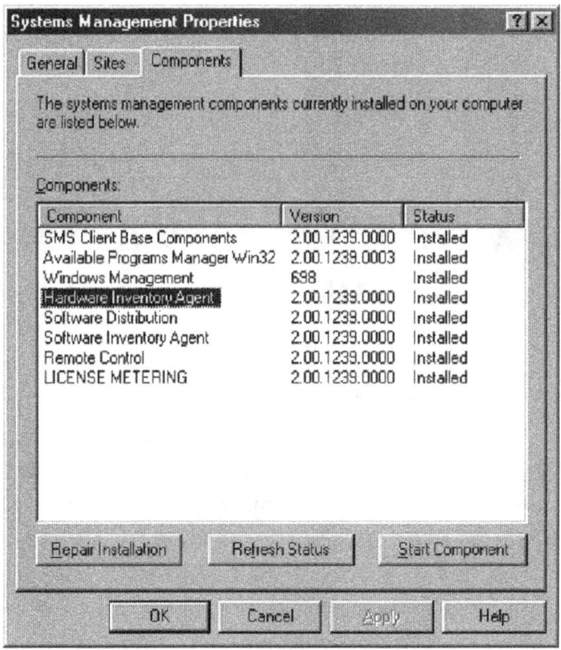

Figure 10-6 Properties of the Software Inventory Client Agent.

Setting the Software Inventory Schedule

The inventory and file collection schedule can be set in one of two ways: through a simple schedule or the full schedule.

1. *Simple Schedule* Enabling the simple schedule allows the schedule to be set by hours, days, or weeks.
2. *Full Schedule* Selecting the full schedule allows the selection of a start date and time with recurring plan:
   - *Interval* Inventory collection can restart every minute, hour, or day
   - *Weekly* Inventory collection can restart on a weekly schedule
   - *Monthly* Inventory collection can restart on a specific day in the month on a custom monthly schedule

Selecting Files to Inventory

The Inventory Collection tab holds the extensions that will be inventoried across the SMS site by software inventory; the default file extension that is searched is .EXE. Right-clicking on the "Yellow Star" button displays the New File Type dialog box for adding to the file types list, as shown in Figure 10-7.

At the base of the Inventory Collection tab, you can select the amount of reporting detail that Resource Explorer can report on. If the following information exists in the header of the discovered file type(s), the product version details of the registered file type can be reported on, along with files that are associated with known products and files that are not associated with known products.

Selecting Files to Capture

The File Collection tab allows you to define what files will be searched for at the SMS clients and stored at the primary site server. Wildcard characters can be used, as can full filenames, as shown in Figure 10-8. Selecting the Yellow Star button displays the New File Type dialog box for adding to the file types list.

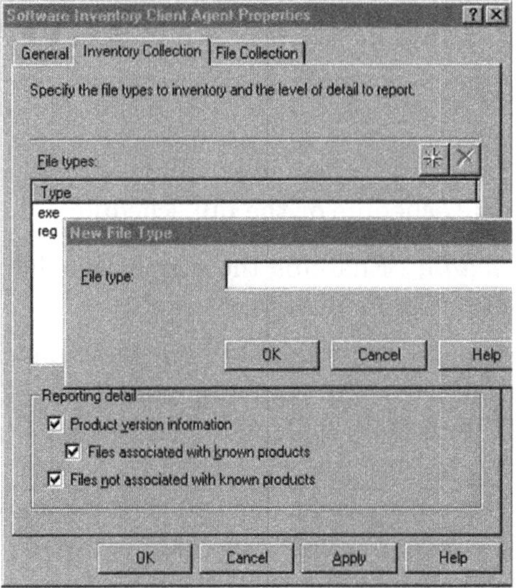

Figure 10-7 Inventory collection properties.

Software Inventory Resynchronization

If the Software Inventory Client Agent attempts to update software inventory data to the site server database that has no previous history record, or if existing inventory data is found to be corrupted, the

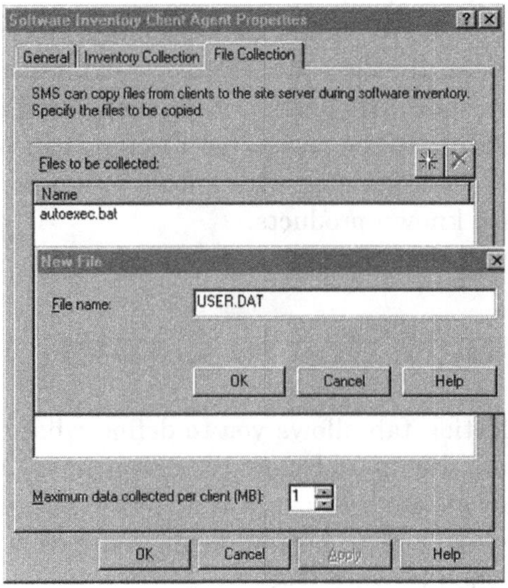

Figure 10-8 File collection properties.

Software Inventory Client Agent initiates a process, mentioned earlier, called *resynchronization*. This process causes the client agent to perform a complete inventory (just like the first time the software inventory process was performed), replacing the client's complete data record at the site server.

This process cannot be manually started; the Software Inventory Client Agent is responsible for starting the resynchronization process.

Software Inventory at the Client

Any SMS client that is discovered has the Software Inventory Agent installed on the local PC. To access the installed software agent, select the *System Management* icon in the Control Panel, then select the *Components* tab. See Figure 10-9.

The hard drive space and memory resources required by the Software Inventory Client Agent to complete the software inventory process are not excessive: 3 MB is needed for virtual memory, and 2 MB of free hard drive space is used to create a temporary file, a history file, and the resulting inventory file that is sent to the primary site server.

The combined size of the collected files at the client cannot exceed 1 MB by default, although you can increase this limit to 20 MB through

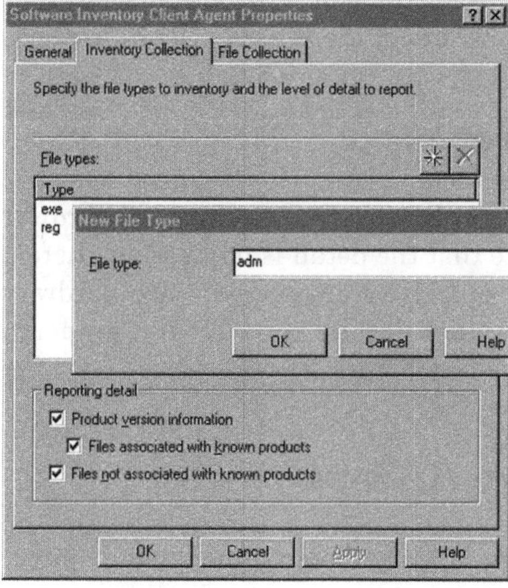

Figure 10-9 The Software Inventory Client Agent.

the properties of the Software Metering Client Agent. One MB may not be sufficient when you consider the size of the user's profile could exceed 4 to 5 MB.

If a client has a very large number of software applications installed, along with a large number of files to be monitored and collected, it is conceivable that network bandwidth will be tasked when the software inventory data and collected files are sent across the network. Try to remember to schedule software inventory and hardware inventory in the early morning hours (2 a.m.) to avoid any network congestion.

Viewing Hardware and Software Inventory

To view the hardware and software inventory collected at a discovered SMS client, start the Resource Explorer applet from the SMS Administrative console. The hardware and software detail can be very useful for troubleshooting.

1. Select the *Collections* folder to view the current client systems in the details pane.
2. Right-click on a client system, and from the displayed context menu, choose *All Tasks | Start Resource Explorer*.

The Resource Explorer will open and display the hardware, hardware history, and software of the selected client, as shown in Figure 10-10.

Hardware

Selecting the Hardware folder displays the hardware inventory that was collected. Note that the detail is impressive; there can be over 650 possible hardware properties discovered. Each hardware inventory item can provide additional details through the properties for each selected device, as shown in Figure 10-11.

Hardware History

The Hardware History folder contains the stored hardware history of prior hardware inventory sessions. This history can be manually deleted,

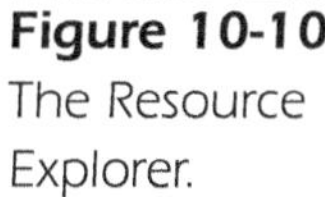

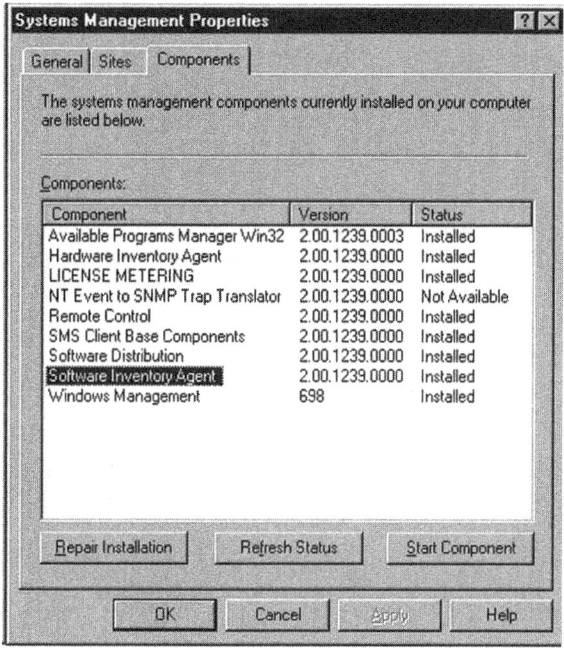

Figure 10-10 The Resource Explorer.

or it can be automatically deleted using a predefined database task under the Database Maintenance|Tasks folder in the SMS Administrator console.

Software

The Software folder holds information about each registered file extension specified to be collected by software inventory. Much detail for each client is shown, including:

- Filename
- File description

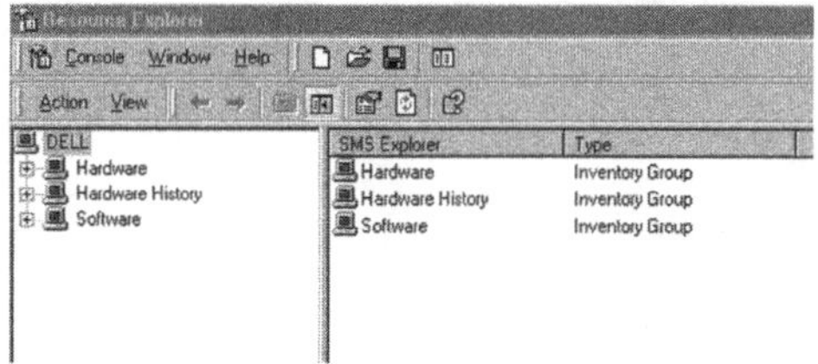

Figure 10-11 Hardware properties shown with Resource Explorer.

- File version
- File size
- File count—How many copies of the file exist on the client PC
- Creation date—Date and time stamp indicating when the file was created

The software inventory displayed through Resource Explorer is categorized under the Manufacturer folder if the software file is known. If the file type is not known, it is stored under the Unknown Files folder. The software inventory information is displayed in Figure 10-12.

Viewing the Collected Software Files

If file collection was configured through the Software Inventory Client Agent, a folder called Collected Files will be displayed in the Resource

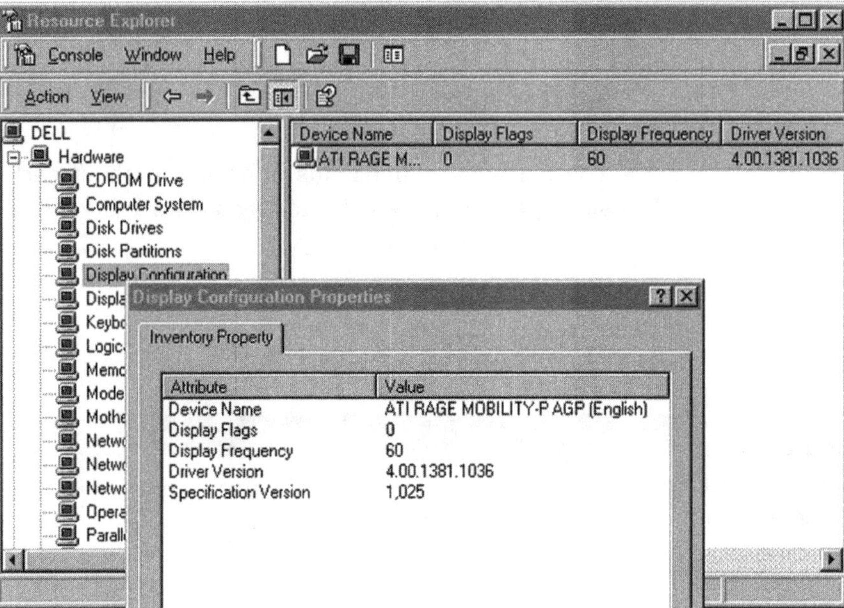

Figure 10-12 Software inventory.

Explorer. This folder will contain information about the collective files, as shown in Figure 10-13, including:

- Filename.
- File path on the client.
- File size in bytes.
- The date the file was last modified.
- The date the file was collected from the client.
- The revision ID; the number corresponds to the number of times this file was collected.

Maintaining Hardware Inventory History Records

Hardware history records are stored for 90 days before they are deleted at the site server. It depends how valuable the hardware information is in your organization. If your users are constantly changing their computer configurations, you may require an even longer storage period.

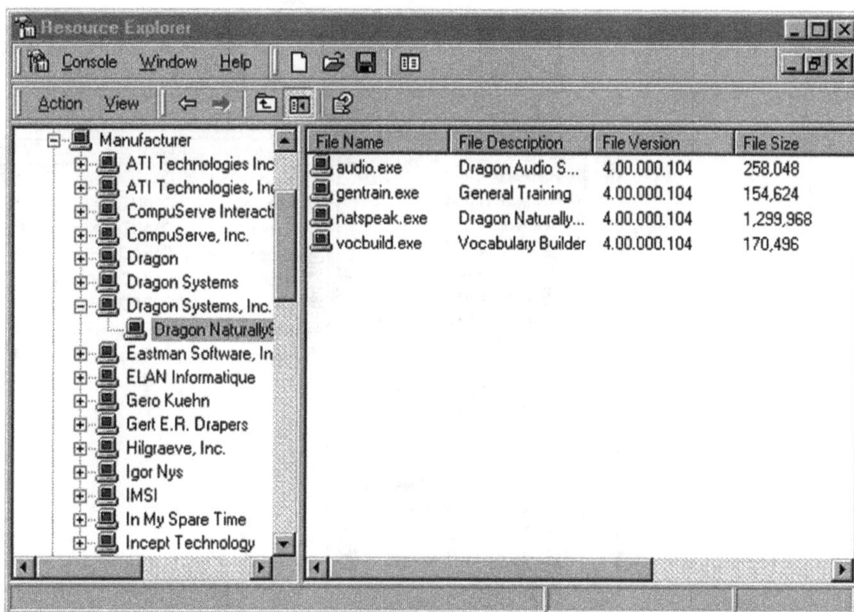

Figure 10-13 Collected file detail.

To change the default time period that history records are kept, use the SMS Administrative console. Navigate to the Database Maintenance folder and then select the *Tasks* subfolder.

Next, double click on the *Delete Aged Inventory History* task to show the properties.

By checking the *Enable this task* option, you can choose the schedule and the timeframe required for maintaining the aged hardware inventory in the SQL database at the site server as shown in Figure 10-14.

Inventory Collection with Multi-Site SMS Clients

If your network environment includes users with notebook PCs rather than standard desktop systems and multiple SMS sites, it's possible that some of your mobile clients might end up being registered at multiple sites. In SMS lingo this is called a *multisite* or *roving client*. Windows 2000 has many features for this type of client; roaming data folders and roaming user profiles, to name a few. Only time will tell if the features will be usable in the corporate world.

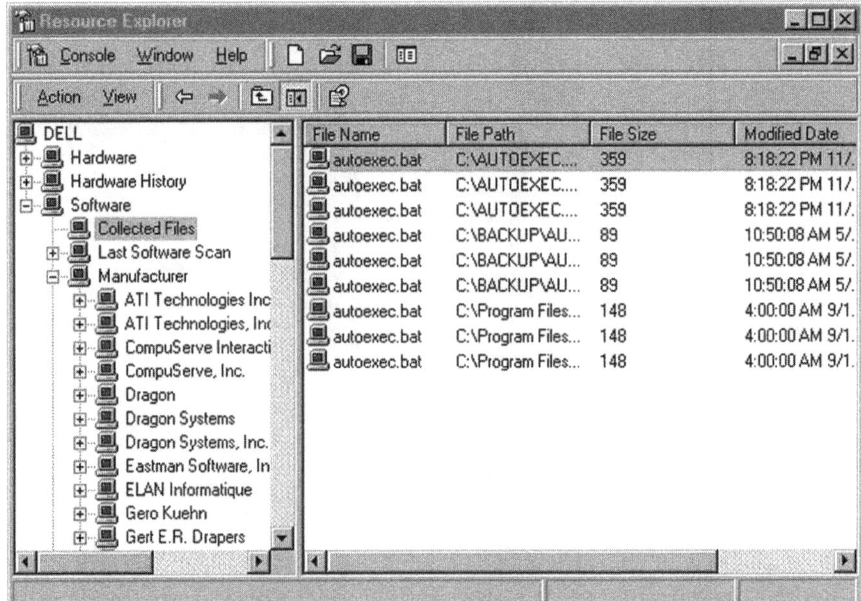

Figure 10-14 Inventory history records.

For SMS, multiple registration of hardware and software inventory should be recognized as a situation that may happen with a multiple-site SMS hierarchy.

The client system can be configured to get around this roaming problem. In the Control Panel of the local client, the System Management icon allows you to disable or enable *traveling mode*.

By checking the Mobile Computer option that reads "This computer connects to the network from different locations," traveling mode is enabled. The Sites tab shows the sites where the client PC has attached; the listed sites priorities can also be switched.

When this mode is enabled, and the client logs on to a new site, the user will be prompted as to whether he or she would like to change the principal site for SMS to the new location. This "feature" may also cause more confusion than it's worth, especially if the idea behind implementing SMS was to lock down the user. Both Windows 95 and 98 clients can change this feature without reprise; NT and Windows 2000 users need Administrative privileges to make the change, as shown in Figure 10-15.

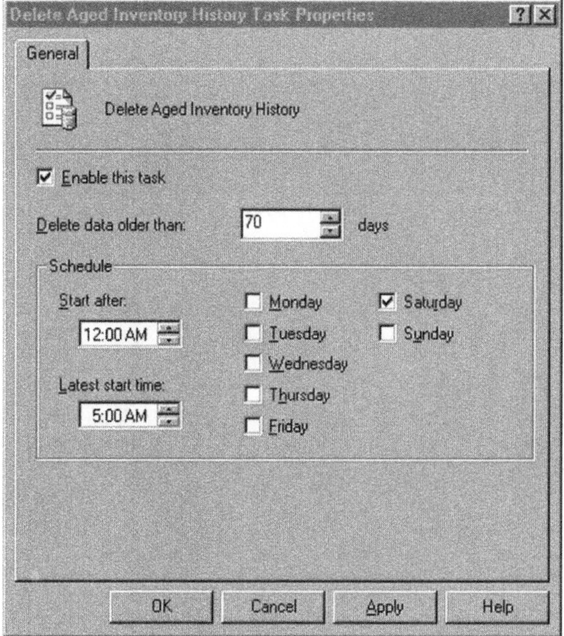

Figure 10-15 Mobile computer settings.

CHAPTER 11

Distributing Software with SMS

In this chapter you will learn about:

- Software distribution components
- Creating programs, packages, and advertisements
- Defining collections
- Installing the Windows operating systems
- Creating package definition files
- Using the SMS wizards to generate programs, packages, and wizards
- Deploying Office 2000 with SMS 2.0

SMS and Software Distribution

Software distribution is a feature that Microsoft has been fine-tuning since NT 3.1 and Windows 3.1 were released. Both of these operating systems provided syntax that would read and obey a text-based script, resulting in a custom deployment of each operating system. The Windows 3.1 world took almost no notice or advantage of this feature, and to be fair, why would we have? After all, the number of hardware changes and mutations back in those heady days meant that fine-tuning your script took much longer than installing the operating system manually. Windows 3.1 was stored on five full floppy disks (sigh).

Windows NT 3.X used a software utility that is still available on the NT 4.0 Server CD-ROM called SETUPMGR.EXE. Through a menu-driven interface, you created what is referred to as an "answer" file. When you install Windows NT Workstation the same way on 50 computer systems 50 times by inserting the CD-ROM and executing SETUP.EXE, you are performing the same role as the answer file. You are selecting choices and supplying information for a successful installation.

The answer file is a text-based script that can be used to install NT Workstation and Server the same way on every computer system using the syntax:

```
WINNT/U: scriptfile
```

Again, this feature is rarely used by the masses because hardware choices for NT for video display adapters and network adapters are in the thousands; the time it would take to modify your scripts for a wide variety of computer workstations, even if they are one national brand, becomes much longer than the manual install.

The fact is that the version of the Windows operating system of choice used in your organization is probably preinstalled, and these scripts can only install the operating system. What's needed is a tool that can handle the operating systems and the software applications and Internet settings.

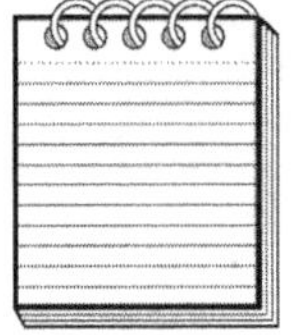

NOTE *Microsoft also provides a software utility called SYSDIFF for cloning an NT workstation's operating system and software. However, it's quite difficult to master and was an early attempt at software distribution. Windows 95 and 98 systems also have a utility called BATCH that creates custom scripts for operating system installation.*

At this stage you're probably thinking about computer system cloning—that is, using various third-party software tools that make an exact image of the complete hard drive and store the compressed contents on a network server or CD-R (CD recorder). Microsoft is betting (and hoping) you'll use SMS and software distribution rather than rely on a third-party alternative. They have good reason to be hopeful, since the software fixes, service pack updates, and virus software updates are sometimes a weekly occurrence.

Any software application, data files, or scheduled maintenance tasks can be distributed with SMS 2.0 for all clients or a group of discovered SMS clients. Again, you might be saying, "We use InstallShield, or WinINSTALL." Microsoft's response is the SMS Installer 2.0, which can create customized self-extracting installations for any software package.

Since the long-range plan is that SMS will be a component of a future release of Windows 2000 Server, Microsoft will certainly have a large segment of the network market captured as more and more features are bundled into the operating system.

SMS Software Distribution Components

Four main network components are involved in the software distribution process to the SMS client's PC:

1. *At the site server* Using the SMS Administrator console, a package is created at the Package folder. The following package criteria are defined:
   - The distribution point, if required
   - The program that will be distributed, if any
   - Security rights for the package

   Also at the site server, via the SMS Administrator console, an advertisement is created at the Advertisement folder. The following advertisement criteria are defined:
   - The package that is linked to the advertisement
   - The program contained in the package to be executed
   - The schedule for the advertisement to be advertised
   - Security rights for the advertisement
   - The collection that will be targeted

2. *At the distribution point* The package is stored on the site server, NetWare server, or network share that has been defined as the distribution point.
3. *At the client access point* The instruction files are stored on the defined client access point, either a NetWare or NT server, along with the listing of users that are to receive each advertisement.
4. *The SMS client* When the client logs in to a client access point, the Advertised Programs Client Agent reads the list of available advertisements. The client's unique Registry identifier (called a GUID), user name, or group is used as the identifier for matching the client's PC with the available advertisements.

A successful link to the defined distribution point storing the package, if needed, allows the software distribution process to begin. Figure 11-1 summarizes the software distribution steps carried out by SMS.

The Software Distribution Process

The first task to complete in the software distribution process is the creation of a *package*, which contains the software program or data file(s) that are to be distributed along with the installation instructions of the software program.

Installation instructions are enclosed in the package itself, and this is usually the command line to execute the installation. However, the instructions can be advertised without any accompanying package—for example, you may want to clean out the temp folder once a week so only the command to carry out this task would be distributed.

If a package has been defined with a collection of needed source files, a master copy is first stored and then compressed on the site server in the folder \SMSPKG. Then a copy of the package is sent to the defined distribution point.

The files can be decompressed or left in the compressed state, depending on storage limitations at the distribution point. If a package has been defined and created with no source files needed, just instructions, it is sent to the defined distribution point.

NOTE. *The SMS Executive service contains a thread called the Distribution Manager that is responsible for copying the package source*

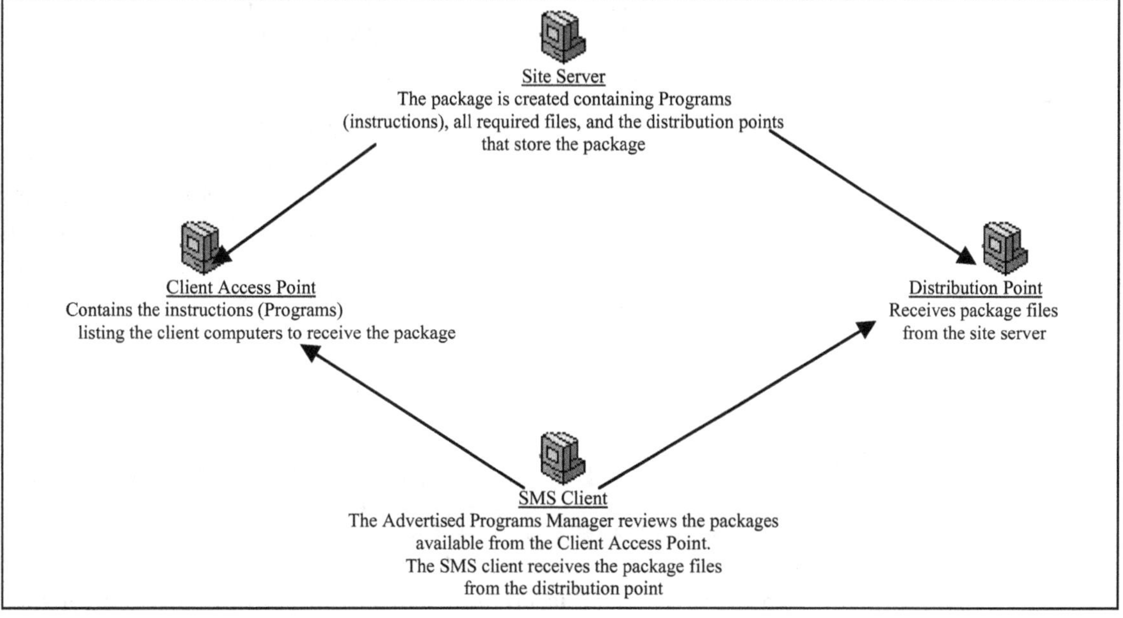

Figure 11-1 Software distribution relies on these four SMS components.

files to the distribution point and the programs to the client access points (CAPs).

Once the package has been created, the program (which contains the instructions for the package) is delivered to the CAP by the Distribution Manager. Two files and a folder are created for each generated package and stored in the folder \SMS\INBOXES\PKGINFO.BOX folder on the site server:

- *packageid.PKG* This file contains all program files and settings for the specific package and the client platforms that will be installing the package.
- *packageid.NAL* This file details the location of the distribution point for the Advertised Programs Client Agent at the SMS client.

- *Package icon folder* This location contains the icons that are associated with the package. For example, if Microsoft Word was contained in the package, the icons would be supplied for Microsoft Word.

Once the files and folder have been created and delivered to the distribution point, another thread of the SMS Executive, the Inbox Manager, notices them on the site server in the \SMS\INBOXES\PKGINFO.BOX folder. They are then copied to the defined client access point at the network path \\CAP\<site code>\PKGINFO.BOX. These files will remain dormant until an advertisement for the package is created and distributed.

The Software Distribution Process: Advertisement Creation

Next, an *advertisement* is created at the SMS Administrator console. Once accepted at the client (or mandated by an administrator) the Advertised Programs Client Agent delivers the package and program information to the defined collection of discovered SMS clients. The advertisement is also sometimes called an *offer*.

The creation of the advertisement wakes up the offer notification trigger, whose job is to wake up yet another SMS Executive thread, the Offer Manager, which oversees the copying of the package to the distribution point or points. If successful, another three files are created for each advertisement that are stored in the \SMS\INBOXES\OFFERINF.BOX folder on the site server.

1. *The offer file (.OFR)* Another name used for the offer file is the advertisement file. Contents include the advertisement ID, the program instructions, and the designated collection or collections for the advertisement.
2. *The lookup file (.LKP)* There is a possibility of three lookup files being created, and the contents catalog two main criteria: the collection type and what instruction file each collection uses to carry out installation of the package. The client computer can be targeted by user name (USER.LKP), group belonged to (USRGP.LKP), and the computer system globally unique identifier found in the local Registry (SYSTM.LKP).

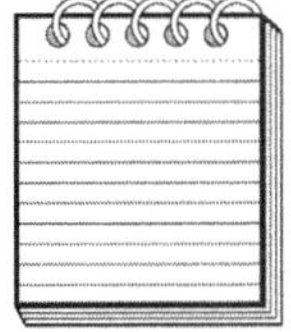

NOTE *The* globally unique identifier *(GUID) may not be a unique number if the client's PC was cloned.*

3. *The instruction file (.INS)* This file links the advertisement ID contained in the advertisement, or offer, to the collection ID of the collection where the software distribution is to take place.

These three files are created on the site server in the \SMS\ INBOXES\OFFERINF.BOX folder. Next, the Inbox Manager copies these files to the defined client access point or points in the common location \\CAP\<site code>\OFFERINF.BOX.

The Software Distribution Process: The SMS Client

When the SMS client logs on to the network, the client access point delivers any valid advertisements to the Advertised Programs Manager (APM) component installed at the SMS client. Any new offers discovered at the client access point are sent from the Advertised Programs Manager to the Advertised Programs Wizard, which, in turn, displays to the user any programs available for installation.

The APM reads the program (the installation instructions) bundled with the package (the software or data files), resulting in the software distribution process being started at the SMS client's PC. If the software distribution includes a package with software source files, the PACKAGEID.NAL on the CAP is read to find the required distribution point. If there are only instructions and no packages for the particular software distribution, the command lines are executed from the client access point.

Both 16-bit (Windows 3.X) and 32-bit Windows clients (Windows 95/98, NT, and 2000) that have been discovered by an SMS discovery process and that have the Advertised Programs Client Agent installed can participate in software distribution.

The applets that are installed to the client's Control Panel are the Advertised Programs icon, and the Advertised Programs Monitor icon. The Advertised Programs icon starts any programs that are all set to be installed, while the Advertised Programs Monitor displays a list of the programs that are present for the client to install.

Options can also be set for how advertisements, once available, are handled by the client's PC from the System drop-down menu, as shown in Figure 11-2. These settings can also be mandated and set by the administrator through the SMS Administrator console by selecting Properties, then the Notification tab of the Advertised Programs Client Agent.

Enabling Software Distribution

As mentioned, setting the properties of the Advertised Programs Client Agent, found in the SMS Administrator console in the Client Agents folder, provides the administrator with complete control, if desired, of the software distribution process. Selecting the General tab and checking the Clients Cannot Change Agent and Settings selection stops the client from changing or stopping the software distribution process.

The Notification tab allows you to define whether sounds, a Status icon, or a time countdown notify you before a schedule program is about to be deployed. Selecting No Options allows the software distribution process to proceed in the background without the user's knowledge.

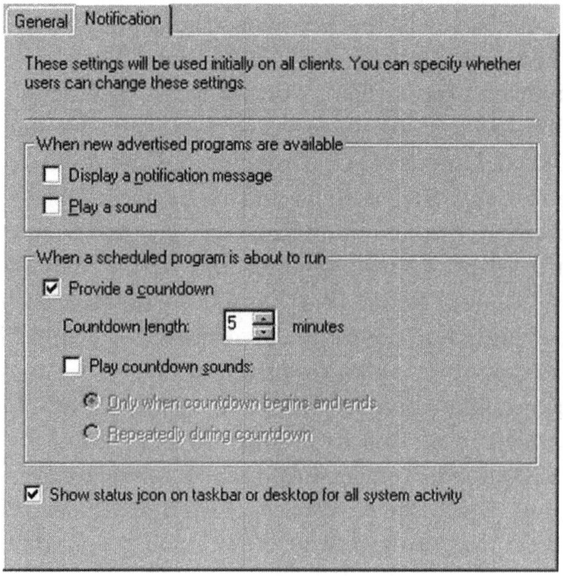

Figure 11-2 Defining software distribution criteria for clients.

SMS Task: Enabling the Advertised Programs Client Agent

Once the Advertise Programs Client Agent is enabled and installed on the SMS client, its job is to query the client access point for any new offers on a set schedule. The default schedule is every 60 minutes, although this can be changed. The user interface to the SMS client is through the Control Panel via the Advertised Programs Monitor and the Advertised Programs Wizard icons. To enable the Advertised Programs Client Agent:

1. Open the SMS Administrator console, and select the *Client Agent* folder.
2. In the details pane, double-click on *Advertised Programs Client Agent* to display its properties and the General tab.
3. Check the option *Enable software distribution for clients.*
4. Determine and change the time frame for checking for new programs on the client access point.
5. Choose the *Notification* tab, and choose the type of response the client receives when a new advertisement is available: through a notification message, a sound, or by a displayed countdown in minutes. Click on *OK* to save your changes.
6. Test your settings by logging in at a discovered SMS client.
7. In the Control Panel, open the *Systems Management* icon, and select the *Components* tab; make sure that the Available Components Manager Win32 is present with a status of "Installed." If these changes are not present, check in 60 minutes.

Checking Available Client Access Points and Distribution Points

In the SMS Administrator console, right-clicking the desired site server in the Site System folder and selecting Properties from the context menu displays the roles that can be assigned to a site server (see Figure 11-3). Selecting either the Client Access Point or Distribution Point tab and checking the "Use This Site System as a Client Access Point" selection

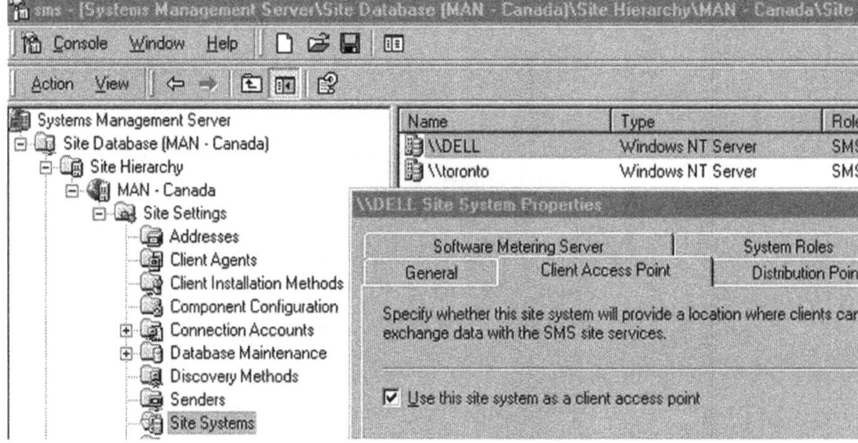

Figure 11-3 Site system properties for each installed site server.

enables the SMS role for this site server. The Distribution Point tab also allows you define a group membership list for including other site systems also functioning as a distribution point. This would be for a very large network with multiple distribution points.

Defining Software Distribution Properties

Software distribution properties are set through the SMS Administrator console. By highlighting the Component Configuration folder in the console tree and checking the properties of the software distribution component, you can define the common storage location at the distribution server for all packages. The number of threads that are allocated for processing packages can be increased from the default number of three to a maximum of seven, depending on the size and number of packages being deployed.

You can also mandate the number of times to retry the deployment of advertisements or software distribution—the System Status folder in the SMS Administrator console will track both advertisement and package status.

Distribution Tasks to Consider

Although deploying software applications is usually mentioned as the main reason for using software distribution, this is by no means the only reason to consider this feature. Any repetitive maintenance task that you manually perform at the client's PC is also a candidate for software distribution using SMS. Tasks are detailed in Table 11-1.

Building a Package with SMS 2.0

The software application or the executable files to be distributed must be close at hand for creating a package. A client access point and a distribution point are also required; if you have multiple site servers defined with these roles, the location of the client(s) will determine which ones are chosen.

Available bandwidth is the important factor to always keep in the back of your mind. Remember that when SMS was first installed, the site server automatically became a CAP and a distribution point.

To create packages, in the SMS Administrator console, right-click on the *Packages* folder, and from the New context menu, select *Package*. After selecting the package creation process, you must now define the

TABLE 11-1 Software Distribution Tasks to Consider Deploying.

Software Task	Details	Required Bandwidth
Virus Software Update	A weekly task that can be automated	Low
Service Pack Update	A task performed several times a year	Medium
Software Update	As required	Medium
Software Installation	Every new PC	High
Operating System Installation	Every failed PC	High
Software Feature Update	A possible weekly update	Low
Maintenance Task	Weekly update	Low
Scripting Update	As required	Low
Registry Update	Every new PC	Low

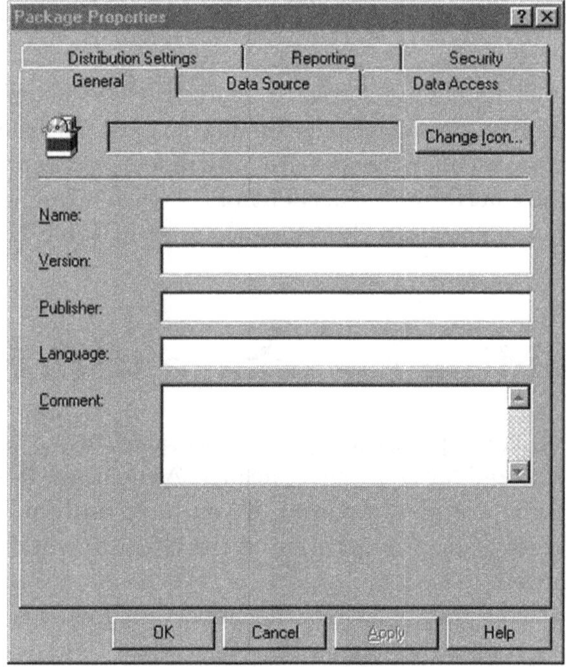

Figure 11-4 The package properties must be defined.

properties of the package being created by entering the criteria through the six tab screens displayed in Figure 11-4.

The tabs are as follows:

General The information entered in the General tab of the package properties should be as detailed as possible; it will come in handy when troubleshooting problems.

Data Source If the package being created contains source files, the source directory, which is usually the CD-ROM drive, must be entered. The package may also be re-created from a previously compressed copy of the source files. Due to the huge size of software today, it is recommended that you compress the software files.

Data Access This tab defines the distribution point or distribution folder when the client computers will access this package.

Distribution Settings This tab allows you to select the priority called the "sending priority" of each package when it is being sent to other distribution points. Choices are low, medium, and high. Once you have more than one package created, the packages with a higher priority are sent first.

Reporting Reporting information about the successful or unsuccessful results of software distribution can be logged from the client's PC to the site server. The MIF (Management Information Format) reporting file will be created using the information entered in the General tab.

- *Security* Class and instance security rights define who has the permissions to modify the packages.

After you define the property sheets for your package and click on OK, the package will be created and appear in the details pane of the Packages folder.

Constructing a Program with SMS 2.0

The *program* contains the instructions that detail how a package will be installed. Each package will have at least one program and perhaps more. For example, deploying Office 97, the choices could be Typical, Minimal, or Complete. Several programs could be created utilizing different command lines that all access the same package.

Programs are created several ways. The easiest method is through the SMS Administrator console by highlighting and then right-clicking any package shown in the details pane of the Packages folder. From the All Tasks context menu, select *Distribute Software*. This launches the Distribute Software Wizard, which will step you through the program creation process, as shown in Figure 11-5.

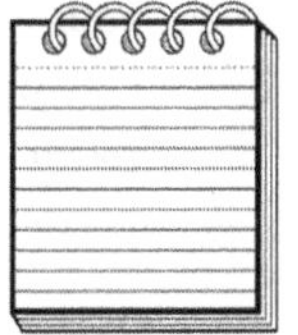

NOTE. *Selecting the Programs subfolder below the Packages folder displays the properties of the defined program that can be reviewed and edited.*

The tabs are as follows.

General The tasks are as follows. Both the name and other command line of the program to be installed must be entered in the General tab. If

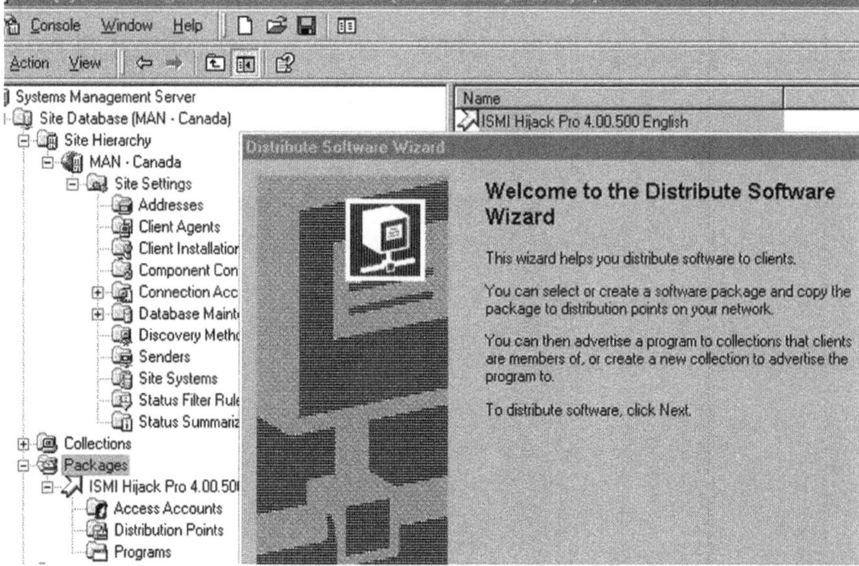

Figure 11-5 Creating a program from the SMS Administrator console.

the software application needs an absolute path on the client, this path information is entered in the Start In option. The Run option defines how the installation process will appear on the client's PC: Normal, Minimized, Maximize, or Hidden. The last option on the General tab defines what action is required after the installation has completed. Following are the four choices:

1. No action
2. SMS restarts computer
3. Program restarts computer
4. SMS logs user off

Requirements Here you can define the operating system platforms that can execute this application. The choices are all supported SMS 2.0 clients; note that MS-DOS and Apple clients are no longer supported. The estimated disk space required and the estimated runtime of the installation can be specified. You can even issue an apology to the user if the program runs 15 minutes longer than estimated.

Environment This tab defines the operating conditions that must be met before program execution begins. For Windows NT and Windows 2000 clients, the security system defined at the local PC can thwart software distribution if the logged-on user does not have the required security permissions. If your clients are Windows NT Workstation or Windows 2000 Professional, a Windows NT client software installation account can be created for software distribution. Using this account, software distribution can be carried out even when no one is presently logged in at the client PC. Other environment settings allow you to define either a drive letter or a UNC (Universal Naming Convention) path required for the software application installation.

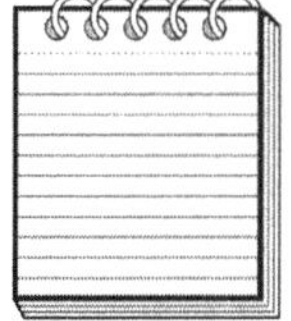

NOTE. *The client software installation account is discussed in the next few paragraphs.*

Advanced Details for installing, executing, and uninstalling the software program is defined in the Advanced tab. If you need to execute programs in a sequence and the client has the choice of selecting multiple programs, you can mandate that another program must execute first. Once the program has been installed, depending on the installation method or the number of users that share the PC, you can set the program to run once, or for every user when they log in.

Uninstalling the program, if allowed, requires an uninstall script that can be specified here for 32-bit Windows clients.

Defining the NT Client Software Installation Account

Most Windows NT clients don't have the required Administrative permissions to install software applications and utilities, and that's usually the main reason that NT Workstation is popular: unlike Windows 95/98, it has a security system.

Therefore, deploying software distribution with SMS requires the setup of the Windows Client Software Installation account SMSNTClient_<site code>. The installation account will be a member of the local Administrative group, so the permission "Act as part of the operating system" will be granted. However, adding this account to every local NT workstation would be a tedious task. When you add this account to the Domain Admin global group at the server, the Domain Admins group is automatically added to the Administrators local group for every NT workstation in the domain.

SMS Task: Setup the NT Client Installation Account

To set up the NT Client Installation account:

1. From the Administrative Tools program group, start User Manager for Domains.
2. From the User drop-down menu, select *New User*. This creates a new user account.
3. For Username enter `SMSNTClientInst_<site code>.`
4. For Description enter `NT client software installation account.`
5. Disable the *User must change password at next login* checkbox option, and select the *User cannot change password* and the *Password never expires* options.
6. Select the *Groups* button, and add the Domain Admins group to the list of groups to which this user account belongs.
7. Add the user to the domain, and then close the dialog box.
8. Open the SMS Administrator console, and highlight the *Component Configuration* folder found in the site settings.
9. Right-click on *Software Distribution*, and from the context menu, select *Properties*. The General tab appears, as shown in Figure 11-6.
10. Clicking the *Set* button, enter the user name and password for the Windows NT Client Installation account. Click on *OK* to finish the configuration of the installation account.

Defining Collections for Software Distribution

If appliance PC has not been discovered by one of the SMS discovery methods, software distribution is obviously not an option. SMS is installed with a list of fixed collections, defining all of the supported SMS 2.0 clients. Another type of collection that is supported by SMS is the query-based collection that is built from a defined list of criteria gathered

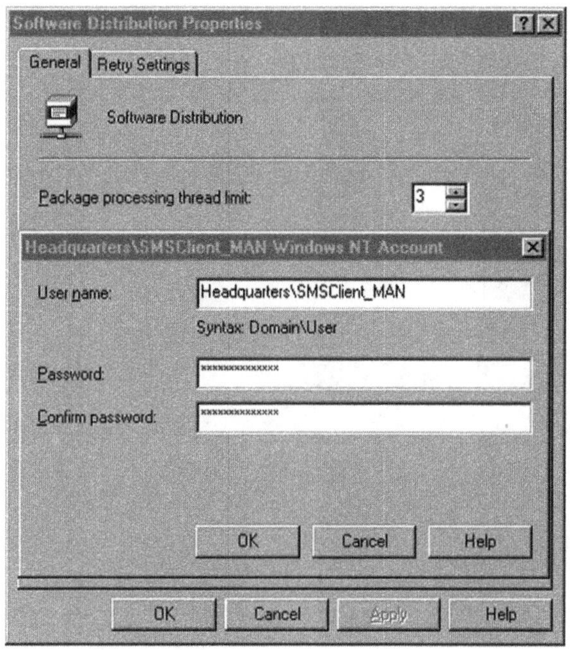

Figure 11-6 Setting up the Windows NT Client Installation account.

from the SQL site database. This type of collection has a much more specific set of membership rules; packages can be deployed only when all of the membership rules have been met.

Collections are viewed and defined using the Collections folder through the SMS Administrator console; the predefined fixed collections appear in the details pane. To define a new collection, right-click on the *Collections* folder, and from the New menu, select *Collection*. Then define the new collection through the property sheets, as shown in Figure 11-7.

The tabs are as follows.

General The name of the collection and any comment must first be entered.

Membership Rules Membership criteria can be either direct assignment or query-based. Selecting Direct Assignment launches the Create Direct Membership Rule Wizard, which allows you to select the class of resource to be used for your collection criteria from drop-down dialog boxes. Query-based Membership allows you to craft the query statement from the same resource classes. Resource class and attribute choices are listed in Table 11-2.

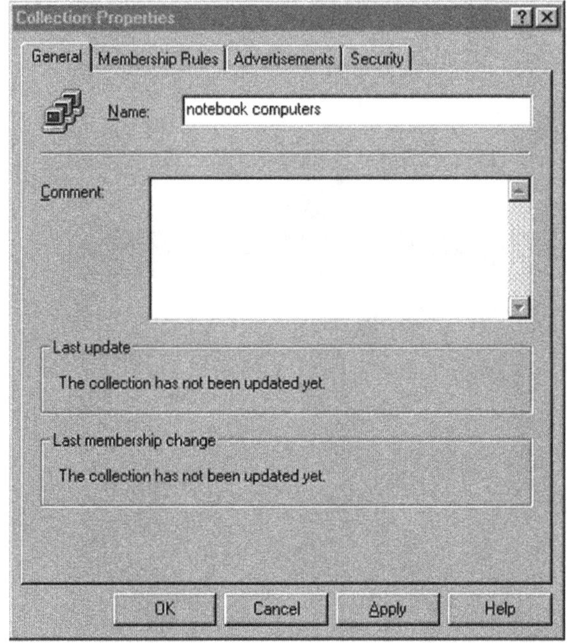

Figure 11-7 Creating a new collection through the SMS Administrator console.

TABLE 11-2 Direct Membership Queries are defined with Resource Classes and Attributes.

Resourc Class	Attributes that Can Be Assigned
User	Agent name, agent site, agent time, name, network operating system, resource ID, resource type, SMS assigned sites, unique user name, user group name, or Windows NT domain
User Group	Agent name, agent site, agent time, name, network operating system, resource ID, resource type, SMS assigned sites, unique user name, user group name, or Windows NT domain
System	Agent name, agent site, agent time, client, client version, IP addresses, IP subnets, IPX addresses, IPX network numbers, last logon user domain, last logon user name, MAC addresses, name, NetBIOS name, operating system name and version, resource domain or workgroup, resource ID, resource names, resource types, SMS assigned sites, SMS installed sites, SMS unique identifier, SNMP community name, system rolls
IP Network	Agent name, agent site, agent time, name, resource ID, resource type, SMS assigned sites, subnet address, subnet mask

Advertisement Any defined advertisements created for the collection will be displayed here.

Security The setting of class and instance security can be applied to the collection to protect any changes.

Creating Advertisements

Once packages and programs have been created and collections have been established, advertisements are created to link a collection to a specific package and program. Advertisements are defined through the SMS Administrative console at the Advertisements folder. By right-clicking the Advertisement folder and selecting Advertisement from the New menu, you can display the properties, as shown in Figure 11-8.

The tab screens are as follows.

General The name of the advertisement must be entered first.

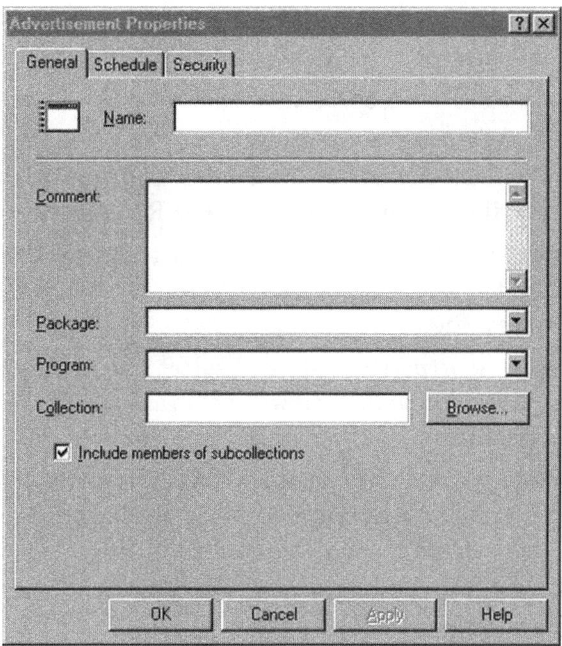

Figure 11-8 Advertisements are defined with the General, Schedule, and Security tabs.

Schedule Define the schedule when the advertisement is available, if it is mandatory, and when it is due to expire, if at all. Mandatory dictates that the user cannot cancel this advertisement.

Security Both link and instance security can be applied to the advertisement.

SMS Task: Building a Package for HiJaak Pro

For this example of creating a package, a 32-bit graphics program called HiJaak Pro version 4.0 will be packaged.

1. Open the SMS Administrator console at the site server, and select the *Packages* folder. Right-click on the details pane; from the New context menu, select *Package*.
2. From the package properties, the General tab is displayed: Enter the name of the software, the version, the software publisher, and the language, as shown in Figure 11-9. (This information will be useful shortly.)
3. From the Data Source tab, select the checkbox *This package contains data files*.
4. Click on the *Set* button, and define the network or local path to the source files, probably the local CD-ROM drive on the site server.
5. Select the *Distribution Settings* tab, and change the Sending Priority to `High`. Leave the preferred sender at `<No Preference>`.
6. Select the *Reporting* tab, and select *Use package properties for status MIF matching*. This will generate a MIF file with the General tab details.
7. Select the *Security* tab. The default security settings for both the class security and instance security settings are defined for the users that can modify this package.
8. Select *OK* to save your changes. You will be returned to the SMS Administrator console.

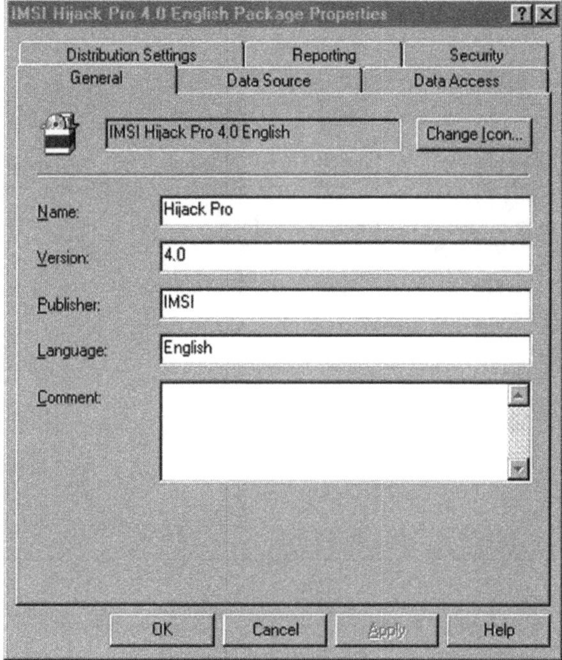

Figure 11-9 Defining the software contained in the package.

Package Subfolders

Once a package is created, a folder structure is generated below the Package folder created and named for the just-generated package (see Figure 11-10).

Access Accounts

An access account allows you to specify the permissions for the users and group of users that are allowed to access the package. The default setup is that all users have access to the package stored at a distribution point. For each account added to the user account folder, the permissions that can be added are as follows:

- *No Access* No allowance for reading, writing, or deleting the package.
- *Read* The account is allowed to read, copy, and execute the program.

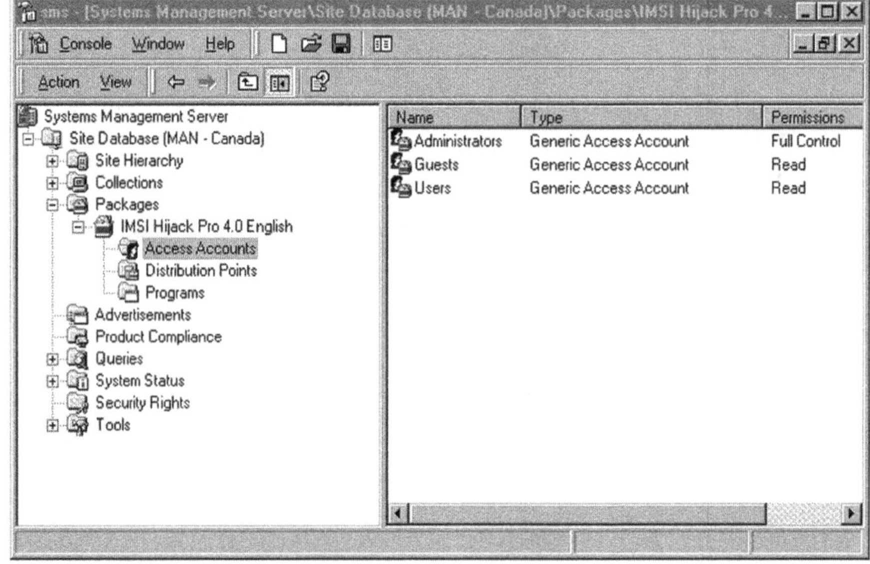

Figure 11-10 Each package has its own folder structure.

- *Change* The account can change the contents of the folder containing the package, as well as delete files.
- *Full Control* Administrators have full control by default.

Distribution Points

This folder contains the distribution points for the package stored at the root of this folder structure below Packages.

Programs

This folder contains the programs that are linked to the package stored at the root of this folder structure below Packages.

SMS Task: Generating a Program for HiJaak Pro

A program must be created for each package. To generate a program for HiJaak Pro:

1. Open the SMS Administrator console at the site server, and select the *Packages* folder. Select the *Programs* subfolder, and right-click on the details pane. From the New context menu, select *Program.*
2. Click on the *Change Icon* button, and browse and select the executable file for the software application. The icon should change to reflect the software being installed.
3. Select the *Requirements* tab, and change the values for the estimated disk space required at the client and the time the installation will run.
4. Select the *Environment* tab. Check the option *User input required.*
5. Select the Advanced tab. Select the option *Run once for first user who logs on.*
6. Click on *OK* to save your changes. The installation should appear in the Programs folder, as shown in Figure 11-11.

SMS Task: Enabling the Distribution Point for HiJaak Pro

The package and program for HiJaak Pro must now be sent to the distribution point and then scheduled for distribution. To enable the distribution point:

1. Open the SMS Administrator console, and select the *Distribution Point* subfolder, which is under the HiJaak Pro Package folder.
2. From the details pane, right-click just below the listed distribution point, and select *New*, then *Distribution Points*; this will launch the Distribution Points Wizard.

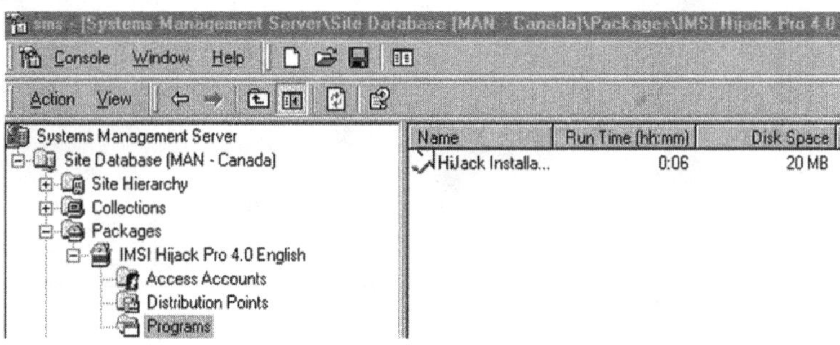

Figure 11-11 A program created for a package.

3. From the Distribution Points dialog box, choose the distribution point to send the package and program to. For this example, the Dell distribution point is selected, as shown in Figure 11-12.

SMS Task: Advertising the HiJaak Pro Package

Now the package must be advertised to a collection. For this example, all Windows 98 clients were chosen.

1. Open the SMS Administrator console at the site server, and select the *Advertisement* folder. Right-click on the details pane, and from the New context menu, select *Advertisement.*
2. From the displayed properties in the General tab, the name of HiJaak Pro is entered. Select the Hijaak Pro 4.0 English package and HiJaak Installation program, as detailed in Figure 11-13.

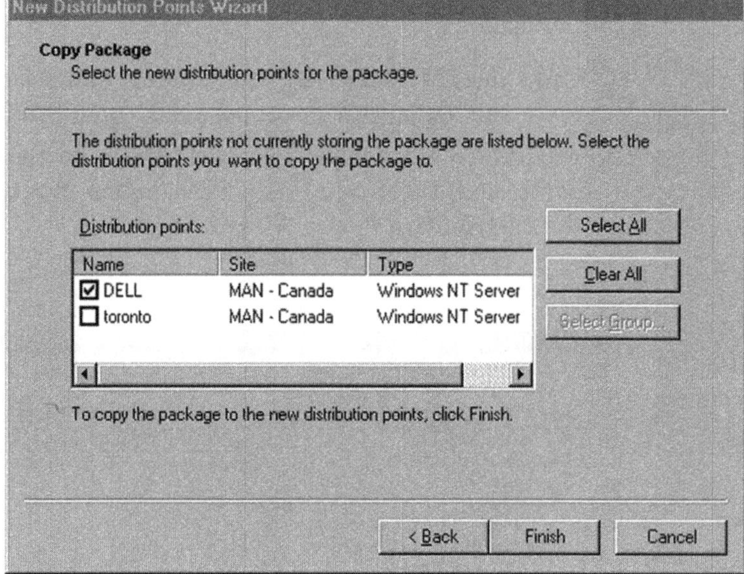

Figure 11-12 The distribution point is selected for the package.

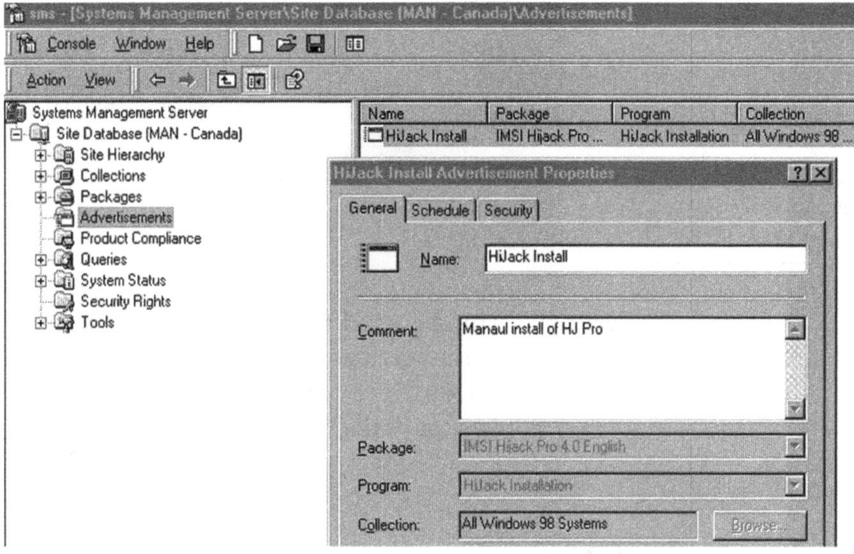

Figure 11-13 Advertised properties for HiJaak Pro.

SMS Task: Running the HiJaak Pro Program at the Client

This package was created and defined for all Windows 98 systems, so logging in with a Windows 98 system results in a message from the Advertised Programs Monitor, as shown in Figure 11-14.

Depending on the notification options set by the administrator, the user may or may not receive any notifications. In this example, the user received the message, as shown in Figure 11-14, along with a Notification icon in the system tray in the bottom right-hand corner of the display.

Package Definition Files (PDF)

Most new Microsoft software applications are bundled with a package definition file (PDF; not to be confused with the Adobe Acrobat PDF data files—for Portable Document Format). A PDF is configured for SMS to automatically distribute the software application.

Several PDF files are installed with SMS for Microsoft applications, and more are appearing every week at www.microsoft.com. A PDF is

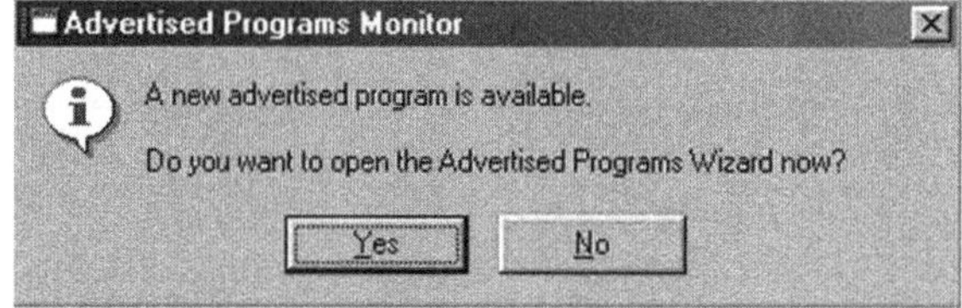

Figure 11-14 The Advertised Programs Monitor indicates a new program is available for installation.

written in standard INI file format containing certain sections and keys. There are three sections: [PDF], [PACKAGE DEFINITION], and [PROGRAM], and they are always enclosed in square brackets. Each key value within a package follows the format of `name = value1, value 2,....`

[PDF]

The first section is always the PDF section. This section contains the following line to distinguish it as a PDF for SMS 2.0:

```
VERSION=2.0
```

[PACKAGE DEFINITION]

The fields in Table 11-3 are usually the sections that can be found in the Package Definition section. There can be additional sections for defining MIF file information if you wish to generate status information about the package deployment.

[PROGRAMS]

This section defines the program that is contained in the package detailed in Table 11-4.

If the Programs section in the Packages sections contains multiple values, there must be multiple Program sections. Creating a PDF for HiJaak Pro would require the keys and sections shown in Figure 11-15.

```
[PDF]
VERSION=2.0
```

TABLE 11-3

Package Key Options in PDF File.

Key Heading	Required	Details	Displayed in the Package Properties
NAME	Yes	Name of the software, maximum 50 characters	Name shown in General tab
VERSION	No	Version of the software, maximum 32 characters	Version shown in General tab
ICON	No	File containing the icon for the software	Change icon in General tab
PUBLISHER	Yes	Publisher of the software; maximum 32 characters	Publisher option in General tab
LANGUAGE	Yes	Language of the software; maximum 32 characters	Language option in General tab
COMMENT	No	Any comment about the software; maximum 127 characters	Comment option in General tab
PROGRAMS	One at a minimum	The program defined for this package: X86 or Alpha, Typical, or Complete	Not shown

```
[PACKAGE DEFINITION]
LANGUAGE=English
VERSION=2.0
PUBLISHER=IMS
NAME=HiJaak Pro for Windows 98 and NT 4.0
PROGRAMS=x86

[x86]
ADMINRIGHTSREQUIRED=True
USERINPUTREQUIRED=True
ESTIMATEDRUNTIME=10
ESTIMATEDDISKSPACE=11MB
COMMANDLINE=install.exe
STARTIN=INSTALL
NAME=x86 systems
CANRUNWHEN=AnyUserStatus
```

Using a PDF for Package and Program Creation

Using a PDF for package and program creation does not guarantee a perfect package and program completion, since mistakes do happen.

TABLE 11-4 Program Key Options in PDF File.

Key Heading	Required	Details	Displayed in the Program Properties
NAME	Yes	Name of software; maximum 50 characters	Name in General tab
ICON	No	The icon will be shown on the client's PC	Change Icon option in General tab
COMMENT	No	Notes up to 127 characters	Comment option in General tab
COMMAND LINE	Yes	Command line for the program	Command-line option in General tab
STARTIN	No	Working directory for the program	Start option in General tab
RUN	Default is Normal	Can be normal, maximized, minimized, or hidden	Run option in General tab
AFTERRUNNING	No	Can be SMSRestart, ProgramRestart, or SMSLogoff	After running in General tab
ESTIMATEDISK SPACE	Defaults to Unknown	KB, MB, or GB needed	Estimated disk time in Program tab
ESTIMATED RUNTIME	Defaults to Unknown	Time in minutes	Estimated runtime in Requirements tab
ENABLE RUNTIME MONITORING	No	Warns the user if estimated runtime is over 15 minutes off	Notify use if the program runs 15 minutes longer than estimated in Program tab
SUPPORTED CLIENTS	No	Supported platforms included Win 9x, Win NT, and Win 16	Program can run only on specified programs in Program tab
ADDITIONAL PROGRAM REQUIREMENTS	No	Optional text up to 127 characters	Additional require-ments in Requirements tab
CANRUNWHEN	Defaults to User Logged On	Can specify UserLoggedOn, NoUserLoggedOn, or AnyUserStatus	Program can run in Environment tab
USERINPUT REQUIRED	Defaults to True	True or False for requiring user input during in stallation	User input required in Environment tab
ADMINRIGHTS REQUIRED	Defaults to False	True or false for needing Administrative rights	Run with Admini-strative rights in Environment tab

TABLE 11-4 (Continued)

Key Heading	Required	Details	Displayed in the Program Properties
USEINSTALL ACCOUNT	Defaults to False	True or False for using the Windows NT client installation account	Use Windows NT Client Software Installation account in Environment tab
DRIVELETTER CONNECTION	Defaults to False	True requires a drive letter; False uses UNC	Requires drive letter in Environment tab
SPECIFYDRIVE	No	Drive letter at the distribution point	Requires specific drive letter in Environment tab
RECONNECT DRIVEATLOGON	Defaults to False	Set to True if user must reconnect to the distribution point	Reconnect to distribution point at logon in Environment tab
DEPENDENT PROGRAM	No	Any program that must be executed first	Run another program first in Advanced tab
ASSIGNMENT	Defaults to First User	The first user received the program, or Every User	When program is assigned in Advanced tab
DISABLED	Defaults to False	True disables the program for the client	Disable this program on computers where it is advertised in Advanced tab
REMOVE PROGRAM	No	True or False. True removes program from client when the advertisement is no longer valid	Remove software when it is no longer advertised in Advanced tab
UNINSTALLKEY	No	Name of the Uninstall in Registry	Uninstall Registry key in Advanced tab

However, if you test and retest software distribution using a package definition file, I think you can see their advantages in weekly software distribution tasks such as antivirus DAT file updates. Since the file name of the antivirus update DAT filename would be the same, it would be a snap to use a PDF for automating the update process with SMS.

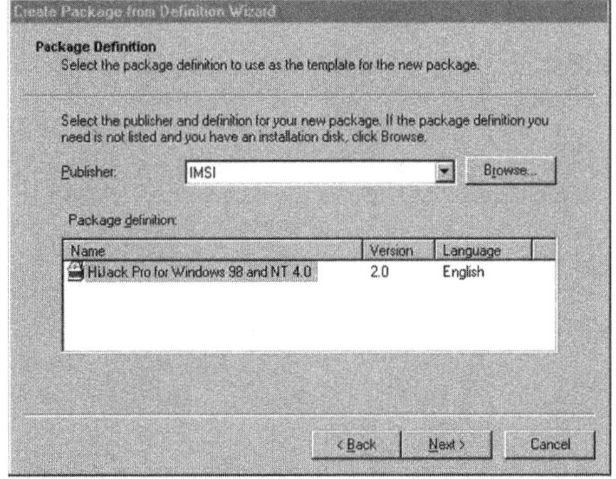

Figure 11-15 A program definition file for HiJaak Pro.

SMS Task: Using a PDF for Package and Program Creation for HiJaak Pro

To use a PDF to create packages and programs:

1. Open the SMS Administrator console at the site server, and select the *Packages* folder. Right-click on the details pane; from the New context menu, select *Package from Definition*.
2. The Create Package from Definition Wizard is launched. Click on *Next* to display the package definition screen.
3. From The Publisher drop-down menu, a list of defined packages is displayed. Microsoft is of course present, as is IMSI, the publisher of HiJaak Pro. See Figure 11-16.
4. The remaining steps are similar to the creation of the package and program earlier in this chapter. To complete this task, enable the distribution point and create the advertisement for the clients.

Package Definition Files from Microsoft

The following package definition files are created and supplied by Microsoft at this time of writing:

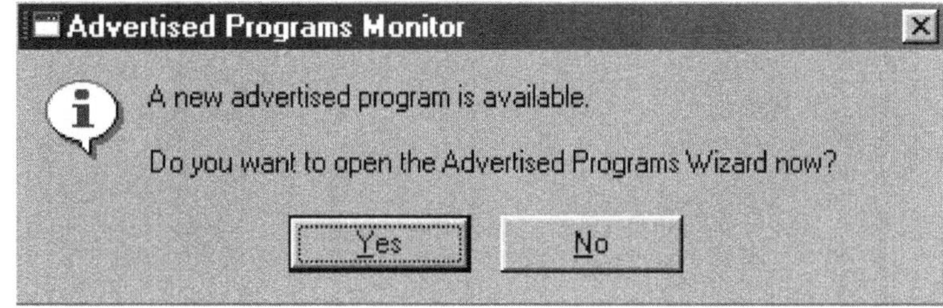

Figure 11-16 The PDF for HiJaak Pro is loaded.

- NT to Event to SNMP Trap Configuration Modification tool
- SMS Healthmon Agent
- SMS Healthmon Console
- Service Pack 4 for Windows NT 4.0
- Windows NT Server
- Windows 98
- Windows NT Workstation
- Windows 2000 Server
- Windows 2000 Professional
- Office 97
- Internet Explorer 5.0
- Office 2000
- Software Distribution Status

Rolling Out Office 2000 with SMS 2.0

When Office 2000 is installed to Windows 95/98 clients, there is no security system to deal with. However, when you install Office 2000 on Windows NT and 2000 Professional clients, the installation must be performed with administrative rights. Office 2000 is bundled with a variety of PDF files for different situations, as detailed in Table 11-5.

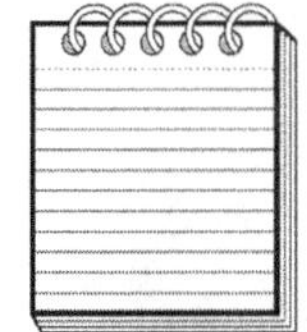

NOTE. *The extension for package definition files has changed to .SMS; however, the extension .PDF is still recognized.*

TABLE 11-5

Space Required for Office 2000 Installation with SMS 2.0.

Office Version	PDF	Distribution Point Required (MB)	Client Space Required
Premium	Off9pre.sms	544	626
Professional	Off9pro.sms	530	400
Small Business	Off9sbe.sms	407	360
Standard	Off9std.sms	484	189

The Office 2000 Resource Kit also contains PDFs only for the installation of individual Office 2000 products that were purchased separately. If you wish to install a single Office 2000 product from the software suite CD-ROM—for example, Microsoft Word 2000—the Offrpre.sms file must be modified using the Custom Installation Wizard (CIW) from the Resource Kit. Office 2000 has three options that can be implemented with SMS 2.0. The options available are as follows:

- *Transform Files* These are used for customizing the Office 2000 installation or adding additional files to the installation. Transform files have an .MST extension.
- *Install on Demand* A "new" feature used by Office 2000, the Windows Installer is really a repackaging of advertisements performed by SMS. The Windows Installer places icons in the Start menu or on the Desktop. When the user selects the icon or shortcut, the installer installs the application on the user's hard drive. SMS 2.0 uses the Control Panel and the Advertised Programs Wizard.

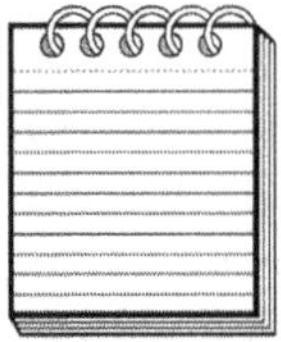

NOTE *Install on Demand needs the active desktop software code to be presently installed on the client PC. Therefore, Internet Explorer 4.01 or later must be installed.*

- *Resilient Source* The resilient source is an "installation point" that remains available to the client as Office 2000 is used by the organization. The Windows Installer is the backbone of the new Office 2000 features: Install on Demand and application repair. A valid network path for the source files can be defined for the Office 2000.

Office 2000 Installation Notes

There are four [Programs] sections contained inside Off9pre.sms. Three deal with installation, and one is for the uninstallation of Office 2000 Installation.

- *Typical Installation* All error messages are suppressed, only a progress indicator is shown; the assumption is an unattended installation.
- *Custom Installation* This option is the same as the typical installation but with a transform file.
- *Manual Installation* The default install with the full user interface; the assumption is that the client will be present during the install to answer questions.

To install Office 2000, perform these steps:

1. An administrative installation point must first be created for Office 2000. The source files will be installed at this location first, and then on the client PCs. Create a network share on a server that the SMS Service account can access. Insert the Office 2000 CD-ROM, and in the Start menu's Run box, enter the following syntax pointing to the CD-ROM drive:

```
<Drive Letter> SETUP.EXE /a data1.msi
```

After the installation screens have been dispensed with, the setup program copies the Office 2000 software files from the CD-ROM to the administrative installation share.

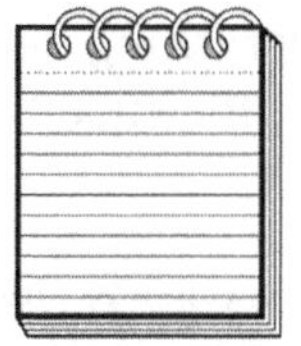

NOTE. *From the Office 2000 Resource Kit, the SMS 2.0 hotfix (SMS2000K.EXE) must be applied if the installed Advertised Programs Manager (found in Control Panel on your SMS clients) version is earlier than 100.1239.003.*

2. Open the SMS Administrator console, and highlight the *Packages* folder.
3. Right-click the details pane, and from the displayed context menu, select *New* and *Package from Definition*. The Create Package from Definition Wizard should start.

4. From the Package Definition dialog box, select the publisher *Microsoft*. You may have to use the Browse button to locate the Office 2000 Off9pre.pdf file. Press *Next*.
5. From the Source Files Wizard screen, choose *Always obtained files from a source directory*.
6. From the Source Directory screen, enter the network location of the Administrative installation point for Office 2000.
7. Verify your installation information on the completion screen, and click on *Finish*.
8. Next, from the SMS Administrator console in the Packages folder, right-click on your package, and from the All Tasks context menu, choose *Distributed Software*. This launches the Distribute Software Wizard.
9. From the Distribute Software Wizard screen, choose *Distribute an Existing Package*, making sure to select *Office 2000*.
10. From the Distribution Points screen, choose the distribution point to use.
11. From the Advertise a Program screen, select *Yes* to the question `Do you want to advertise a program to a collection?`
12. From the Advertisement Target screen, choose *Advertise the program to an existing collection*, and then select the collection to use.
13. From the Advertisement Name Wizard screen, enter a name for the advertisement that will appear at the client's PC.
14. From the Advertisement Schedule Wizard screen, choose the schedule of deployment that you want and any expiration date for the advertisement.
15. From the Completing the Distribute Software Wizard screen, review the information in the details pane. If everything seems correct, click on *Finish* to start the distribution of Office 2000.

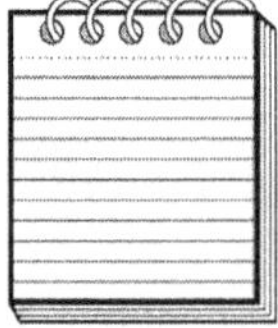

NOTE. *If your clients are all Windows NT 4.0 or later, your servers are all NT servers, and you require some custom setup, I recommend that you check with Microsoft and TechNet for complete instructions for installing Office 2000 with SMS 2.0.*

CHAPTER 12

Using the SMS Installer

In this chapter you will learn about:

- The SMS Installer and its features
- Creating scripts and variables with the Script Editor
- Installing a 32-bit application with the SMS Installer
- Installing Internet Explorer 5 with the SMS Installer
- Windows 2000 and the Windows Installer
- Side-by-side component installations for Windows 2000

Automating Installations

In the last chapter, we dealt with the process of software distribution, including creating packages and programs and advertising these programs to the end user. Unfortunately, there are still many times that the packaged installation still requires a great deal of user intervention. By the time you plan for all of the possible situations and combinations that you will run into, you might as well have installed the application manually.

Although the manual installation is not exactly considered proactive administration, you could probably live with that fact if the client's PC never had to be touched again. However, reality dictates that software upgrades, damaged files, and other problems created by the user ensure that you will be back to visit the end user again and again. What is needed is a utility like the SMS Installer that will allow the scripting of installations that will install themselves correctly every time without user intervention.

As we all get ready for Windows 2000 upgrades, one main advantage is that the hardware world is becoming completely plug and play for both the Windows 98 and Windows NT client base. The operating system in most cases will now be able to fix itself. Although plug and play isn't perfect, it's getting much better.

Turning to the software world, well, that's another matter. The biggest headache in the 32-bit software world is "DLL hell," as it has been described. Every single DLL on your system is a complicated library of software components registered to a process.

The information message "A file older [or newer] has been found on your system" that you often see while installing software is the best example of the current DLL problem: The installation doesn't know what to do about multiple DLL versions. At least in this instance, however, it's informing you that a DLL or other system components being copied onto your system don't match or may conflict with currently installed software. In addition, the same scenario can repeat itself when you uninstall software, as the uninstall routine may remove certain DLLs and other system components, messing up other software that is installed on the computer system that must use those same DLLs.

The SYSTEM folder for Windows 95 or 98 clients, or the SYSTEM32 folder for Windows NT or 2000 clients is the usual global location for dynamic link library files.

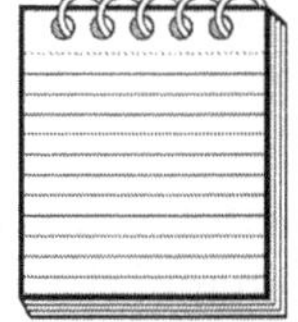

NOTE. *Microsoft is changing the global location for DLLs back to private folder locations in an attempt to stop the "DLL hell" scenario from continuing. This "new" way of thinking is called "side-by-side installation" and is discussed later in this chapter.*

InstallShield Express, InstallShield Professional, PC-Install Pro, Setup Factory, Setup Wizard, and Wise Installation System are just some of the competing script editing packages available today for automating the software installation. Microsoft's response to these competing products depends on the version of the Windows operating system you use: The launch of Windows 2000 introduces the new Windows Installer service, discussed later in this chapter; in the NT 4.0 world, when SMS 2.0 is installed, the SMS Installer is included.

The SMS Installer allows you complete control in the way the software installation process occurs by creating and compiling an executable file and script that reproduces a software installation exactly the same every time.

NOTE. *The earliest version of a Microsoft-based software installer program was a utility called SYSDIFF.EXE, still bundled on the Windows NT 4.0 Server CD in the \SUPPORT folder. The Windows Installer is a core component of Windows 2000 Server. If you have experience with using SYSDIFF, then you will recognize some aspects of the Windows installer service.*

The SMS Installer program is provided in two versions: one for 16-bit software applications (Windows 3.X) and another for 32-bit (Windows 95/98 and NT/2000).

Regardless of the type of SMS installation, Custom or Express, the SMS Installer software is stored on the site server ready for installation. Depending on the type of clients that you support, you may have to install the SMS Installer in two client locations: once on a Windows 95/98 computer and on a Windows NT or Windows 2000 Professional Workstation.

The term used to describe these installer installations is a *reference computer* installation. The SMS Installer works in the background on a reference client computer, comparing the file structure and Registry settings before and after the installation has been performed and generating an installation script containing the application file and Registry settings, along with the installation options that were selected during the installation.

The generated script can also be customized, producing a completely unintended installation, or some information can be left for the user to input, such as his or her user name and personal information.

SMS Task: Installing the SMS Installer on a Reference Computer

The following steps install the SMS Installer on the desired reference PC:

1. On the reference computer, using the Windows Explorer through Network Neighborhood, navigate to SMS\SMS_Inst\i386 on the site server.
2. Execute SMSINSTL.EXE.
3. You will be prompted as to the type of software environment to install: 16-bit, 32-bit, or both. After making your choice, the installation proceeds and finishes. The Microsoft SMS Installer program group appears on the Start | Program menu.

When you start the SMS Installer, the opening screen of the SMS Installer displays the Installation Expert, as shown in Figure 12-1.

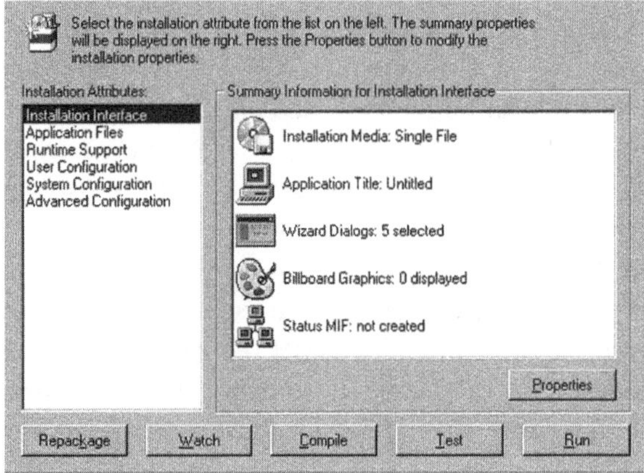

Figure 12-1 Viewing the SMS Installer Installation Expert interface.

Choosing a Reference Computer

The reference computer must have the same hardware and software mix as the client's computer where the installation script will be installed. Obviously, with plug and play hardware, it's perhaps easier to solve any hardware differences for Windows 95/98 and Windows 2000 PCs, but the sameness of each PC's hardware and software installed is very important. Table 12-1 lists the other problem areas to check out.

TABLE 12-1

Settings to Check Before Choosing the Reference Computer.

Operating system version and service pack	Windows 95 has four versions, Windows 98 has three versions, NT 4.0 has six service packs.
Internet Explorer version and service pack	Internet Explorer 4, 5, plus service packs.
Software applications in the same folders with service packs, and updates	Always accept the default \Program Files suggestion on all PCs.
Video and network hardware and driver versions	Check every three months on manufacturer's Web site.
BIOS version	Flash BIOS upgrades on the manufacturer's Web site are regularly available.
Hard drive partition(s)	Use the same drive letters for easier script reading and assigning.
Drive letter assignment	CD-ROM drives should be the same on all PCs.
User profile (Local, Roaming, Mandatory)	Mandatory profiles save no Registry changes.
System policy or group policy settings	Policy settings may interfere with the installation.
Security permissions	User settings on NT 4.0 Workstations and Windows 2000 Professional Workstations.
Startup files	AUTOEXEC.BAT, CONFIG.SYS, and SYSTEM.INI settings.

Using the Installation Expert Interface

The Installation Expert interface comprises five buttons that launch wizards to quickly step you through the testing and creation of your package.

The Repackage Wizard

This button starts the Repackage Wizard, which is then used to create a new installation procedure in script format from monitoring the software installation procedure carried out on the reference computer. After the Repackage Wizard has finished, the Script Editor or the Installation Expert can be used to change the created script before compiling. Then the software application files and the executable script are stored in the same location.

The Repackage Wizard carries out the following tasks:

1. The reference PC's file structure and local Registry is scanned and logged.
2. The SETUP.EXE for the desired application is executed and completed through the Repackage Wizard.
3. The reference PC is scanned again to detect the changes that have occurred during the software installation.
4. The detected changes to the reference PC are used to create the new installation script.

The Repackage Wizard scan performed on the reference PC can search up to 32 subfolders and up to 64 subkeys in the Registry hierarchy. The completed script can be a maximum of 8,192 script lines. Specifying specific file and Registry locations to be searched, or to be ignored, can also be added through the Repackage properties of the Installation Expert interface.

The Watch Wizard

This wizard does not install the application as the Repackage Wizard did; its job is to watch the application as it starts and executes, building a list of files required, software components required, and Registry settings accessed. If custom software is being installed, you may not be aware that the software requires specific software components to be installed on the client's computer in order to run the software successfully. Before a custom application is packaged, it's a good idea to first install the application and then use the Watch Expert to track the files and components the application uses.

The Compile Wizard

Once the software application has been installed on the reference computer, generating a satisfactory script, it is necessary to compile the script created during the installation into an executable file that contains the script; all of the software files required for the software application's successful installation are needed as well in the same location.

During the compile procedure, if any failures occur, the SMS Installer will prompt you as to whether the current script error should be viewed through the Script Editor in order to be corrected. Changes or additions can be inserted in the script, and then you can start recompiling at the point where the failure first occurred.

The Test Wizard

The Test button allows you to test the installation script before it is compiled. Although it looks like the installation is proceeding, no actual modifications or changes to the computer system are being made at this time.

The Run Wizard

The Run button executes the installation package created by the SMS Installer.

Working with the Installation Expert Interface

Any changes to the reference PC monitored through the Installation Expert interface will be reproduced in the script that is created. There are six attribute windows selected from the main window of the installer.

Changes made through the installation interface are detailed in Table 12-.2 Dialog box options are shown in Figure 12-2.

Application Files

This section defines the files required for the installation. Choices are for the application components and installation files as detailed in Table 12-3.

TABLE 12-2

Installation Script Interface Options and Details.

Installation Media	From a single EXE package or from floppy disks.
Application Title	Name of software application and default folder to be installed into. Choosing Place Default Directory... installs under Program Files folder.
Wizard Dialogs	Five default dialog boxes are presented during installation, and five are disabled, as shown in Figure 12-2.
Billboard Graphics	Provide a custom install graphic.
Status MIF	Create a custom MIF for SMS software inventory.

Figure 12-2 Dialog box choices shown during the installation.

TABLE 12-3

Application File Choices.

Application Components	Installation choices: Typical, Custom, Full, or Minimal.
Installation Files	Add custom file(s) to the package, such as templates or form letters.

Runtime Support

The Runtime Support attributes are for detailing any components that may be needed for database support, such as ODBC, Visual Basic, or Visual FoxPro, as described in Table 12-4.

User Configuration

This section lists any icons, registered file types, Registry settings, or INI files to be added to the script, as described in Table 12-5.

System Configuration

This section lists operating system components such as VxDs, Windows NT services, or AUTOEXEC.BAT or CONFIG.SYS settings, as described in Table 12-6.

TABLE 12-4

Runtime Support Options.

Runtime Options	Support components needed for successful installation: ODBC, OLE, COM, Access, Oracle, dBase, Paradox, and 16-bit sharing. Uninstall support enabled here.
Visual Basic	Folder location for VB plus additional components for runtime and OCX support.
Visual FoxPro	Folder location for FoxPro plus additional components for runtime and OCX support.

TABLE 12-5

User Configuration Details.

Icons or Shortcuts	Define Start menu program groups and software icons. Additions allowed.
File Associations	Lists the file types to be registered in the Registry. Additions allowed.
INI Files	Any INI files that will be changed during the installation. Additions allowed.
Registry Keys	Any user or system Registry settings that will be changed. Additions allowed.

Advanced Configuration

This section lists details on the installation variables required for operating system installations and Web-based applications as described in Table 12-7.

Using the Script Editor

The Script Editor can be used after a script has been generated with the Repackage Installation Expert, as shown in Figure 12-3.

The Script Editor can be used for adding the following customizations to the installation script:

- Stopping and asking the user for any additional information during the installation
- Uninstall and rollback options should the installation run into problems

TABLE 12-6

System Configuration Details.

VxD Devices	Device drivers for Windows 95/98 systems.
Windows NT Services	Installs needed for Services for NT systems.
AUTOEXEC.BAT Commands	Add commands that will be required.
CONFIG.SYS Commands	Add commands that will be required.

TABLE 12-7 Advanced Configuration Details.

Global	Set password protection, Install.log location, platform type, compression type, Zip compatible install packages, turn-off boot messages, and more.
Screen	Set background size, color, and placement of install screen.
Font	Define font size used for installation messages and text.
Installation Languages	Configure default language.
Options	Setup options for the Script Editor, Compiler, and Watch Wizards, as shown in Figure 12-3.
Settings	Define folders used during the installation script.
Patching	Define the options for creating updates that install after the current software packages installs.
Compiler Variables	Configure the variables used by the compiler.
Code Signing	Employ digital code signing if installation package is over the Internet.

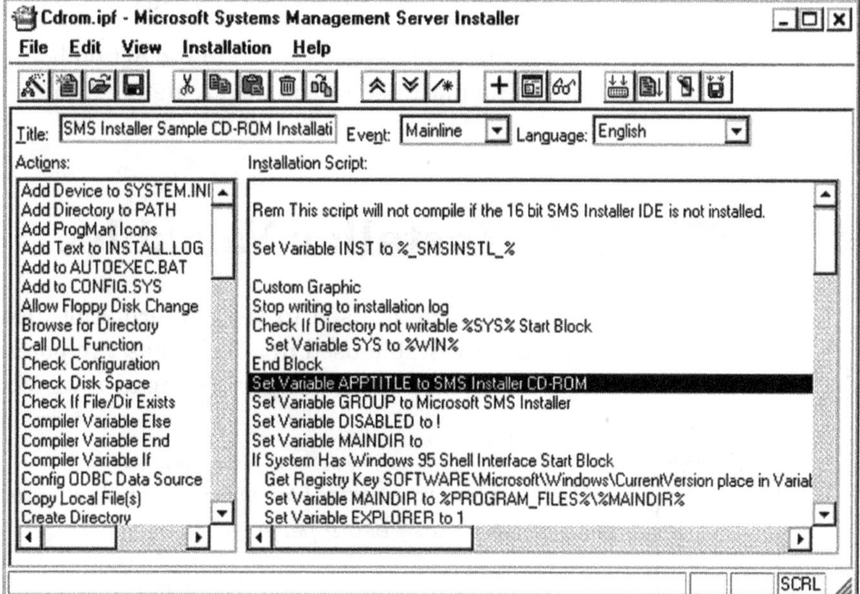

Figure 12-3 Viewing a script with the Script Editor mode of the SMS Installer.

- Customizing the SMS Installer messages that are displayed during the installation
- Add additional Registry settings such as uninstall scripts or user customizations
- Execute additional utilities or software applications when an application first starts

To edit any line of the script in the details pane of the Script Editor, just double-click any highlighted line. The best plan of attack is to first use the Installation Expert to create the basic script, and then load the Script Editor to make modifications and additions. Options to be aware of when creating or modifying a script are as follows:

- *Title* The displayed title shown while the installation executes
- *Event* Three event choices are available:
  - Mainline—Displays the installation script
  - Exit—Displays the script that executes once the installation has completed successfully
  - Cancel—Displays the script that executes if the installation fails to finish successfully or the user cancels the installation.
- *Language* The language used for the displayed script
- *Actions* Shown in the left-hand column of the display window listing all tasks that installation scripts can carry out

There are many actions listed in the Action listing in the Script Editor. Some of the most useful actions are detailed in Table 12-8.

SMS Installer Variables

A script variable is used to store information used by the installation script. Each variable used in a script has two potential roles: performing as a destination variable or performing as a variable reference.

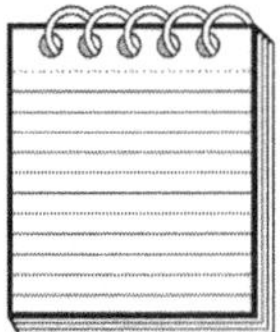

NOTE. *The term "variable" means it is changeable or adaptable to the current job or task being performed.*

TABLE 12-8 A Summary Listing of the Actions Used by the Script Editor.

Action	Description
Add Device to SYSTEM.INI	Add or change an entry in the [386enh] section
Add Directory to Path	Adds the directory to the environment path
Add Text to INSTALL.LOG	Add a remark to the installation log file for checkpoint tracing
Add to AUTOEXEC.BAT	Add or change commands
Add to CONFIG.SYS	Add `Device=` statements
Call DLL Function	Call WIN16 and WIN32 DLLs
Create Shortcut	On the desktop or Start menu of Windows clients
Display Graphic	A bitmap graphic shown during installation
Display Message	Show a message to the end user and capture the user's answer
Get Registry Key Value	Read data values from the Registry
Read INI Value	Read an INI file entry on the client's PC
Remark	Add a comment to the script
Search for File	Find a file located on the client's PC
Set File Attributes	Set a file's or a group of files' attributes
Win32 System Directory	Produces the path to the Windows client's system folder

Destination Variables

When the installation script receives information and places it into a variable, it is called a *destination variable*. The contained information is being used for the destination where the installation is being performed. For example, a predefined variable used in SMS scripts is WIN. The path of the local Windows directory is usually C:\WINDOWS.

Rules for a destination variable include that it must begin with a letter, be a maximum of 14 characters, and can include numbers, letters, and the underscore character (_).

Variable Reference

Once a variable has been created or defined by the installation script, the contained information can be referenced and used multiple times throughout the script through a *variable reference*. To use the variable information contained in the reference variable, the variable name is referenced in the script enclosed in percent signs %—for instance, %Variable Name%.

Predefined Variables

Variables shown in Table 12-9 are created and defined when the SMS Installer is installed. The table shows the common list of variables bundled with the SMS Installer.

Creating a New Script Variable

To create or change a value in the SMS Installer, the `Set Variable` command is used from the Actions menu. To change a defined value in

TABLE 12-9

Predefined Installation Script Variables.

APPTITLE	DOBACKUP
BACKUP	DOBRAND
BACKUPDIR	EXPLORER
BRANDING	GROUP
CDESKTOPDIR	GROUPDIR
CGROUP_SAVE	INST
CGROUPDIR	MAINDIR
COMMON	MAINDIR_SAVE
COMPANY	NAME
COMPONENTS	PROGRAM_FILES
CSTARTMENUDIR	STARTMENUDIR
CSTARTUPDIR	STARTUPDIR
DESKTOPDIR	SYS
DIRECTION	TEMP
DISABLED	WIN
DISPLAY	

the script, double-click on the line containing the variable, as shown in Figure 12-4.

SMS Installer Checklist

The process of creating an SMS installer executable file is a detailed process. The checklist shown in Table 12-10 summarizes the tasks involved.

SMS Task: Automating a 32-Bit Software Application with the SMS Installer

To automate a 32-bit software application:

1. Open the Microsoft SMS Installer 32 by selecting *Start | Programs | SMS Installer*

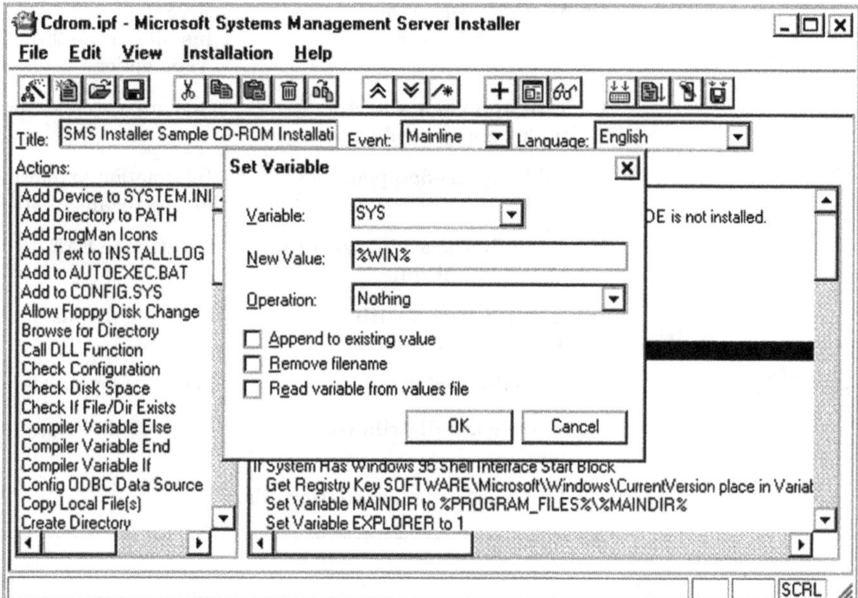

Figure 12-4 Create a new variable in your script with the Add option.

TABLE 12-10

Tasks for Creating the Software Installation Executable File.

Task	Notes
1. **Install the SMS Installer on the reference computer.**	16-Bit or 32-bit versions available.
2. **Copy the installation file to the reference computer.**	If an existing installation script is available.
3. **Run the Repackage command option.**	By installing the software application, you create an installation script.
4. **Load the SMS Installer, open the Installation Expert, and load the installation file.**	Choices are Installation Expert or the Script Editor.
5. **Edit Installation Interface choices.**	
6. **Edit Application Files choices.**	
7. **Edit Runtime Support choices.**	
8. **Edit User Configuration choices.**	
9. **Edit System Configuration choices.**	
10. **Edit Advanced Configuration options.**	
11. **Run the Watch Application Wizard.**	Test for any additional software components.
12. **Load the installation script in Script Editor.**	Save the script first, then toggle the SMS Installer mode through the View drop-down menu option.
13. **Edit and review script, making any needed changes.**	Add any variables as required.
14. **Add any needed prompts.**	Information to inform or help the end user during the installation.
15. **Compile the script with the Compile button.**	Creates the EXE, PDF, IPF, and WSM files.
16. **Test the script with the Test command button.**	Simulate the installation.
17. **Save the script.**	With a recognizable name.
18. **Choose the distribution method.**	SMS, CD-R, Floppy, or Web.
19. **Distribute the installation file.**	

2. Insert the CD-ROM containing the software to be installed into the reference computer's CD-ROM drive.
3. From the bottom of the Installation Expert, click on The *Repackage* button.
4. The Repackage Installation screen prompts you for the path and name of the installation executable file, as shown in Figure 12-5.
5. Type in the local path where your software files are located, for example, `G:\SETUP.EXE`. Click on *Next*. The Repackage Installation screen is displayed, and the reference PC is scanned, as shown in Figure 12-6. Then the installation starts.
6. The installation starts, continuing until it is finished. Then the message "Installation Completed" appears on the screen.
7. Click on *Finish*. The Repackage Installation dialog box appears. Click on *Next*.
8. The rescan procedure of the reference computer system after the installation begins and eventually completes. Once it has finished, click on *Next*.
9. The Installation Interface screen appears, displaying the Wizard Dialog options.

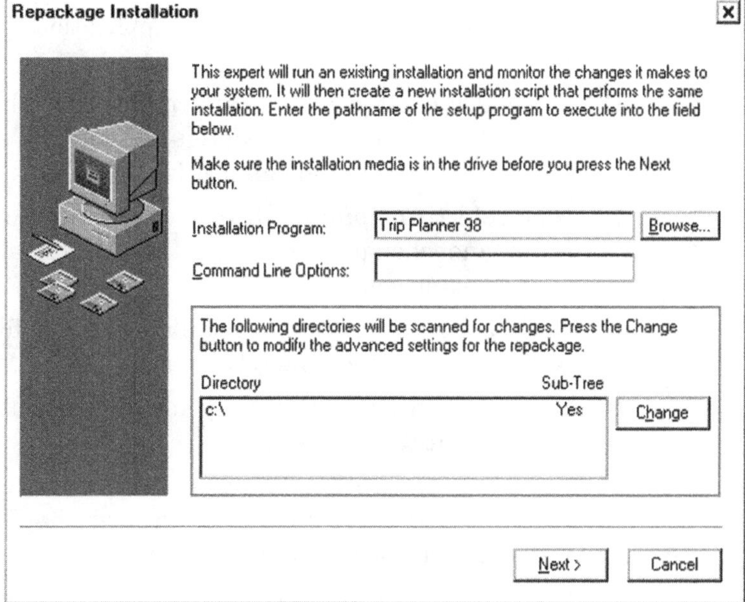

Figure 12-5 Enter the location and name of the installation file.

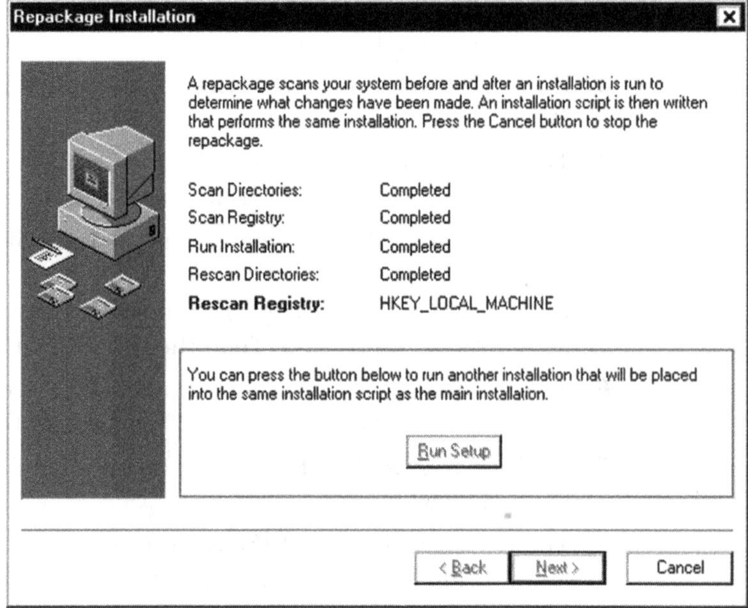
Repackage Installation
A repackage scans your system before and after an installation is run to determine what changes have been made. An installation script is then written that performs the same installation. Press the Cancel button to stop the repackage.
Scan Directories: Completed
Scan Registry: Completed
Run Installation: Completed
Rescan Directories: Completed
Rescan Registry: HKEY_LOCAL_MACHINE
You can press the button below to run another installation that will be placed into the same installation script as the main installation.
Run Setup
< Back
Next >
Cancel

Figure 12-6 The reference computer system is scanned before the installation starts.

10. Select the *SMS* tab from the Installation Interface, and enter MIF product information in order to include this software for software inventory. See Figure 12-7.
11. Select the *Place default directory under program files* checkbox if you wish to install the software application under the Program Files folder.
12. Select *Runtime Support*, and make sure that the Uninstall Support checkbox is selected; this provides the ability to uninstall the software application after it has been installed.
13. Now select *Compile* to start the compiling of the installation script, and when prompted, save the SMS Installer script file with an .IPF extension.
14. Click on *Test* to check the installation script file to make sure it installs as expected. The results are shown in Figure 12-8.
15. Now click on *Run* to actually install the software application using the installation script.
16. Once the installation has been verified as successful, you can remove the software application through the Control Panel using the uninstall script displayed in the Add/Remove Programs applet.

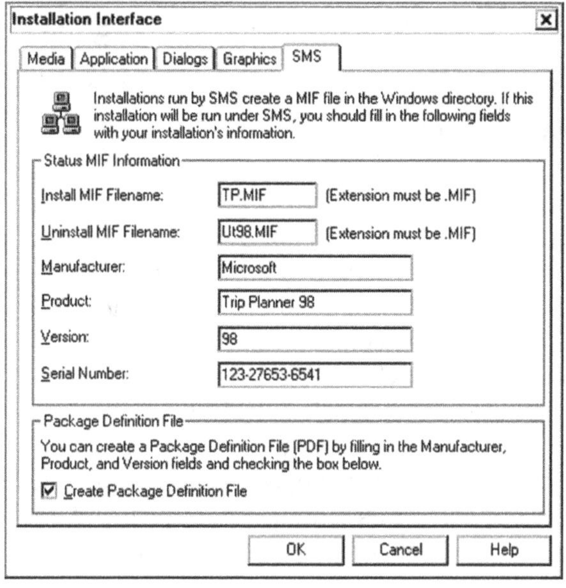

Figure 12-7
MIF information is used by the SMS inventory.

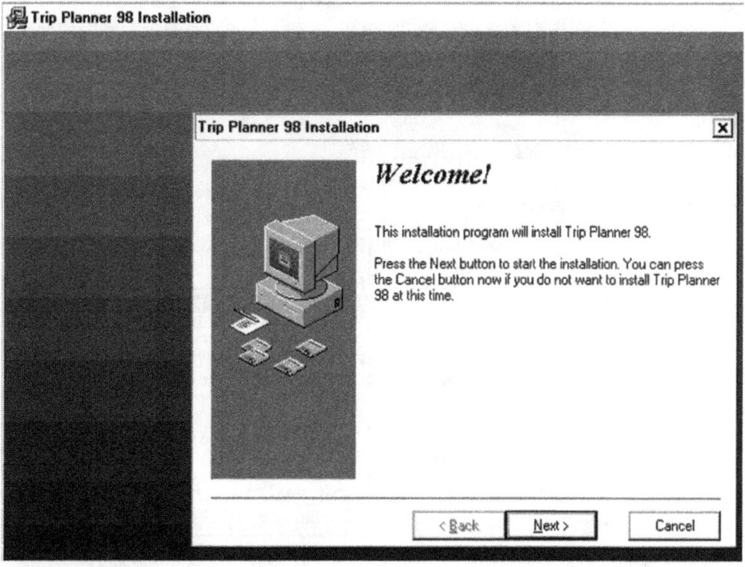

Figure 12-8
Run the Test option to check the installation script.

SMS Task: Automating Internet Explorer 5 for NT with the SMS Installer

When installing Internet Explorer for NT Workstation clients, the security system must be recognized; that is, the user installing IE 5 must have Administrator rights in order to complete this installation successfully. In addition, the installer script relies on a utility called SHUTDOWN.EXE; it is included in the NT Resource Kit and can also be found on the monthly TechNet CD labeled "Server Utilities" (along with the SMS Installer script for IE 5, IESETUP.IPF) in the folder SMS\SMSIE.

The SMS Installer script for Internet Explorer 5 (IESETUP.IPF) must be customized to match the user's security and domain settings. The initial settings are left as comment fields, which for a Windows 95/98 installation would be left in this format, since there is no security system to plan for.

To automate Internet Explorer:

1. Open the script IESETUP.IPF with the SMS Installer. It will switch into script mode, as shown in Figure 12-9.

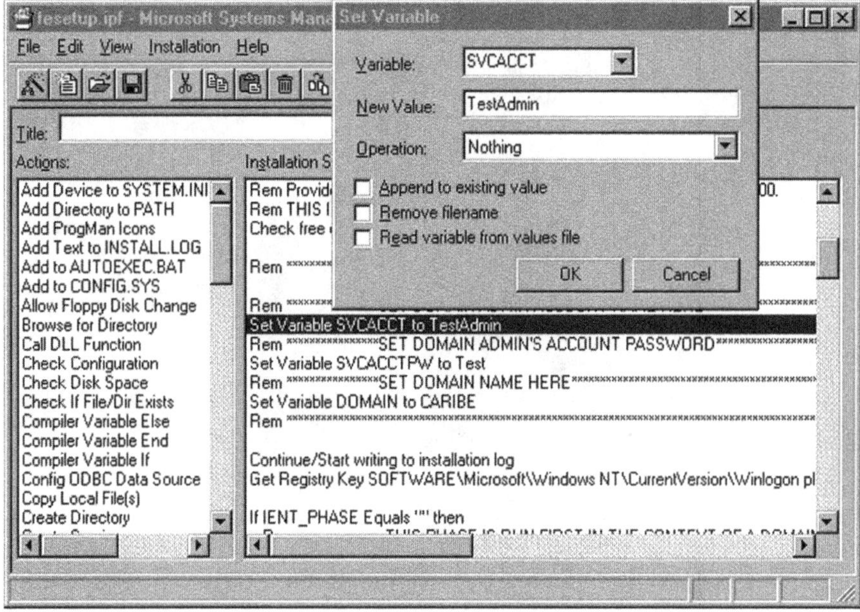

Figure 12-9 Debugging the Internet Explorer installation script with the SMS Installer.

2. Locate the variable `SET DOMAIN ADMIN'S ACCOUNT NAME HERE`, and change this variable to the name of the account with domain admin permissions that SMS and software distribution can use.
3. Next, locate and change the `SET DOMAIN ADMIN'S ACCOUNT PASSWORD` variable to the password for the domain admin account. (This should be the next setting, as shown in Figure 12-9).
4. Then locate and change `SET DOMAIN NAME HERE` to the name of the domain admin account belongs. (This again should be the next setting, as shown in Figure 12-9).
5. Save the file as IESETUP.IPF.
6. From the SMS Installer main windows, click on *Compile*. This will create the EXE file with the name IESETUP.EXE. Make sure that IESETUP.EXE and SHUTDOWN.EXE is placed into the same network folder as the IE 5 installation files.

Creating the SMS Package for Internet Explorer 5

To create the SMS package:

1. Open the SMS Administrator console, and right-click on the Packages folder details pane. From the context menu, click on *New* and then *Package*.
2. On the displayed General tab, name the package.
3. Open the *Data Source* tab, and check the *This Package Contains Source Files* checkbox.
4. Next, click on the *Set* button, and at the Source Version Source Directory option, enter the path to the IE 5 setup files in the network or CD-ROM source directory.
5. Open the *Distribution Settings* tab, and change the Sending Priority to `High`.
6. Click on *OK*. The package should now be shown in the new Packages section.
7. Expand the IE 5 package under Packages, and right-click on the Distribution Points details pane. From the context menu, select *New* and *Distribution Points*. This should launch the Distribution Points Wizard.

8. Click on *Next*, and select the server to be used as the distribution point by putting a check in the checkbox on the server to be used. Then click on *Finish*.

SMS Task: Creating a Program for the IE 5 Package

To create a program:

1. At the SMS Administrative console, right-click on the *Programs* subfolder details pane, and from the context menu, select *New* and then *Program*.
2. From the displayed General tab, name the program that will launch IE 5.
3. In the Command Line field, enter the full path to the IE 5 script executable file.
4. Open the *Environment* tab, and clear the *User input required* checkbox.
5. Check the *Run with Administrative rights* checkbox. This must be checked for an NT installation. Now click on *OK*.

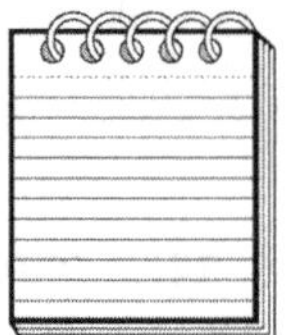

***NOTE**. Since the run with Administrative Right option was selected, and the script has been changed to add the domain account, this account will run as part of the operating system on all NT workstations across the domain. See Chapter 11 for more details on creating the Windows NT Client Installation Account.*

We have now created the IE 5 package, distributed the IE 5 software application files, and created the program that is linked to the IE 5 package. Now IE 5 must be advertised to the NT clients.

SMS Task: Creating the IE 5 Advertisement for NT Clients

To advertise IE 5:

1. At the SMS Administrator console, open the Queries folder and select the collection of users to advertise IE 5—for this example, the collection Windows NT 4.0 users. You may have a different name for your NT Workstation users.
2. Right-click on the collection to advertise, and install the package; from the context menu, select *All Tasks* and *Distribute Software*. The Distribute Software Wizard is now launched.
3. Click on *Next*, select the IE 5 package.
4. Click on *Next*, and check that the correct distribution site is selected.
5. Click on *Next*, then choose the IE 5 program to install.
6. Click on *Next*. On the displayed Advertisement Target tab, choose the *Create a New Collection Containing This Resource and Advertise To the New Collection* radio button.
7. Move through the last few wizard tab screens until the Assign Program screen is displayed. Select *Yes* to assign the IE 5 program.
8. Click on *Next*, and then click on *Finish* to complete the advertisement assignment.
9. When an NT user logs on to the network at a CAP from a client machine included in the collection, the server will recognize and install IE 5 to the NT client.

Internet Explorer 5 Installation at the Client

Once the client PC's Advertised Program Manager is informed that an advertisement is now available, the IE 5 installation process will begin. IESETUP.EXE carries out the following tasks:

- Modifies the local Registry in HKEY_LOCAL_MACHINE\SOFTWARE\Microsoft\Windows\NT\CurrentVersion\Winlogon to allow automatic logon
- Disables keyboard and mouse services for the end user through HKEY_LOCAL_MACHINE\SYSTEM\CurrentControlSet\Services
- Sets the path to the Systems Management Server distribution server, the location the script is being executed from

- Calls the SHUTDOWN.EXE utility to restart the client computer

1. Now the client's PC restarts, with automatic logon enabled and with the keyboard and the mouse services disabled. IE5SETUP.EXE runs from the Registry and starts Internet Explorer Setup in "quiet" mode, finishes the first phase of its installation, and calls SHUTDOWN.EXE to starting the client's PC.
2. IESETUP.EXE restarts again. First, it disables automatic logon. Next, the Administrator account and password is removed from the Registry. Finally, the keyboard and mouse services are enabled.
3. After finishing the last segment of the installation, the client PC is restarted.

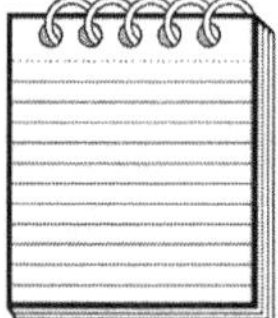

NOTE*. There are many syntax choices for the starting of the Internet Explorer 5 installation. At the command prompt, check out IESETUP.EXE /?*

Delivering the Finished Product

Once the script file has been created, tested, and compiled, it can be delivered through the SMS software distribution process by a CD-R or floppy disk installation. Table 12-11 lists the files that the SMS Installer creates when the installation script is compiled using the Compile Expert.

Following are a few notes regarding the distribution options:

- Choosing SMS for distributing the installation script requires that the settings in the Installation Interface SMS tab be defined to create a package definition file used for SMS software distribution.
- Using a CD-ROM installation is smart; it is unchangeable, cheap, and requires no network bandwidth if all required files are included on the CD-R.
- Choosing a floppy-based installation, although not fast, is still available by selecting the Floppy-Based Installation option found on the Installation Interface installer attribute. Then when you have finished your script, from the File menu of the SMS Installer, choose

TABLE 12-11

Files Created by the SMS Installer When a Script Is Compiled.

Filename	Description
APPLICATION_NAME.EXE	The installation files, including the installation script and a compressed version of the software application files
APPLICATION_NAME.PDF	The package definition file for SMS software distribution
APPLICATION_NAME.IPF	A text version of the installation script
APPLICATION_NAME.WSM	A working file used by the installation script file

Make Floppies. Be sure to have lots of coffee and preformatted floppy disks on hand!

Rolling Back an Installation

If a software installation produces the wrong results due to improper planning before the installation proceeded or some other failure, SMS has two features to consider. Uninstall, for uninstalling the software just installed, or, Rollback, for returning the client PC to the state before the installation was attempted.

Uninstall. Removes all new files installed and all added Registry entries. Support for using the Uninstall option must be enabled before the installation script is compiled in the Runtime Support attribute in the Installation Expert. After it is enabled, the UNINSTAL.EXE utility is placed in the installation package once it is compiled.

When the installation script is executed, installing the application, a LOG file called INSTALL.LOG is produced; this information will be used if the Uninstall feature is selected, removing the software application. An entry is inserted in the LOG file for every file copied, every Registry change, and every DLL change.

Rollback With Rollback, the uninstall is first performed, then all replaced files and Registry settings are restored. Note that the Uninstall feature must be performed before the Rollback feature can occur.

To use the Rollback feature, before the information script is compiled, you must check Backup Replaced Files in the Dialog tab of the

Installation Expert. When the installation script is running on the client's computer, the message "Backup Replace Files?" will be displayed on the computer screen. Assuming that the user does not answer No, a folder called BACKUP directly below the Software Applications folder will hold any files changed during the installation process.

In addition, in order to suppress the backup message, the line `Set Variable dobackup to B` must be changed to `Set Variable dobackup to A`.

***NOTE**. After you install the SMS Installer contained with Service Pack 1, there are some very helpful debugging features added to this release. You can set breakpoints, variable watches, and a single stepping mode, allowing you to watch what is happening to your variables during the actual execution of a script.*

Using the Installer Setup Utility

A forthcoming utility you should be aware from Microsoft is the Installer Step-up Utility (ISU) specifically for SMS 2.0 and installation scripts. This command-line tool migrates any scripts previously created with the SMS Installer to the Windows Installer format. This converted setup package can be used with the Windows Installer service in the Windows 2000 environment.

Any SMS Installer executable scripts that were created using the Repackage Installation Wizard, the Installation Expert, or the Script Editor can be converted. However the Windows Installer does not support the SMS Installer features listed in Table 12-12.

All uninstall logs created with the SMS Installer are not migrated, since the Windows Installer service provides support at the component level for uninstalling and removing applications. The features of the SMS Installer that are supported are listed in Table 12-13.

Understanding Side-by-Side Component Sharing

The software that we use on our PCs uses many software components, and these components are usually stored in the same system folder. This

TABLE 12-12

SMS Installer Features Not Supported by the Windows Installer.

The SMS Installer Feature Not Supported	Located in the SMS Installer
Add Text to INSTALL.LOG	Script Editor
Allow Floppy Disk Change	Script Editor
Open and Close INSTALL.LOG	Script Editor
Modify Component Size	Script Editor
Remark	Script Editor
Floppy-Based Installation	Media tab: Installation Interface
16-Bit FoxPro Options	Visual FoxPro tab: Runtime Support
16-Bit VB Options	Visual Basic tab: Runtime Support
OLE2 Support	Options tab: Runtime Support
16-bit Windows Clients	Global tab: Advanced Configuration
Beep in New Disk Prompt	Global tab: Advanced Configuration
No Installation Log	Global tab: Advanced Configuration
Install Log Pathname	Global tab: Advanced Configuration
Maximum Compression	Global tab: Advanced Configuration
Control Installation Speed	Global tab: Advanced Configuration
Changes Made During Setup to the Uninstall.Log	Anywhere in the installation script
Timing Loops	Anywhere in the Installation Script

TABLE 12-13

Windows Installer Features Supported with ISU.

Windows Install Feature	Support in ISU Converted Package
Install on Local Hard Drive	Fully supported
CAB Files	Fully supported
Install on Demand	Fully supported
Feature-Level Install on Demand	SMS Installer components are treated as one feature; therefore, the entire app would be installed.
Dynamic Repair	Fully supported
Installation Rollback	Fully supported
Uninstall	Fully supported

design was encouraged in the past, since software was large and hard drive space was expensive. The shared components are also version-dependent; every software and operating system process (EXE) demands access to a specific version of the DLL or COM component in order to work properly.

For example, on a Windows NT 4.0 workstation with Service Pack 3 installed, you will have no success installing a brand-new ATI video adapter with video drivers that take advantage of the latest version of DirectX. That's because the DLLs available on an NT 4.0 SP3 system have no idea what DirectX is; they don't support it.

Installing Service Pack 4 and up, however, installs the up-to-date DLLs with the newer operating system software components that recognize the new video adapters, and the new video adapter is at last recognized. Although today's software is even larger, hard drive space is cheap. At the present time, Windows 95, Windows 98, and Windows NT 4.0 install both software applications and operating system components in the same shared and stored locations on the local PC in the following areas:

- The system Registry and user profile
- System folder locations
- Windows API function calls

Once an application is installed, it becomes totally dependent on a specific version of a shared component; it can work with no substitutes. Then, another software application is installed with either a newer or older version of the shared Registry setting, DLL, or Win32 API component, and the older application fails.

Side-by-Side Sharing

The solution offered by Microsoft, and a solution that makes sense, is to isolate key components into private locations in both the Registry and in hard drive folders. Both Windows 2000 and Windows 98 Second Edition feature this new form of component sharing, called *side-by-side sharing*, which uses isolation to minimize the so-called DLL hell.

Implementing side-by-side sharing allows multiple versions of the same component to execute simultaneously in different processes. New software applications, such as Office 2000, use the exact version of the component that they were designed for and tested with.

Creating New Side-by-Side Components

Side-by-side sharing rules mandate that when a new application is created for the Windows 32-bit world, the software developer must write and design the software's execution using side-by-side components. These can be the very same COM or Win32 components used in older versions of the software, except that they are installed into the software application directory and not into the system directory.

Then the side-by-side components are registered into the local Registry in their singular location, isolating them to the specific software application. So, if another installed software application on the same PC requires and has installed a different version, each software application is unaffected by the decisions of each installation program.

Each of the software applications on the local PC now runs with its individual version of the needed software and Registry components. The end result: The operating system can load and use both versions at the same time.

When the uninstall routine of either application is executed to remove either software application, because each side-by-side component is "private" to the software application that installed it, the uninstall routine safely removes the side-by-side components without asking you if it's safe to remove the following component, since it "appears" that no other application needs it.

Windows 2000 and the Windows Installer Service

A new operating system component has been included with Windows 2000 called the Windows Installer service. The service will carry out the installation requirements for each software application through three linked but separate sections: Components, Features, and Products.

Components

The Components section consists of the software application files, Registry keys, and other software resources that are required for installation. The Windows Installer also follows the side-by-side installation rules if a required DLL or COM component is installed several times on the local PC by different applications; each component is assigned a globally unique identifier (GUID) pointing to its private copy of the software component.

Features

The installed features of a software program are at the top Explorer shell interface level; however, these features may overlap between two installed products from the same manufacturer. Although the features are not globally unique, the underlying components that make up the feature remain so. Applications installed with the Windows Installer present their features or subapplications in one of four states:

1. *Installed on local hard drive* The required software files are copied to the local PC.
2. *Installed to run from source* The software files are left on a network share or CD-ROM drive. When they are required, the application reads the required files from the prescribed location.
3. *Advertised* The software files are left at the source location but are automatically installed the first time the feature is accessed. This is now called "Install on Demand." In the SMS world, the word *advertised* is used in a slightly different manner. The software distribution process can be selected by the user or mandated by the administrator.
4. *Not installed* No software files are copied.

Products

A product symbolizes a software product that is installed in the form of a package file with the MSI extension—for example, Microsoft Office 2000. Each product lists each of its features with a unique product code, and each component, in turn, has a unique GUID identification stored in the local Registry of the PC where the installation takes place.

The package file is a database of the required features, components, and software resources needed for the given product. It is then linked to the software applications files stored in compressed CAB files on the CD-ROM.

Features of the Windows Installer

The Installer does its work though the Windows 2000 operating system, providing the ability to enumerate all supported products, features, and components installed on the local PC. Windows 2000 provides the Windows Installer as a system service so it can execute in the background as a local service with more rights than the local user. This is much like the Windows NT Client Installation account used with SMS. Other features of the Windows Installer are as follows:

- *File and File Path Management* Multiple locations can be specified for the location of the source files for on-demand installations, fixes, or reinstallations. These locations can be located anywhere in the active directory hierarchy used by Windows 2000.
- *Runtime Resource Resiliency* In English, the Windows Installer can perform dynamic repairs of a software application if the required components are damaged or missing. This type of repair is called an "on-demand repair."
- *Rollback* For every operation performed by the Windows Installer, it maintains an undo operation for every task that it carries out. Using temporary file locations, the Installer can restore deleted files, Registry settings, or any other resources used and changed by the installation or task performed.

CHAPTER 13

Using Remote Tools

In this chapter you'll learn about:

- Using SMS Remote Tools and properly setting up user and administrator options
- Using Chat, Reboot, and File Transfer, and starting a remote session
- Troubleshooting with Remote Tools for Windows 95/98 and NT clients
- Using the Resource Explorer
- Using the Health Monitor

Remote Tools: Overview

The term *remote tools* can be misleading sometimes, as there are many software utilities that proclaim themselves remote tools. Consequently, Remote Access Service (RAS) is called a remote tool and so is pcAnywhere, a popular remote control utility from Symantec. To clarify, following are two types of remote tools available in the industry today:

- *Remote Node* A remote connection to a server using a modem (in most cases) to make the connection. RAS is a Remote Node utility; it allows you to connect and be authenticated to an NT domain and that's all. By itself, it does not allow you to take control of a remote PC from your location
- *Remote Control* A software utility like pcAnywhere that allows you to take control of a user's PC from a remote location. SMS Remote Tools belong in this category as well.

The Remote Tools that are bundled with SMS are, depending on the installation method, an optional set of software tools for both the server and the client side of SMS. If you installed SMS with the Express Setup, the Remote Tools were installed and initialized. If you chose Custom Setup, you may have to install the Remote Tools.

To check if Remote Tools have been installed:

1. Open the SMS Administrator console, and select the site database.
2. Open the site database, and navigate to the *Collections* folder.
3. Select the collection *All Systems*, and select a displayed computer in the details pane.
4. Right-click on the selected resource, and in the All Tasks menu, Start Remote Tools should appear, as shown in Figure 13-1.

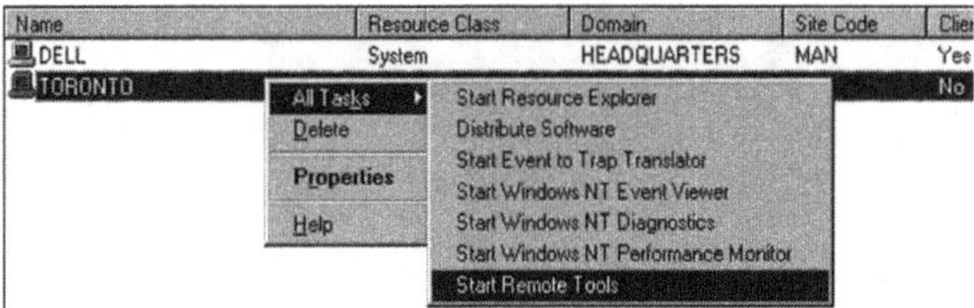

Figure 13-1 Checking if Remote Tools have been installed.

Server components can be installed on any SMS primary site, secondary site, or any Windows NT server. Client components can be installed on any supported SMS client (Windows NT 3.51, 4.0, or 2000, Windows 95/98, Windows 3.1, or Windows for Workgroups 3.11) that has been discovered within the SMS site boundaries.

The basic suite of SMS Remote Tools is detailed in Table 13-1.

Enabling Remote Tools for SMS

The files that are installed for enabling Remote Tools at the site server are REMOTE.EXE. LDFTRANS.DLL, LDWMNT.DLL, and MULTPROT.DLL.

Remote Tools can be executed at the command prompt or through the SMS Administrator console. Although the server component may be installed and enabled, steps must be taken if you want to enable the installation of the Remote Tools components onto all discovered SMS clients.

TABLE 13-1

Remote Tools for SMS 2.0.

SMS 2.0 Remote Tools	Details
Remote Control	Take control of a remote PC.
Remote Reboot	Reboot the remote PC.
Remote Chat	Chat with a remote user.
File Transfer	Copy files from one computer system to another.
Remote Execute	Execute files on the remote PC.
Windows 3.X/95/98 Diagnostics	Check RAM, Software Modules, Current Tasks, CMOS, ROM, MS-DOS RAM.
Windows NT	Remote Tools can launch the Windows NT Diagnostics found in the Diagnostics Administrators program group.
Ping Test	Check for network speed by sending test packets.

SMS Task: Enabling Remote Tool Installation

To start a Remote Tools installation:

1. At the site server, start the SMS Administrator console, and select the desired site hierarchy. Move down the console tree, and select the *Client Agents* folder.
2. From the details pane, highlight and right-click on *Remote Tools Client Agent*, and select *Properties*.
3. On the displayed General tab, check the *Enable Remote Tools on Clients* box, and then click on *OK*, as shown in Figure 13-2.

Defining Site Settings for Remote Tools

The properties of the Remote Tools Client Agent contains the settings that must be set up in order to succeed with Remote Tools.

General—*Clients cannot change Policy or Notification settings.* Selecting this option enables a lock-down scenario, and none of your clients contained in the entire SMS site can change any Remote Tool settings on their computer system through Control Panel. This would be the

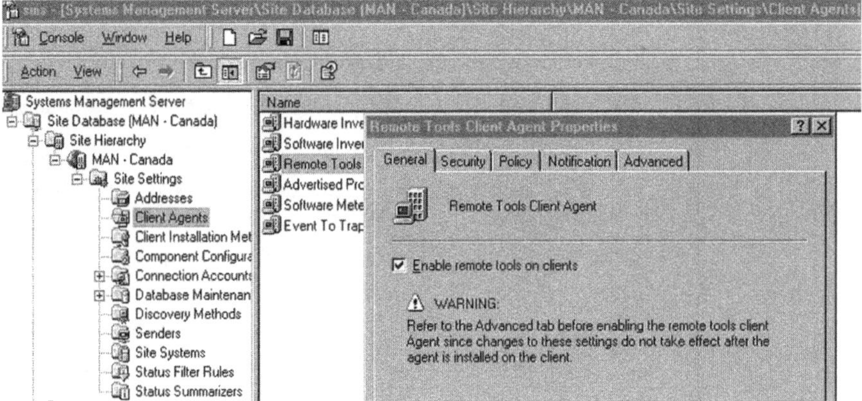

Figure 13-2 Properties of the Remote Tools Client Agent.

safest setting for some sites—for example, a school or college—because the worst-case scenario would be that you are trying to start a remote session with a client, but the client has turned off or changed their settings, making any remote session attempt fail.

However, you may prefer to give your users a little more leeway. If this option is not checked, the client can change the following options for Remote Tools by accessing the Remote Control icon in Control Panel (SMSRC.CPL).

- What tasks a support person can perform at their (or your) PC
- If permission must be requested before a remote session can begin
- Whether remote access will be Full, Limited, or None.

Security—*Add the names of users and groups allowed to use Remote Tools on NT clients.* This setting does not mean that non-Windows NT clients are not allowed to use Remote Tools, merely that Windows NT is the only client-based operating system with a security system. Once you enable Remote Tools through the General tab, you have enabled Remote Tools on all Windows 95, 98, 3.1, and 3.11 clients at once. For all collections, you may have to add the Remote Control permission to allow Remote Control of the remote PC.

By default, the person who installed SMS will be able to perform Remote Control on all collections. For all other support personnel—for example, for the Windows NT client collection—a security right must also be created for the collection of NT workstations that will be accessed by Remote Control. Then the security right must be granted to the NT user or group that will be performing Remote Control.

SMS Task: Adding Permissions for Remote Control Access

To add permissions:

1. At the site server, open the SMS Administrator console and navigate to the *Collections* folder.
2. Highlight the desired NT collection (for this example, All Windows NT 4.0 Workstations).
3. Right-click on the collection, and select *Properties*. Then select the *Security* tab.

4. Click on the "yellow star" button to the right of the Class Security Rights title. The Object Class Security Right Properties dialog now appears.
5. Add the user or group that you wish to assign the task of Remote Control.
6. Using the scroll bar, select the *Use Remote Tools* permission, as shown in Figure 13-3, along with any other permissions you want to grant. Select *OK* to save your changes.

If you are not running a network that is multilingual, then you should remove the foreign-language equivalent to Administrator. You also may want one of the other displayed Administrators presented in various languages; in this case, remove all the languages that are not needed on your network. The best administrative practice would be to add groups only, either a group of administrators or support or help desk personnel that will be executing Remote Tools.

Policy—*Set the level of remote access and access permission at the client's PC.* Choices for the level of remote access at the client PC are Full, Limited, and None. If you select Limited, you display your configuration choices by selecting the Settings button, as shown in Figure 13-4.

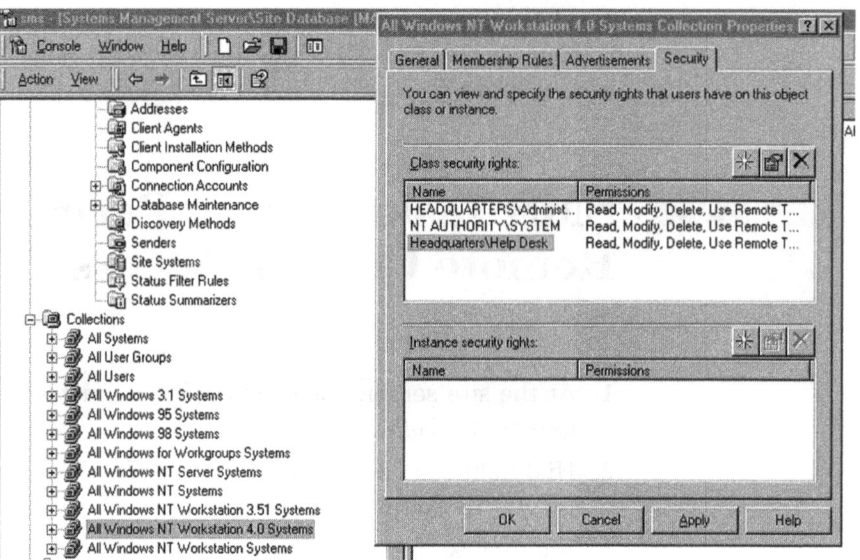

Figure 13-3 Defining permissions for collections for Remote Control.

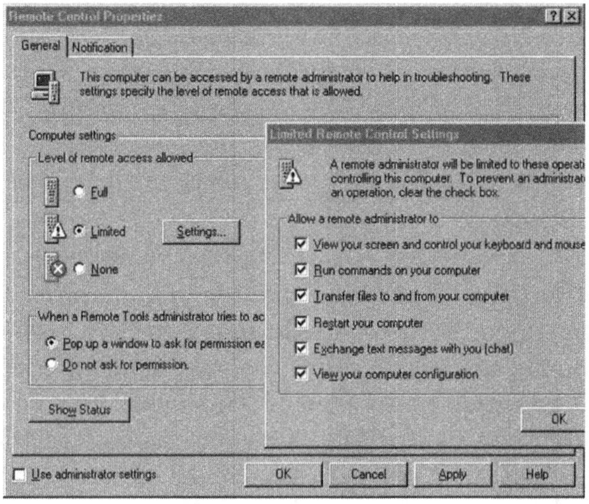

Figure 13-4 Remote Tools settings.

These settings were discussed earlier in the chapter; you could completely restrict these through the properties of the Remote Tool Client Agent at the General tab.

SMS Registry Notes

These checkbox settings for Remote Control are stored in the local system Registry under the key HKEY_LOCAL_MACHINE\SOFTWARE\Microsoft\SMS\Client\Client Components\Remote Control. The following DWORD settings are present with a value of 1 to enable, or check, the checkbox, or with 0 to disable, or clear, the checkbox:

- Allow Chat
- Allow File Transfer
- Allow Ping Test
- Allow Reboot
- Allow Remote Execute
- Allow Takeover
- Permission Required

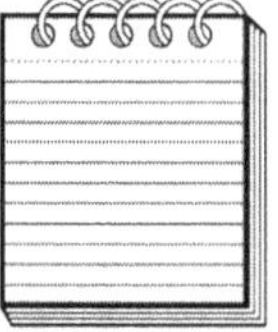

NOTE. *Note: If you want to change these settings on a networkwide basis, you could create a REG file containing just the above settings, either enabling or disabling the settings found in Control Panel. Then you could use a login script with the command* `REGEDIT /S "Regfile.REG`. *The* `/S` *syntax forces the import of the REG file in silent mode.*

Notification—*Enable or disable visual indicators to the end user.* Choices to notify the end user that a remote session is currently active include status icons, desktop icons, or sounds that occur when the session begins and ends or throughout the session. Two types of Remote Control indicators are used during a remote session. In the taskbar beside the clock, a Computer icon indicator can be initiated that changes appearance by displaying a green triangle when a remote session is in progress.

A second indicator, called a high-security indicator, appears at the top right-hand corner of the client's PC (shown in Figure 13-7 later in the chapter). By checking the properties of the high-security indicator, the client can see who has initiated the remote session. This information can also be viewed after the session has ended. Sounds can also be used at the start or end of the remote session or throughout the session.

Advanced—*Set compression, protocol, and video drivers for the client's PC.* Choices for the compression ratio for Remote Control include Low Compression, which utilizes the Run Length Encoding (RLE) algorithm, for slower PCs or in situations where the network bandwidth is 100 MHz, and High Compression, which uses the Lempel-Ziv (LZ) method. For client PCs with Pentium 150 MHz or greater, High Compression can be chosen. You can also choose the default setting of Automatic; with this option, the client's PC will be queried as to the type and speed of CPU. If the speed is greater than 150 MHz, High Compression will be chosen.

The protocol used by the client for the remote session—TCP/IP, NetBIOS, or IPX—can be selected. However, the client will only use the protocol that is bound—that is, active—at the time the report session started.

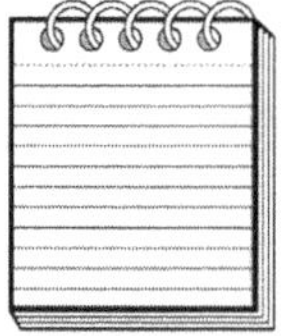

NOTE. *If you have a network with multiple protocols, this could pose some problems, since the initiator of the remote session can use all of the protocols in the priority in which they were bound, but the client cannot switch on the fly. If possible, try to use TCP/IP exclusively across your networks.*

You can also choose to install drivers for a collection of popular video adapters; in fact, you can even add your own video drivers to the default collection. Beware, though: These settings are for Windows NT or Windows 2000 clients only. Assuming that your client base is indeed NT, take the time to add your NT clients' video drivers to this list before enabling Remote Control so the advanced screen transfer settings will be installed on all clients at the same time.

Using these accelerator drivers means the entire remote PC's video screen does not have to be sent, just the changes. Obviously, bandwidth could be a problem; since all of your clients that are Windows 95 or Windows 98 can't use these accelerated drivers, their entire screens must be re-sent. However, Remote Control of Windows 95/98 clients works well.

NOTE. *Before a remote session can be initiated at a client's PC, that client must have been discovered by SMS and the client Remote Tool components installed from an SMS primary site.*

Starting a Remote Tools Session

There are several ways that you can start a remote session:

1. At the site server, using the Run dialog box, you can start a session by entering `D:\SMS\bin\I386\REMOTE.EXE`, which will start a remote session at the command prompt. The Remote Tools utility will load and prompt you for one of three choices:
   1. NetBIOS name
   2. IP address
   3. IPX address

Once you enter one of the address selections, the utility will attempt to connect to the remote PC, as shown in Figure 13-5.

2. You can also start a remote SMS Administrator console session and select the Collections folder containing the client you want to support with Remote Control. Details for starting a remote session with the Administrator console are as follows:
   1. Start the remote or local SMS Administrator console, and select the *Collections* folder.
   2. Next, select the desired collection of clients, for example, *All Windows 98 Systems* or *All Windows NT Systems*.

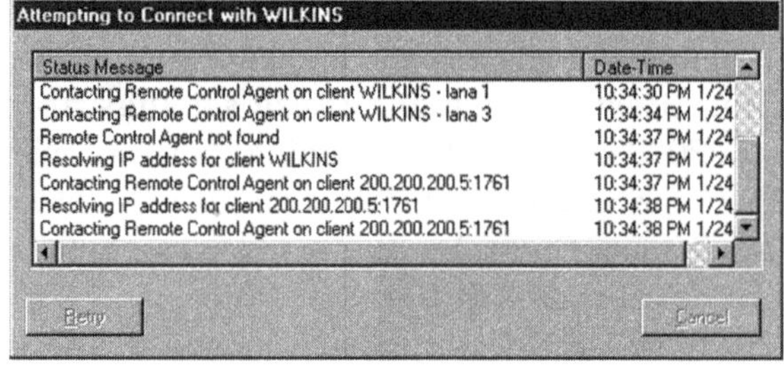

Figure 13-5 Attempting to start a remote session with a remote PC.

3. Now highlight and right-click on the selected client system you wish to start a remote session with.
4. Select *All Tasks* from the context menu; then select *Start Remote Tools.*
5. The Remote Tools utility screen will appear with a dialog box that reads, `Attempting to connect to <computer name>`, as shown in Figure 13-4. Once the remote user allows the session to begin, the dialog box will disappear.
6. To start the remote session, click on the *Remote Control* button (that's the far-left hand button on the toolbar), as shown in Figure 13-6.
7. Depending on your configuration, two dialog boxes appear, one on your PC (the site server or wherever you are executing the remote SMS Administrator console) and one on the remote PC. The per-

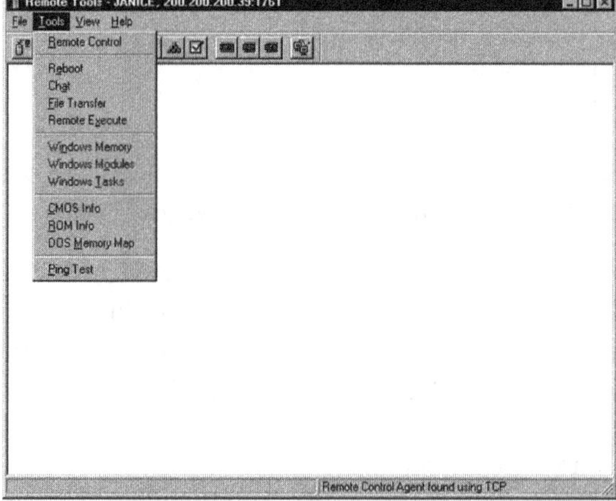

Figure 13-6 The Remote Tools starting screen and Tools menu options.

son who initiated the remote session can ask the client's permission to start a Remote Control session. Once the client agrees, a new screen appears on the server's screen, showing you the remote client's current screen (see Figure 13-7). It will be outlined in a yellow and black dashed picture frame.

8. You now can control the client's computer.

At the top right-hand corner of the remote client's PC screen is the high-security indicator, as shown in Figure 13-8. There are five buttons that you can utilize during your remote session. Starting from the left side:

- *Key button* On NT systems this button invokes the Ctrl-Alt-Del keystrokes so you can log out or log in.
- *Arrow button* Lists the current applications open and running on the client PC (as if you pressed Alt-Tab).
- *List Button* Activates the Start menu on the remote PC (as if you pressed Ctrl-Esc).
- *ALT button* A toggle key for changing the keyboard control. When you issue Control key combinations at your PC, the codes are sent to the remote PC, or if the Alt button is pressed again, performed on your PC.
- *Hand button* Allows you to move yourself quickly to a location on the client's screen.

Figure 13-7
A successful Remote Control session has started.

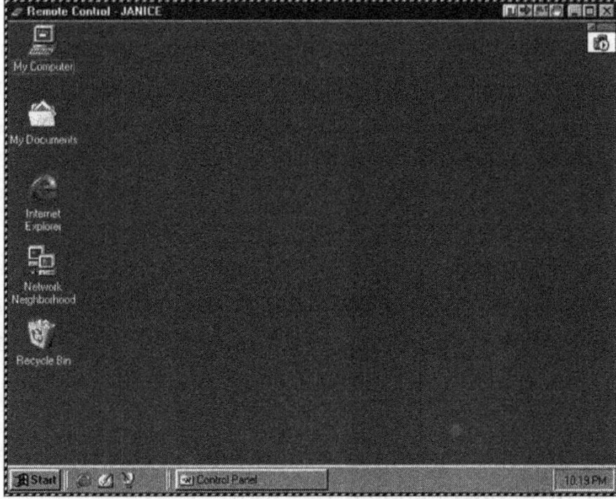

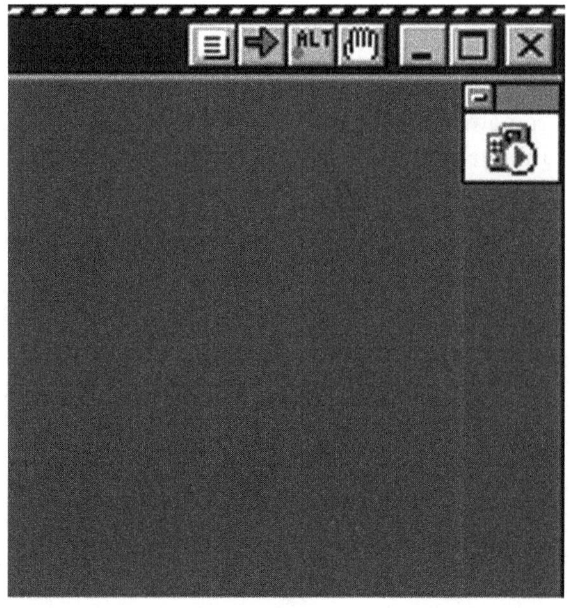

Figure 13-8 High-security indicator buttons on the remote client's PC.

High-Security Indicator Options

The larger button in Figure 13-8, showing the computer graphic, is the Control icon. Right-clicking and selecting this icon allows you to adjust the control parameters of the remote PC. If bandwidth is a problem, the most important setting to enable is the Suppress Client Wallpaper option. The other options that you can set are 16-color Viewing, which speeds up the remote PC's video refresh, and Hot Keys.

When you select Hot Keys, a dialog box is displayed that lists the default Ctrl-keyboard combinations for quickly performing the seven tasks detailed in Table 13-2.

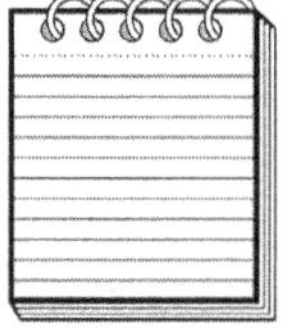

NOTE. *Through the Remote Control Tools' Policy Properties tab, you can mandate that no permission is needed to access the client's PC. To do so, under Access Permissions, check the* Do not ask for permission *option.*

From the Tools menu, you can now select the options you wish to perform, as previously shown in Figure 13-6.

TABLE 13-2

Hot Key settings for Remote Control Sessions.

Hot Key Settings	Details
Ctrl-Alt-M	Full screen toggle
Ctrl-Alt-R	Refresh viewer
Ctrl-Alt-T	Restart viewer
Ctrl-Alt-S	System key routing
Ctrl-Alt-H	Enable hot keys
Ctrl-Alt-A	Accelerated mode
Ctrl-Alt-Q	Close viewing session

Starting a Remote Control Support Session

One of the first potential hurdles to overcome when using Remote Control is determining just who the user is calling for help and where he or she is located. This may not be a problem if users don't move around the network; however, in many situations, users may use many PCs during the course of a day, and they may not know where they are or who they are logged in as.

A quick solution is having the user exit to the command prompt (if they are allowed) and typing in the `IPCONFIG` or `NET NAME` command, shown in Figure 13-9, if the client type is Windows 95/98 or NT and the network protocol is TCP/IP.

You could also check the Start button menu. If the user's PC has Internet Explorer 4.0 installed, the current user's logon name will be just above the Shut Down option on the menu.

Another method would be to use Network Neighborhood. Right-click on the *Network Neighborhood* icon and select *Properties*; this will display the Network icon information in Control Panel, along with the computer name and workgroup/domain.

Yet another method is to use the SMS client software installed in the Control Panel. When the SMS Remote Tools are installed on the client's PC, the Control Panel will have new applet called System Management. Have the client at the remote PC open this icon; the General tab will display the following information to help you identify the user in need of help:

```
(C) Copyright 1985-1996 Microsoft Corp.

D:\>IPCONFIG

Windows NT IP Configuration

Ethernet adapter NP1001:

        IP Address. . . . . . . . : 200.200.200.60
        Subnet Mask . . . . . . . : 255.255.255.0
        Default Gateway . . . . . :

Ethernet adapter NdisWan5:

        IP Address. . . . . . . . : 0.0.0.0
        Subnet Mask . . . . . . . : 0.0.0.0
        Default Gateway . . . . . :

Ethernet adapter NdisWan6:

        IP Address. . . . . . . . : 0.0.0.0
        Subnet Mask . . . . . . . : 0.0.0.0
        Default Gateway . . . . . :

D:\>
```

Figure 13-9 Running `IPCONFIG` for identifying the client.

- User's SMS unique identifier
- Computer NetBIOS name
- Current IP address and IP subnet
- Network adapter's MAC address
- Resource domain the user logged in to
- Last logon user name
- Last logon user domain

Finally, you could use the SMS Administrator console to perform a query as follows:

1. Open up an SMS Administrator console, and highlight and open the *Queries* folder.
2. Highlight the query *Systems by Last Logged On User*.
3. Right-click and select *Run Query*. You will be prompted with `Input Query Value`.
4. Enter the user's name, and click on *OK*; in the details pane, a listing of every client PC that the user has logged in to will appear, along with the IP address and computer name.

Supplying Support with Remote Control

OK, we've made a connection. Now let's go to work. Just what type of support can we offer the remote end user? We have a suite of Remote Tool choices.

Remote Chat

Once the remote session is established, from the toolbar of Remote Tools, select the *Remote Chat* icon (that's the third button from the left), or from the *Tools* drop-down menu, select *Chat*. The Remote Chat window should appear, as shown in Figure 13-10.

The window in Figure 13-10 will appear for the remote client and the support person's screen, allowing a conversation to take place. (This insulates you from the upset user, which sometimes is a blessing.)

Solving Software and Hardware Problems

Using SMS Remote Tools, you can run both hardware and software diagnostics for Windows 95, Windows 98, and to a lesser degree, Windows NT systems. For Windows 95/98 clients, you run the diagnostics from the Remote Tools window by selecting the Diagnostic icons found in the toolbar or from the Tools drop-down menu. Diagnostic checks can be performed for both hardware and software components, saving an incredible amount of time when you are trying to pinpoint a problem with an inexperienced user. The diagnostic tests that you can perform are detailed in Table 13-3.

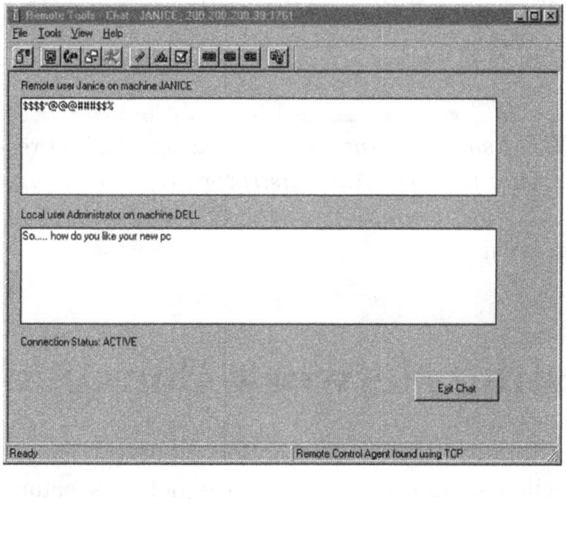

Figure 13-10 A Remote Chat session.

TABLE 3-3

Windows Diagnostics for Windows 95/98 clients.

Remote Diagnostic Test	Details
Windows Memory	Shows the amount in % of the user's memory used. Also details the swap file size and shows the use of the memory heaps for the User and GDI (Graphic Device Interface).
Windows Modules	Lists the DLLs and other system drivers that are loaded at the present time. Memory details can also be viewed.
Windows Tasks	Displays all current tasks and command-line options in process.
CMOS Information	Displays the current CMOS settings for the remote client's PC.
Device Drivers	Lists the current device drivers loaded on the remote client's PC. Includes the address and name of each device driver.
ROM Information	Lists the ROMs in use on the client's PC and any IRQ information.
Interrupt Vectors	Lists the hardware and software interrupts on the remote client's PC.
DOS Memory Map	Provides details about the use of conventional memory and upper memory by the loaded software modules.

The Windows NT client cannot be monitored with these diagnostics tools; however, you can execute Windows NT Diagnostics in several ways. From the SMS Administrator console, select either the collection of NT clients that have been discovered, or by using the Queries folder, run a query on a selected collection for an up-to-date listing of NT clients. Now right-click on the desired client, and from the *All Tasks* menu, select *Run Windows NT Diagnostics* to start diagnosing your NT clients. (See Figure 13-11).

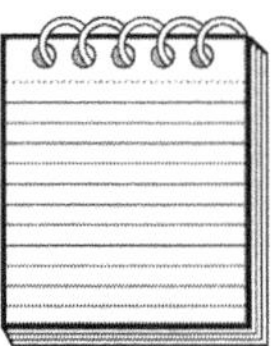

NOTE. *I should point out that you could also execute Windows NT Diagnostics from the Administrator program group and by using the Select Computer option from the File drop-down menu to check on another remote PC.*

Testing Network Connectivity

Using another Remote Tool option called the Ping Test, you can find out what clients are connected on your network before you initiate Remote

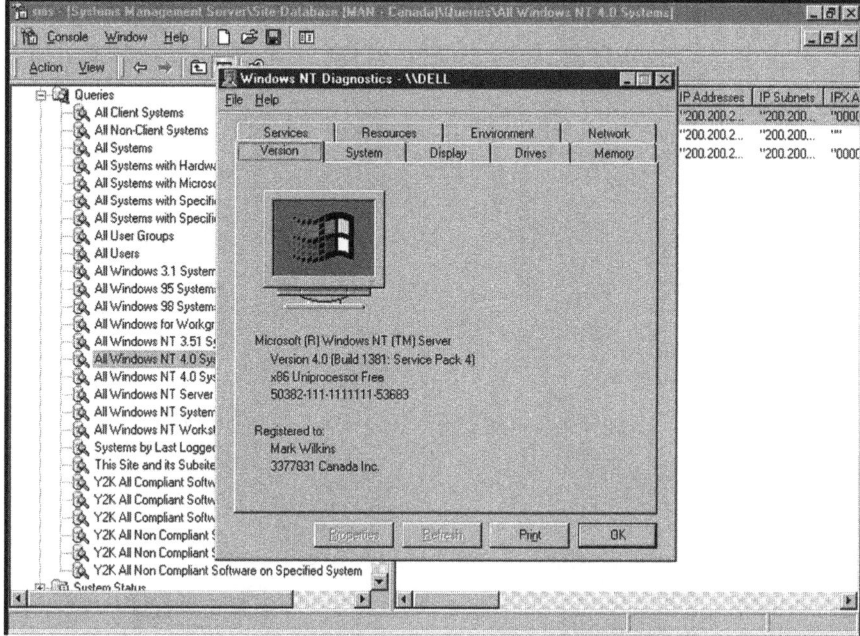

Figure 13-11 Using NT Diagnostics from the SMS Administrator console.

Control. This test works with all network protocols and sends a stream of packets to the selected computer. Once the remote computer replies, additional 4-second barrages of packets are sent to the remote client. The packets returned to the source computer that initiated the test are captured and analyzed, and the results show you a snapshot view of your network's speed and reliability at the present time (see Figure 13-12).

Searching the Remote Client's PC

Once you have connected to a user's PC through a Remote Tools session, it may take a few sessions to become comfortable with the fact that the Start button used in the remote session is the remote user's Start button. If you have any experience with Cytrix or Microsoft's Terminal Server, you will recognize the technology being used with SMS Remote Tools. The remote client is operated just like a terminal server session between a terminal server and a terminal server client, except it's in reverse. You are controlling the Remote Client through the SMS Administrator console.

Therefore, you can use the user's Explorer shell to search and compare filenames, folder structure, Registry settings, or Control Panel settings.

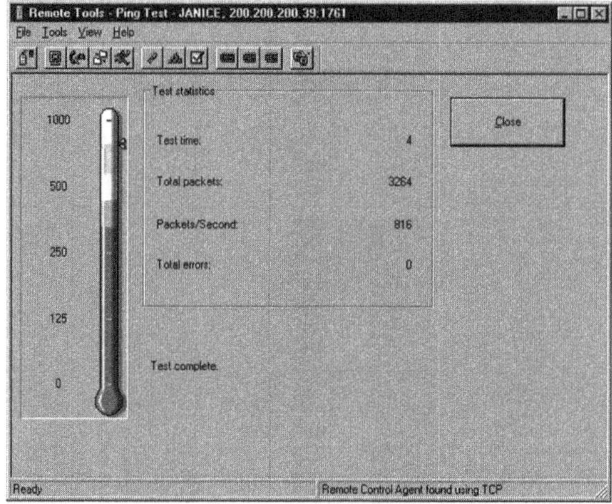

Figure 13-12 Analyzing network performance with the Ping test.

Troubleshooting sessions with a remote user will be much more productive if you or your support staff use the same Windows client at both the remote and local computers. (Obviously, this is not always possible.)

Executing Commands at the Remote Client

Using the Remote Execute support tool allows you to run commands that execute at the command line at the remote PC. This allows you to quickly execute any commands that require specific syntax, such as backing up a Windows 98 client's local Registry, as shown in Figure 13-13.

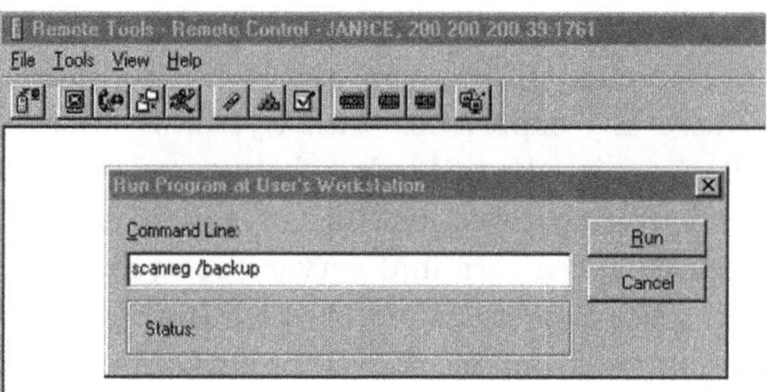

Figure 13-13 Using Remote Execute for command-line commands.

Transferring Files to the Remote Client

After starting a remote session, you may find that specific system or software application files are missing or damaged, or you might want a copy of certain files that have appeared on the client's PC. In such cases you can use the File Transfer remote tool to transfer files to the client from your PC or vice versa. This tool can be accessed from the Tools drop-down menu or by selecting the File Transfer button.

Once the File Transfer process is selected, the File Transfer Agent is launched. The resulting screen shows you a split view of both the local PC, called the "Console" at the top of the display and the "Remote Machine" at the bottom. Using the button bar menu on either the local or remote PC, you can delete and copy files, make new folders, and change the details of the file listing, as shown in Figure 13-14.

Rebooting a Remote Client

Using the Reboot option, you can choose to reboot a remote client's PC after you have made a change that will only be active after a physical reboot. If there are dialog boxes that require acceptance and closing before the remote system can be rebooted, a Remote Control session can be started to prepare the system for shutdown and restart.

SMS Task: Remote Troubleshooting Using Remote Tools

If you have administrative privileges on the remote client's PC, you can perform most, if not all, troubleshooting tasks at a user's PC when the user is not even there.

Problem 1: A user gets a DLL error whenever she tries to start Microsoft Word.

A help call comes in from Janice in the records department. She is having a problem whenever she tries to start using Word/Office 97. The

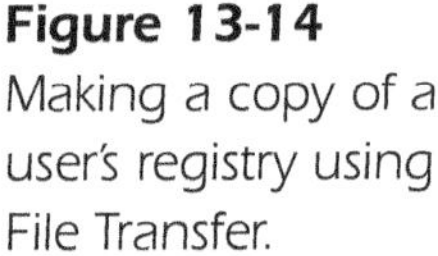

Figure 13-14 Making a copy of a user's registry using File Transfer.

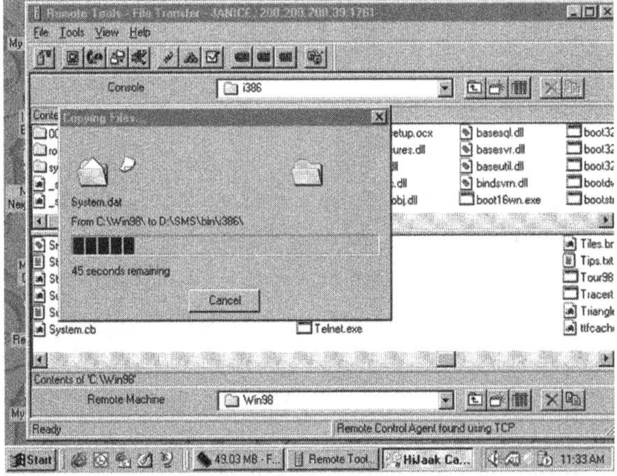

error message is unfamiliar to her and she needs help, as she is under a deadline.

1. The support person opens a remote session of the SMS Administrator console and selects Janice's Windows 98 PC from the current computers under the Collections folder. From the details pane, the support person selects Janice's PC by right-clicking from the All Tasks menu. Then Start Remote Tools is selected.
2. The remote session starts, and from the Tools menu, the support person starts Remote Control. In a few seconds Janice's computer screen is displayed with the error message `A required .DLL file, MS097.DLL, was not found`, as shown in Figure 13-15.
3. The support person closes the error message on the remote PC after carefully noting the name of the missing DLL.
4. Starting a chat session, he informs Janice that the error message helps and that he will be back to her in a few seconds.
5. When checking on the local workstation, which also had the same version of Office 97 installed, the support person finds the DLL file that is missing on Janice's computer in PROGRAM FILES\MICROSOFT OFFICE\OFFICE.
6. When Janice restarts the Chat session, she is told that a search is going to be performed on her PC and to please be patient for a few more seconds.
7. Using the File Transfer tool, the support person checks Janice's PC for the missing DLL file. The file is not in the required location. A

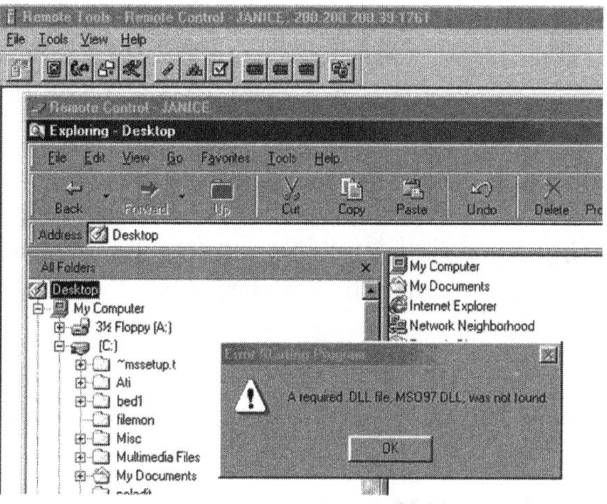

Figure 13-15 The error message viewed through a remote session.

copy of the file is transferred to Janice's PC and placed in the PROGRAM FILES\MICROSOFT OFFICE\OFFICE folder.

8. After starting a Remote Control session, the support person starts and tests Microsoft Word. It starts normally. The user is thrilled, and the support person gets free coffee for a week.

Problem 2: Support wants to remove a Windows NT 4.0 user's ability to change his video settings by adding a Registry setting disabling the Settings tab.

1. The support person starts a remote session for the desired NT user by starting the SMS Administrator console and selecting the Collections folder for Windows NT 4.0 Workstations. From the details pane, she selects the user's PC, and after right-clicking from the All Tasks menu, selects Start Remote Tools.
2. The remote session is started, and the Remote Tools screen appears.
3. From the Tools menu, the support person selects Remote Control. The user's PC is displayed.
4. Next, from the desktop, she checks the current video settings. They are still available.
5. Running REGEDT32 so the remote user can't watch, the support person selects the remote PC's Registry from the Registry drop-down menu, and Select Computer.

6. Navigating through the keys to HKEY_CURRENT_USER\SOFTWARE\MICROSOFT\WINDOWS\CURRENT VERSION\POLICIES\EXPLORER\SYSTEM, the DWORD setting NoDispSettingsPage with a HEX value of 1 is added, as shown in Figure 13-16.
7. After starting the remote session, the support person tests the new setting on the remote PC by again selecting and checking the current video settings; the Settings tab is removed.

Using the Resource Explorer

The SMS Administrator console contains an additional remote support tool called Resource Explorer, which allows you to check out a remote client's software and hardware inventory. Hardware and software inventory must first be enabled in order for this utility to perform its job. Using the Resource Explorer on a particular client allows you to perform a real-time view and search of installed hardware, software applications, and unknown files.

SMS Task: Using the Resource Explorer

1. After opening the SMS Administrator console, open the site database and select the *Collections* folder.
2. Highlight one of the groups that inventory has been performed upon.

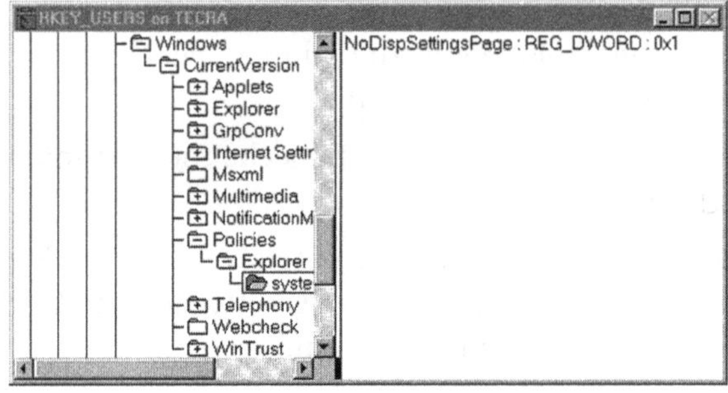

Figure 13-16 Using REGEDT32 to remotely add an NT user setting.

3. Right-click on a listed client from the details pane, and from the *All Tasks* menus, select *Start Resource Explorer*.
4. The Resource Explorer loads as a separate MMC as a snap-in component (you can load multiple copies of the Resource Explorer for comparison purposes), showing the selected client's hardware and software inventory data. (See Figure 13-17.) This allows you to browse the remote client. By selecting a particular software application, you can drill down and find out the file size, the file version, and the creation date.

The Resource Explorer is a great troubleshooting aid. Note that the folder called Unknown Files lists DOS software components (In the current Microsoft world, DOS is indeed unknown.)

Using the Health Monitor

The Health Monitor utility supplied with SMS version 2.0 is a new twist on the Performance Monitor. Usable for Windows NT 4.0 and Windows 2000 systems, the Health Monitor can be used to check the overall physical health using counters for the following:

- Faults
- Logical disk
- Memory

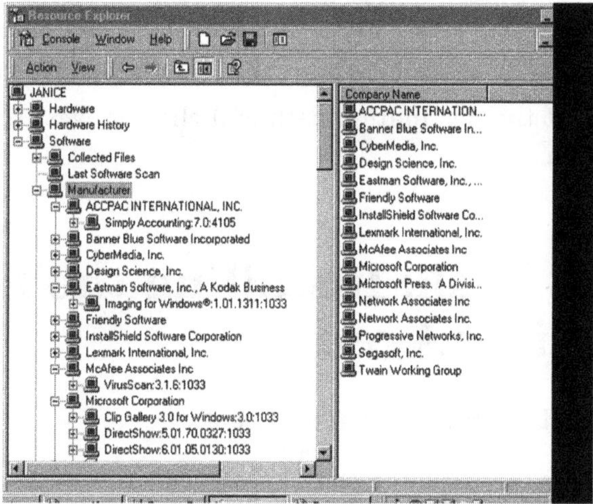

Figure 13-17 Using the Resource Explorer.

- Paging file
- Paging disk
- Network interface
- Server work queues
- Processor

Using monitoring policies that you define, the data is passed through the existing WMI (Windows Management Instrumentation) providers to a Health Monitor Agent that is resident on the Windows NT 4.0 or 2000 computer system. When system events occur that match the health policy criteria that has been set, an event is written to the Windows event log, and the WBEM (Web-Based Enterprise Management) events are also passed on to the SMS Administrator console for posting.

Each of the monitoring events has a predefined threshold; however, you can change the thresholds for each event. In order to begin using Health Monitor, you must install both the Health Monitor console and Health Monitor Agent.

SMS Task: Installing the Health Monitor

To install Health Monitor:

1. Using the Explorer shell, select your CD-ROM drive that has the SMS 2.0 CD-ROM inserted.
2. Run the SETUP.EXE program in the folder HEALTHMON\I386\00000409\Console to start the Health Monitor selection.
3. Select the destination path and click on *Next* to finish the installation.

SMS Task: Installing the Health Monitor Agent

To install the Health Monitor Agent:

1. Using the Explorer shell, select your CD-ROM drive that has the SMS 2.0 CD-ROM inserted.

2. Run the SETUP.EXE program in the folder HEALTHMON\I386\00000409\Agent to start the Health Monitor selection.
3. You are then asked whether you would like to turn on the DISKPERF counters. You will need to enable these counters if you wish to monitor hard drive performance. A reboot will be required if you select Yes.
4. Select the destination path and click on *Next* to finish the installation.

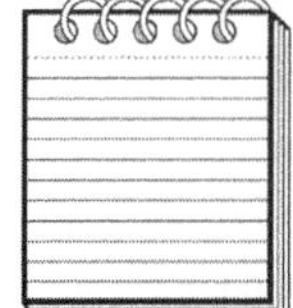

NOTE. *Once a Health Monitor is enabled on a site system, the performance counters will take a fair bit of system resources.*

SMS Task: Using the Health Monitor

To use the Health Monitor:

1. Select the site server where you have started Health Monitor, and start the Health Monitor from the Systems Management Server program group.
2. Expand the console tree to show HealthMon | Monitored Systems
3. From the details pane, right-click on *All Systems*, and select the option *New Monitored System*, as shown in Figure 13-18.

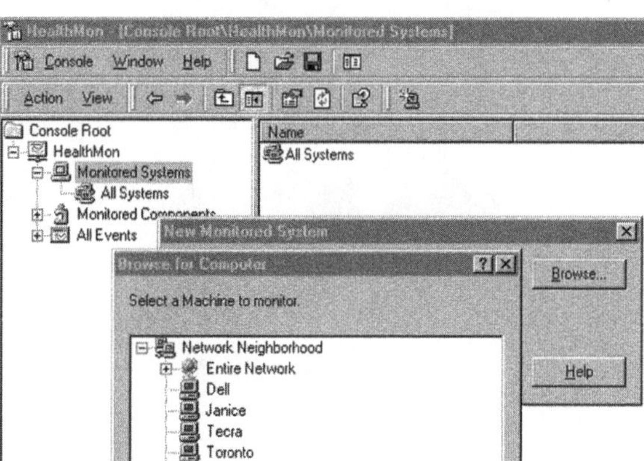

Figure 13-18
Selected a system for Health Monitor.

4. After selecting the computer that you added to the Health Monitor, double-click to display the Components and Events subfolders. The Events subfolder should show a Normal icon—that is, a green checkmark in a round white circle. The icons used with health monitor are the same as the Status Message Viewer found in the SMS Administrator console: Normal, Warning, and Status messages.
5. Select the *Components* folder. This will show you the components monitored by the Health Monitor. Right-clicking on any of the displayed components allows you to enable it from the context menu. Double-clicking on a component allows you to view the properties of the component and the default thresholds, or trigger points.
6. Once you have enabled the component or components that you wish to monitor, select the *Monitor Components* folder to view details of each selected component, as shown in Figure 13-19.

Monitoring the selected components provides you with an easier interface to set up and manage than Performance Monitor. Make sure that any components you wish to analyze with the Health Monitor are then included as part of your daily maintenance routine so you will note any patterns develop before problems occur.

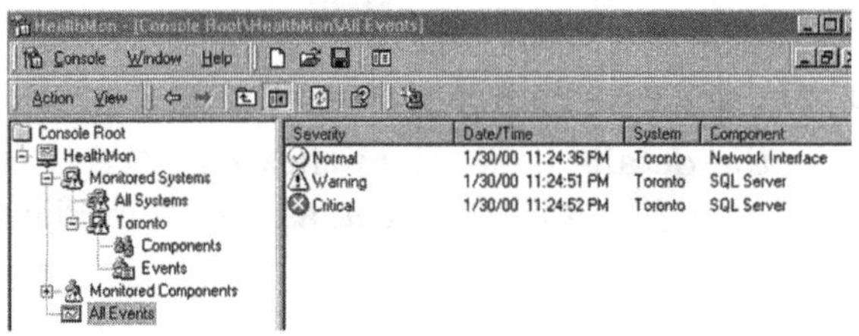

Figure 13-19 Monitoring selected components with Health Monitor.

CHAPTER 14

Maintaining SMS

In this chapter you will learn how to:

- Be proactive about your SMS maintenance
- Set and maintain a proper maintenance cycle
- Maintain your SQL databases and key Registry and file settings
- Backup and restore SMS and SQL components
- Set status message alerts for detailed monitoring
- Use Network Monitor and the Monitor Control tool
- Optimize SMS with SQL for the best performance

Becoming Proactive

Are you a proactive type of person when it comes to network maintenance? I sure hope the answer is "Yes," because a properly followed maintenance schedule can make your working life so much easier and more stress-free. Long-term planning helps you become a proactive and much better network support person.

However, the benefits of long-term planning do not appear overnight; it takes a few months or more for the proactive approach toward support and maintenance to show tangible benefits.

Most of us (myself included) spend too much time reacting to problems that occur every day, having to stop and put out random fires. Now that you have SMS and SQL Server installed, you hopefully will have some additional motivation for becoming more proactive in your approach toward network maintenance, as the SMS/SQL system is large and complicated.

The initial installation of SMS comes with preset values and numerous checks and balances found in the SMS Administrator console and the SQL Server Enterprise Manager. However, these monitoring options are most useful after SMS site systems are up and running; you also really have to be prepared *before* your SMS hierarchy goes live.

There are, at a bare minimum, specific startup maintenance tasks that should be put in place and properly documented for a truly proactive environment.

Proper Documentation Is Essential

You can sometimes survive for a longer time if you are the entire network support staff. If this is the situation, you have my sympathy. However, if you work as part of a support team, clear and essential documentation of what tasks have been performed and what tasks need to be done at present and in the future is essential for maintaining proper communications among team members when problems occur and when you or somebody else is attempting to solve the problem. Proper documentation allows you and everyone else concerned to see at the glance what has been done and what hasn't.

Essentially, documentation sets the stage for successful troubleshooting in advance of problems. If you haven't started writing down network changes and system information in a network log, now is the time to begin. Over a time line of several days or weeks, you will absolutely see patterns begin to develop when you start to write down tasks, errors, and technical notes to yourself. Without paper notation, successful network troubleshooting is almost impossible.

SMS Tasks: After the Installation

- *Plan and test your backup and restore plan for all SMS and SQL servers.* It's quite prudent to check your backup procedures, but make sure that you test—and I mean really test—your restore procedures. Unfortunately, the day that you have to restore important data is not the time that you can be proactive, because you usually won't know when disaster is going to strike. If you have custom scripts written for your backup, make sure you have backup software copies and a hard copy as well.
- *Create backup copies of the system Registry, SMS 2.0, SQL 6.5/7.0, and Windows NT 4.0 Server, and the current installed service pack.* Each NT 4.0 site server and NT system participating in a site server role should have a freshly created and labeled emergency recovery disk (ERD). This disk holds a copy of all security, software, and system settings that are stored in the system portion of the Registry (HKEY_LOCAL_MACHINE).

  To create an ERD, open up the *Run* box from the *Start* menu and enter `RDISK/S`. The `/S` is very important; this tells the utility to back up the entire system Registry to the `\WINNT\REPAIR` folder and also to a floppy disk. Next, you should burn backup CD copies of SMS, SQL Server, and the service pack. Then you should store all of these disks, along with the weekly data backups, off-site in a safe place.
- *Save any unique system configuration information.* If you have any unique RAID hard disk subsystems or other one-of-a-kind hardware, then make backups of all required driver disks. Do you have any specific variables set under the Control Panel | System Icon | Environment tab? Make careful notations in your network logbook.
- *Save SMS and SQL configuration data.* After SMS and SQL have been installed, you should record any database configuration settings that you may have modified during the installation, such as the num-

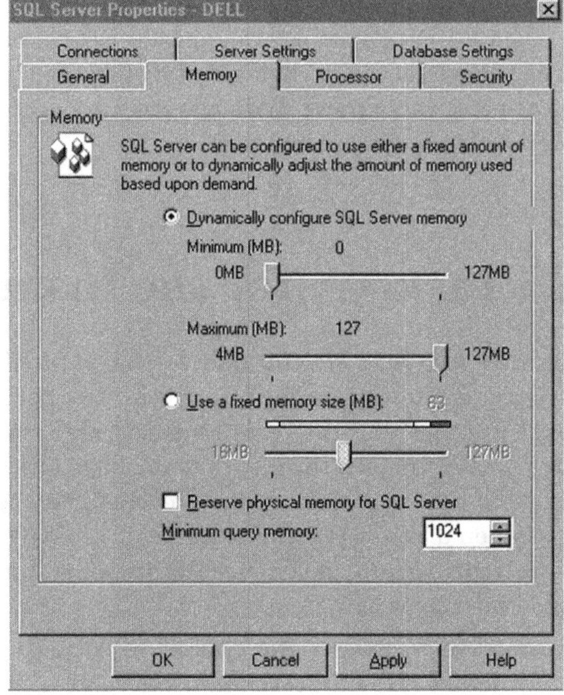

Figure 14-1 Viewing SQL Server properties through the SQL Server Enterprise Manager.

ber of user connections or memory allocation, as shown in Figure 14-1. The SQL Server properties are found by running the SQL Server Enterprise Manager, located in the Microsoft SQL Server 6.5/7.0 program group.

As your SMS/SQL system runs day in and day out, over time you may need to make adjustments—for example, changing the number of user connections as your user base expands. These changes should be also carefully logged and dated in your network log.

Setup Performance Monitor Alerts

On each SMS site system, you should activate Performance Monitor, setting up important alerts for key SMS and SQL system components. These should include the objects shown in Table 14-1.

The Performance Monitor is found in the Administrator Tools program group on the local site server. From the drop-down menu options, select

TABLE 14-1

Performance Monitor objects to set alerts for tracking performance.

Performance Monitor Object	Details
Processor—% Processor time	If your processor time is above 80 percent, then your site server(s) are overburdened.
Memory—% Available bytes	Set a minimum footprint of memory space that you are comfortable with, for example, 20 MB.
Network Segment—% Network utilization	Refers to how much overall network activity there is.
Physical Disk—% Disk time	Refers to how busy your hard drive is while servicing your read and write requests.
Paging File—% Usage	Refers to how large your virtual memory is.
SQL Server General Statistics—User connections	Traces the number of users connected to SQL Server.

View and then *Alert*. Clicking on the plus button from the button menu allows you to add many different objects, defining when you would like Performance Monitor to alert you that the selected objects are over or under your defined benchmark, as shown in Figure 14-2.

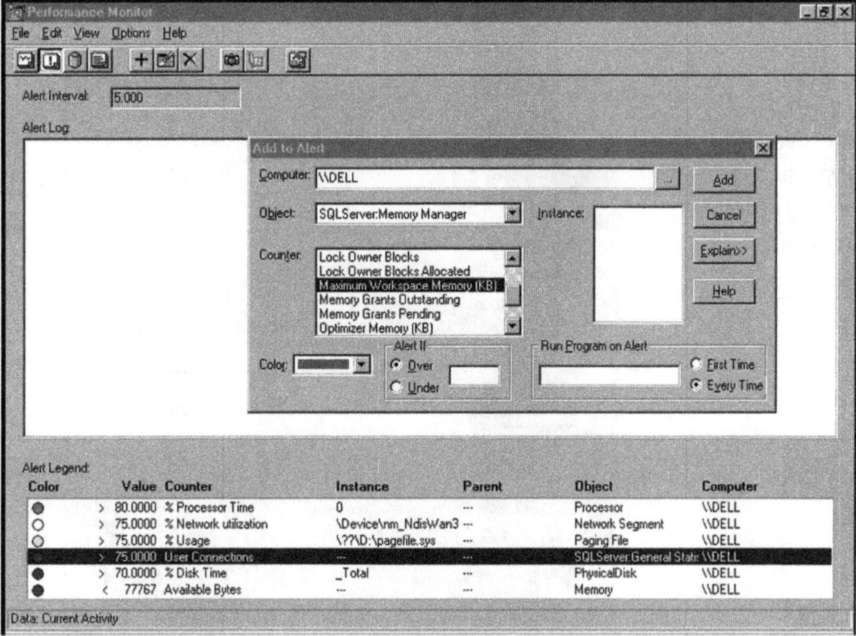

Figure 14-2 Setting alerts with Performance Monitor.

Once you have finished setting your alerts, from the Options drop-down menu, select *Alert* options. Choices for tracking your preset Alert options are to:

1. Log each event in the application log of the Event Viewer.
2. Specify a network alert, which sends a network alert to a specific Event Viewer location on the network.

SQL Server Alerts

SQL Server alerts are set up through the SQL Enterprise Manager found in the SQL Server program group. Navigating to the Management folder and right-clicking on Alerts accesses the New Alert Properties tab screen, as shown in Figure 14-3.

Two types of SQL alerts are enabled by default for SQL Server:

1. SQL Server event alerts
2. SQL Server performance condition alerts

Event alerts are generated based on a severity coding, as detailed in Table 14-2. The simplest way to create an alert is by using the SQL

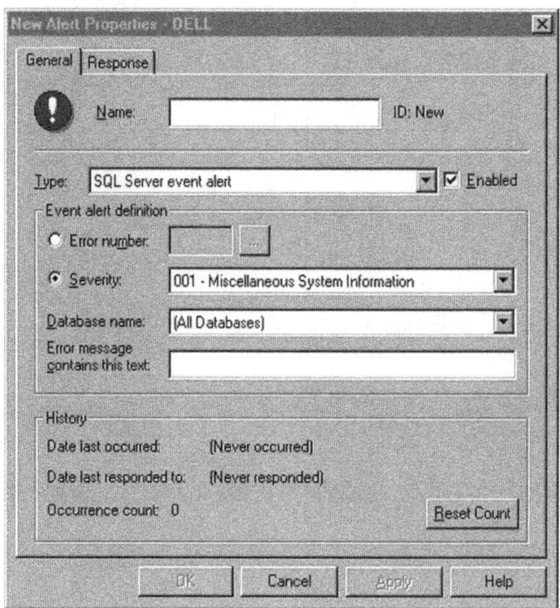

Figure 14-3 New Alert Properties viewed through the SQL Enterprise Manager.

TABLE 14-2

SQL database event alert error codes.

Alert Severity Code	Details
001	Miscellaneous system information
002	Notification: Status information
008	Notification: User intervention required
009	User defined
010	Information
011	Specified database object not found
013	User transactions syntax error
014	Insufficient permission
015	Syntax error in SQL statements
016	Miscellaneous user error
017	Insufficient resources
018	Nonfatal internal error
019	Fatal error in resource
020	Fatal error in current process
021	Fatal error in database process
022	Fatal error: Table integrity suspect
023	Fatal error: Database integrity suspect
024	Fatal error: Hardware error
025	Fatal error

Enterprise Manager. Click on the *Administer SQL Server* wizard shortcut shown in the Details pane to the right of the highlighted SQL Server. This will display the Create an Alert wizard, which is then started by clicking once. The wizard will then step you through defining the alert, specifying the database you want to assign the alert to, and adding any error keywords.

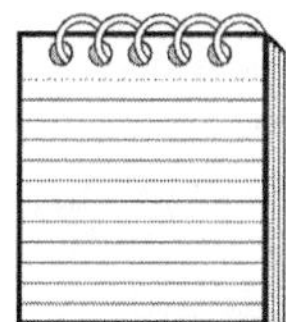

NOTE. *Alert codes for 019 through 025 are enabled by default when SQL is installed.*

Performance condition alerts can also be defined for the following operating areas of SQL Server:

- SQL Server: Access Methods
- SQL Server: Buffer Manager
- SQL Server: Cache Manager
- SQL Server: Databases
- SQL Server: General Statistics
- SQL Server: Latches
- SQL Server: Locks
- SQL Server: Memory Manager
- SQL Server: SQL Statistics

Either the event or performance condition alert can be sent to respond in three ways: to the Event Viewer application log, by e-mail, or by pager.

Remember that SQL Server has the ability to generate numerous alerts. If you are not using SQL Server for your databases other than SMS, knowing what type of errors are generated and reported is essential for monitoring and troubleshooting. Luckily, since SQL 7.0 is self-tuning by default, most performance settings are dynamically adjusted based on the size of the defined databases.

The current settings are viewed through the SQL Enterprise Manager by right-clicking on the icon for the installed SQL Server and selecting Properties. This will display the Memory and Database settings and other system details, as shown in Figure 14-4. It's a good idea to make sure that the memory settings are set to Dynamic and Default, respectively.

Setting Up the Windows NT Event Viewer Logs

In the NT Administrator, the Event Viewer utility is the central holding location for Windows NT, SMS, and SQL error messages. Make sure that you set the log settings of the Event Viewer to match the reporting detail that you require.

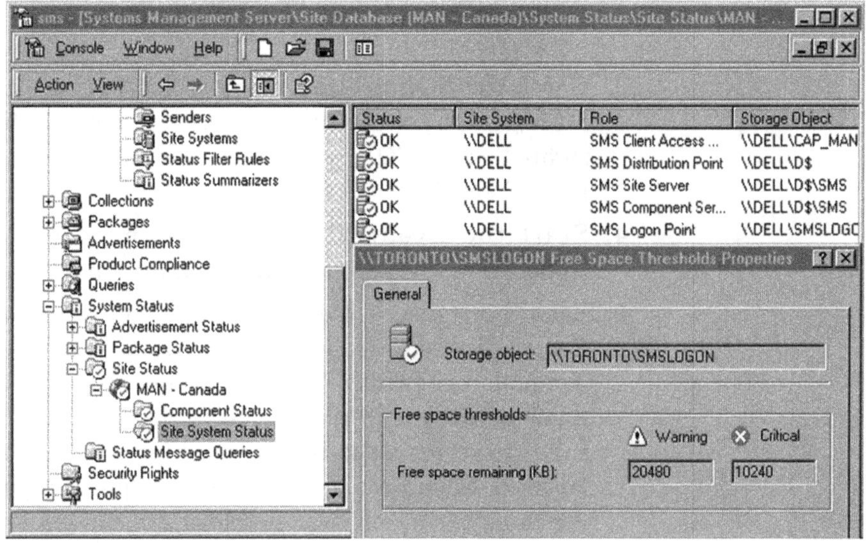

Figure 14-4 Checking SQL Server properties with the SQL Enterprise Manager.

Open up the Event Viewer and from the *Log* menu, select *Log Settings*. It's a good idea to set the *Overwrite Events* option to `21 days` to allow you an error history longer than the default of one week.

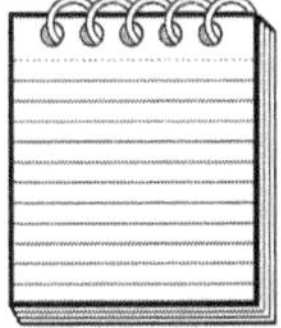

NOTE. *The Event Viewer also shows SQL counters. In fact, there are more counters to set through the Event Viewer than in the SQL Server Enterprise Manager. The additional counters shown here deal exclusively with internal database replication.*

Daily SMS Tasks

The following SMS tasks should be performed on a daily schedule:

1. First thing in the morning, check all tape backups before completion, along with any errors that may have occurred. Update the network log with this information. If you decide on a daily backup for SMS data only (SMS and SQL data), these tapes should be then locked in the appropriate secure location.
2. Check all status messages on all SMS site servers by using the SMS Administrator console to view the status summarizer infor-

mation. Any severe error messages should be documented in the network log.

3. Check the SQL Server error log by opening the SQL Enterprise Manager and selecting the Management folder. Highlight and right-click the *SQL Server Agent* object; from the displayed context menu, select *Display Error Log*.
4. Start the Event Viewer utility, and check all three logs: Application, System, and Security, for any new error messages.
5. Load the Network Monitor utility from the *Systems Management Server* program group. Start a network capture, and check the available bandwidth. Choose the time assuring the date when you know network traffic will be at peak. This is advance troubleshooting. There may not be any problems now; however, using the Network Monitor utility effectively requires regular usage. Day-to-day monitoring of your network traffic will help you recognize when network problems are occurring, especially if you monitor your network at the same time every day.
6. Remove and archive any created advertisements or packages that have been used.
7. Deploy any created advertisements or packages as needed.

Weekly SMS Tasks

The following tasks should be performed on a weekly basis:

1. Perform week-ending data and system backups, then make sure the backup media is taken off-site and stored in a safe location.
2. Check all systems that belong to your SMS hierarchy and document the size of free hard drive space on all servers.
3. Run disk defragmentation utilities on all NTFS (NT file system) partitions. Contrary to popular belief, NTFS partitions can become quite fragmented.
4. Produce and read any reports you have generated for your SMS environment—for example, hardware and software inventory, or software license metering.
5. Track and delete any inventory, bad MIF (Management Information Format) files, aged software inventory, and any old SQL Server maintenance log files.

6. Delete any packages and advertisements that have been deployed.
7. Load any new advertisements and packages as needed.

Monthly SMS Tasks

You should perform the following tasks monthly:

1. Check your current security levels for all SMS administrators. Depending on the level of security within your organization, you may want to change these passwords on a monthly basis.
2. Test your backup and restoration procedures. This can involve using a temporary location on the server to back up, delete, and restore.
3. Using the Network Trace SMS utility, generate a real-time trace of your network environment.

Maintenance Tasks for the SMS Databases

As you know by now, SMS stores all of its data components through SQL Server using two SQL databases. Therefore, it stands to reason that SQL Server utilities can also be used to back up and restore the SMS databases.

Like any backup and restore archive, your data backups are only as good as their date. That is to say, regular and complete backups are essential to successfully restoring data when it is damaged.

The databases that we are concerned about backing up in a timely fashion are the SMS site database and the software-metering database. The data structure in the SQL Server database is made up of tables, indexes, views, stored procedures, and triggers. Table 14-3 describes these terms in some detail.

The SMS databases can grow quite large over time, so it's essential to make sure adequate free space in the database is maintained. You're probably using SQL Server 7.0, which allows you to set the database and a transaction log to grow automatically to a predetermined size once the current database file is full.

TABLE 14-3

SQL database component details.

SQL Server Database Objects	Details
Tables	Think of a *table* as a collection of records made up of rows and columns. There are over 200 tables in the SMS site database.
Indexes	An *index* is a search engine within the database. Indexes can be clustered, i.e., in a sorted order, or nonclustered, i.e., stored in a nonsorted order.
Views	*Views* allow the creation of queries.
Stored Procedures	A *procedure* is a collection of SQL commands statements for carrying out tasks.
Triggers	*Triggers* are executed when data is changed in a table to ensure that all database components are aware of the changes.

To find the current status of your database, open up the SQL Server Enterprise Manager and open the *Databases* folder. Select your SMS database, and then after right-clicking on the highlighted SMS database folder, select *Properties*.

In the General and Transaction Log tabs, you can set the properties for how you wish your database files to grow—in MB or by a defined percentage—as shown in Figure 14-5.

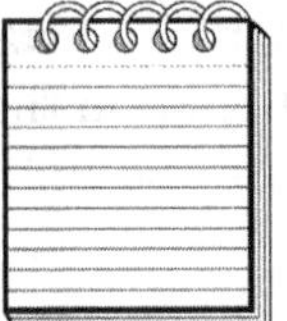

***NOTE**. There could be two databases: the SMS database called SMS and the software-metering database called <Name> LicDB.*

As your SQL databases are used by SMS, a temporary database file called tempdb is used for holding the temporary working tables. During peak usage, the temporary database size should never be more than 60 percent full. You can set this to grow dynamically via the properties of tempdb in the SQL Enterprise Manager.

SMS Database Integrity Checking

At least every four weeks, you should run an integrity check on both the SMS database and log. The Database Consistency Checker (DBCC) checks for the physical and logical consistency of the named database.

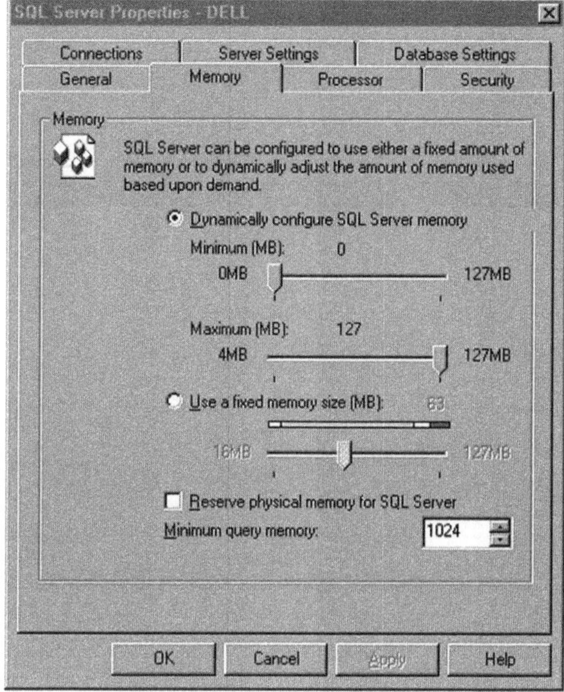

Figure 14-5 File properties for the SMS database.

The graphical interface that you can use to perform this query is called the SQL Server Query Analyzer. The Database Consistency Checker is found on the drop-down Tools menu located at the top left-hand corner of the SQL Server Enterprise Manager. The command-line sequence and parameters are as follows:

- **Sample syntax:** `Dbcc checkalloc ('name of database')`
- **Sample command:** `Dbcc checkalloc ('sms')`

This command and syntax checks the specified database, reporting on the allocated space and used space. At the end of the generated report should be a line that reads as follows: `CHECKALLOC found 0 allocation errors and 0 consistency errors in database`, as shown in Figure 14-6.

Other commands that should be executed on a weekly basis are as follows:

`Dbcc checkdb` Checks the databases for table linkage and index page errors

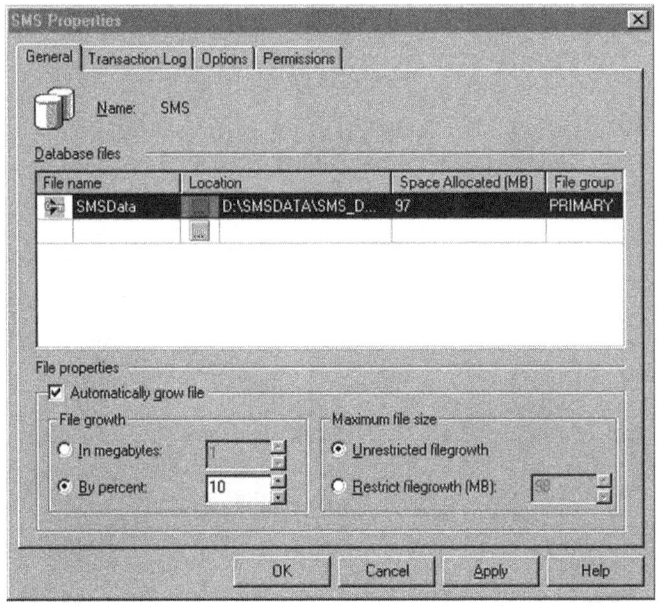

Figure 14-6 Checking for database errors using the SQL Server Query Analyzer.

`DbcC checkcatalog` Checks the system table for any allocation and corruption errors

Backing Up Your SMS Components

There are predefined database maintenance tasks already set up in the Database Maintenance folder found in the SMS Administrator console. The tasks that should be enabled are listed below. (Obviously, if you have not installed software metering, you can ignore the last two backup procedures.)

- Export Site Database
- Export Site Database Transaction Log
- Back Up SMS Site Server
- Export Software Metering Database
- Export Software Metering Transaction Log

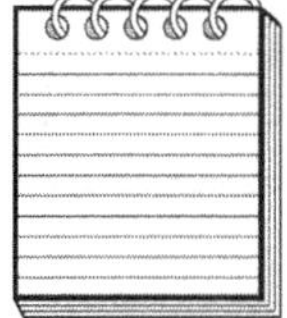

NOTE. The term "export" can be confusing because in this case it really means "back up." All of the SMS database backup options found in the SMS Administrator console are called "export tasks," with the exception of the SMS site server backup, which is called "backup."

The other database maintenance tasks that are defined and enabled in the Database Maintenance | Tasks folder are as follows:

- Update statistics every second day after SMS is installed.
- Rebuild indexes once a week.
- Monitor keys and re-create views once a week.

NOTE. You cannot add additional tasks to this preset list. However, you can add any one-line SQL scripting command to the SQL Command folder also found under the Database Maintenance folder, and you can also define when your custom script will execute.

SMS Task: Creating a Custom SQL Command Line

To create a custom SQL command line:

1. Open up the SMS Administrator console and navigate down to the console tree to *Database Maintenance*. Now select and highlight the *SQL Commands* folder.
2. Right-click and from the context menu, select *New* and then *SQL Command*.
3. In the Name field, enter the name `Check SMS site database free space`.
4. Next, check the checkbox to enable the SQL command.
5. Now enter the SQL command `sp_spaceused`.
6. Enter the log status path: `\\NTSERVER1\SMS\LOGS\SQLDB-SPACE.LOG`.
7. Set your schedule to once a week in the early morning hours.
8. Select *OK*. Your new command should appear in the details pane as shown in Figure 14-7.

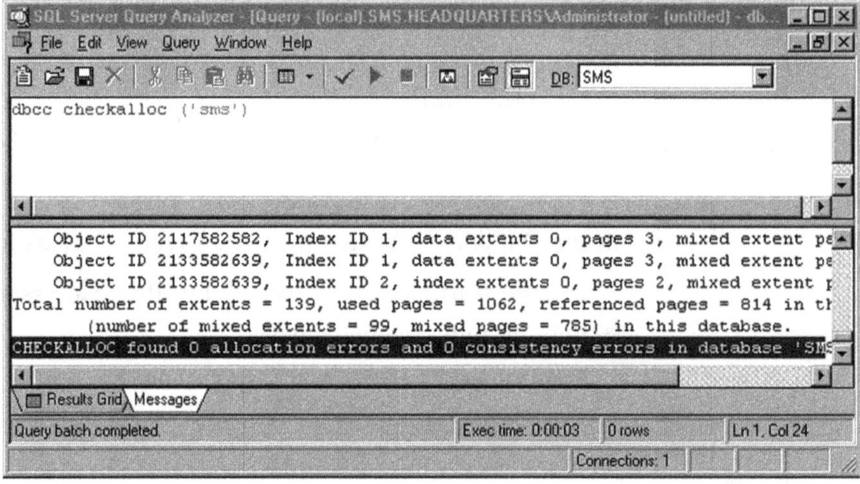

Figure 14-7 Creating an SQL command to execute automatically.

Task: Back Up the SMS Site Server

This backup task does not require you to create a backup device before executing the task, since SMS will automatically create a backup device. All backup files are then backed up to the network location that you have entered in the properties of this task, as shown in Figure 14-8.

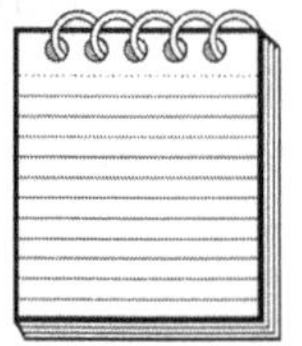

NOTE. *During the backup procedure, the SQL database is not accessible by the other installed SMS components in order to maintain a complete data backup.*

When executed, the site server backup task backs up the following data components:

1. The SMS site server database
2. The SMS software-metering database (if applicable)
3. HKEY_LOCAL_MACHINE\SOFTWARE\Microsoft\NAL
4. HKEY_LOCAL_MACHINE\SOFTWARE\Microsoft\SMS
5. The SMS main site folder SMS <site code>

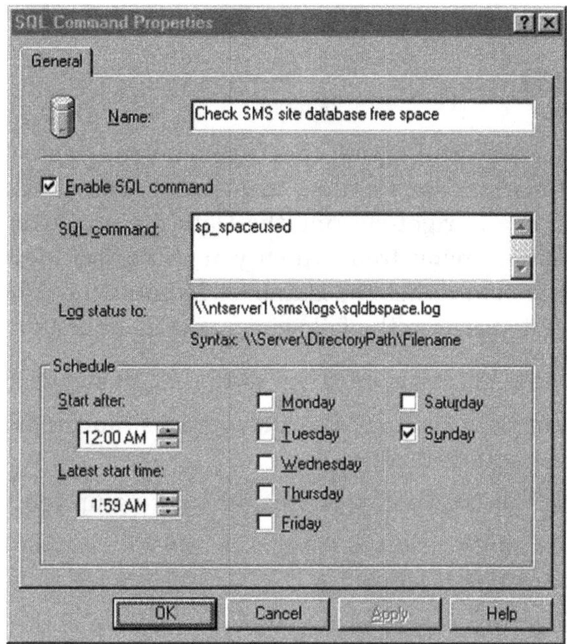

Figure 14-8 Enabling the backup task for the SMS site server.

Adding a Tape Device

All of the other data backup tasks that are defined in the Database Maintenance Tasks folder require that you first create a backup device in SQL Server before enabling and executing. (Export Software Metering Database, Export Software Metering Transaction Log, Export Site Database, and Export Site Database Transaction Log are the other predefined backup options.)

Opening up the SQL Server Enterprise Manager and selecting and opening the Management folder will display the Backup option. Selecting and right-clicking the Backup object reveals the context menu from which you can select New Backup Device.

The backup device can be a network hard drive location or a tape backup device; the tape backups that NT 4.0 supports are fully supported by SQL Server.

Creating a Database Maintenance Plan

Another powerful option that I recommend you set up is the Database Maintenance Plans option, also found under the Management folder. Selecting and right-clicking the Data Maintenance Plan object displays the context menu from which you can select New Maintenance Plan. This action launches the Database Maintenance Plan Wizard, which you can use to perform the following tasks on an automated schedule:

- Execute database integrity checks on all of your databases.
- Optimize your data and index pages, and remove unused database space automatically.
- Check database integrity before backing up your databases.
- Back up the selected databases and transaction logs to either tape or a hard disk location.
- Generate a report on the success or failure of this maintenance task.

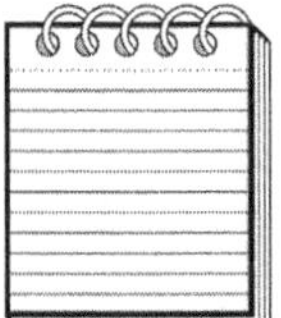

NOTE. *You could also choose to define two separate maintenance tasks: one for tape backup and another for a hard disk backup to an alternate location. The beauty of these tasks is that they're automated; you set them up, and they do their job.*

Database and Log File Backup Choices

Over time, as SMS executes, performing its job in the background, all components of the SQL database(s) will continue to get larger. Part of your overall proactive strategy should be full and periodic backups of the SMS site and software-metering databases.

Predefined database maintenance tasks allow you to choose what and when you want to backup, by separating the site database and software-metering transaction logs from the site database and software-metering database backup.

Removing Database Objects

Several tasks in the database maintenance subfolder allow you to delete specific database objects on a predefined schedule. Depending on the size of your SMS site, you may choose to change the frequency of the predefined tasks once they are enabled. The choices are as follows:

- *Status Messages* By default, system messages that are produced by SMS are stored in the SMS site database. Over time, these messages stack up, becoming quite large and possibly causing system performance problems (to say nothing of the hard drive space used). By default, SMS enables the task of deleting the aged status messages that are more than seven days old.
- *Software Inventory Data* When software inventory is Ronan SMS clients software inventory files e outdated at the site server. Again, this information will grow over time. If you also collect files from the users, even more space is required. After 90 days, the aged software inventory is deleted once this task has been enabled.
- *Hardware Inventory History Data* As just mentioned, the default for removing older hardware inventory, once the task to delete the aged inventory history is enabled, is every 90 days. You can choose to increase and decrease this value through the properties of the task, as shown in Figure 14-9.

Database Maintenance Tasks

Part of your periodic database maintenance should include enabling the following tasks for proper optimization of your SQL database:

- *Rebuild Indexes* Enabled by default, your system rebuilds its indexes once a week. If you have a large network implementation of SMS with many clients, your database values may be changing quickly. Rebuilding your indexes reorganizes your searches and can repair disk fragmentation if your indexes are clustered.
- *Update Statistics* Statistics are used to perform queries on the stored SQL data. By default, the statistics are updated every second day. This setting should be sufficient.

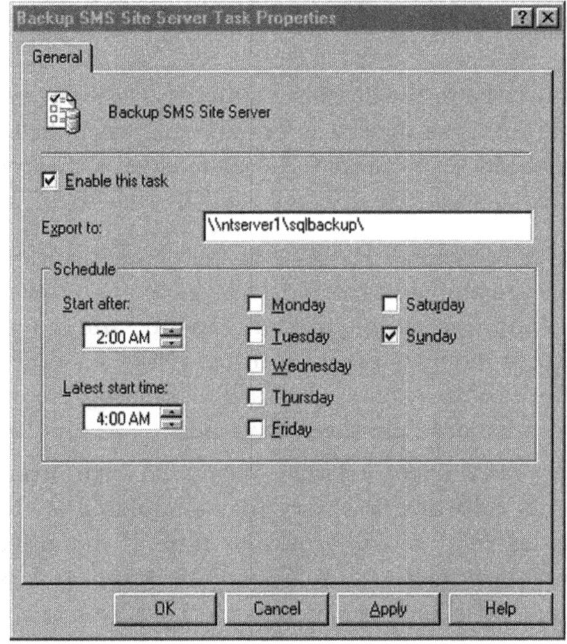

Figure 14-9 Viewing the current properties for the Aged Inventory History task.

- *Monitor Keys and Re-create Views* This task checks the primary keys that uniquely identify each table in the SMS site database for data integrity once a week. This setting should be sufficient.

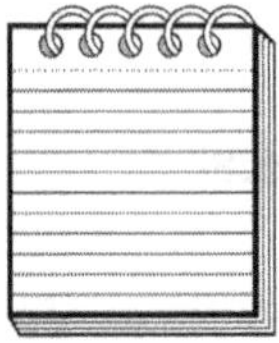

NOTE. *Another option, which is handy if you are new to SQL Server, is to use the Tools menu in the SQL Enterprise Manager to select the Wizard option. This will allow you to view all of the preset wizards. Under Management, you will find the Backup Wizard, which allows you to back up any or all databases to either a hard drive location or using an installed tape device.*

Moving Your SQL Databases

Hopefully, you won't have to move your database records in the near future, but you probably will over the life of your network. Reasons for the database move could be hardware problems or upgrading to a more powerful server. There are two common ways that you can move your SMS databases:

1. First, configure a computer system running SQL Server, making sure it has an identical computer name, database(s) name, SMS system files, and Registry settings. Then restore your databases.
2. Restore a backup copy of your SMS databases to a computer running SQL Server. Then run SMS Setup, and select the Installation option to reset the restored database with the new SQL database server.

NOTE. *You must also make sure that the same database sort order is used on the new SQL Server and the restored database files, or the restore will fail.*

Rebuilding a Failed SMS Site Server

If you have a failed SQL database or SMS site server that you need to rebuild, you must have certain components in order to successfully rebuild your site server, along with copies of the relevant SMS site database(s) or the SQL databases and the associated transaction logs. The essential databases and transaction logs are shown in Table 14-4.

The essential pieces that you must also have backups for are copies of the relevant Registry keys, the site control file, and the SMS directory. These essential pieces may be safe in your regular tape backup procedure; however, I strongly recommend backing up the following three components as part of your daily backup process.

1. *Registry keys* The following Registry keys should each be exported using REGEDIT (a Registry editor) to a REG file on either a Zip or floppy disk for safekeeping:

TABLE 14-4

Database and transaction log detail.

Database Name	SMS Use	Transaction Log
Master Database (master.dbf)	Initial configuration settings	MSSQL \ data \ mastlog.ldf
SMS (SMS_Data_7.MDF	Site server database	SMSDATA \ SMS_Log_7.ldf
SMSLicData (LicDB_Data.Mdf_8)	Software-metering database	LicDB_Log.ldf_8

- *HKEY_LOCAL_MACHINE\SOFTWARE\Microsoft\NAL*—CAP and protocol information for SMS clients and servers
- *HKEY_LOCAL_MACHINE\SOFTWARE\Microsoft\MSSQLServer*—SQL information
- *HKEY_LOCAL_MACHINE\SOFTWARE\Microsoft\MMC*—Microsoft Management Console setup information
- *HKEY_LOCAL_MACHINE\SOFTWARE\Microsoft\SMS*—SMS configuration information
- *HKEY_LOCAL_MACHINE\SYSTEM\CurrentControlSet\Services*—SMS services that are installed

2. *Site Control File* The site control file is the initial file that is checked when the SMS site server is first started. The name of the site control file is Sitectrl.ct0, which is located in the SMS directory in the path \INBOXES\SOTECTRL.BOX
3. *SMS Site Server Directory* The entire SMS directory should be backed up onto separate backup media for the purpose of disaster recovery. Most of the files are not modified on a day-to-day basis; however, a service pack upgrade will. Inventory, error logs, packages, and scripts are just a few of the folders that will have changes on a regular basis. Rather than trying to back up a handful of folders regularly, it's more proactive to back up the entire SMS directory and the subdirectory.

Restoring the SQL Database and SMS Components

To restore your database properly, complete the following steps:

1. First, install a fresh copy of the SMS and SQL Server
2. Next, all running SMS services should be stopped before starting the restore process. Using the Services icon in Control Panel, select and stop each service so they don't try to respond to a client or server request during the restore process. Also make sure that no attempts are made to access the database(s) being restored by a remote SMS Administrative console.
3. Now open the SQL Enterprise Manager, and from the drop-down Tools menu, select *Restore Database*. (There are numerous locations from which to activate the backing and restoring of the

desired databases. I am just showing you one example.) The resulting dialog box allows you to pick the database you wish to restore, along with the location.

4. If you had to reinstall SQL Server, you must restore the master database. It holds the initial settings and options that you had selected. If you need to restore the SMS site database, then you also must restore the site control file, as well as the Registry keys that you also backed up. These backed up files match the backed up site system database.
5. Finish the restoration by also restoring the site server's SMS directory. This will ensure that your inventory history, collected files, and trace logs are up-to-date.
6. Apply any service packs and back up all your key components once again.

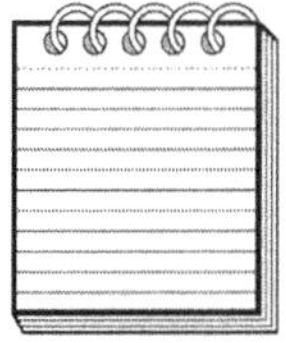

NOTE. *If you find that there is no backup of the site control file, you can generate a new one by using the supplied utility called Perinst.exe found on the SMS CD-ROM in the SUPPORT\RESKIT\BIN\platform\DBMAIN folder. Running this utility will regenerate a copy of the site control file. The syntax to use is as follows:*

```
Preinst/DUMP
```

The resulting process generates a site control file called SMS_<site code>.SCF in the root of the drive that contains the SMSDIR folder. The file should then be renamed SITECTRL.CT0.

Monitoring Your SMS Site Systems

SMS includes several tools and software utilities that you can use to monitor your SMS site systems. The performance and acceptable execution of your SMS site(s) depends on several factors: the network infrastructure, the types of computers where SMS has been installed, the number of SMS clients, and the amount of day-to-day monitoring. Obviously, if so many factors are involved in defining your overall performance, it can sometimes be a tough job to determine where the actual problem source actually is.

This is why SMS has a predefined reporting system detailing all installed site components and their overall activity. Under the surface, there are many points being monitored 24 hours a day, and all of the data relevant to your SMS sites is delivered to the SMS Administrator console. Status reporting can be initialized, which starts the capture of specific status messages from both the site server and SMS clients.

In the Site Status folder you can view the relevant status messages and quickly see what is right and what is wrong with your SMS sites, as shown in Figure 14-10.

Configuring Status Message Reporting

These status messages can be directed to the NT Event Log on the site server, or they can be stored in the SMS site server database. You can even have a command execute when a critical number of error messages have been generated, by applying a status filter rule to a status filter.

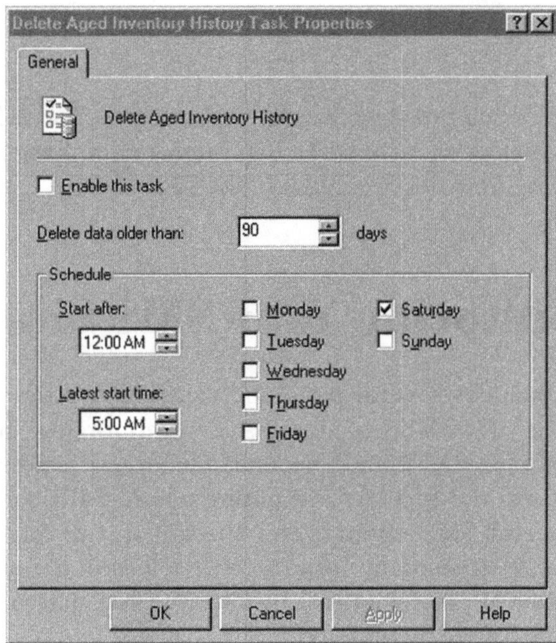

Figure 14-10 Current status messages viewed in the site status folder.

Both server and client components report based on a defined level of status message:

- *All Milestones* All messages are logged to the selected destination.
- *All Milestones with All Details* Only milestone messages are logged to the selected destination. Anytime an SMS component or activity completes the complete process, a "milestone" message is generated.
- *Error Milestones* Only event error messages are logged to the selected destination.
- *Error and Warning Milestones* Only major errors and milestone messages are logged to the selected destination.

The icon beside each status message displayed in the Site Status folder has three possible status filter states, shown in Figure 14-11.

These summaries of SMS status messages are an attempt to help you pinpoint the area of your site that is not functioning up to par. The threshold levels that trigger reporting are OK, Informational, Warning, and Error. The four areas that are summarized are as follows:

- *Component Status Messages* These status messages summarize the site server's operation and can also be configured to report to the parent site automatically. Thresholds are defined for every SMS Server service and thread; once the number of status messages goes over the

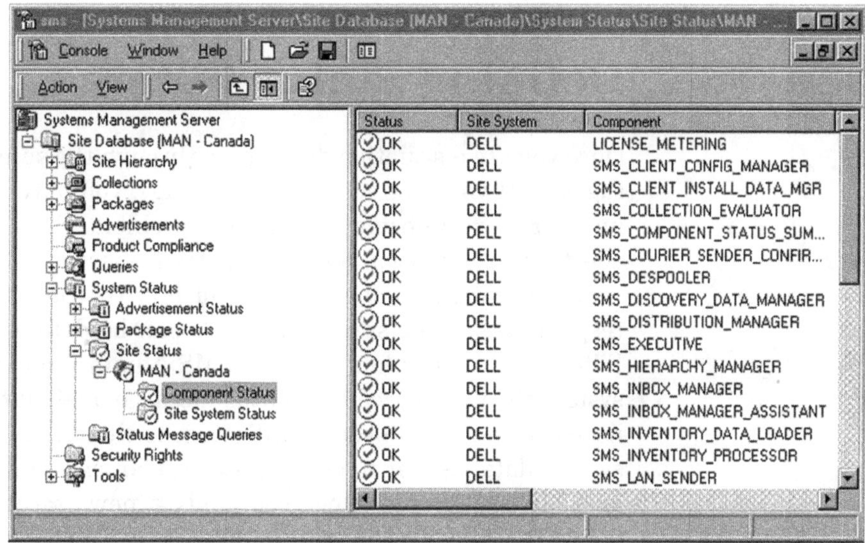

Figure 14-11 Site status states shown in the Site Status folder.

defined number, a summary message is created and sent to the SMS Administrator console.

- *Site System Status Messages* These status messages provide tracking of the site server's free hard drive space allotted for SMS and the amount of free SQL database space left. Settings can be defined for Windows NT hard drives, NT shares, and NetWare volumes, plus SQL settings for the data and log devices used for both the SMS site server and software-metering database. You can increase or decrease the defined warning and critical levels of each summary status message through the Thresholds tab.
- *Advertisement Messages* The current state of all advertisements across your site is summarized here in the SMS Administrator console. Find out what clients have received, started, and successfully executed the advertised program. The summary details are grouped by site and specific advertisement. Further details of software distribution, including distribution failure and client's successes and errors, are also logged here.

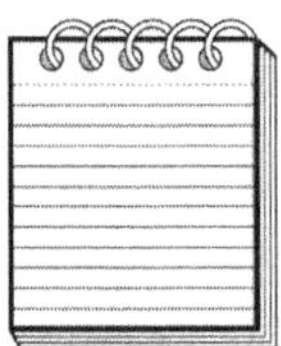

NOTE. *The Package status folder also found in the SMS Administrator console holds the details on all packages you have created. Details can be viewed by package, by site, and by distribution process.*

Defining Status Filters

Once you see a situation developing through the summarized status messages, or if you receive an error message, you may want to dig deeper to uncover more information about a problem. SMS allows you to set in effect a trap condition for when a status message is generated.

An unlimited number of rules for how the SMS status system should respond to specific status messages can be defined through the Status Filter Rules folder found in the SMS Administrator console. The status system then compares any status message against the defined rules you have set, in order to send notification to the NT Event Log or to the site system database, or to actually execute an executable command such as an EXE or BAT file. Once you apply a new status filter rule, you also define the rules by the criteria detailed in Table 14-5.

Once your status filter trap has been set and a status message is trapped that matches your criteria, the status system then deals with the captured message by the actions that you have defined through the status filter rules Actions tab, as listed in Table 14-6.

TABLE 14-5

Status filter details.

Status Filter Rules	Details
Source	Server, client, SMS provider.
Site code	The site where the status message was first generated.
System	The site system or client's NetBIOS name.
Component	All SMS components are listed.
Message type	Milestone, detail, or audit.
Severity	Informational, warning, or error.
Message ID	The message identifier.
Property	Some messages have specific properties.
Property value	Some messages have specific property values.

TABLE 14-6

Status filter rules actions that can be defined.

Status Filter Actions	Details
Write the status message	To the SMS site database and retain by default for 30 days or as defined.
Replicate the status message	To the parent SMS site server at the defined priority level.
Execute	An executable program, or have a message displayed on the site server by using the `NET SEND` command.
Do not send the status message	Ignore the status filter actions that are set.
Do not process	Any lower-priority status filter rules that are defined through the Actions | All Tasks menu.

Examples of Threads and Their Associated Log Files

Data Discovery Records

When the Data Discovery Manager creates and processes data discovery records, the following SMS threads log their activity to the log files as detailed in Table 14-7.

Hardware Inventory

When hardware inventory for 32-bit clients is executed, the server-side threads log their activity to the log files listed in Table 14-8.

Secondary Site Installation

When a secondary site server installation is started from a primary site server using the SMS Administrator console, the threads log their activ-

TABLE 14-7

Data discovery threads and log files.

Thread	Log File	
Inbox Manager	\SMS\Logs\Inboxmgr.log	
Inbox Assistant	\SMS\Logs\Inboxast.log	
Replication Manager	\SMS\Logs\Replmgr.log	(Secondary site location)
Discovery Data Manager	\SMS\Logs\Ddm.log	(Primary site location)

TABLE 14-8

Hardware inventory threads and log files.

Thread	Log File
Inbox Manager Assistant (at the CAP)	SMS\Logs\Inboxast.log
Inventory Processor	SMS\Logs\Invproc.log
Inventory Dataloader	SMS\Logs>Dataldr.log
Replication Manager	SMS\Logs\Replmgr.log

ity to the log files at the primary site and at the secondary site as listed in Table 14-9.

Software Inventory

When software inventory is performed for a 32-bit client, the threads perform the task and can log their activity to the log files at the client and the client access point as detailed in Table 14-10.

Using the SMS Service Manager

The SMS Service Manager is found in the SMS Administrator console under the Tools folder. This tool shows a real-time view of the SMS site components, including the current working status of the installed SMS

TABLE 14-9

Secondary site installation threads and log files used.

Primary Site Thread	Log File
SMS Provider	SMS\Logs\SMSprov.log
Hierarchy Manager	SMS\Logs\Hman.log
Scheduler	SMS\Logs\Sched.log
Sender (Standard Sender)	SMS\Logs\Sender.log
Despooler	SMS\Log\Despool.log
Replication Manager	SMS\Logs\Replmgr.log
Secondary Site Thread	**Log File**
SMS_Bootstrap Service	<Installation Hard Drive>\SMS_bootstrap.log
Setup	SMSsetup.log
Site Component Manager	SMS\Logs\Sitecomp.log
Hierarchy Manager	SMS\Logs\Hman.log
Replication Manager	SMS\Logs\Replmgr.log
Scheduler	SMS\Logs\Sched.log
Sender (Standard Sender)	SMS\Logs\Sender.log

TABLE 14-10

Software inventory threads and log files.

Client-Side Thread	Log File
Software Inventory Agent	SMS\Logs\Sinv32.log
Client Component Installation Manager	SMS\Logs\Ccim32.log
Client Service	SMS\Logs\Clisvc.log
Copy Queue	SMS\Logs\Cqmgr32.log
Client Access Point Thread	**Log File**
Inbox Manager Assistant	\SMS\Logs\Inboxast.log
Software Inventory Processor	\SMS\Logs\Sinvproc.log
Replication Manager	\SMS\Logs\Replmgr.log

services and the SMS executive threads on a specific site server. Administrative tasks include the following:

- Connecting to a specific site server
- Controlling SMS components by starting, stopping, pausing, and resuming them
- Logging the activity of a selected component to a text log file
- Checking the current status of SMS components

SMS Task: Using the SMS Services Manager

To enable the logging of the SMS components using the Service Manager:

1. Open the SMS Administrator console and find the Tools folder. After right-clicking on the SMS Service Manager object, select *All Tasks* | *Start SMS Service Manager*.
2. Select and expand the desired server to display the Components and Servers subfolders.
3. Select the Components folder. Then from the Components drop-down menu, choose *Select All*.
4. Then from the Components drop-down menu, choose *Logging*.

From this point on, logging will be enabled for all components. The log files are stored in SMS\LOGS.

To query the SMS components current status using the Service Manager:

1. Open the SMS Administrator console and find the Tools folder. Right-clicking on the SMS Service Manager object, and select *All Tasks | Start SMS Service Manager*.
2. Select *Servers* and highlight the server shown (or one of the installed servers).
3. Select the *Component* drop-down menu again, and choose *Select All*.
4. From the Component menu, choose *Query*. All of the SMS installed components will be queried for their current status, and in a few minutes, the results will be shown in the details pane, as shown in Figure 14-12.

To stop an individual SMS component using the Service Manager:

1. Open the SMS Administrator console and find the Tools folder. Right-click on the *SMS Service Manager* object, then select *All Tasks | Start SMS Service Manager*.
2. Select a running component from the details pane, and right-click on the highlighted component. From the context menu, select *Stop*.

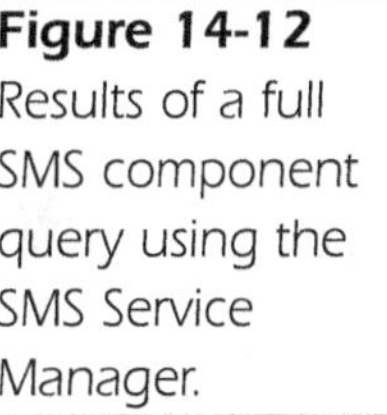

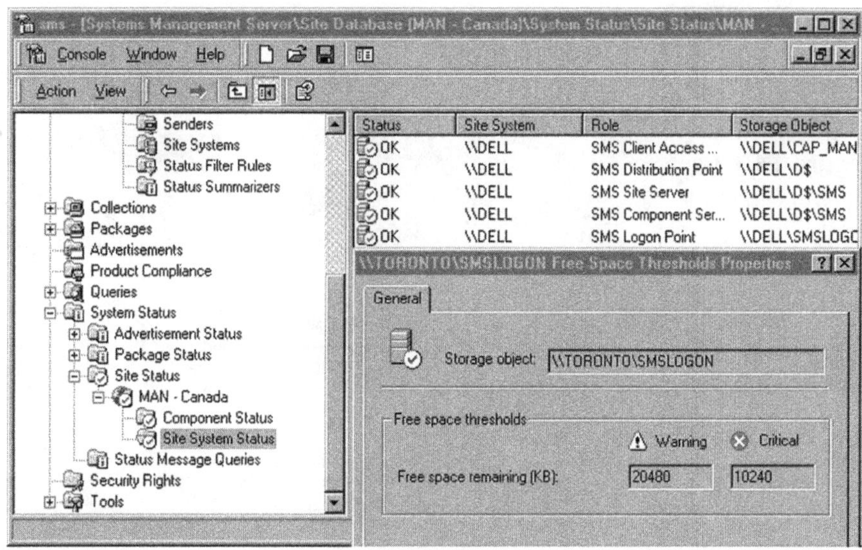

Figure 14-12 Results of a full SMS component query using the SMS Service Manager.

3. If the status of the component that you just stopped does not initially change, execute a query on the individual component in order to update the component's status in the details pane.

Using Network Trace

One helpful tool that can be used to check on your site servers and their current working status is Network Trace. This is started by selecting the desired site server listed in the SMS Administrative console's Site Systems folder. Right-clicking the selected site server displays a context menu showing All Tasks.

Selecting this option accesses another menu; the last menu option is the Network Trace menu. Starting Network Trace causes the data to be collected from Network and Server Discovery to generate a map of the SMS site systems and the network connections, as shown in Figure 14-13.

From the Tools menu, you can also ping all servers and routers to ensure their network components are functioning properly.

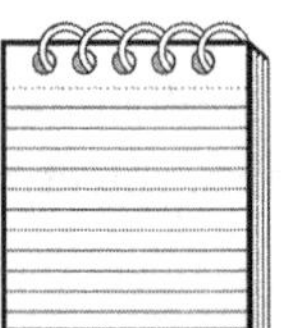

***Note**. Network Discovery must first have been run at least once before you can use Network Trace.*

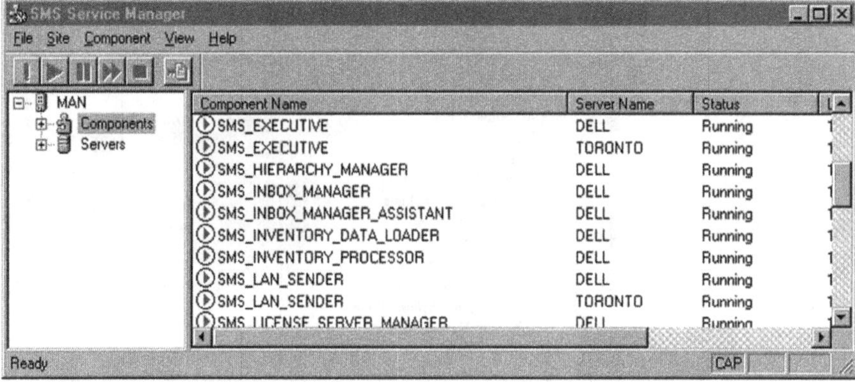

Figure 14-13 Network Trace results.

Using the Network Monitor (NetMon)

The Network Monitor is a tool that first appeared in the NT world as part of Windows NT BackOffice Server and later as Windows NT 4.0 Server in a more restrictive version. Using Network Monitor and the companion NetMon Agent, you can monitor network traffic by capturing and displaying the network packet traffic flow across your network from any computer or selected computer systems, as shown in Figure 14-14.

NDIS 4.0 (Network Device Interface Specification) network drivers must also be installed in order for this utility to operate in what is called *promiscuous mode.* Network Monitor is bundled with six software filter tools called "experts." Once you have saved a capture of network traffic, you can use one or more of the included experts to summarize the captured data. The installed experts are listed in Table 14-11. To activate use of the experts, you simply follow the following steps.

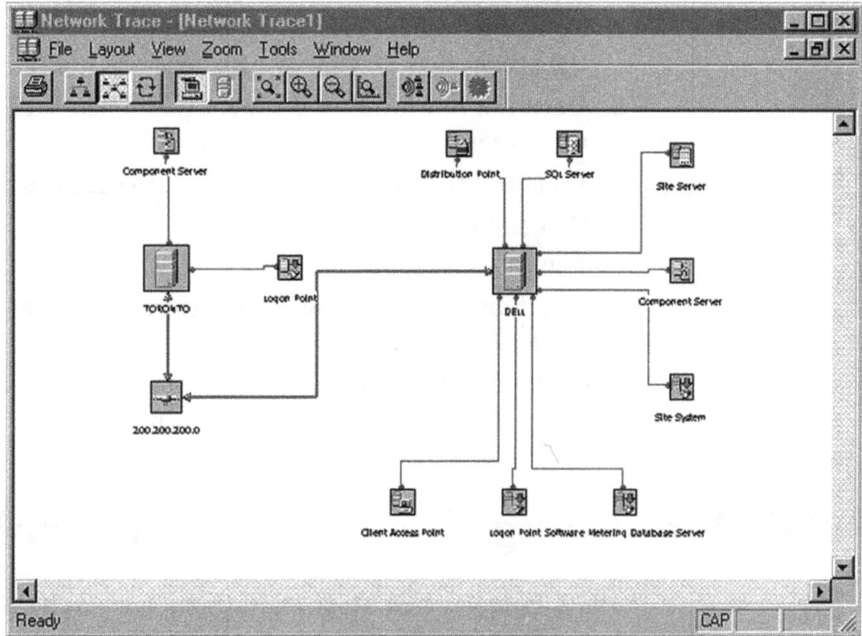

Figure 14-14 Capturing packet flow with Network Monitor.

TABLE 14-11

Network experts included with the SMS Network Monitor.

Network Monitor Experts	Details
Average Server Response Time	Resolves the average response time of a specific server to network requests.
Property Distribution Expert	Calculates statistics for a specific property within a selected network protocol, for example, the protocol DHCP and the property Server Host Name.
Protocol Coalesce Tool	Creates a summary capture of a specific protocol. Choices are IP, TCP/IP, NCP, or SPX.
Protocol Distribution	Produces a summary list of all protocols discovered.
TCP Retransmit	Calculates the current level of TCP retransmissions.
Top Users	Shows the busiest users based on transmit and receive packets summarized by MAC or link-layer addresses

Using Experts with Network Monitor

1. Open up Network Monitor from the Systems Management Server program group.
2. From the Capture drop-down menu, select *Start* to begin capturing the packet flow flowing by your network interface card.
3. Once you have captured the desired amount of frames, select the *Capture* menu and select the *Stop and View* option.
4. From the Tools drop-down menu, select *Experts*.
5. The Network Monitor Experts screen is displayed, as shown in Figure 14-15.
6. Select and highlight the desired experts, and then click on the *Add to Run List* button.
7. Click on the *Run Experts* button to have the expert complete its query of the collected network capture.

Using the Monitor Control Tool

Along with Network Monitor, SMS 2.0 has a collection of network monitors that are used to analyze the network traffic for specific events. The network monitors are set up and configured by opening up the Monitor

Figure 14-15 Expert choices for Network Monitor.

Capture: 1 (Summary)

Frame	Time	Src MAC Addr	Dst MAC Addr	Protocol	Description
1107	254.86...	LOCAL	TORONTO	TCP	.A...., len: 0, seq: 217110-21711
1108	254.86...	TORONTO	LOCAL	NBT	SS: Session Keep Alive, Len: 0
1109	255.06...	LOCAL	TORONTO	TCP	.A...., len: 0, seq: 160035-16003
1110	260.24...	LOCAL	030000000002	BONE	Security Check (0x03)
1111	267.08...	WILKINS	LOCAL	NBIPX	Session Data, Keep Alive
1112	267.08...	LOCAL	WILKINS	NBIPX	Session Data, Ack, Recv Seq 0x0F, 0x14
1113	267.92...	LOCAL	WILKINS	NBIPX	Session Data, Keep Alive
1114	267.92...	WILKINS	LOCAL	NBIPX	Session Data, Ack, Recv Seq 0x0E, 0x13
1115	270.25...	LOCAL	030000000002	BONE	Security Check (0x03)
1116	280.25...	LOCAL	030000000002	BONE	Security Check (0x03)
1117	288.13...	TORONTO	*BROADCAST	SAP	General Svc Resp [TORONTO - RPC Server
1118	290.26...	LOCAL	030000000002	BONE	Security Check (0x03)
1119	299.13...	WILKINS	LOCAL	NBIPX	Session Data, Keep Alive
1120	299.13...	LOCAL	WILKINS	NBIPX	Session Data, Ack, Recv Seq 0x0F, 0x14
1121	299.58...	LOCAL	*BROADCAST	RIPX	RIP Response [Net 0x00000001: 1 Hops]
1122	299.97...	LOCAL	WILKINS	NBIPX	Session Data, Keep Alive
1123	299.97...	WILKINS	LOCAL	NBIPX	Session Data, Ack, Recv Seq 0x0E, 0x13
1124	300.27...	LOCAL	030000000002	BONE	Security Check (0x03)
1125	304.97...	LOCAL	*BROADCAST	SAP	General Svc Resp [DELL - RPC Server]
1126	310.27...	LOCAL	030000000002	BONE	Security Check (0x03)
1127	313.73...	WILKINS	*BROADCAST	SAP	General Svc Resp [WILKINS - RPC Server

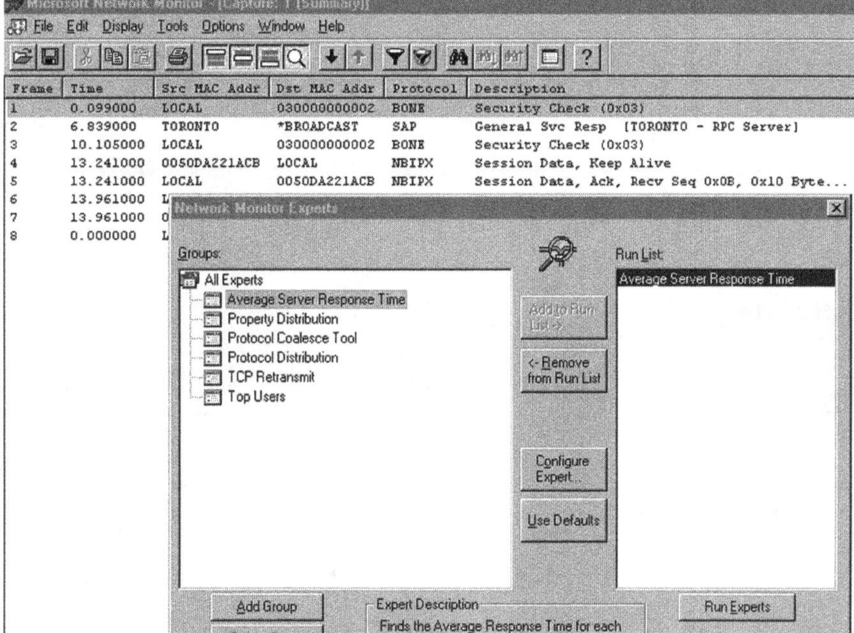

Figure 14-16 Running the Monitor Control tool.

Control tool, also found in the Systems Management Server program group, as shown in Figure 14-16.

The Monitor Control tool can be configured to run locally or on a remote computer system or systems, allowing you the ability to monitor network traffic from several network locations at the same time. Your choices for monitors are listed in Table 14-12. Once you have selected a monitor, you then configure the monitor's range criteria through the Configure button.

Tuning SQL Server for SMS

If you are using SQL Server 6.0, this book is not going to help you tune your server because that's a book in itself. More likely, however, you are using SQL Server 7.0, so most of the tuning chores are automatically set and maintained by SQL. Memory allocations, user connections, and the sizing of the databases, the transaction logs, and the tempdb database are all automatic. Earlier in this chapter we covered setting a database maintenance plan and using the SQL Server Query Analyzer to maintain your SQL databases.

To speed up your SQL Server's overall response time, the following areas (in order of ease) should be analyzed:

- Add additional memory for more RAM caching of data and also to minimize swap file paging.
- Locate the data and log devices for both the tempdb and SMS databases on separate hard drive subsystems.

TABLE 14-12

Details on network monitors.

Network Monitors	Details
ICMP Redirect Monitor	Checks for the presence of any unauthorized routers and router table corruption.
IP Router Monitor	Monitors specified IP routes and reports on any failures.
IPRange Monitor	Checks for frames from specific IP addresses.
IPX Router Monitor	Watches specific IPX routes and reports on any failures.
Rouge DHCP and WINS Monitor	Monitors any unauthorized DHCP or WINS servers.
Security Monitor	Reports on any authorized Network Monitor session.
SynAttack Monitor	Monitors and reports on any half-opened server connections established by unauthorized clients.

TABLE 14-13

Task-by-task analysis.

SMS Task	Check and Analyze
Installation of Clients	■ Number of available client access points ■ Number of available logon points ■ Overall available network bandwidth
Site-to-Site Connectivity	■ Number of senders installed ■ Overall available network bandwidth
Remote Control	■ Overall available network bandwidth
Software Distribution	■ Number of available distribution points ■ Number of available client access points ■ Overall available network bandwidth
Software Metering	■ Location and power of the software-metering server
Hardware and Software Inventory	■ Power of the site server assigned this task ■ Number of available client access points ■ Overall available network bandwidth

- Upgrade your hard drive subsystem to RAID 5 to increase input and output operations.
- Add an additional CPU for more processing power.

The best proactive optimization techniques are found when the tasks that your SMS system performs are analyzed task by task, as shown in Table 14-13. Careful planning and scheduling of the installed SMS tasks can help improve overall performance without a lot of money changing hands.

CHAPTER 15

Troubleshooting SMS 2.0

In this chapter you will learn about:

- Troubleshooting memory leaks and excessive file activity
- Tuning NT before troubleshooting
- Using SMS Trace and log files to track SMS
- Troubleshooting the core functions of SMS
- Solving SMS client problems
- Implementing SMS Resource Kit tools
- Using WBEM (Web-Based Enterprise Management)

SMS Troubleshooting

There is still nothing like a complicated network anchored by NT to bring even the most experienced network support people to their knees. NT humbles every one of us every now and again. This isn't a Microsoft rant; it's just a fact that a system designed and built with many hands and brains will have some bizarre problems surface every now and then that takes time to solve. Frequently the solution is not complicated. However, it can sure feel daunting when it's late at night and your list of to-dos is interrupted by a problem for which you are expected to know the answer immediately.

A common suggested starting point when troubleshooting is to first take a visual look at the problem. This is much easier when you are performing hardware troubleshooting or cable testing; however, discovering what is happening under the hood of a site server with respect to memory (and in the NT world, that means RAM, paging file usage, and current hard drive activity) is the best starting point.

The best software utility for both NT servers and workstation systems is Task Manager (TASKMGR.EXE). This utility is directly started by pressing Ctrl-Shift-Esc.

By selecting the Performance tab, as shown in Figure 15-1, you can see at a glance the Physical memory map summary: Total, Available, and what has been allocated as a RAM file cache.

If the free RAM is lower than you had expected, you might not have enough to begin with. Another possibility, however, is that a program may be eating up valuable memory resources when it is running, and when it's finished, the program is not returning its slice of chip memory back to the Memory Manager. (This situation is called a "memory leak." Coming up, we will look at several ways to discover just when our systems are misusing resources.)

The bottom left option on the Performance tab, called Commit Charge, details the total allocation of both chip memory and swap file. If the swap file is too small and over 75 percent full, then the NT operating system will be in a panic to find additional hard drive space to use for virtual memory/swap file.

The Process tab displays the current 16-bit and 32-bit executables processes. By using the View drop-down menu and selecting Columns, you can access a detailed view. Make sure that the following stats are selected and monitored on a regular schedule:

- *Memory usage* Per process.

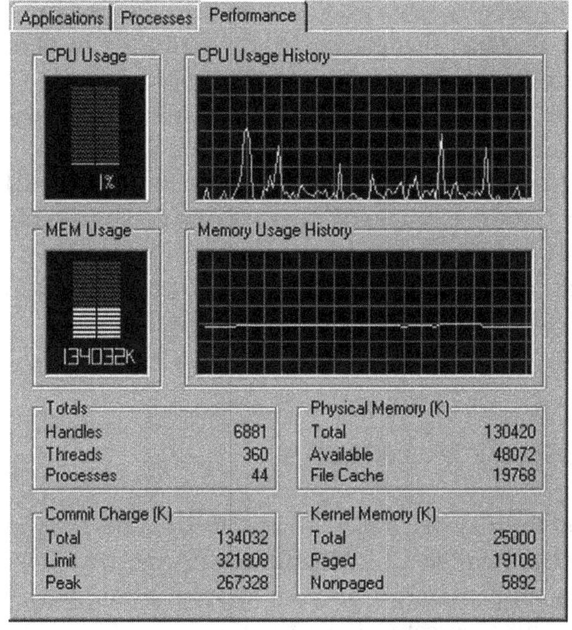

Figure 15-1 Task Manager can report many current details about the NT system and its overall health.

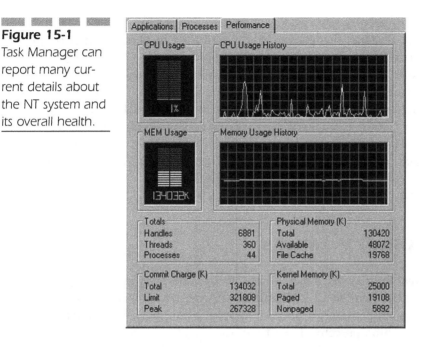

- *Page faults* A page fault indicates that the swap file was checked for a file. However, it wasn't present, and as a result, the operating system had to search the hard drive, wasting processing time.
- *Virtual memory size* Per process.

Setting the Page File Minimum and Maximum Size

Terminology can be confusing, as *paging* file, *swap* file, and *virtual memory* stand for the same darn feature. The rule of thumb for setting virtual memory/paging file initial and maximum thresholds with Windows NT is to set both values at the same time. Initial paging file size should be at least 200 MB, with a maximum swap file size set at 600 MB. If possible, the location of the paging file should always be on a separate partition, away from where the operating system is installed. This way, it will become much less fragmented over time.

The suggested paging file values are minimums; you will have to be proactive in checking and rechecking the current virtual memory size of all your servers with Task Manager while they are under working conditions. Setting the paging file thresholds is performed through the Control Panel | System Icon | Performance tab, as shown in Figure 15-2.

Next, after selecting the Virtual Memory section, adjust the paging file Initial and Maximum sizes, and then click on *OK* to accept the changes. A reboot is required before the settings take effect. Setting the swap file size properly also increases the maximum size that your Registry is allowed to expand to; take careful note that the maximum Registry size value shown at the bottom of the Virtual Memory tab screen does not increase automatically.

Memory Leaks

To test for memory leaks, Microsoft has a Server Resource Kit command-line utility called CLEARMEM.EXE, and that's exactly what it does: it cleans chip memory as your system runs, with no reboot required. Ninety-nine percent of the time, this utility recovers 4 to 6 MB of chip memory and sometimes much more. It really depends on how many

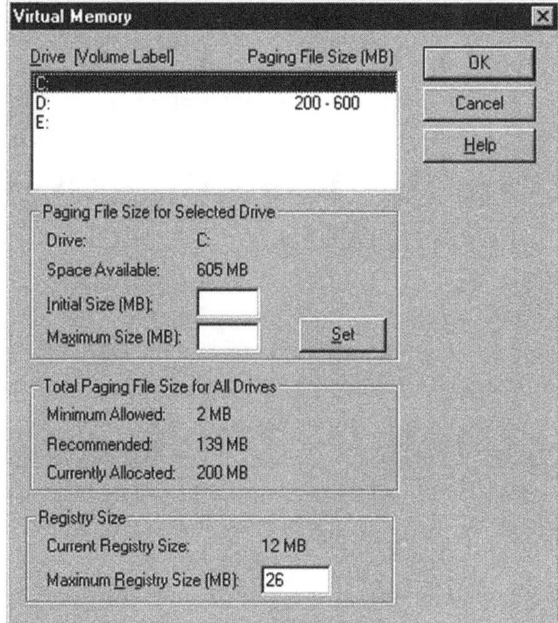

Figure 15-2 Paging file and Registry size settings must be set correctly.

startup tasks the site server is configured for, how busy it is with other system tasks, and the number of software applets that affect memory usage.

First, use Task Manager to take a read of the physical memory available, then run CLEARMEM. The results may surprise you. On a trusty Dell notebook with 120 MB, where much of my writing is done while on the road, when I start up and load NT, then SQL and Word, the amount of free memory available is around 30 MB. Add in the 20 MB reserved for file cache, and it's up to 50 MB. Running CLEARMEM gets back an additional 23 MB in free memory.

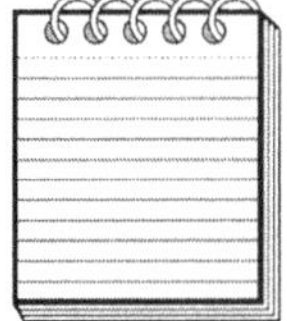

NOTE *On a site server that seemed sluggish, I ran CLEARMEM.EXE and gained back 40 MB of RAM.*

Now you may be thinking, "Doesn't the NT operating system get this memory back for me?" And the answer is... sometimes. If your system is underutilized, after several hours, most of the memory *may* be recovered. If the system is a busy site server or distribution point, you may never get all of your valuable memory resources back. Make sure that memory consumption is checked under a variety of conditions. Adding additional memory resources over and above the expected amount is necessary to always have available a certain working size of RAM when it is needed.

Hard Drive Activity

An all-too-common scenario is excessive hard drive activity. Although Task Manager lists the processes that are currently in RAM, it doesn't tell us what process is busy at any given point. And sometimes several of the listed processes are not even supposed to be running!

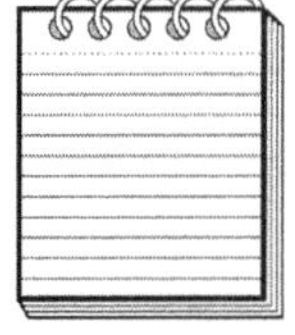

NOTE. *The classic example is when a process called RUNDLL32.EXE is listed in the current processes in Task Manager and has finished its job, yet it hasn't been removed from RAM. Selecting the End Process button will remove the process if it has indeed finished. (If it hasn't, you won't be allowed to remove it.) RUNDLL32 is a worker process that opens up dynamic link library files as needed. It sometimes seems to get lost and ends up hanging out in RAM.*

To deal with these situations, I recommend two free software tools: FILEMON and REGMON. You can download these tools at www.sysinternals.com, a terrific Web site for NT utilities and knowledge. (Be sure to check out the Blue Screen of Death screen saver as well.)

FILEMON runs at the Explorer shell, needs no installation, and reports on all real-time file activity for NT and Windows 95/98 systems. You can even filter the file activity and log the results to a text file. For troubleshooting hard drive activity, this tool is terrific. As shown in Figure 15-3, you can see the current detail on the site server activity and what LOG and EXE files are currently performing their jobs in the background.

REGMON works the same as FILEMON, but its focus is reporting on real-time Registry access. Using a filter, you can find out most anything about any software that writes to the Registry.

Defragmentation Issues

So, when's the last time you checked file defragmentation on your server's hard drives? Curiously, a strange myth has developed over the

File Monitor - Systems Internals: http://www.sysinternals.com

File Edit Options Drives Help

#	Time	Process	Request	Path
147	10:51:03 AM	smsexec.exe	IRP_MJ_CLEANUP	D:\WINNT\system32\DBMSSHRN.dll
148	10:51:03 AM	smsexec.exe	IRP_MJ_CLOSE	D:\WINNT\system32\DBMSSHRN.dll
149	10:51:03 AM	smsexec.exe	FSCTL_IS_VOLUME_M...	D:\WINNT\system32
150	10:51:03 AM	smsexec.exe	IRP_MJ_CREATE	D:\SMS\Logs\sitestat.log
151	10:51:03 AM	smsexec.exe	FASTIO_QUERY_STAN...	D:\SMS\Logs\sitestat.log
152	10:51:03 AM	smsexec.exe	IRP_MJ_WRITE	D:\SMS\Logs\sitestat.log
153	10:51:03 AM	System	IRP_MJ_CLOSE	D:\SMS\Logs\sitestat.log
154	10:51:03 AM	smsexec.exe	FASTIO_QUERY_STAN...	D:\SMS\Logs\sitestat.log
155	10:51:03 AM	smsexec.exe	IRP_MJ_CLEANUP	D:\SMS\Logs\sitestat.log
156	10:51:03 AM	System	IRP_MJ_WRITE*	D:\SMS\Logs\sitestat.log
157	10:51:03 AM	System	IRP_MJ_SET_INFORM...	D:\SMS\Logs\sitestat.log
158	10:51:04 AM	explorer.exe	FSCTL_IS_VOLUME_M...	D:\
159	10:51:04 AM	explorer.exe	FASTIO_QUERY_OPEN	D:\MSSQL\Binn\sqlmangr.exe
160	10:51:04 AM	explorer.exe	FSCTL_IS_VOLUME_M...	D:\
161	10:51:04 AM	explorer.exe	FSCTL_IS_VOLUME_M...	D:\
162	10:51:04 AM	explorer.exe	FASTIO_QUERY_OPEN	D:\MSSQL\Binn\sqlmangr.exe
163	10:51:04 AM	explorer.exe	FSCTL_IS_VOLUME_M...	D:\
164	10:51:05 AM	HJCAP.EXE	IRP_MJ_READ*	D:\pagefile.sys
165	10:51:05 AM	System	IRP_MJ_WRITE*	D: DASD
166	10:51:05 AM	System	IRP_MJ_WRITE*	D: DASD
167	10:51:05 AM	System	IRP_MJ_WRITE*	D: DASD

Figure 15-3 FILEMON provides details on all file activity.

years about NT hard drive subsystems not fragmenting as badly as Windows 95/98. It's just that, though—a strange myth.

Download a copy of Diskeeper Lite from www.execsoft.com, and test all NT site servers. NT systems must be defragged on a timely basis—at least once a week (in my humble opinion), or you're going to be in trouble. The full version allows the setup of a defragmentation schedule for all your site servers and NT workstations. If these first few pages seem like tuning rather than troubleshooting, remember, systems must be properly tuned in order for successful troubleshooting to take place.

NOTE. *Diskeeper is bundled with Windows 2000. Also, at www.sysinternals.com, you can try out their utility PAGEDFRG.EXE for defragging the system Registry hives and the pagefile.*

Service Pack 1 Fixes

If you encounter a strange SMS situation, or you attempt to carry out an SMS task and it just won't work, remember Service Pack 1 for SMS 2.0. (At this writing, Service Pack 2 was in beta test and will probably be available by the time this book is published.) Please do yourself a huge favor: Print out and read the release notes and service pack fixes, with highlighter in hand. Your unsolvable problem could very well be a service pack bug fix. A summary of fixes is listed in Table 15-1.

SMS is still a new software application. The service packs for NT are also worthy of a mention here.

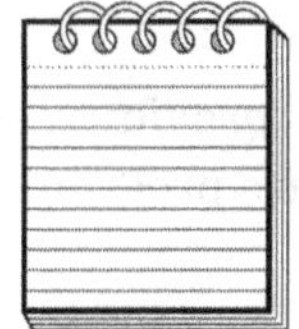

NOTE. *My best results at this time of writing have been with Service Pack 4 for NT Server and Service Pack 1 for SMS 2.0.*

Using Status Messages for Troubleshooting

There are four objects defined through the System Status folder in the SMS Administrator console that summarize status messages generated by SMS components as they perform their scheduled tasks:

TABLE 15-1

Service Pack 1 fixes for SMS 2.0.

KB Article	Problem Report
Q214979	Service Manager Does Not Connect to Secondary Site Servers.
Q215018	Cannot Add Local Groups in Manage User Wizard.
Q221481	WMI Fails to Install on Windows NT 4.0 SP 5.
Q223755	SMS Executive Crashes When Enumerating Non-Microsoft Server.
Q226114	Advertisement Fails When Sent to Win95 & Win98 Users in more than 10 Groups.
Q228276	Software Inventory Processing Degrades Foreground Performance on Win95 & Win98 Clients.
Q230128	SQL Monitor Reports "Cannot Connect to Site Server Registry."
Q232240	Specifying Long File Name for Status MIF Causes Error.
Q233395	SNMP Access Violation After Installing Windows NT 4.0 Service Pack 4.
Q235735	Site Backup Only Occurs Once a Week and Does Not Adhere to Schedule.
Q235745	Setup Does Not Create "SMS Admins" Group When Installing SMS on a Backup Domain Controller.

1. *Advertisement Status* Server status messages report on the advertisements that are distributed to client access points. The SMS client computers provide details about the advertisements that are received and the success or failure of the program installation.
2. *Package Status* Status messages are generated, providing current information about package creation and software program distribution.
3. *Site Status* The top site status Fuller provides a summary listing of the SMS components running on all site servers. Subsequent subfolders provide details on each individual SMS component.
4. *Status Message Queries* Many status message queries are created by SMS. You can also create your own custom status messages by using the SMS Query Builder. Right-clicking on the Status Message folder in the SMS Administrator console allows you to create a status message query from the New context menu.

NOTE. Each site server's status message thresholds for the individual SMS components, the site server, and advertisements can be defined through the SMS Administrator console Status Summarizers folder.

SMS Architecture

SMS uses multiple locations to store the data and configuration files needed and used by each site server and the data sent to each site server from the SMS clients. The SMS Executive Service assigns multiple threads to carry out the completion of all SMS tasks of the installed SMS services. You must keep in mind the following structure of SMS when solving an SMS problem, since the entire architecture is usually involved.

SMS Site Database

The SQL database is stored on the local site server or located at a remote server location. It can be accessed through the SQL Enterprise Manager or the SMS Administrator console.

Site Control File

The site control file is a text file named Sitectrl.ct0. It lists the current site configuration with the help of a copy of the site control file that is stored in the SMS site database, as well as the delta site control file, which contains the changes made to the actual site control file. Because each child site sends its site control file to its parent site, which then sends both site control files up the SMS tree to the next parent site, ending at the central site, each central site contains the site control files for both the primary and secondary sites throughout the SMS hierarchy.

Any changes made to the site control file are done through the SMS Administrator console.

Registry

All of the server and client configuration settings, including the enabling and disabling of SMS components and the location of the installed components, are stored and updated in the Registry on the site server. The SMS client also has many Registry settings that define the SMS components that are installed and how they will operate through the SOFTWARE and SYSTEM system hives and the NTUSER.DAT user hive.

SMS Services and Threads

The server and client components that make up SMS are essentially services; another term for these services is "SMS software components." These services provide a custom service depending on the assigned task. Some of these services start automatically at system startup; others start and stop as needed. As shown in Figure 15-4, all SMS services can be viewed, initiated, and stopped through the Services icon in Control Panel for each site server and each installed SMS client.

The threads are the workers that carry out the installed services as directed by the SMS Executive Service. You can start and stop each thread component through the SMS Administrator console by using the SMS Service Manager located in the Tools folder. More importantly, each individual SMS server thread can be set to log its progress to a LOG file. Although the SMS LOG files are not the easiest to read in text format, they contain essential real-time information. (More details on LOG files follow in the next few pages of this chapter.)

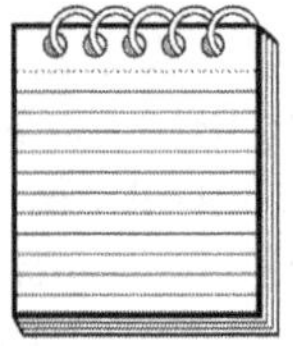

NOTE. *Each server LOG file is limited to a maximum of 1 MB so they won't clog your hard drive space. After you have finished using the log to solve your problem, remember to disable the logging process. The downside of server LOG files is that once they are enabled, you lose at least 15 percent of your performance if your hard drives are IDE-based*

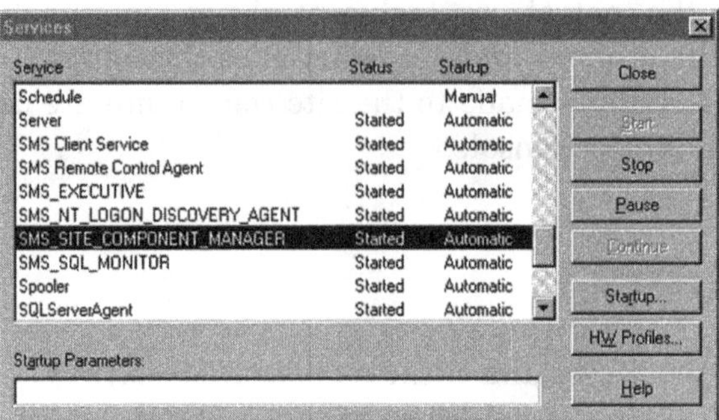

Figure 15-4 SMS services as viewed through the Control Panel.

(Integrated Device Electronics). If you use SCSI adapters and hard drive subsystems, the percentage drops to between 6 and 10 percent.

SMS Task: Enable Logging of SMS Server Components

To enable logging:

1. Open the SMS Administrator, and select the *Tools* folder and the *SMS Service Manager.*
2. Right-click on the *SMS Service Manager*. From the *All Tasks* menu, choose *Start SMS Service Manager*.
3. Select the site server shows. The Components and the Services icons appear.
4. Select *Components*. Next, choose the desired component, and select the Logging tab.
5. Check Logging Enabled to log activity to the specified LOG file. All logs are stored in <site Server> SMS\Logs.

A complete listing of server and client LOG files is shown in Table 15-2.

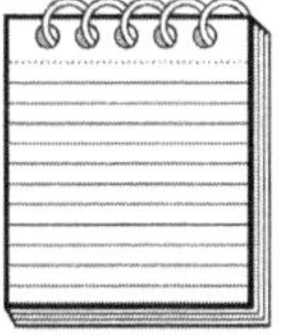

NOTE. *You can also use the Status Filter Rules folder through the SMS Administrator console to create a custom filter for any SMS component for the local site.*

SMS Client LOG Files

Client LOG files are enabled by default for SMS clients and stored in the %SYSTEM ROOT%\MS\SMS\LOGS folder for each client. The client logs are initially limited in size to 100 KB; however, you can change the size through the Registry at HKEY_LOCAL_MACHINE\SOFTWARE\Microsoft\SMS\Client\Sites\Shared\MAN\Configuration\Client Properties by changing the default decimal DWORD value.

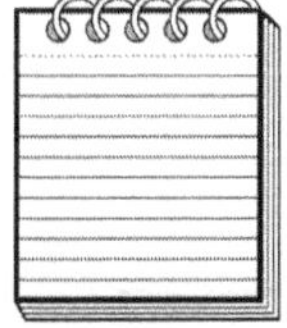

NOTE. *The user LOG file Clicore.log contains the latest installation information for the SMS client.*

TABLE 15-2

SMS LOG files for server and client components.

Log Type	LOG Filename (.LOG)	Component Name
Server	CCM	Client Config Manager
Server	CIDM	Client Install Data Manager
Server	Colleval	Collection Evaluator
Server	Compsumm	Component Status Summarizer
Server	Dataldr	Inventory Data Loader
Server	DDM	Discovery Data Manager
Server	Despool	Despooler
Server	Distmgr	Distribution Manager
Server	Hman	Hierarchy Manager
Server	Inboxast	Inbox Manager Assistant
Server	Inboxmgr	Inbox Manager
Server	Invproc	Inventory Processor
Server	Licsrvc	License Metering
Server	Licsvcfg	License Server Manager
Server	Netdisc	Network Discovery Agent
Server	NT_logon	NT Logon Server Manager
Server	NTlgdscm	NT Logon Discovery Manager
Server	Ntlginst	NT Logon Installation Manager
Server	Offermgr	Offer Manager
Server	Offersum	Offer Status Summarizer
Server	Replmgr	Replication Manager
Server	Sched	Scheduler
Server	Sender	Sender
Server	Sinvproc	Software Inventory Processor
Server	Sitecomp	Site Component Manager
Server	Sitectrl	Site Control Manager
Server	Sitestat	Site System Status Summarizer
Server	Smsdbmon	SMS SQL Monitor
Server	Smsexec	SMS Executive
Server	Statmgr	Status Manager

TABLE 15-2

(Continued)

Log Type	LOG Filename (.LOG)	Component Name
Client	Clicore	Client Component Installation
Client	Wn_logon	Windows Client Logon and Automatic Install
Client	Wnmanual	Windows Manual Client Installation

Using SMS Trace with Log Files

SMS Trace is provided for easier reading of SMS LOG files. It can be found on the SMS CD-ROM in the Support\Reskit\Bin\I386 folder. Running SMSTRACE.EXE launches the GUI interface, and from the drop-down File menu, you can navigate to the SMS\Log folder and select a LOG file to load. (See Figure 15-5.)

SMS Trace can read both Server and LOG files in real-time mode; this means that a LOG file can be loaded for a particular SMS component, monitoring the work of the component as it executes. A command-line utility TRACER.EXE is also included, which allows you to view one single LOG file at a time.

NOTE. *If you have the SMS Resource Kit, you will have access to the Reset Log tool RESETLOG.EXE, which resets the site server LOG files back to the installation defaults at the command prompt without having to use the SMS Administrator console.*

Troubleshooting SMS Using Performance Monitor Counters

When SMS is installed, several new performance object and counters are added for monitoring SMS systems with the Performance Monitor detailed in Table 15-3. The Performance Monitor is started from the Administrator program group. These counters allow you to get a feel for the overall working level of your site servers by monitoring the queuing levels, number of threads in use, and the workload of the Standard Sender.

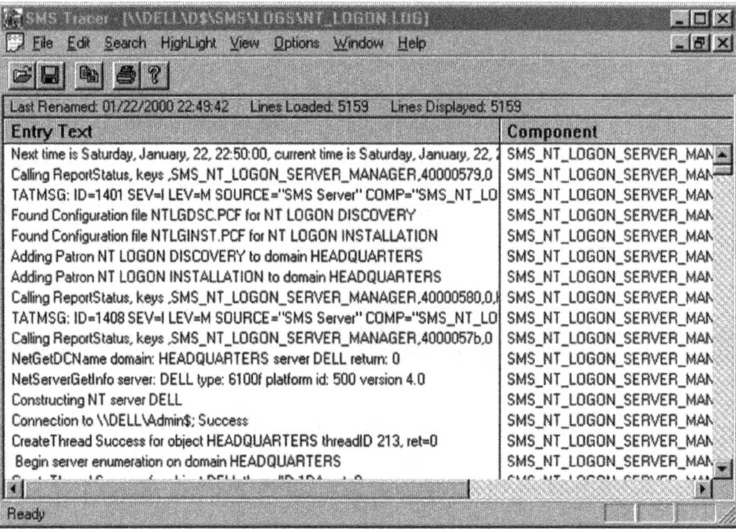

Figure 15-5 Running SMS Trace with SMS LOG files.

TABLE 15-3 Performance counters for monitoring SMS.

Performance Counter	Details
SMS Discovery Data Manager	Discovery data records that are held in the input queue, processed per minute, or totally processed. Also, any bad DDRs.
SMS Executive Thread Status	How many threads controlled by the SMS are running, sleeping, or yielding to another process.
SMS In-Memory Queues	Total number of objects that are being held or discarded in the queue by a process.
SMS Inventory Data Loader	Inventory records that are held in the input queue, processed per minute, or totally processed, along with any bad MIFs (Management Information Format).
SMS Software Inventory Processor	Software Inventory records held in the input queue, processed per minute, totally processed, and any bad SINVs.
SMS Standard Sender	Check the workload of Standard Sender in total, current, and average bytes sent and thread count across the LAN/WAN
SMS Status Messages	Track number of status messages sent by the SMS Status Manager.
SMS Software Metering	Track license processing data.

Remember that the choices for using Performance Monitor include the real-time chart view, as well as the ability to log the results to an event log anywhere on the network, or into an report or event log LOG file.

Troubleshooting the SMS Installation

If you are having problems completing the installation of SMS, the first place to check is the Smssetup.log file that SMS uses to log the installation success for failure. A careful read of the LOG file can reveal that the last installation of SMS was a success. Figure 15-6 shows the LOG file in Notepad. Keep in mind, however, that using SMS Trace would've been easier.

Following is a quick summary of the most common SMS setup and installation areas to check and verify:

- *Security* The SMS Service account must be part of the Domain Admin group and have the advanced right "Log on as a service."
- *Hard Disk Space* At least 1 GB must be available.
- *Hard Disk Partition Type* NTFS partitions must be available.
- *User Connections* Must be at least 55 set by SQL Server Enterprise Manager.

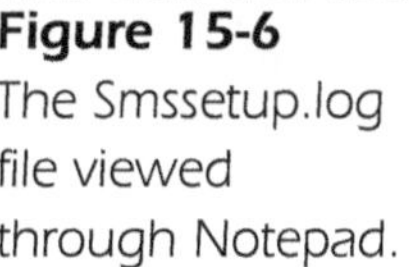

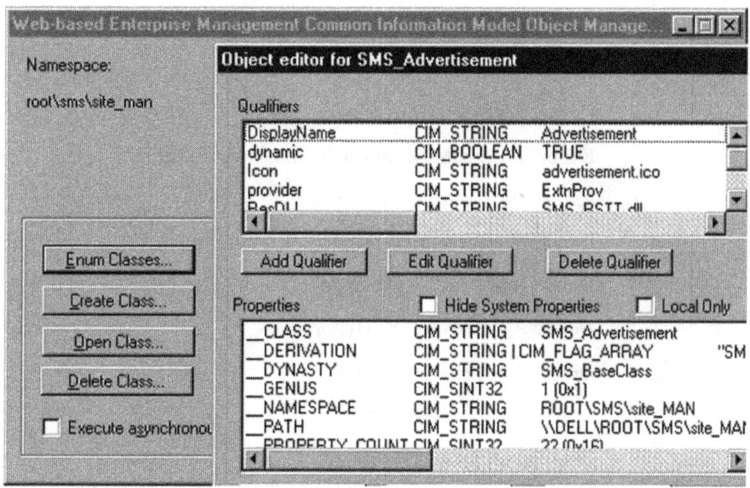

Figure 15-6 The Smssetup.log file viewed through Notepad.

- *Service Pack* At a minimum, must be Service Pack 4.0 for NT Server.
- *Internet Explorer* IE 4.01 must be installed.
- *Data Component Tools* Version 2.0 must be installed.

Troubleshooting the SQL Site Server Databases

SMS SQL Monitor carries out weekly maintenance of the SQL databases; it is an installed SMS service component that executes on the SMS site server containing the SQL database.

By reading specific Registry entries stored on the SMS site server and from the site control file, this service carries out nine predefined database tasks, as detailed in Table 15-4. By default, tasks are performed once a week on Saturday or Sunday between 12:00 midnight and 5:00 a.m.

Using SMS Trace, you can review the SMSdbmon.log if you find that these tasks are not being carried out. You can also verify that the SMS SQL Server service is running, the SMS Site Database service is running, and the SMS site database, transaction log, and tempdb are not full (although SQL Server 7.0 automatically adjusts for free space).

Through the SQL Enterprise Manager, you can check the properties of each database and the schedule that the default maintenance is working on.

TABLE 15-4

Weekly SQL database tasks performed.

Export SMS Site Database
Export SMS Site Database Transaction Catalog
Export for Metering Database
Export Software-Metering Transaction Log
Delete Aged Status Messages
Delete Aged Inventory History
Delete Aged Discovery Data
Delete Aged Collected Files
Rebuild Indexes

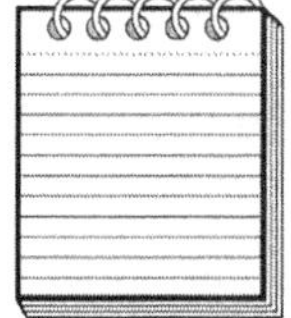

NOTE. If a task is more than one hour away, the SMS SQL service sleeps until it's time to wake up and carry out the assigned task.

Troubleshooting Site System Installation

First, you should make sure that you have assigned the proper SMS role to your site server by checking its defined role through the SMS Administrator console. A specific chain of command occurs when a new site system is defined and set up by you, the administrator. Specific site control files that are created and changed involve the SMS SQL Monitor, the Hierarchy Manager, and the Site Control Manager.

This chain of processing is an example of the complicated data flow within a site system:

1. The SMS SQL Monitor receives the site database change and, in turn, tells the Hierarchy Manager.
2. The Hierarchy Manager then creates a delta site control file containing the change with an extension of .CT1 and sends it to SMS\Inboxex\Sitectrl.box on the site server.
3. This wakes up the Site Control Manager, which, in turn, copies the older CT0 file into the History folder and then creates a new CT0 file reflecting the new changes.
4. The Site Control Manager then sends a new CT2 to the Hierarchy Manager's inbox, detailing the new changes to the site.
5. The Hierarchy Manager uses the newly received CT2 file to update the site database.

Troubleshooting Logon Point Installation

If logon points are not discovering any new SMS clients, make sure that you have enabled the defined site servers as logon points by checking the properties of the site server through the SMS Administrator console.

Make sure that the assigned logon points have the following:

- A file called NTLGDSC.PCF, which is created and stored in the Nt_logon.box folder on the logon point
- A folder called SMSLogon, which is created on the logon point
- A SMSLogon share
- New logon script files, which are copied to the NETLOGON share on the logon point

Troubleshooting Client Access Point Installation

Make sure that the assigned client access points follow these rules:

- A CAP must be installed on an NTFS partition.
- A directory CAP_ <site code> should be created and shared.
- The SMS service must have permission to access the new CAP server.
- The service SMS_Executive should be running on the NT server.

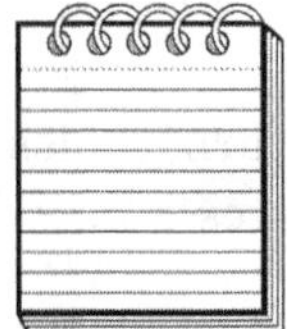

NOTE. *Using SMS Trace and the Inboxmgr.log file, you can trace the inbox activity.*

Troubleshooting Distribution Points

Distribution points must be installed on an NTFS partition. There must also be enough space for storage of the packages at this server location. If the created advertisement is not appearing at the client's PC at the expected time, there are several settings to reverify at the SMS Administrator console:

- Check that the start time for the advertisement is correct in the Schedule tab of the advertisement.
- Make sure that the Greenwich Mean Time checkbox has not been checked, or if it has, ensure that GMT, and not your local time zone, will be the starting reference point.

- Make sure that the client has enough network and local permissions to carry out the installation.
- If you have a mixed client base of Windows 95/98 and NT workstations, make certain you have checked off all of the supported platforms in the Requirements tab.

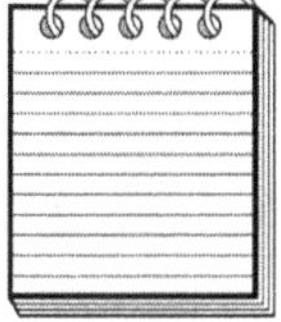

NOTE. *Using SMS Trace and the Despool.log file, you can trace package activity. Distmgr.log details the package construction, and Offermgr.log lists the clients that have not yet been contacted about the new advertisement.*

Troubleshooting Secondary Site Installations

You can narrow down problems with secondary site installations by reading the installation LOG file Sms_bootstrap.log that is stored on the secondary site server hard drive. The application event log on the secondary site server should also be checked for any bootstrap errors that may have occurred. A quick summary of the most common setup problems are as follows:

- *Partition type and size* An NTFS partition with an absolute minimum of 223 MB must be available.
- *Address* An address must be set up for communication with the parent site, along with the correct domain name and SMS service account name.
- *Name of Secondary Server* The name cannot have underscores (_) used
- *Security* The SMS Service account named at the secondary site must not have the advanced user right "Log on as a service" or must not be an Administrator at the secondary site server.

  In addition:

- Make sure that the secondary site server has never been installed as an SMS client. The client software must be removed before the secondary site can become active.

- Make sure that the primary site contains an address for communicating with the secondary site.

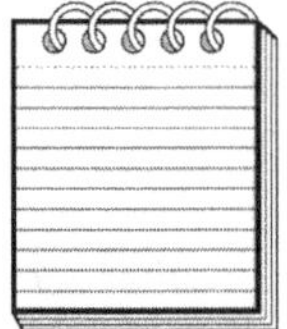

NOTE. The Senders.log file will provide evidence of any wrong details, such as the wrong domain name, site server name, or user account.

Troubleshooting Windows NT Remote Client Installation

Following are a few troubleshooting tips:

1. Make sure that Windows NT Remote Client Installation has been enabled for the site through the SMS Administrator console.
2. The client IP addresses must be within the defined IP address entered in Site Boundaries through the SMS Administrator console.
3. Check to make sure the Discovery Data Manager has generated a client configuration request (CCR) file in the SMS\Inboxes\Ccm.box on the site server.
4. Make sure that the NetBIOS name of the computer system has not been changed since the computer was discovered.
5. Ensure that all SQL Server services are currently running.
6. Make sure the SMS can access the SMS database.
7. Check the SQL Server error logs

Troubleshooting Software Metering at the Site Server

Check that software metering has been enabled through the SMS Administrator console through the properties of the site server; if it has been enabled, make sure that the database location and time zone are correct, as well as the Service account. Next, review the properties of the software-metering component located further down the console tree in the Component Configuration folder. The General and Local tabs should be checked for correct settings. Finally, open Software Metering in the Tools folder, and make sure all of your software has been registered per your company's metering rules.

Next, verify on the named site server that the SMS services have properly loaded and started. Then through the Control Panel | Services icon, make sure that the Software-Metering Server and the SMS License Metering service are operational. Other items that must pass inspection are as follows:

1. The proper users and groups must have the right to the program that is being tracked by software metering. Permissions for each product are set through the properties of the Software Metering tool's listed license program properties.
2. The client agent on the user's PC has not been installed.

Troubleshooting Software Distribution at the Site Server

Software distribution involves many SMS components that must work in harmony for successful software distribution:

- *Clients' PC* Properly functioning SMS components can be checked through the Control Panel; the Advertised Programs, Advertised Programs Manager, and Systems Management icons should be present. Software distribution components can be verified and repaired through the Components tab of the System Management icon. The clients' PC must also have enough space to install the package and the required security permissions. Most importantly, the client's system time must match the SMS database time.
- *Client access point* The CAP stores the controlling "parts" for a package installation, including the instructions, the advertisement, package description files, lookup files, and NAL files (Network Application Layer). These pieces do not take a lot of space on the site server.
- *Advertisement*
- *Package*
- *Distribution point server* The package containing the software application will be small, so the site server that is a distribution point should have a substantial amount of free space. Since every program

is MB in size, calculate your needed space and then add 50 percent additional space.

Status Message and LOG Files

By opening the System Status folder in the SMS Administrator console, you can view the current status of both advertisements and packages.

- Package detail includes Package Name, Targeted, Installed, Retrying, Failed, and Source Site.
- Advertisement detail includes Advertisement Name, Received, Failures, Programs (Started, Errors, Success), and Target Collections.

NOTE. *Distmgr.log details the package creation and copying to the distribution point. Offermgr.log lists the clients that have not received the advertisement.*

Troubleshooting Hardware and Software Inventory Collection

After checking that the inventory has been enabled at the site server, you can view several site server LOG files with SMS Trace to track the inventory progress (or lack thereof):

- *Inboxast.log* Details the movement of hardware and software inventory data files to the site server
- *Invproc.log* Details the creation of each client's hardware inventory file and traces the processing cycle
- *Dataldr.log* Details that the client's inventory file was accepted by the inventory processor
- *Sinvproc.log* Details the creation of each client's software inventory file and traces the processing cycle

Other SMS settings that can be checked and verified at the site server where inventory has been installed are as follows:

1. Make sure that your collections are accurate, and then manually refresh the collection through the SMS Administrator console.
2. Make sure that the schedule for both hardware and software inventory collection is accurate by checking the Inventory Collection properties on the site server.
3. Make sure that the client's time and the site server's time are synchronized. Use the `NET TIME` command in the user's logon script.
4. Through the SMS Administrator console, check the status messages pertaining to inventory to see if any errors have been reported. The following components should be checked:
   - Inbox Manager
   - Inventory Processor
   - Software Inventory Processor

Troubleshooting 32-Bit SMS Clients

The SMS client is the engine that drives entire the process of Systems Management Server. If you're having problems with your clients been discovered and SMS components being installed, there are many LOG files listed in the next few pages that you can check to see what client component is not responding. Using the System Management icon in the Control Panel, select the *Components* tab and verify that the Hardware Inventory Agent has been installed.

Next, select the *Hardware Inventory Agent*, and click on the *Repair Installation* button. You can also force the Hardware Inventory Agent to install (if the component is enabled but not installed) by selecting the Sites tab and clicking the Update Configuration, as shown in Figure 15-7.

If the reinstallation of the component does not solve the problem, the Systems Management Installation Wizard SMSMAN.EXE can be used to remove the component and then reinstall again. If you choose to follow this track, check out the Client Cleaner tool (20CLICLN.EXE) in the SMS Resource Kit. This utility removes all traces of the SMS client installation, including local Registry settings.

Another handy troubleshooting tool included with the Resource Kit is the Client Utilities tool (CLIUTILS.EXE). This utility can used at the command prompt to start and stop the installed SMS client components.

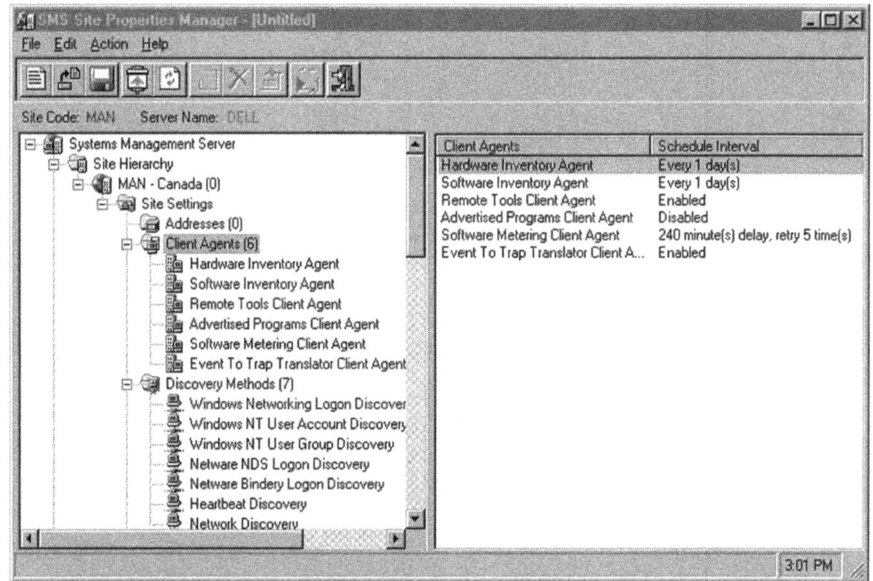

Figure 15-7 Forcing the Hardware Inventory Agent installation through the client's Control Panel.

Troubleshooting Logon Discovery for Windows 32-Bit Clients

Following are a few troubleshooting tips:

1. If Windows clients are being discovered but software is not being installed, the first thing to check is that a discovery agent has been initialized for the SMS site.
2. The most common agent would be the Windows Networking Logon Client Agent.
3. If batch files are being utilized to perform the installation of the SMS components, make sure that the SMSLS.BAT is part of the user's logon script.
4. Also make sure that the user's IP address falls within the assigned site boundaries.
5. Check that the user has the read permission on the NETLOGON share if you have not been using logon scripts prior to installing SMS.
6. Make sure that the client has enough permissions to edit the local Registry.
7. Check that the SMSCliSvc account is a member of the local Administrators group.

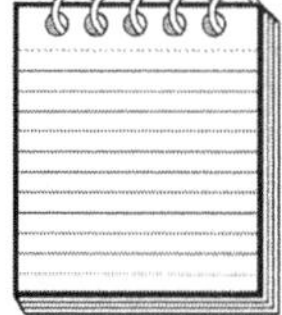

NOTE. The LOG files that can be enabled and monitored for both the server and the client are listed in Table 15-2. Read the Ntlginst.log on the server, and check if the DDR was received and then processed; the DDR for the discovered computer must be accepted before installation will take place.

Troubleshooting 32-Bit Client Hardware Inventory

Troubleshooting tips for hardware inventory are as follows:

1. Check to make sure that the Hardware Inventory Agent is enabled at the site. Also ensure that the schedule is set to when you expected it to execute.
2. Make sure that the agent was installed correctly by reading the Hinv.log file on the site server.
3. Make sure that the client's IP address is within the defined site boundaries.
4. Check the logs for the Hardware Inventory Agent (Hinv32), the Client Component Installation Manager (Ccim32), the client service (Clisvc), and the copy queue (Cqmgr32).
5. By viewing the Cqmgr32.log and the Inboxast.log file, check that the client's INV file has been sent to the client access point and the extension has changed to .nhm.

Details about the entire process of hardware inventory can be found in the following LOG files:

- *Cqmgr32.log* Hardware inventory data and status file details
- *Inhinv32.log* Tracks installation of the Hardware Inventory Client Agent
- *Hinv32.log* Tracks hardware inventory data to determine whether it is generated on schedule

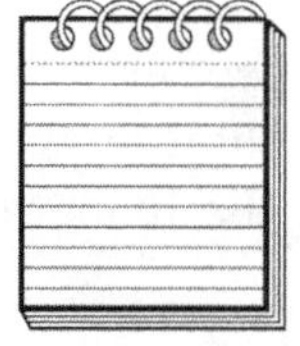

NOTE. The initial hardware inventory takes place 15 minutes after the client software is installed.

Troubleshooting 32-Bit Client Software Distribution

When software is distributed to a Windows NT or Windows 95/98 client, it is carried out with the use of advertisements that are usually targeted to a group of users. Once the Software Distribution Agent is installed on the client, the agent checks the client access point on a schedule to see if any advertisements have been set up for processing. When an advertisement is made available, the software distribution process begins from a defined distribution point within the SMS site. Software distribution is set up and scheduled using the SMS Administrative console, and the Software Distribution Agent runs on each discovered SMS client.

At the client, the schedule for checking for new advertised programs takes place every 60 minutes. The current schedule can be checked on the client through the Advertised Programs Manager icon in the Control Panel. Several LOG files are used that track the software distribution process at the SMS client's PC:

- *Smsapm32.log* Tracks the schedule of advertised programs, as well as CAP connections
- *Pipcap32.log* Tracks the found location of the advertised program
- *Odpusr32.log* Displays the users that are to run the listed advertisements
- *Odpwnt32.log* Displays the groups that are to run the listed advertisements

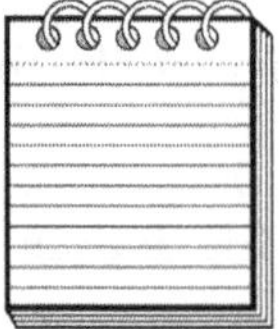

NOTE. *Another Resource Kit utility (APMSPY.EXE) can be used to determine what background tasks the local Advertised Program Manager is performing.*

Troubleshooting 32-Bit Client: Remote Tools

Fixing a Remote Tool session that does not start properly usually involves addressing more problems at the client end than at the SMS Administrator console. The first item to verify is that the Remote Tools have been installed. You may know that they were installed at one time; however, the user may have removed them. (Why users do this is a whole other matter. Perhaps they had the required permissions at their local PCs, or they may have disabled all remote sessions involving their PC through the Remote Control icon in the Control Panel.) A quick check in the user's Control Panel is the place to start.

Assuming all settings are found to be okay, the next item to review is the protocols that are installed on the client's PC. The remote client computer will only establish a session with the host with the default protocol that was selected in the properties of the Remote Tools Client Agent.

Remember: The host can use multiple protocols; the remote client cannot. If a user had multiple protocols with NWLink bound as the first protocol (LANA0) and TCP/IP bound as the second (LANA1), but the site server had TCP/IP as the sole bound protocol (LANA0), the client would not be found with Remote Control. Also keep in mind that the host can search up to eight protocols; the client uses only its primary bound protocol.

Remote Tool components report their status differently than other SMS components—LOG files and status messages are not used. Instead, security events are generated in the event log of the remote client using log codes 1 through 7, detailing what components are being used during the remote session. Table 15-5 lists the event log codes. Figure 15-8 shows the security event log.

TABLE 15-5

Event log codes used for Remote Control sessions.

Security Log Codes	Event Detail
1	Remote reboot was performed.
2	Chat session was started.
3	File transfer took place.
4	Remote execute was performed.
5	Remote Control session was started.
6	Remote Control session ended.
7	Local user on the remote PC granted permission to start a Remote Control session.

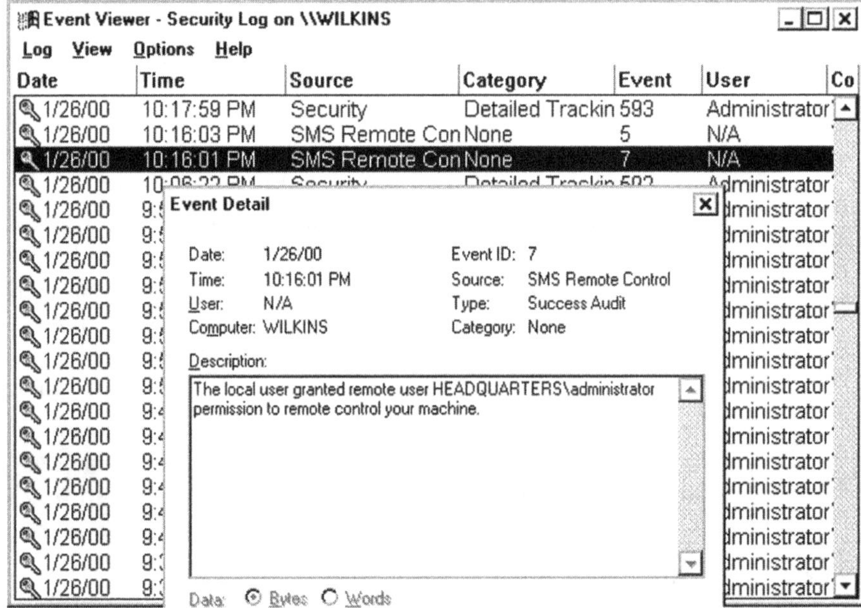

Figure 15-8 Security event log details on the client's PC.

Using the SMS Site Properties Manager

The SMS Resource Kit has many powerful tools to complement your SMS installation. One tool is the SMS Site Properties Manager (SMSSPMAN.EXE). Although its main use is for exporting and importing objects from one SMS site to another, it's also a very handy troubleshooting tool on a local site.

Executing this utility shows you at a glance the current properties of all installed components. You can check your addresses and view the current schedule of your client agents, discovery methods, collections, queries, packages, and advertisements, as shown in Figure 15-9.

Filename Extensions for SMS

Knowing the file extensions that SMS uses can be a great help when troubleshooting an error message. Table 15-6 lists the extensions and descriptions used by the Systems Management Server features.

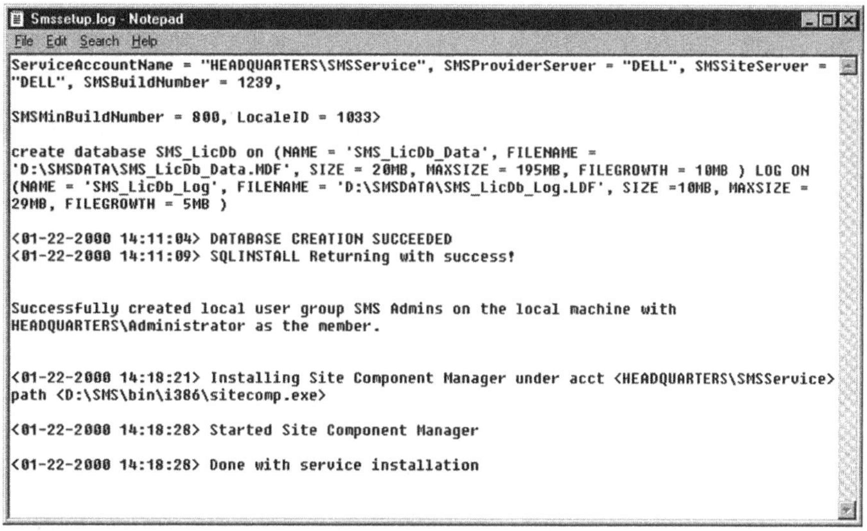

Figure 15-9 Using the SMS Site Properties Manager to check current schedules.

Smssetup.log - Notepad

File Edit Search Help

```
ServiceAccountName = "HEADQUARTERS\SMSService", SMSProviderServer = "DELL", SMSSiteServer =
"DELL", SMSBuildNumber = 1239,

SMSMinBuildNumber = 800, LocaleID = 1033>

create database SMS_LicDb on (NAME = 'SMS_LicDb_Data', FILENAME =
'D:\SMSDATA\SMS_LicDb_Data.MDF', SIZE = 20MB, MAXSIZE = 195MB, FILEGROWTH = 10MB ) LOG ON
(NAME = 'SMS_LicDb_Log', FILENAME = 'D:\SMSDATA\SMS_LicDb_Log.LDF', SIZE =10MB, MAXSIZE =
29MB, FILEGROWTH = 5MB )

<01-22-2000 14:11:04> DATABASE CREATION SUCCEEDED
<01-22-2000 14:11:09> SQLINSTALL Returning with success!


Successfully created local user group SMS Admins on the local machine with
HEADQUARTERS\Administrator as the member.


<01-22-2000 14:18:21> Installing Site Component Manager under acct <HEADQUARTERS\SMSService>
path <D:\SMS\bin\i386\sitecomp.exe>

<01-22-2000 14:18:28> Started Site Component Manager

<01-22-2000 14:18:28> Done with service installation
```

SMS Site Server Folder Structure

Once a primary site server has been installed, there is a huge folder structure created for the initialization and day-to-day running of the SMS system. Although Table 15-7 is quite long, it contains essential information that can help in troubleshooting the primary site.

Client Access Point Folder Structure

Once a client access point has been installed, a folder structure will be installed containing the needed software files, folders, and LOG files, as detailed in Table 15-8. This information can be valuable in determining what components should be present and what data should be in each folder during the working cycle of the client access point.

Logon Point Folder Structure

Once you have installed a logon point, a folder structure will be installed containing the needed software files, folders, and LOG files, as detailed in Table 15-9. This information can be valuable in determining what components should be present, as well as the current status of the logon point.

TABLE 15-6

Filename extensions used by SMS.

File Extension	Details
.ADC	Contains a collection to be added to the Collection Evaluator
.BOX	Contains temporary files used by SMS components
.CCR	A client configuration request
.CFG	A configuration file containing parameters for a client component
.CMN	A collection membership update to the Offer Manager
.CT0	The master site control file
.CT1	A proposed site control file sent from the Hierarchy Manager
.CT3	A proposed site control file from other SMS services
.DAT	Contains inventory data for the parent's site
.DC	Will delete a collection from the Collection Evaluator
.DDR	Discovery data record
.INS	An instruction file for advertisements for a specific collection
.IST	A compressed instruction file sent from another site
.JOB	A job file waiting to be processed
.LKP	A lookup file containing Registry GUIDs (globally unique identifiers)
.LO_	An old LOG file
.LOG	A current LOG file
.MIF	Management information format file
.MOF	Managed object format file—a template file for package data
.NAL	Network Abstraction Layer file containing directions for packages
.NCF	Network configuration file
.NHM	Contains data inventory from SMS clients
.OFN	Contains a notification for the Offer Manager
.OFR	An offer file that details the package and program being offered
.P*	A package file that will be sent to another site
.PCF	A configuration file holding details of a manager or agent installation
.PCK	A package file received from another site
.PDF	A package definition file
.PKG	A package file that describes the contents of a package
.PKN	A package creation notification sent to the Distribution Manager

TABLE 15-6
(Continued)

File Extension	Details
.RPL	A replication file that does not need transaction processing
.RPT	A replication file that does needs transaction processing
.SCA	A site control file addition
.SCD	A site control file deletion
.SCU	A site configuration update
.SHA	A site hierarchy addition
.SIC	Contains full software inventory data from clients
.SID	Contains the delta software inventory from clients
.SVF	A status file sent from both client and server components
.UDC	Updates a collection to the Collection Evaluator

Status Messages

A status message is reported to a primary site server when an SMS task that is attempted causes errors. All facets of SMS generate status messages: the client, site servers, hardware and software inventory, to name but a few. Each status message has three sections: Message ID, Severity, and Message Text. The status messages are in the hundreds and are not detailed here, as the majority are informational messages.

The *Systems Management Server 2.0 Resource Guide* has a complete listing of all status messages for all SMS components. Table 15-10 lists the most common error messages for the SMS client. Table 15-11 lists some of the more common error messages for SMS Server.

Removing SMS Manually

If you have a catastrophic system failure with the site server database or the software-metering database, you will not be able to reinstall Systems Management Server or uninstall Systems Management Server using the standard SMS setup; the previous version of SMS must be manually uninstalled first. Follow these step before attempting to reinstall SMS:

TABLE 15-7 SMS site server folder structure.

Folder	SMS Component	Use of the Folder or Configuration File
\Bin\i386	Base SMS Components	Storing SMS executables.
\Bin\i386\00000409	Base Client Components	Storing SMS executables.
\Bin\i386\Routing	SMS_SQL_ Monitor	Inbox for SQL Monitor.
\Bin\i386\System32	Base SMS Components	DLLs and support files.
\Data\ND_Logon	NetWare NDS Logon Manager	Logon point installation details.
\Data\Ndlgdsc	NetWare NDS Logon Discovery Agent	Discovery agent installation details.
\Data\Ndlginst	NetWare NDS Logon Installation Manager	NDS logon installation details.
\Data\Nt_logon	Windows NT Logon Manager	Windows NT logon point installation details.
\Data\Ntlgdsc	Windows NT Logon Discovery Manager	Discovery agent installation details for NT systems.
\Data\Ntlginst	Windows NT Logon Installation Manager	Setup file detailing the networking logon installation components.
\Data\NW_Logon	NetWare Bindery Logon Manager	Setup file detailing NetWare bindery logon point components.
\Data\Nwlgdsc	NetWare Bindery Logon Discovery Manager	Setup file detailing discovery agent installation at login point.
\Data\Nwlginst	NetWare Bindery Logon Discovery Manager	Setup file that details a NetWare logon point installation.
\Inboxes\Asstdata.box	Discovery Data Manager	Master copy of assignment list.
\Inboxes\CCRDist.box	CCR Distributor	The CCRs distributed to CAPs.
\Inboxes\Clicfg.src	Client Installation Data Manager	Master copies of CFG, NAL, and PKG files for SMS clients.
\Inboxes\Clicomp.src	Client Installation Data Manager	PDF files for all SMS client computers.
\Inboxes\Clicomp.src\Base	Client Installation Data Manager	Master copy of files for installing SMS client components.
\Inboxes\Clicomp.src\Swdist	Client Installation Data Manager	Master copy of the advertisement components.
\Inboxes\Clicomp.src\Hinv	Client Installation Data Manager	Master copy of the Hardware Inventory Agent.
\Inboxes\Clicomp.src\Licmtr	Client Installation Data Manager	Master copy of the software-metering client components.

TABLE 15-7 (Continued)

Folder	SMS Component	Use of the Folder or Configuration File
\Inboxes\Clicomp.src\Remctrl	Client Installation Data Manager	Master copy of the Remote Control Agent components.
\Inboxes\Clicomp.src\Sinv	Client Installation Data Manager	Master copy of the Software Inventory Agent.
\Inboxes\Clicomp.src\Smsapm32	Client Installation Data Manager	Master copy of the software distribution components.
\Inboxes\Clicomp.scr\Snmpela	Client Installation Data Manager	Master copy of the NT event to SNMP trap translator components.
\Inboxes\Clicomp.src\Wbem	Client Installation Data Manager	Master copy of the WBEM components.
\Inboxes\Clidata.src	Client Installation Data Manager	Master copies of existing CAPs and SMS client Registry installation settings and parameters.
\Inboxes\Colfile.box	Inventory Data Loader	Collected SMS 1.2 delta MIF files.
\Inboxes\Coll_out.box	Collection Evaluator	Holds collected information for child sites.
\Inboxes\Colleval.box	Collection Evaluator	Files received from the SMS_SQL_Monitor about existing collections.
\Inboxes\Courseend.box	Courier Sender	Compressing files and packages for Courier Sender.
\Inboxes\Dataldr.box	Inventory Data Loader	Receives delta MIF files for the hardware inventory database.
\Inboxes\Dbm.box	Discovery Data Manager	Receives DDRs for the discovery database.
\Inboxes\Despoolr.box\Receive	Despooler	Main receiving area from other sites; files are then sent to the proper inbox.
\Inboxes\Distmgr.box	Distribution Manager	Receives package notification files when a package needs processing.
\Inboxes\Hman.box	Hierarchy Manager	Receives site updates from the SMS Trigger Manager.
\Inboxes\Inventory.box	Inventory Processor	Receives inventory files from client access points and converts them to delta MIF files.
\Inboxes\Invproc.box	Inventory Processor	MIF files are stored here if history is enabled.

TABLE 15-7 (Continued)

Folder	SMS Component	Use of the Folder or Configuration File
\Inboxes\License.box	License Server Manager	Used for communication across the site for software metering.
\Inboxes\NT_logon.box	NT Logon Server Manager	Setup details for installing Windows networking logon.
\Inboxes\Offerinf.box	Offer Manager	Master copies of advertisement, instruction and lookup files.
\Inboxes\Offermgr.box	Offer Manager	Updates, creations, and deletions of advertisements through notification files from the SMS Trigger Manager.
\Inboxes\Pkginfo.box	Distribution Manager	Master copies of NAL, PKG, and \Ico folders.
\Inboxes\Replmgr.box	Intersite Replication Manager	Receives requests for data transmission to other SMS sites.
\Inboxes\Schedule.box	Scheduler	Receives the details necessary to create packages, instruction files, and send requests.
\Inboxes\Sinv.box	Software Inventory Process	Receives SIC and SID files from client access points.
\Inboxes\Sinv.box\Badsinv	Software Inventory Processor	Contains files that attempted to install three times and failed.
\Inboxes\Sinv.box\Filecol	Software Inventory Processor	Contains files collected from software inventory.
\Inboxes\Sinv.box\Orphans	Software Inventory Processor	Holds software inventory files that do not have a valid DDR.
\Inboxes\Sinv.box\Retry	Software Inventory Processor	Holds software inventory files that are waiting for access to the site database.
\Inboxes\Sinv.box\Temp	Software Inventory Manager	Used as workspace for manipulating collected files.
\Inboxes\Sitectrl.box	Site Configuration Manager	Master copy of the site control file. Also processes CT1 and CT3 files.
\Inboxes\SiteStat.box	Site Summarizer	Deals with status message from other sites.
\Inboxes\SiteStatmgr.box	Status Manager	Receives status messages from CAPs and passes them to the NT application log.
\Licmtr	License Server Manger	Holds the master copy of the data cache and files used for the software-metering server.

TABLE 15-7 (Continued)

Folder	SMS Component	Use of the Folder or Configuration File
\Logs	Site server components	Logs files for each SMS component.
\Netmon	Network Monitor	Contains software files, saved captures, and address filters.
\Scripts	SQL Server	Contains master script files (MOF) used to import package files into the SMS site database.
\SMS_Inst	SMS Installer	Holds SMS installer software.

1. All SMS services must first be stopped. Open the *Control Panel*, and select the *Services* icon. Select and stop the following SMS services:
   - SMS_EXECUTIVE
   - SMS_HIERARCHY_MANAGER
   - SMS_INVENTORY_AGENT_NT
   - SMS_PACKAGE_COMMAND_MANAGER_NT
   - SMS_SITE_CONFIG_MANAGER
2. Make a backup of the system Registry by executing `RDISK /S`, creating both an updated copy in the \\WINNT\REPAIR folder and also on floppy disk.
3. Start the Registry Editor REGEDT32.EXE, and opening the HKEY_LOCAL_MACHINE key, select and delete the following keys:
   - SOFTWARE\Microsoft\SMS
   - SYSTEM\CurrentControlSet\Services\SMS_EXECUTIVE
   - SYSTEM\CurrentControlSet\Services\SMS_HIERARCHY_MANAGER
   - SYSTEM\CurrentControlSet\Services\SMS\INVENTORY_AGENT_NT
   - SYSTEM\CurrentControlSet\Services\SMS_PACKAGE_COMMAND_MANAGER_NT
   - SYSTEM\CurrentControlSet\Services\SMS_SITE_CONFIG_MANAGER
4. Select the drive where you installed SMS, and remove the SMS folders and subfolders, along with CAP_<site code>, Config.Msi, and MSSQL.
5. Delete the Smssetup.log file from the root of the boot drive of the site server.

TABLE 15-8 Client access point folder structure.

Folder	SMS Component	What's the Folder or File Used For?
\CCR.box	Client Component Request Manager	Holds CCR requests from NT clients with insufficient permissions.
\Ccrretry.box	Client Component Request Manager	Stores CCRs that can't be processed.
\Clicomp.box	Inbox Manager	Stores all client component (CFG, NAL, PKG, OFR) configuration files.
\Clicomp.box\Base	Inbox Manager	A copy of the base client installation files.
\Clicomp.box\Swdist	Inbox Manager	A copy of the software distribution installation files.
\Clicomp.box\Hinv	Inbox Manager	A copy of the Hardware Inventory Agent installation files.
\Clicomp.box\Licmtr	Inbox Manager	A copy of the Software Metering Client Agent installation files.
\Clicomp.box\Remctrl	Inbox Manager	A copy of the Remote Control Client Agent installation files.
\Clicomp.box\Sinv	Inbox Manager	A copy of the Software Inventory Agent installation files.
\Clicomp.box\Smsapm32	Inbox Manager	A copy of the core distribution installation files.
\Clicomp.box\Snmpela	Inbox Manager	A copy of the Windows NT event to SNMP trap translator components.
\Clicomp.box\Wbem	Inbox Manager	A copy of the WBEM components.
\Clidata.box	Inbox Manager	A copy of client Registry settings and a listing of all installed CAPs.
\Ddr.box	Inbox Manager	Used by clients to write DDRs to; DDRS are then moved to the site server's box \Inboxes\Ddr.box file.
\Inventory.box	Inbox Manager	Used by clients to write hardware inventory data to. The data is then moved to the site server's \Inbox\Inventory.box file.
\Offerinf.box	Inbox Manager	Copies of all advertisements (OFR, INS, and LKP).
\Pkginfo.box	Inbox Manager	Copies of all package files (PKG, NAL)
\inv.box	Inbox Manager	Used by clients to write software inventory files (SIC, SID), which are then moved to the site server \Inboxes\Sinv.box file.
\Statsmsgs.box	Inbox Manager	Used by clients to write status message files (SVF), which are then sent to the site server's \Inboxes\Statmgr.box file.

TABLE 15-9 Logon point folder structure.

Folder	SMS Component	Uses of the Folder or Files
\Alpha	NT Logon Manager	Stores alpha logon point files.
\Config	NT Logon Manager	Stores client configuration files for Windows 95/98 and NT users, along with a listing of member sites.
\Ddr.box	NT Logon Discovery Agent	If Windows Networking Logon Discovery is enabled, the DDRs are first written here, and then at the site server.
\I386	NT Logon Manager	Holds the Windows NT Logon Discovery Agent and associated dynamic link library files.
\Logs	NT Logon Discovery Agent	Contains Ntlgdsca.log, which is updated when DDRs are sent to the site server from the logon point.
\Sites\<site code>	NT Logon Manager	A copy of Caplist.ini that details client Registry settings and CAP information for the SMS site.
\X86.bin	NT Logon Manager	Contains Smsboot.exe and Boot32wm.exe, SMS startup utilities, and other base files used for installing client components.
\V.86.bin\00000409	NT Logon Manager	Contains Smsman.exe used for manual discovery and installation of 32-bit Windows clients.

Running the WBEM Support Tool

One SMS utility that will not be executed on a weekly basis but still needs to be mentioned is the WBEM (Windows-Based Enterprise Management) support tool. It is used to check and verify the internal operating system hooks used by the SMS Administrator console when it is interfacing with the SMS site databases through the Windows Management Instrumentation interface (WMI). When you are executing SMS tasks, the WMI is operating in the background for accessing the SMS database, performing hardware inventory, or connecting to the site server through the SMS Administrator console.

To execute and test the WBEM connectivity test, follow these steps:

1. Through the Windows Explorer, open the WINNT\System32\WBEM folder.
2. Execute WBEMTEST.EXE.
3. Select *Connect to the Site Server*, and enter ROOT\SMS to test the SMS namespace. The Web-based Enterprise Common Information

TABLE 15-10

SMS client status messages.

Message ID	Message Text and Solution
10000	Data integrity error. A bad or missing advertisement file (.OFR). Re-create or resave the advertisement at the SMS Administrator console.
10001	Data integrity error. A bad or missing package file (.PKG). Open and resave the package to force the Distribution Manager to rewrite the package files.
10004	The program for the named advertisement could not be executed. Check that the right EXE file is in the correct location.
10010	An error occurred when the SMS Advertised Program Manager was preparing to run the Uninstall program. The Uninstall program could not be found or is incorrect.
10017	The uninstall for the named advertisements failed. The uninstall path in the user's Registry is missing. The Add/Remove Programs icon in Control Panel also lists the uninstall Scripts that are present on the user's PC.
10021	The program for the named advertisement failed. The user's PC was restarted during the advertisement process and failed. Check your properties, and make sure they have been set for a restart during the installation.
10100, 10101	The Client Component Installation Manager encountered an error or cannot generate the client's Heartbeat Discovery Data Record. For both of these errors, check for low hard disk space on the clients PC.
10105, 10106	Both of these error messages indicate that a component has failed on the client's PC. Open the *System Management* icon in the client's Control Panel, and in the Component tab, select *Repair Installation*.
10209–10212	For these five error messages, check and make sure your users have a reliable network connection to their assigned CAP.
10213,10214	SMS Client Component Installation Manager errors, indicating low disk space on the user's PC.
10218, 10219	SMS Client Component Installation Manager errors generated when trying to communicate with the SMS Available Programs Manager. Using the System Management icon in the client's Control Panel and in the Component tab, select *Repair Installation*.
10501-10502	SMS Hardware Inventory Agent cannot connect. Make sure that the WinMgnt service is running on the client's PC.
10506	SMS Hardware Inventory Agent cannot update the hardware inventory schema. Reinstall the Hardware Inventory Agent.

TABLE 15-11

SMS Server status messages.

Message ID	Message Text and Solution
1016–1020	The SMS Site Component Manager failed to install or reinstall this component. By stopping and restarting the SMS Site Component Manager using the SMS Service Manager, the component installation will be carried out once again.
1049	SMS Site Component Manager could not find an NTFS partition on the named site system. Convert the existing FAT partitioned NTFS or make sure that the default root administrative shares required by SMS have been disabled.
1076	SMS Site Component Manager could not copy files from one location to another. Check your security permissions.
1108	SMS Executive could not start this component because it could not load off the named DLL. This DLL is missing, or it depends on another DLL that hasn't loaded. Use the Dependency Walker utility DEPENDS.EXE found in the SMS Resource Kit to find out what other DLLs this DLL required to be loaded first.
1109	SMS Executive could not start to this component because it could not determine the address by this named DLL. The named DLL is corrupted.
1420	SMS NT Logon Server Manager failed to read the site control file. The file is corrupt. Restore from backup or reset the current installation of SMS.

Model Object Manager should appear, with all of the buttons enabled. This indicates that the internal structure is working properly.

4. Now use the Connect to load your local site server by entering `ROOT\SMS\SITE_SITE-CODE`, and click on the *Login* button.
5. If the WBEM console appears, your site has been loaded successfully (See Figure 15-10.)

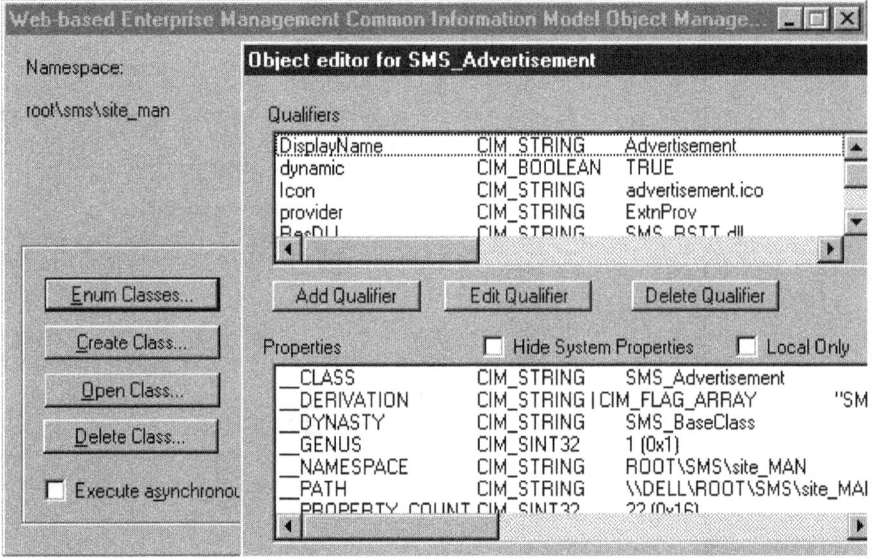

Figure 15-10
A successful WBEM interface and site connection.

APPENDIX

This appendix contains information on several support options for administering and supporting SMS versions 1.2 and 2.0, including:

- BackOffice Resource Kit Support Tools for SMS
- Installing SMS and SQL Server 7.0 in Unattended/Batch Mode
- Knowledge Base Resources for SMS 1.2 and 2.0

BackOffice Resource Kit Tools for SMS

This section provides, in alphabetical order, documentation for the BackOffice Resource Kit 4.5 tools for use with managing both clients and site servers running Systems Management Server version 2.0.

Add/Remove 1.2 Console: V12Admin.ipf

This utility allows you to either add or remove the SMS 1.2 Administrator console from a computer system that also has the SMS Administrator 2.0 console installed. This tool could be useful after you have migrated from SMS 1.2 to 2.0.

The SMS Installer must also be installed on the selected computer for this utility to work. Using the SMS Installer, open the V12ADMIN.IPF file and create an executable file for installing the SMS 1.2 Administrator console. If you wish to have both 1.2 and 2.0 consoles on the same PC, you must first remove the SMS 1.2 console, then install the SMS 2.0 console, and finally use the Add/Remove 1.2 Console utility to reinstall the SMS 1.2 console.

Syntax that can be also used is `/ s` - The setup program is executed in silent mode.

Add System Tool: AddSystem.exe

This tool simulates the remote client installation method, locally installing the required SMS client software on a Windows NT computer system. A discovery data record (DDR) is also then created and sent to the site server for processing. The syntax required for the utility must all be specified at the same time and in the correct order of:

```
addsystem system domain IP_Adress subnet address file.ddr
```

Where:

`system` The NetBIOS name of the computer where software is to be installed

`domain` The current domain that the computer is installed in

`IP_Adress` The current IP address of the computer system

`subnet address` The IP subnet address of the computer system

`file.ddr` An optional syntax field

Administrator Console Setup: v20Admin.ini, v20Admin.sms

This tool is used to install the SMS Administrator console on computers that are not the site server. Some initial setup must be performed before using this tool:

1. First, create an image of the SMS 2.0 CD, and store the image in a package source folder.
2. Copy V20ADMIN.INI to the SMSSetup\BIN folder in the package source location you created in Step 1.
3. Generate a software distribution package, and define V20ADMIN.SMS as the PDF and the folder created in Step 1 as the package source directory.
4. Create an advertisement for the package, and list the computer systems where the SMS Administrator console is to be installed.
5. The package will then be installed through the advertisement.

Advertisement Info: AdvInfo.exe

This tool can be used during troubleshooting to gather and display header information from either a package file (PKG) or an advertised program offer file (OFR), usually located in the folders SMS\INBOXES\OFFERINF.BOX and SMS\INBOXES\PKGINFO.BOX. The information that can be displayed is the package ID, name, version, language, MIF file information, program command line, and disk space requirements.

APM Spy: APMSpy.exe

This utility can be used to view and search Advertised Program Manager data records on an SMS client in readable format to troubleshoot problems that may occur with software distribution. The APMSPY.EXE should be copied to the MS\SMS\CORE\BIN folder on the SMS client. Once the APM Spy utility is executed at the client, you will be prompted for a number value that corresponds with the information you wish to view.

The values that can be entered are as follows:

- `0 program_number` Shows the offer received by the client for the program
- `1 program_number` Lists the information that is displayed in the Advertised Program Monitor and the Advertised Programs Wizard
- `D program_number` Lists the program's properties that are displayed in the Advertised Program Monitor and the Advertised Programs Wizard
- `S program_number` Lists the programs that are scheduled to be run at the client
- `T program_number` Lists the programs that require a set-point (logon, logoff, or another program must be executed first) before it can proceed
- `C program_number` Shows the IPC (Interprocess Communications Connections) components that are used to communicate with the Advertised Program Manager
- `X program_number` Stops and exits the APM Spy tool

The output of the APM Spy tool lists various job, run, advertisement, and program status codes and data/time flag codes. Some examples are listed in Tables A-1 and A-2.

Client Cleaner Tool: 20CliCln.bat

This batch file launches the Client Cleaner tool for completely removing a Windows 95, Windows 98, or Windows NT SMS client and all installed components. Administrator permissions must be granted for the use of

TABLE A-1

Job status codes.

Job Status	Name	Details
0	Success	The advertised program was successfully run. baked beans
1	Not yet run	The advertised program has not started.
2	Stopped waiting	The advertised program was too long and was stopped by the user.
3	Check at restart	The advertised programs restarted the computer.
10	Internal error	The advertised programs did not execute because of an internal error.
11	Program error	The advertised program did not work.
12	Network down	The client PC could not access the network.
13	Unknown	Unknown error.
14	Could not find file	The executable file of the software program could not be found.
15	Access denied	Access to the executable program was denied.
16	Insufficient memory	Not enough memory was available on the client PC.
17	Disk full	The hard drive on the client PC was full.
18	User cancelled	The advertised program was stopped by the end user.
20	Bad removal key	The uninstall command line for the advertised software program was not found.

this utility in order to completely remove all files and Registry settings. The Client Cleaner tool uses the following files: 20CliCln.bat, Hammer.exe, Kill.exe, and SerEvnt.exe.

Client Preload: CliStage.ipf

This utility allows you to install the SMS client components on a standalone computer before it is added to an SMS site. The SMS Installer must be used to change the script into an executable file. The computer system where the compiling takes place must be logged on to the network and have access to the share where the SMS client components are located—they will be included in the final executable file.

TABLE A-2

Date/time flag codes.

Date/time flag	Name	Details
0x00000001	Presented	The advertised program is displayed but will not execute before the listed time.
0x00000002	Expires	The advertised program is not available after the listed expiration time
0x00000004	Available	Future use.
0x00000008	Unavailable	Future use.
0x00000010	Mandatory	The advertised program is mandatory.
0x00000020	ASAP	The advertised program will run at once unless the trigger is defined.
0x00000040	Scheduled	The end user scheduled the advertised program to run on the listed date and time.
0x00000080	Last run	The last time the advertised program was run.
0x00000100	On startup	The advertised program will execute when the computer is started.
0x00000200	On logon	The advertised program will run when a user first logs on.
0x00000400	On logoff	The advertised program will run when the user logs off.
0x00000800	Modified	Displays the last time the advertised program was modified.
0x00001000	Recurring	The advertised program has a recurring schedule.
0x00002000	Start run	Displays when the command line was last carried out.

Client Utilities Tool: CliUtils.exe

This tool can be used on Windows NT and Windows 95 and 98 SMS clients to perform several SMS functions, including:

- Starting or stopping various SMS client components—Starts and monitors all service components (Clisvc95 for Windows 95/98 systems or Ccim32 for Windows NT systems), the Client Configuration Installation Manager, the Available Programs Manager, or the Advertised Programs Monitor.
- Displaying the schedule of a client component.
- Registering a software application to be started at the client.

- Requesting a Start Cycle event for a client component; this starts the component cycling continuously for testing purposes.

The syntax used for the client utility tools is as follows:

`CLIUTILS` command parameter_list

`/KICK` component_name Begin the Start Cycle event for the listed component.

`/START` component_name Begin the Start event for the listed component.

`/SCHED` component_name Begin the Stop event for the listed component.

`/APPREG` component_name Register a software application to be advertised and started.

Configure Client Desktop: SetStart.exe

This tool can be used on Windows NT and Windows 95 and 98 SMS clients to deliver or remove program shortcuts on the client's Start menu or have them placed on the client's desktop.

Syntax that can be used with the SetStart utility is as follows:

```
SETSTART /? /S /NAME /EXE /GROUP /KEY /ICON /COMMON /DIR / ARGS
```

Where:

`/?` Lists help for the utility.

`/S` Runs the script in silent mode.

`/NAME` The friendly name of the shortcut.

`/EXE` The program's executable file.

`/GROUP` Where the shortcut is to be placed: `desktop` or `start` (Start menu).

`KEY` The uninstall key to be accessed by Add/Remove Programs.

`/ICON` The icon file to be used.

`/COMMON` A shortcut is created that is common to all user profiles.

`/DIR` The path to the folder where the executable file is stored on the client's PC.

`/ARGS` Lists any command parameters that are to be passed to the shortcut's command line.

Convert Schedule Tool: SchedCnv.exe

This utility is handy when you are troubleshooting scheduling problems—it can be used to convert the schedule string data into readable format, indicating start time, the next scheduled start time, and any defined intervals. Most of the schedule strings are stored in the site control file: The graphical interface will guide you through the steps of converting schedule string data.

Delete Group Class: DelGrp.exe

This tool is used to delete a group class and all of its tables from the SMS site database. You must first know the name of the group that you wish to delete. Running the SQL query `select GroupClass from GroupMap` will display the current groups. Make sure to surround the group last name with double quotations, or errors will result.

Delete PDF: DeletPDF.exe

This tool is used to delete any unwanted package definition files (PDF) from the SMS site database. Using the graphical interface and entering the following syntax allows you to connect to the SMS server and remove the package definition files:

- *Server* Where the SMS Provider is located
- *Site code* The three-digit SMS site code
- *User* The domain and user name
- *Password*

Once you have entered the necessary information, the current PDF files that are installed will be displayed. Each can be highlighted and then deleted.

Dump Discovery Data: DiscDump.exe

This utility can be used on both Windows NT and Windows 95/98 computer systems. The Dump Discovery Data tool is used to review local network discovery data stored at the client in readable format.

Dump Error Message: Error32.exe

This utility is used to show the text of an error message generated by the Win32 subsystem, drivers, or services. By using the error code that the Event Viewer displays, or an event code generated by SMS, additional details can be displayed.

Dump Scheduler Data: DumpSend.exe

This tool can be used to view data generated by a scheduler request (SRQ) file for troubleshooting software distribution or sender errors. The SRQ files are stored in the following folder on the site server: SMS\INBOXES\SCHEDULE.BOX\OUTBOXES.

Inventory Synchronizer: InvSync.exe

This tool is operated from a primary site server to send either a hardware or software inventory request to an installed SMS client to force the sending of resynchronized inventory from the client to the parent site.

License Reports: LicenseReports.mdb

This tool is used to generate reports using Access 97 from the software-metering database stored on the site server. Before this tool will work, an ODBC data source connection must be configured and Access 97 must be installed.

Load Network Discovery: NDiscLdr.exe

This tool can be used to load resources for network discovery from a text file. Resources that can be defined are subnets, domains, SNMP devices, and DHCP servers. The text file follows an IN file format with resource headings in square brackets and the resource listing below.

Load Site Boundary: SiteBndy.exe

With the tool, site boundaries can be imported or exported to and from a text file. Syntax for the site boundary tool is as follows:

```
SITEBNDY filename server sitecode /s:sitecode /e /i
```

Where:

`filename` The text filename with the site boundaries

`server` The site server where the SMS Provider is installed

`sitecode` The three-digit site code

`/s sitecode` Used to process site boundaries at a defined site

`/e` Export the existing site boundaries to the listed text file

`/i` Overwrite the existing site boundaries with the values in the text file

Local Server Tool: LocalSvr.exe

This tool can be used to query the SMS site database for all network paths of all installed site systems. This information can then be used with the Set SMS Server utility to specify exact distribution point groups and CAPs for an SMS client to use.

Log Span: LogSpan.exe

This tool can define a specified time to read and compile a real-time listing of all SMS log file activity into a single text file for troubleshooting purposes.

Make CAP: MakeCAP.exe

The Make Cap tool can be used to assign a client access point to a server. The syntax that can be used is as follows:

- `server` The name of the site server where the SMS provider is installed

- `cap_server` The name of the NT server that is to become the CAP
- `/s: sitecode` The site code of the site the new CAP will belong to

Make Collection: MakeColl.exe

After creating a text-based list of computer names or IP addresses, you can use the Make Collection tool to create a new collection. The default is computer names; however, using `/i` syntax prompts the utility to read IP addresses from the text file rather than computer names.

Make Distribution Point: MakeDist.exe

Use the Make Distribution Point tool to configure a distribution point role to an NT server.

Make Distribution Point Group: MakeDPG.exe

This utility allows you to use a text file to create a distribution point group. The servers must already have been assigned a distribution point.

MIF Checker: MIFCheck.exe

This utility can verify the syntax of a Management Information Format file (MIF) before it is sent to an SMS site system. If you are creating custom hardware inventory items, this tool can verify the syntax used.

MIF Form Generator and MIF Entry: MifGen.exe, MifWin.exe

These tools can be used to add to an SMS client's existing computer hardware inventory items, storing them in new groupings that detail the group name, its class, and its attributes.

MOF Manager: MofMan.exe

This utility can be used on both Windows NT and Windows 95/98 computer systems for editing the standard SMS_def.MOF file. This file defines the hardware classes and attributes that are collected by hardware inventory.

NAL Logging: Turn_on_nal_logging.reg, Turn_off_nal_logging.reg

This tool can be used to either enable or disable the network abstraction layer logging performed on an SMS site server. Before NAL logging is enabled, each component must be enabled on the site server. This will also increase network traffic.

PDF Wizard: PdfWiz.exe

This tool allows you to create a PDF from a package ID for software distribution using the SMS Installer.

PGC Migration Wizard: SMS_MPGC.exe

This wizard is used for upgrading PGC (Program Group Control) applications from SMS 1.2 to SMS 2.0. It be installed on an SMS primary site.

Preferred Server Tools: LocalSvr.exe, SetSMSSvr.exe

These tools allow you to specify the preferred distribution point groups and client access point for an SMS client.

```
PREINST /deinstall: sitecode /deljob: sitecode
```

Where:

`deinstall:{sitecode}` Remove the named secondary site from the site hierarchy.

`/deljob: {sitecode}` Delete all jobs or commands that are destined to the named site.

`/delsite: {sitecode}` Remove incorrectly deleted sites from the SMS site database.

`/stopsite` Stop all SMS servers at the site.

`/syncparent` Force all site control images in the SMS site database to move to the parent's site.

Process Viewer: Pview.exe

This utility can be used to monitor EXE and DLL dependencies for both Windows NT and Windows 95/98 clients.

Query Backup and Restore: QryEdit.exe

This tool can be used to back up and restore any queries that have been created by administrators and not the default queries installed by SMS.

Query Extract: SMSExtract.xlt, SMSExtract.xls, SMSExtract.mdb

This tool can extract SMS query results into Excel worksheets or Access tables for creating custom reports.

Random Login: RndLogin.exe

This utility can be used to limit the discovery and installation of SMS clients either by a range of computer names or by an average percentage of the time that they log on. Syntax is either `/M start end` for computer names or `/R percent` for the percentage ratio.

Remote Control Settings: RCCliopt.exe

Both Windows NT and Windows 95/98 clients can use this tool to set the default protocol and LANA (LAN adapter) number for remote control settings at the SMS client.

Reset Log Settings: ResetLog.exe

Use this tool to reset the SMS site server log files to the installed default settings without having to individually set each log file through the SMS Administrator console.

Set Client Event Tool: SetEvnt.exe

This tool can be used to trigger both the CCIM (Client Configuration Installation Manager) and Copy queues to cycle at the client without waiting for the scheduled cycle to begin.

Set New ID Tool: NewUID.exe

This tool allows you to assign a unique ID to each SMS client computer. If you have used cloning for creating your SMS clients, this tool can re-create a unique SMS ID.

Set NIC Tool: MultiNIC.exe

This utility can be used on both Windows NT and Windows 95/98 computer systems, with multiple NICs to define what network interface card (NIC) an SMS client will bind to when Remote Tools is executed. The default is the first NIC in the binding order.

Set Preferred Distribution Point and CAP Tool: PrefServ.exe

This utility can be used on both Windows NT and Windows 95/98 computer systems for specifying a preferred distribution point or CAP for an SMS client.

Site Utilities: PreInst.exe

This utility can be used to diagnose problems in an SMS site and to start and stop SMS services. Some of the syntax that can be used is as follows:

Site Properties Manager: SMSSPMan.exe

This tool can be used to import and export any object in the SMS site. If you have a defined site hierarchy in your pilot project that you wish to use in your final installation, this utility can be very useful for exporting the configured objects.

SMS Console Load Simulation: UILoad.exe

This utility can be used to simulate the load that up to 50 SMS Administrator consoles could generate at an SMS site.

SMS Object Generator: SMSObgn.exe, SMSObldr.exe

This utility can be used to generate data that will approximate client load at your SMS sites.

SMS Status Monitor: StatMon.exe

The Status Monitor can report site status and monitor status summarizer thresholds through a status indicator displayed on the system trade of the taskbar. This tool can also be used to connect to the remote site server for monitoring its thresholds.

SMS Toolkit: Software Development Kit

The Software Development K (SDK) provides you with a programming interface for the SMS. Extend both hardware or software distribution and the SMS user interface with the SDK.

SMS Trace and Tracer: SMSTrace.exe, Tracer.exe

These tools present the SMS service log files in real time as they are actually added to the log file. These tools can be used at the client or the SMS site server.

Software Inventory Viewer: SInvView.exe

This token is used to view data processed by software inventory. Both full inventory files (SIC) and delta inventory files (SID), as well as history files (SINV.HIS) can be viewed.

Stop Remote Control: StopRC.exe

This tool can be used for both Windows NT and Windows 95/98 clients to stop the Remote Control Client Agent installed on an SMS client that is connected through a RAS connection.

Test Application: TestApp.exe

This tool can be used for both Windows NT and Windows 95/98 clients to test that a package command line and its location are correct. When it is executed, a dialog box displays the location where it was started and the command line that was used.

UILoad.exe: SMS Console Load Simulation

This utility can be used to simulate the load that up to 50 SMS Administrator consoles could generate at an SMS site.

Zap: Zap.exe

This tool can be used to delete a file that can't be deleted by normal means, or a file that is running and being used by the SMS system. The syntax for this utility is `ZAP` *`filename`*.

Installing SMS and SQL Server in Batch Mode

Installing Systems Management Server 2.0 can take a lot of time and effort. Batch files can be created to install both SMS and SQL Server 6.5 and 7.0 without any user intervention.

Initial Steps before Installing

1. Make sure that all Windows NT 4.0 servers that are to be site servers or site database servers have a minimum Service Pack 4.
2. Execute Y2KSETUP.EXE from the SMS 2.0 CD on the selected Windows NT computers.

Installing SMS 2.0 in Unattended Mode

1. First, create a user account that will be used as the SMS Service account.
2. Grant the account the "Log on as a service" right, and then make the account a member of the Domain Administrators group.
3. Create an initialization file containing the values for the variables: site, domain, and server.
4. Run the SMS 2.0 Setup program from the command prompt using this command and syntax:

```
Setup /Script filename.ini /NoUserInput
```

Where:

`/Script` Mandates that the installation values are read from the initialization file created rather than from the end user through the SMS Setup Wizard.

filename.ini The name of a file containing SMS setup information.

`NoUserInput` No user input will be required for Setup to run to completion.

Initialization File for SMS Setup

The SMS Setup initialization file supplies the answers for the information that the SMS Setup Wizard prompts for during the installation. All values must be entered for the setup keys that apply to installation that you wish to perform—that is, a primary site, secondary site, or the SMS

Administrator console. Each key description specifies the type of installations that can be performed:

- *Primary* Primary site installations
- *Secondary* Secondary site installations
- *Site installation* Primary and secondary site installations
- *SMS Administrator console* SMS Administrator console installations
- *All* All installations

Note that there are no optional keys. The order of the keys within sections, and the order of sections within the file, is also not important for a successful installation. The keys and data are also not case-sensitive.

[Identification]

Action

All One of the following three options can be specified:

1. *InstallAdminUI* Installs the SMS Administrator console only
2. *InstallPrimarySite* Installs the primary site
3. *InstallSecondarySite* Installs a secondary site

[Options]

AddressType

Secondary Specifies one of the following types of address to be used as the default address for communications to the secondary site from its parent site:

- *MS_ASYNC_RAS* RAS communication over asynchronous lines
- *MS_ISDN_RAS* RAS communication over ISDN lines
- *MS_LAN* Communication over LAN/WAN where routers connect multiple LAN segments or subnets
- *MS_SNA_RAS* RAS communication over SNA links
- *MS_X25_RAS* RAS communication over X.25 lines

FullName

All The name of the person or company that this product will be registered to; this matches the Name field on the Product Registration screen of the SMS Setup Wizard.

InstallSQLServer

Primary Enter `1` to install SQL Server; otherwise, enter `0`.

LanUser

Secondary The account name for the standard sender account that will be used at this site.

LanUserPassword

Secondary The password for the account defined in `LanUser`.

NetworkEnvironments

Site Installation Indicate one or more of the following types of network environment support to install, in a comma-separated list with no spaces:

- NetWare
- Banyan
- AppleTalk

NumberOfAdminUI

Primary Stipulate the maximum number of SMS Administrator consoles that the site can have running concurrently.

NumOfClients

Site Installation Indicate the maximum number of clients that the site can concurrently support.

OptionalUnits

Site Installation Indicate one or more of the following SMS components, in a comma-separated list containing no spaces.

- *Crystal Info* In the SMS Setup Wizard, it is called Crystal Reports. Contains many report-generation tools plus a scheduler that allow you to view, modify, and schedule reports using the SMS Administrator console.
- *Crystal Info UI* The Crystal Reports user interface.
- *Installer* In the SMS Setup wizard, it is called the SMS Installer. A powerful utility that creates installation programs that can be distributed through SMS.
- *License Metering* This tool is called Software Metering in the SMS Setup Wizard. The Software Metering tool tracks all software application usage and real-time license allocation across the network. Note that software-metering services are supported only on the Intel platform; however, the software-metering clients are supported on both Intel and Alpha platforms.
- *License Metering UI* This tool is called the Software Metering Console in the SMS Setup wizard; this provides the user interface.
- *Network Monitor* A network analyzer that monitors and troubleshoots network problems by capturing, displaying, and filtering many types of network frames. It can also edit the captured frames.
- *NWbind* Called NetWare Bindery Support in the SMS Setup Wizard, this protocol allows SMS to interface and communicate with NetWare servers and clients still using the NetWare Bindery environment (3.X/4.X).
- *NWNDS* Called NetWare NDS Support in the SMS Setup Wizard, this protocol allows SMS to interface and communicate with servers and clients in the NetWare NDS environment (4.X/5.X)

- *Remote Control* Called Remote Tools in the SMS Setup Wizard, this feature provides the administrator the ability to control remote computers over the network from the SMS Administrator console, allowing support personnel to run local programs, troubleshoot, and reboot the connected client.
- *Scripts* This feature is called Package Automation Scripts in the SMS Setup Wizard. It provides already created scripts for automating the installation and configuration of software applications
- *Y2K* This feature is called Product Compliance Database in the SMS Setup Wizard. This data can be used to create queries on collected SMS data, seeing which products meet Year 2000 and Euro standards. Then, software distribution can be used to distribute any relevant patches or fixes to systems with software that is found not to be compliant. Software metering can also be implemented to restrict access to software applications that are not compliant.

OrgName

All The company name under which SMS will be registered in the Organization field on the Product Registration screen of the SMS Setup Wizard.

ParentSiteCode

Secondary Indicates the site code of the site that will be the new secondary site's parent site.

ParentSiteServer

Secondary Indicates the network name of the site server of the new secondary site's parent site.

ProductID

All The 10-digit key from the yellow sticker on the SMS CD jewel case.

RasUser

Enter the account name for the RAS sender account to be used at this site.

RasUserDomain

Enter the Windows NT domain where the RasUser account was created.

RasUserPassword

Enter the password for the account listed for RasUser.

RasPhoneBook

Enter the RAS phone book name for the RAS sender to use.

SDKServer

Primary Indicate the server where the SDK Provider will be installed.

ServerPlatforms

Site Installation Indicate any site-system support for one or more of the following CPU architectures, in a comma-separated list with no spaces:

- *x86* Any Intel CPU or clone version, such as AMD
- *Alpha* Compaq or Digital Alpha CPU

ServiceAccount

Site Installation Enter the user account to be used as the SMS Service account at this site.

ServiceAccountDomain

Site Installation Enter the Windows NT domain in which the SMS Service account was created.

ServiceAccountPassword

Site Installation Enter the password for the SMS Service account.

SiteCode

Site Installation Enter the three characters that will be the new site's site code.

SiteDomain

Site Installation Enter the Windows NT domain containing the site server.

SiteName

Site Installation Enter the new site's name up to 50 characters.

SMSInstallDir

Site Installation Enter the folder path where the SMS directory tree will be installed, for example, `C:\SMS`. The folder is created if it does not exist.

[SQLInstallOptions]

SAPassword

Primary Enter the password for the database account listed by SQLLoginID in the next section, "SQLConfigOptions."

SQLDevicePath

Primary Enter the folder path where the SQL Server devices and files used by the site database will be installed, for example, `C:\MSSQL\SMSSATA`. The folder is created if it does not exist.

SQLInstallDir

Primary Enter the folder path where SQL Server will be installed if SQL Server containing the site database is to be installed on the site server. For example, `C:\MSSQL`. The directory is created if it does not exist.

[SQLConfigOptions]

AutoConfigSqlConnections

Primary Enter `1` to automatically configure SQL Server connections; `0` not to.

DatabaseName

Primary Enter the name for the site database. For example, `SMS_CDN`.

NumberOfSqlConnections

Primary Enter the number of concurrent connections your site database will have.

SQLLoginID

Primary Enter the SQL Server account for accessing the SMS site database. This account must already exist (SMS Setup does not create it) and have SQL Server system administrator sa permissions, plus Create DB, Dump DB, and Dump Transaction permissions on the master database. The SQL Server's built-in sa account has these three permissions and is the default account used in the SMS Setup Wizard.

SQLLoginPassword

Primary Enter the password for the account specified for SQLLoginID.

SQLServerName

Primary Enter the name of the computer running the instance of SQL Server containing the site database for the site.

SQLServerVersion

Primary Enter the version of SQL Server that will contain the site database: `7.0`.

UseSQLIntegratedSecurity

Primary Enter `1` to have SMS use integrated security when accessing the site database; otherwise, enter `0`.

[LicenseServer]

DatabaseName

Enter the name for the software-metering database.

SQLDevicePath

Enter the folder path where the SQL Server software-metering database device and log device will be created For example, `C:\MSSQL\SMSDATA`.

SQLLoginID

Enter the SQL Server account for accessing the SMS software-metering database This account must already exist, as the SMS Setup does not create it during installation. It must also have SQL Server system administrator sa permissions, plus Create DB, Dump DB, and Dump Transaction permissions on the master database. The SQL Server's built-in sa account has these three permissions and is the default account used in the SMS Setup Wizard.

SQLLoginPassword

Enter the password for the account listed for SQLLoginID

SQLServerName

Enter the name of the computer running the instance of SQL Server containing the software-metering database.

SQLServerVersion

Enter the version of SQL Server running the software-metering database: `7.0`.

UseSQLIntegratedSecurity

Enter `1` to have SMS use integrated security when accessing the software metering database; otherwise, enter `0`.

Example Installation File

```
[Identification]
Action=InstallPrimarySite

[Options]
FullName=Mark Wilkins
OrgName=3377831 Canada Inc.
ProductID=123-4567890
SiteCode=CDN
SiteName=Headquarters
SiteDomain=Wilkins
ServiceAccount=smsadmin
ServiceAccountDomain=Wilkins
ServiceAccountPassword=Servicetech14
NumOfClients=200
```

```
ServerPlatforms=X86
NetworkEnvironments=NetWare
OptionalUnits=Installer,License Metering,Network Monitor
SMSInstallDir=C:\SMS
InstallSQLServer=0
NumberOfAdminUI=4
SDKServer=Dell

[SQLInstallOptions]
SQLInstallDir=C:\MSSQL
saPassword=CraveThirst
SQLDevicePath=C:\MSSQL\SMSDATA

[SQLConfigOptions]
SQLServerName=Dell
SQLServerVersion=70
UseSQLIntegratedSecurity=0
SQLLoginID=sa
SQLLoginPassword=CRaveThirst
CreateSQLDevice=1
DatabaseName=SMS_CDN
DatabaseDevice=SMSdata_CDN
LogDevice=SMSlog_CDN
SQLDevicePath=C:\MSSQL\SMSDATA
NumberOfSqlConnections=75
AutoConfigSqlConnections=1

[LicenseServer]
SQLServerName=Dell
SQLServerVersion=70
UseSQLIntegratedSecurity=0
SQLLoginID=sa
SQLLoginPassword=CraveThirst
CreateSQLDevice=1
DatabaseName=LicDb_CDN
DatabaseDevice=LicData_CDN
LogDevice=LicLog_CDN
SQLDevicePath= C:\MSSQL\SMSDATA
```

Knowledge Base Articles for Troubleshooting and Supporting SMS 2.0

Q229973 SMS: SINV Does Not Report Last Accessed Date or Modified Date

Q231230 SMS: Canned Queries Do Not Complete

Q232653 SMSCliToknAcct& Locked Out When Hardware Inventory Is Enabled

Q235205 Advertised Program Does Not Run with 10003 Status Message

Q235808 SMS: Smsapm32exe May Report Status Incorrectly

Q237752 SMS: Client Discovery Does Not Enumerate over 25 Netcards

Q238302 SMS: Logon Points Are Not Removed Correctly

Q238371 SMS: Network Discovery Causes GPF when Polling DHCP Servers

Q238633 SMS: Unable to Create Collection Based on Direct Rule Membership

Q238762 Software Inventory Creation Date Is Incorrect in SMS Database

Q239130 SMS: 32-Bit Package Does Not Remove Duplicate Registry Entries

Q239136 SMS: Repairing RC Agent Overwrites Custom Viewers List

Q239564 SMS: Client Components Reinstalled during Periodic Verification

Q239590 SMS: SMSCliToknAcct Connection Attempts to Mapped Drives in Path

Q239828 SMS: Access Violation in SMS_SITE_SYSTEM_STATUS_SUMMARIZER

Q239915 SMS: "Insert Disk in Drive A:" Message during Hardware Inventory

Q240056 SMS: Forced Sites Registry Key Entry Causes Multiple Errors

Q240155 MMC Security Rights Do Not Work with More than 64 Global Groups

Q240158 SMS: Logon Server Manager Performs Too Many Work Cycles

Q240250 Migration from SMS 12 to 20 Uninstalls LANDesk Files

Q240426 SMS: Cannot Obtain Performance Data for SMS Counters

Q240783 SMS Installer Does Not Repackage Large MULTI-SZ Registry Values

Q240921 Smsapm32 Consumes 100 Percent CPU Time on Windows NT SMS Clients

Q240980 Smscfgcpl May Not Be Loaded with More than 20 Network Adapters

Q241279 SMS: Client Appears as Not Installed in Administrator Console

Q241419 SMS Executive Causes Access Violation Processing Prochistdat

Q241656 SMS: Memory Leak in Pcmsvc32

Q241734 SMS: MMC Stack Overflow in User Security Wizard

Q242011 SMS: APM Does Not Install Software on BDCs

Q242356 Remote Control Logging Does Not Work in SMS 20 SP1

Q242421 SMS: Offer Summarizer May Process Sum Files Out of Order

Q242477 SMS: Login Script Support Files Not Copied after Applying SP1

Q242489 SMS: Run-Time Error when Advertising MFC-Based Package

Q242490 DistMgr Package Removal Does Not Work If Package Share Not Empty

Q242492 SMS: LSM Can Deinstall Domain If PDC Connectivity Lost

Q242496 Advertisement and Site System Status Summarizer Problems

Q242498 SMS: Component Status Summarizer Has Performance Problems

Q242924 SMS: Client Install Problems Using the SMS_LOCAL_DIR Variable

Q242963 SMS: Slow Enumeration of Existing Collections

Q242965 Collection Based on Query May Display Incorrect Results

Q243179 SMS: Sinvproc Log Error Message: Delete Zero Length File Failed

Q243189 SMS: %SMS_LOCAL_DIR%\MS\CORE\BIN Added to Path Multiple Times

Q243326 SMS: Browsing for PDFs Requires Site Modify

Q243681Copy-Queue Causes "Not Logged In" Requests on NetWare Servers

Q244034 SMS: Window 95/98 Clients Hang Opening E-mail Attachments

Q244157 Preferred Server Selection Does Not Work as Expected with NDS

Q244405 SMS: Distribution Manager May Not Remove Compressed Package

Q244409 Access Account Security on Distribution Points May Be Incorrect

Q244410 SMS: Smsapm32 Uses SMSCliToknAcct& to Search Mapped Drives

Q244630 SMS: Site Status Node May Take a Long Time to Open

Q244633 SMS: Site Status Node is Slow

Q245051 Updated Collections Go to Every Child Site with New Child Site

Q245101 SMS: LSM Is Case-Sensitive When Comparing Domain Names

Q245321 SMS: "Stop 0x0000000A" with SMS Remote Control Installed

Q245579 SMS: Secondary Site Does Not Decompress Package

Q245812 SMS: Visual C++ 6 Run-Time Libraries Installed with SMS

Q246164 intraNetWare Login Dialog Box Appears during Hardware Inventory

Q246527 SMS: Systems Management Server 20 Service Pack 1 Client Hotfix

Q246583 SMS: RC Does Not Work in Master Domain Model Using Global Groups

Q246785 SMS: SMSExec Components Report SQL Error Messages

Q246949 Offer Summarizer Reports SQL Error 105 with Corrupted svf Files

Q247230 SMS: Multiple Advertisements to the Same Program/Package Do Not

Q247543 SMS: Clients Incorrectly Assigned to Multiple Sites

Q248367 SMSINST: Repackager Hangs when the Package Requires a Reboot

Q248969 Sinvproc Leaves Zero-Byte Files in the BADSINV Folder

Q249077 SMS: SP1:Copylogtcf Does Not Show Site that Updated Logon Point

Q249331 Advertisements Received by Clients Outside Targeted Collections

Q251070 SMS: Copylogtcf Does Not Show Site that Updated Logon Point

Q253151 SMS: Systems Management Server 20 Dependency Package Contents

Knowledge Base Articles for Troubleshooting and Supporting SMS 1.2

Q157589 SMS: PGC Does Not Work in a Trusted Domain with Windows 95

Q159087 SMS Does Not Identify Pentium Pro (P6) Processor Speeds

Q160566 SMS: PCM Command Line and "Cannot Find File" Error

Q164204 SMS: PC Memory Reported Incorrectly for Windows 3x Clients

Q168130 SMS: Despooler Service Processes SNI Files Slowly

Q171067 SMSINST: Error Creating Registry Keys with Empty Values

Q172762 Continuous Bhntsys Load and Unload Causes STOP 0xA and 0x7F

Q175077 SMS: Audit Gets "No Data Available" Message after Full Inventory

Q176544 SMS: Err Msg: "Couldn't Save the Query Result Format"

Q181747 SMSINST: Configuration Registry List Box Displays Only 1024 Keys

Q181759 SMSINST: Edit INI File Is Limited to 30720 Characters

Q181761 SMS: Cannot Specify an Inventory Scan Interval for SKIPINV

Q184539 SMS: PGC Shows Long Delay before Completing Normal Process Cycle

Q184858 SMS: CLIMON Consumes PDC LSASS Resources when Password Expired

Q184999 SMS: Software Inventory Wrong after Daylight Savings Time Change

Q185179 SMS: No Retry for "Remove Package" Jobs

Q186255 SMS: File Corruption During File Transfer from Help Desk

Q186827 SMS: Despooler Causes AV while Creating Retry Instruction

Q188578 SMS: PCMWin Exits at Startup If No SMS Logon Server Is Available

Q188779 SMS: Inventory Fails to Properly Identify 400 MHz Processors

Q189304 SMS: Windows NT Processor Speed Incorrectly Reported

Q189530 SMS: Scheduler Never Creates Send Request

Q189723 SMS: Audit Fails on Win95 or Win98 Clients with FAT32 Partitions

Q189844 SMS: PGC Should Ignore Configuration Command Line

Q190135 SMS: Despooler Errors: Compilation Failed, Error Code = cb

Q190832 SMS: RSERVICE Unable to Configure Service to Use the LocalSystem

Q191067 SMS: PGC Fails to Configure Apps when Roaming Profiles Are Used

Q191320 SMS: Getmem Hangs Inventory at 27 to 30 Percent

Q191828 Account Lockouts and 5711 Events on the PDC

Q192439 SMS: Command Line Smsviewexe Leaves Open Window in Background

Q192462 SMS: Client Stops Responding Using DisableFailedServerDialog

Q192788 SMS: Wuser32 Leaks Memory after UDP Port 1762 Attack

Q192920 SMS: Site Attachment Fails when Adding Custom Architectures

Q193015 SMS: Pentium II Processor Detected as 486DX on OS/2 Clients

Q193030 SMS:Logged on User Name Not Reported on OS/2 Clients

Q193031 SMS: INVDOS Reports 2 GB Space on FAT32 Drives Larger than 2 GB

Q193224 SMS: PCMSVC32 AVs If Package Cmd Line Contains a Drive Letter

Q193269 SMS: Remote Control to Win9x Clients Fails w/Winsock2, Using IP

Q193280 SMS: CCM Removes LANDesk Files when Remote Control Isn't Enabled

Q193333 NetMon Fails on Multiprocessor Windows NT Server Under Stress

Q193421 SMS: Audit16 Fails on Long User Names

Q193784PCM "Execute" Button Unavailable or Dimmed

Q194297 SMS: Windows NT Inventory File Collector Causes Access Violation

Q194559 SMS: SNMPELEA May Conflict with Compaq Insight Manager Agents

Q195701 SMS: No System BIOS Information Returned on IBM OS/2 Clients

Q195702 SMS: CHECK20 Misidentifies SMS 12 Client as an SMS 20 Client

Q195823 SMS: Audit Stops If Certain Entries in Smsini Are Blank

Q195936 SMS: Pkg Distribution Fails If Updating of Master Pkg Fails

Q195937 SMS: Pcmsvc32exe Fails to Execute Cmd Line Containing UNC Path

Q195944 SMS: Package Command Manager Preferred Server Selection

Q199974 SMS: Event to Trap Translator Error—Can't Load Message File

Q200713 SMS: Smsiddupexe Fails with Case-Sensitive SQL Server Code Page

Q200791 SMS: SMS 12 SP4 May Cause WinNT Clients Not to Report Inventory

Q207369 SMS: INVOS2 Does Not Report TCP/IP Information

Q214425 SMS: NetMon Fails to Recognize HTTP Packets on Alternate Ports

Q214983 Skipinvexe Fails to Compensate for Change of Month

Q216552 SMS: SMSRUN Hangs at 90% CPU while IE Setup Is Running

Q222988 SMS: SystemRole and SystemType Values Removed from Smsini

Q223009 SMS: Long Paths Make Audit Create a MIF that Cannot Be Processed

Q223143 SMS: AUDIT32 Does Not Delete Temp MIF Created in Ms\Sms\Temp

Q225056 SMS: PCMSVC32 Runs a Job after Expired Date

Q225063 SMS: INVMAC Reports Incorrect Processor Name

Q225064 SMS: INVMAC Software Inventory Performance Decreases over Time

Q229698 SMS: New Functionality Added to Audit

Q229809 SMS: Unexpected Reinstallation of SMS Packages

Q229927 SMS: Long Event to Trap Translator Description Brings Error

Q230242 SMS: PCM May Cause Account Lockouts in a High-Security Domain

Q231362 SMS: Using SmsrunStartupDelay Causes Win 95/98 Clients to Hang

Q231378 SMS: Pcmwin32 Exits when It Is Unable to Initialize

Q231821 SMS: Getdisk and 95Getdsk Display Messages when Verbose Mode Off

Q232242 SMS: Audit16 Stops Responding on Removable Media Drive

Q233545 SMS: Remote Control WinNT to WinNT Drops Connection

Q234750 SMS: Pentium Processor Speed Incorrectly Reported

Q236066 SMS: INVMAC Fails to Report Package During Software Inventory

Q236913 Err Msg: Couldn't Open ISV MIF

Q237690 SMS: Err Msg: The Redirector Has Timed Out to\\

Q238247 SMS: Invdosexe Does Not Compensate for Change of Month

Q239534 SMS: Data Loader Cannot Process MIF Date above Year 2030

Q240786 SMS: Hierarchy Manager Develops Backlog of ct2 Files

Q243159 SMS: Long Path Causes "Access Violation" in Invwin32exe

Q249151 SMS: Getsfwrexe Does Not Report the File Date During Inventory

Q249578 Pcmdump Detects Expiration Date Incorrectly in Instruction File

Q253578 SMS: Error When PCMMAC Runs Job on Multiple Clients at Same Time

www.ingramcontent.com/pod-product-compliance
Lightning Source LLC
Chambersburg PA
CBHW080133060326
40689CB00018B/3768
* 9 7 8 0 0 7 2 1 2 4 2 1 7 *